MW01629798

Halbstark
Baby-Baby
Halbstark!

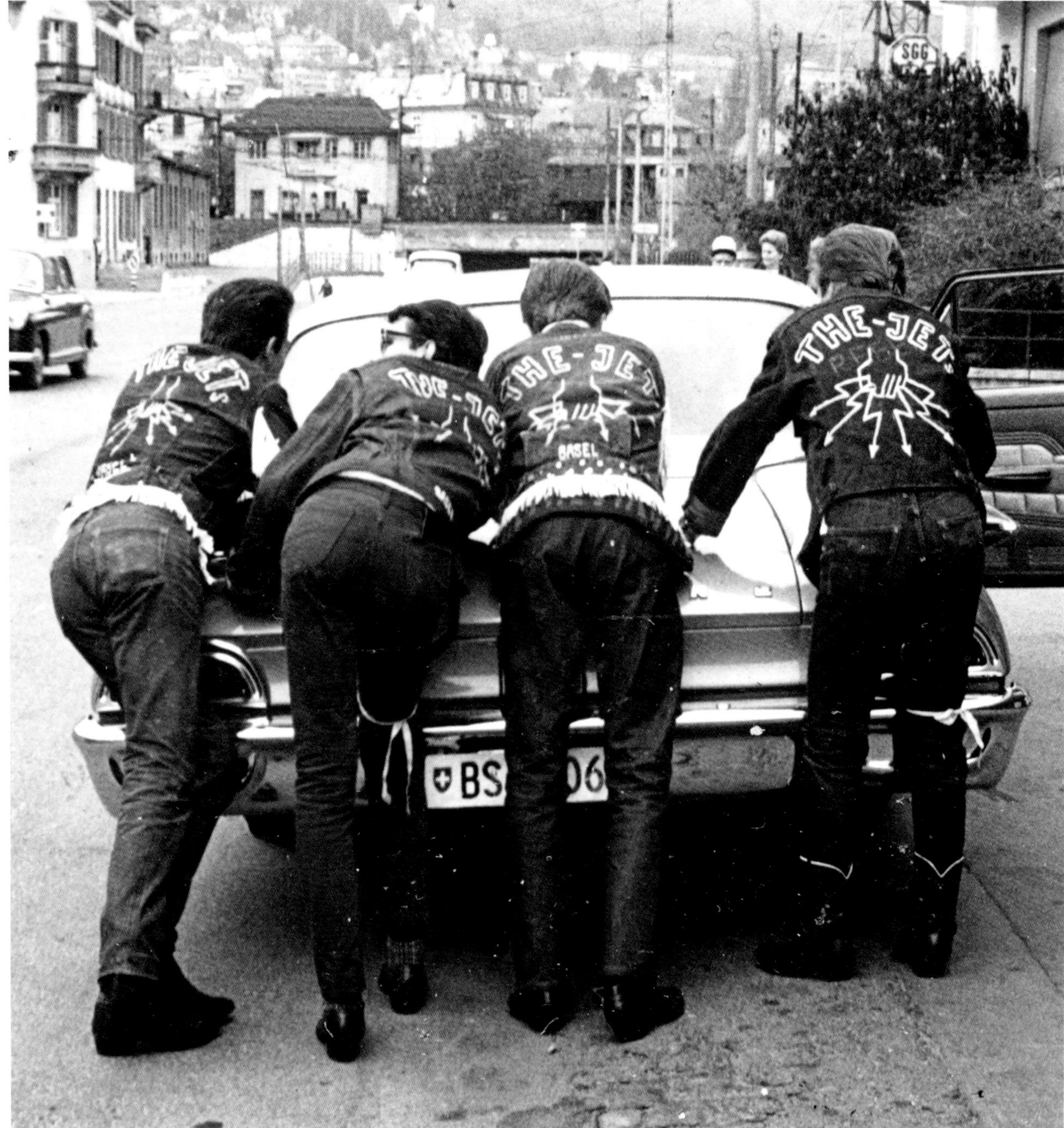

SGG
THE-JET
BASEL
THE-JET

Halbstark Baby-Baby Halbstark!

Teenage Street Gangs in Switzerland 1962-1972 Through the Eyes of Dieter "Igel" Ehrlich

KICKS BOOKS / NYC

Copyright @ 2023 by Kicks Books

All rights reserved. No part of this publication may be used or reproduced in any manner whatsoever without written permission from the publisher, except in the case of brief quotations embodied in critical articles and reviews.

All photographs courtesy Dieter Ehrlich unless noted.

Edited by Miriam Linna
Designed by Elizabeth Van Itallie

Kicks Books
PO Box 646 Cooper Station
New York New York 10276 USA

Printed and bound in China at Union Printing Co., LTD
Ningbo Union Printing Products Co., LTD

ISBN: 978-1-940157-19-1

First edition

For prints and licensing, please contact www.kicksbooks.com

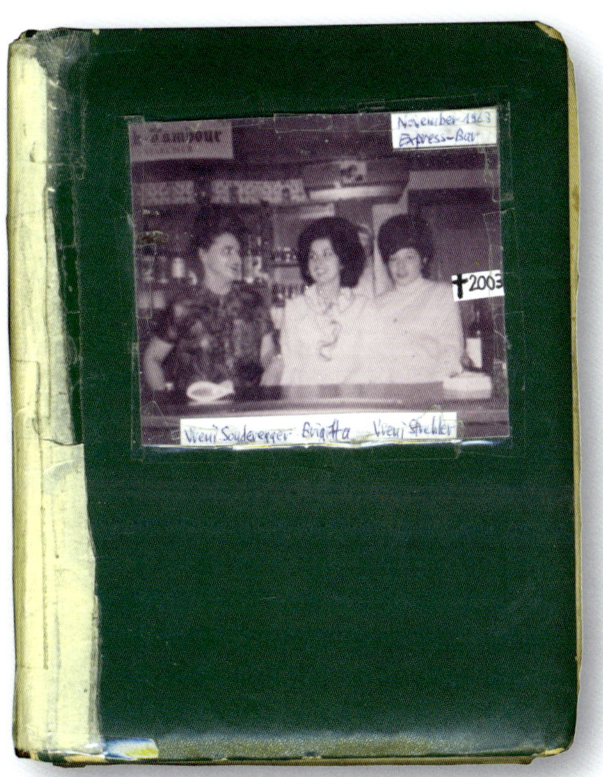
November 1963
Express-Bar
†2003

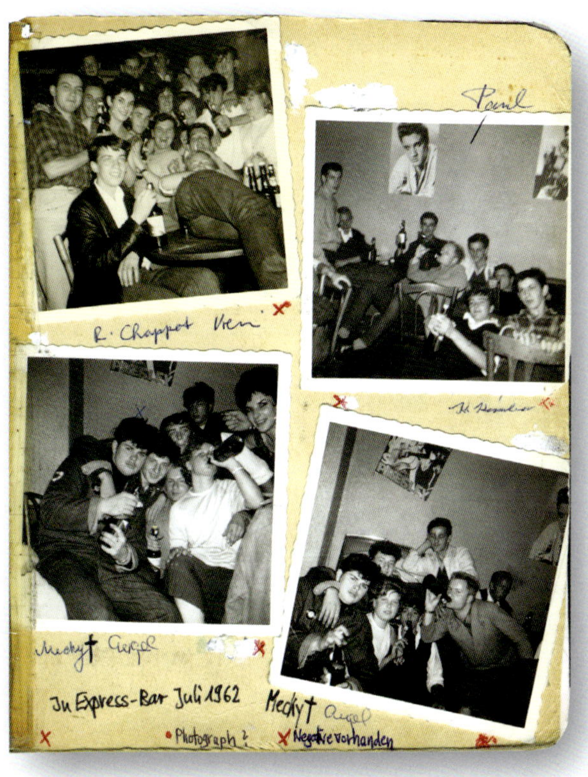
Paul
R. Chappot Vreni
In Express-Bar Juli 1962
Mecky†
Photograph?
Negative vorhanden

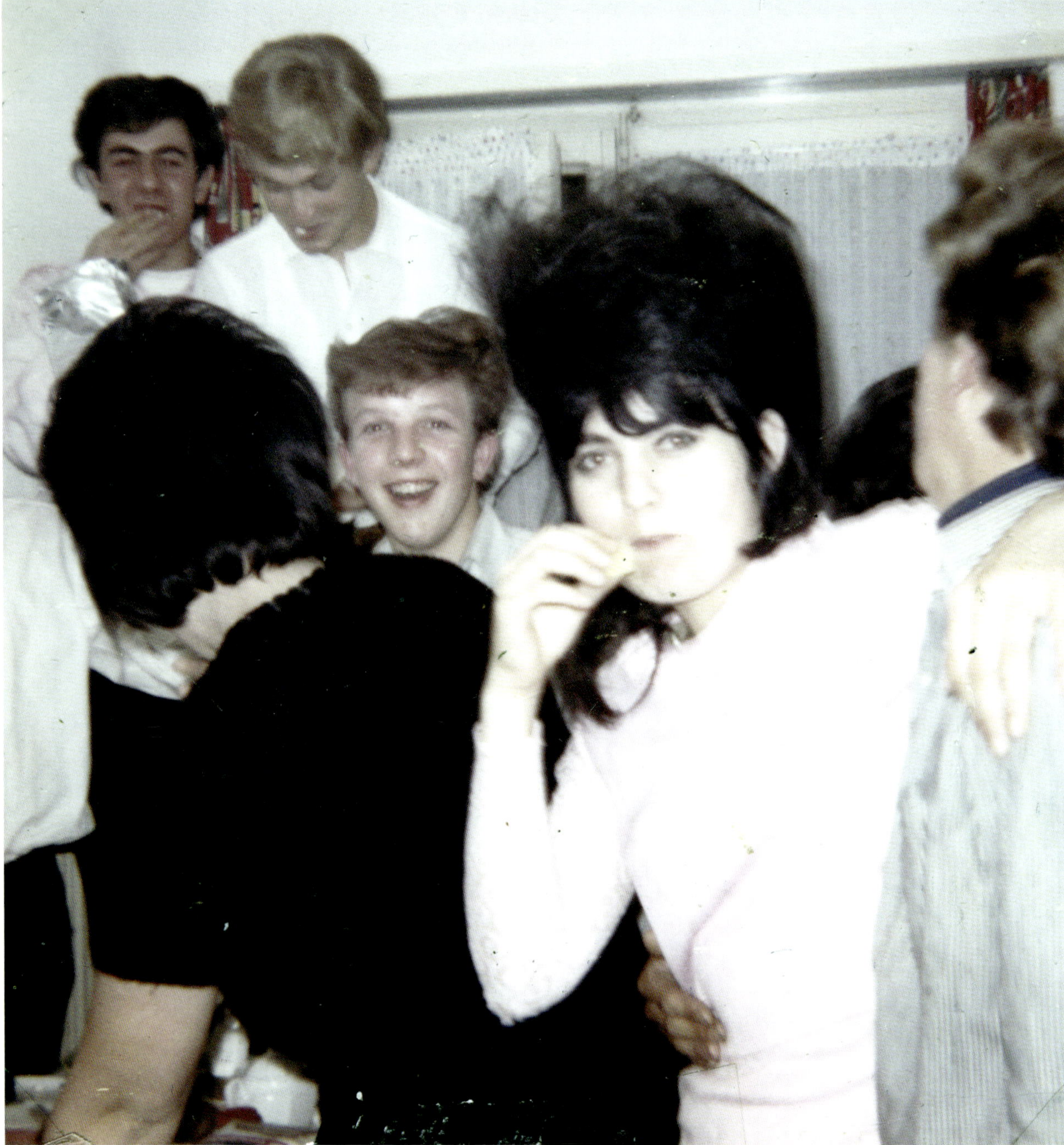

foreword

I began publishing *Bad Seed* forty years ago, an irregular book collectors periodical that focused on juvenile delinquency in popular culture and real life—"torn from the headlines." The original caveat was that all content should be drawn from teenage street life circa 1959-1969 in the USA. At the time, I could never have dreamed that rebellious street packs existed in Switzerland, neutral land of chocolate, cheese, yodeling, lederhosen, and Rolex watches. It was my exposure, decades later, to the iconic portraits of nameless Swiss street toughs by photographer Karlheinz Weinberger that blew a myopic view of teenage cool straight out the window. Here were teenagers dressed in bizarrely altered blue jeans, and sporting massive chains, belts and medallions, the girls with their hair teased a foot into the air and with their rock n' roll idols names crudely bleached into their clothing. Their menacing attitude was colored with a veiled desperation and vulnerability that was beyond appealing. Who were these wild ones, these "half-strengths," these fierce faces without names?

As fate would have it, one of these restless greasers, known in Europe as Halbstark (German for "half-stong"), had carried a camera throughout his gang years during the early 1960s, and had kept a scrapbook containing his own snapshots, which identified members from various gangs in cities across Switzerland, and which documented the private pages of gang life in the streets of Zurich, Basel, Aesch, and across the countryside. That young tyrant was Dieter "Igel" Ehrlich, the young gang boy who had first allowed Weinberger in to photograph his fellow gang members.

Weinberger captured packs of dead-end kids growing up into uncertain, unwelcome futures at odds with the staid, responsible world they deplored. His images are freeze frames caught in a spell of tight pants and dirty boots. Igel's snapshots are from the other side—the inside—a defiant world unto itself, a cultish pack of card-carrying delinquents with one goal—to rebel. Readers will follow Igel here from the early cafe parties in Basel to the day he burns his gang jacket and buries the remains, with Weinberger looking on, mortified, trying to stop him from destroying his identity in the gang.

Hang on tight. It's going to be a wild ride.

Miriam Linna
Kicks Books
Bad Seed International

teen gangs of basel

1960 RESTLESS

Our chronicle begins at the close of the fifties. The city of Basel is in the midst of a postwar boom; its economy is humming. Life for most teenagers is predictable — the squares are taking dancing lessons and Bible classes after school, obediently settling into boring, middle-class futures, and some of these young kids drop out to work at construction jobs or on the Rhine docks. Then there are the others — a small group of toughs with few professional prospects, or objectives of any kind. They hang out in tea rooms or coffee houses with names like the Café Florida at the Voltaplatz, the Café Luxor at Schifflände, the Tea Room Broadway in Steinenvorstadt, and the Café Nord-Süd in Kleinhüningen. The jukeboxes in these establishments are well fed by the kids, where they blast the boxes loudly. Rock n' roll kills the boredom, defines them, just as movies like *Rebel Without A Cause* with James Dean and *The Wild One* with Marlon Brando give them an attitude where a mood will go quickly from a simmer to a boil. You can feel it in the air. Something is going to happen. One night at the Broadway, a bunch of no-counts congregate to form the first of the Swiss street gangs, taking the name of their hangout. They become the Broadway Trampers. At this point their dress code is still denim, and more denim — no belts, no boots, no buckles, and no gang colors emblazoned on the backs of their jackets. It is a start. All systems are go. The wild ride is about to begin.

1961 ENTER THE RED DEVIL

Denim, turtlenecks and leather jackets define the dress code for the Red Devil street gang in their early days. They are founded by Urs Meier and Eugen Muff. Other members were Bruno "Mizge" Meier, Peter Mai, Herbert Häuptli, Tullio, a guy called Schmuddle und Max Wasser. There were also some girls in the group, such as Ruth Bechtel (she was Bruno Meier's girlfriend), the Schellenbaum (sisters from Zurich) and Margrit von Arx. Margrit is also sewing the Red Devil emblems on their jackets. For transfers from Basel to Zurich and other places they drove Kreidler, Florett and Motom, which all went at a much higher speed than normal. The Red Devil headquarter is the restaurant Vogesenstube, but they also were at Oasis, Express Bar, Greifen and Select. All in all they are about thirty persons. As they do lots of forbidden things, they soon get in contact with chief policeman Bulla and his crew at police station Clara in Kleinbasel. But they didn't have to stay under arrest in the police station.

In this time Freddi Madörin and his brother Kurt are known around town as troublemakers. Forming contacts throughout Switzerland, they are soon known to police and the press. Some magazines tried to interview these young men. And when they didn't get an original one, they just invented something. For example, there was published a so called interview by *Schweizer Illustrierte Sie + Er* magazine, Peter Michel (gang name Al Capone). The nineteen-year-old leader of a Zurich gang called Totenkopf Gang (the Skulls-Gang) is cited as follows: "I've been the leader of the gang for six and a half years. If a boy or a girl wants to join us, the minimum age is 16 and there's a trial period for six months. Right now there are full groups with us: Two gangs from Lucerne, two gangs from Basel, one gang from Rüti, one gang from Aesch and one gang from Zurich, they are all in their trial period." Today, Peter Michel tells us that he never had a real interview with this magazine and that some of the things printed in that so called interview are wrong.

What we know for sure is: Al Capone, who founded his Totenkopf Gang around 1959, is in these early days one of the toughest gang leaders around. His right-hand man is Peter Grob, an eighteen year old precision mechanic apprentice. What these gang leaders are up to is well known. Police find undocumented weapons at house searches of the Skulls leaders, and the newspapers zero in on a suspected syndicate of three Zurich teenage gangs. Police action escalates when they are called in on a tip that the gangbangers have plans to wreak havoc at the "Josefwiese" city fair. Federal police officers do house searches and find some weapons in apartments in Zurich: Several pistols, a Browning, ammunition, stiletto knives, sawed-off rifles, brass knuckles, masks and other weapons at house searches. Fifty-five boys and six gang debs are arrested. Police chief Inspector Grunder and his fellow officers are busy around the clock.

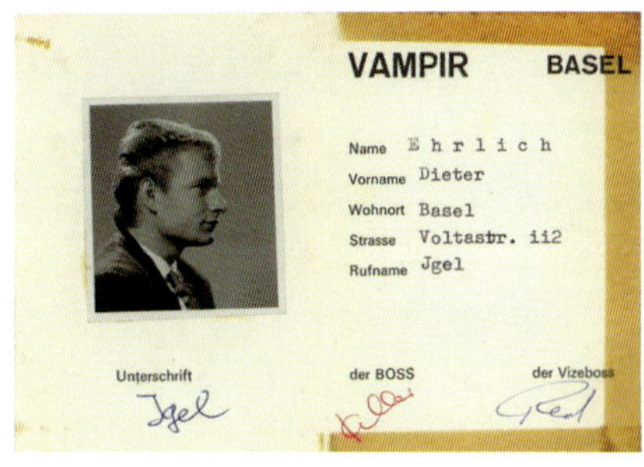

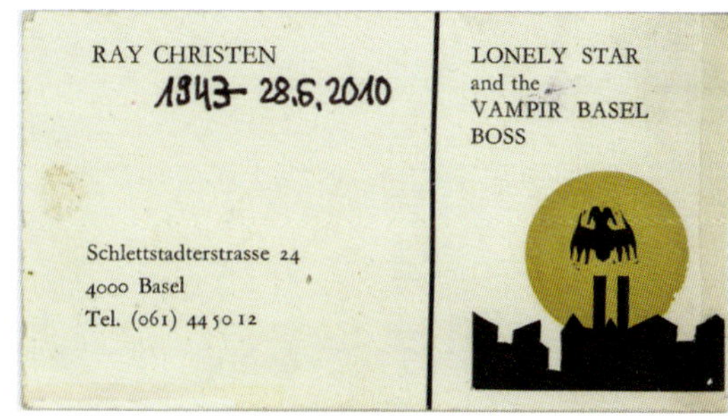

1962 THE EXPRESS KILLERS ARRIVE

The origins of the name the Express Killers Club (EKC) comes from the Express Bar in the Rheingasse. Rita Guyer, who would later work at the Olé-Olé Bar in Zurich, runs the Express Bar. She is beautiful and charming, and on good terms with everyone, even the rowdy young thugs. According to EKC original member Igel, one of the most distinctive members of the Express Killers is René Bösiger, a lean, tough giant who wears size 12 cowboy boots and wraps a massive metal chain around his neck. Aside from criminal activities, he spends his time drinking a lot of beer and roaring around on his motorcycle. By late fall, 1962, the Express Killers Club gang has disbanded, although their hangout, the Express Bar, remains, decorated with Elvis pictures. Barmaid Rita Guyer moves from Basel to Zurich and an equally charming Brigitte takes over behind the bar. Some members of the Express Killers Club head for parts unknown, others completely disappear. Igel continues wearing his rivet-adorned denim jacket with the "Rebell EKC Basel" back patch on it.

THE VAMPIRES EXPLODE

Just as the Express Killers end their reign, the youth gang scene explodes in Basel and an infamous gang called the Vampirs (the Vampires) take over, with Raymond Christen leading the pack. Members are vice boss Red(Ruedi Schmid), Kid (Arnoldo Steiner), Cliff (Werner Kesselring), Ted (Beat Bucher), Jess (Max Gass), and Mucki. In the beginning they wear Spider patches on their jackets, but by 1963 their back patches read "Strangers Gang — Vampir Basel" and a big bat replaces the spider. After Red has left the gang, Kid was nominated as new vice boss. Mexicana Joe, Ted, the Frech brothers Muus (Roger) and Whisky (Peter), Johnny (Arrigo Prestini), Rio (Hanspeter Rütti) and many others joined the Vampirs (Vampires). Raymond provides everyone with official photo ID membership cards. Every member has a small tattoo on their hand — Raymond's is a V1 flying bomb. The citizens of Basel alternately shuns these toughs or attacks them via the press: "The style and attitude of the gang members does not work for the stuffy bourgeoisie," comments Igel some years after.

Dares are part of Vampire culture, members goading each other into precarious situations. Although they clash with law enforcement in Basel, Raymond ultimately has everything in control. He runs the gang within his own set of rules and if someone causes too much trouble, he is expelled from the gang. There are invitations from Al Capone (Peter Michel) of the Skulls gang in Zurich to combine to form an even bigger gang, but Raymond declines the offers. He wants to stay independent from other gangs and their leaders, saying "I want to run my gang by my own principles and rules." One of those principles is to avoid violence when possible. That is important to Raymond and it is what sets the Vampires apart from many other gangs. They see themselves as more down to earth and grounded, and that way they attract more young girls than the others.

Besides the charismatic Raymond, his right-hand Red plays an important role for the Vampires. He was with them from the start, through their Spider, Bat, and Tiger days, and through their Teddy Boy-like phases. Raymond remains their leader until the end. During the six year history of the Vampires, the good looking Red is in a relationship with Sylvia Nebel. In 1969 things begin to crumble for the couple. At a concert at the Hazyland in Basel, Sylvia and her friend Priska Thüring meet the dutch-indonesian rock n' roll band, the Tielman Brothers. The girls start following them around immediately and move to Frankfurt in Germany to be closer to them. In the big city without jobs or money they quickly slip into the local red light scene. Red tries to save Sylvia from the danger that she has gotten herself into and brings her back to Basel, but after a short time she runs away again and ends up in prostitution at the bars and brothels of Zurich. He would never see her again.

Today, when the old members of these gangs take a walking tour around the notorious red light district of Basel, they have bittersweet memories. The Express Bar at Rheingasse 8, the Restaurant Schwarzer Bären at Rheingasse 17, the Restaurant Sonne at Rheingasse 25, and also at Café Oasis at Greifengasse 36 were their stomping grounds.

GANGLAND PEAKS

During the heyday of the local teenage gang culture, between 80 and 100 toughs and their outfits roam the streets

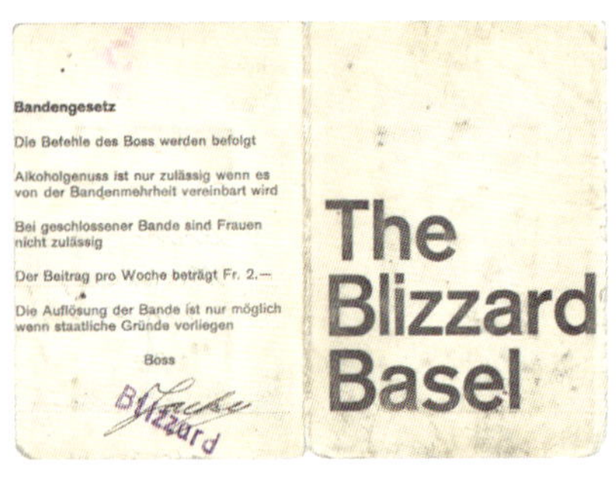

Bandengesetz

Die Befehle des Boss werden befolgt

Alkoholgenuss ist nur zulässig wenn es von der Bandenmehrheit vereinbart wird

Bei geschlossener Bande sind Frauen nicht zulässig

Der Beitrag pro Woche beträgt Fr. 2.—

Die Auflösung der Bande ist nur möglich wenn staatliche Gründe vorliegen

Boss

Blizzard

The Blizzard Basel

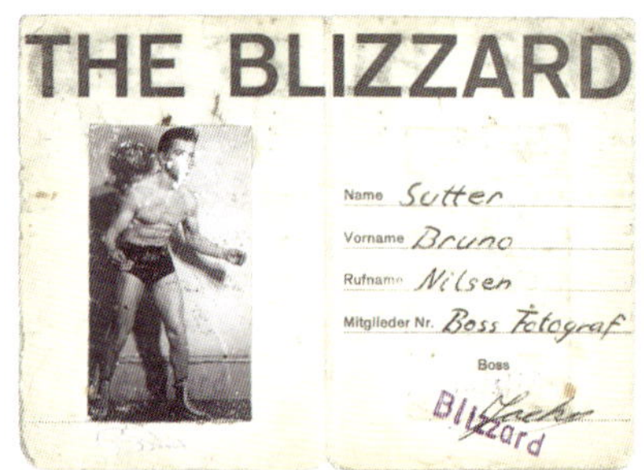

THE BLIZZARD

Name Sutter

Vorname Bruno

Rufname Nilsen

Mitglieder Nr. Boss Fotograf

Boss

Blizzard

of Basel, clashing nightly with the police. Statistics show that between 17,000 and 18,000 young people between the ages of fifteen and twenty-four live in Basel at the time, yet only about a hundred of them are members of street gangs. Yet these relentless squadrons of night boppers make themselves seen and heard. Two of the most dangerous gangs, the Blizzards and Venom, were formed by Jacky (Marcel Zimmerli). He is the boss, he controls and organizes the two lineups into a pair of unstoppable regiments. Venom member Schlangenpfiff ("Snake Whistle") is notorious for inflicting injuries with his signature headbut, alongside henchmen Mario (Michel Clemens) and Yoya. Clochard (René Rütti) is a well-known member of the Blizzards, designing the metallic thunderbolt symbol that the gang members wear around their necks and on the backs of their jackets. The other Blizzards are Ricky (Ferdinand Schäfer, the second in command), Lee (René Schmassmann) and Nilsen (Bruno Sutter, who takes a lot of Venom photos). Boots and bikes and heavy food are important — Clochard once roars right through the door and into the Express Bar on his bike. According to Clochard, they all enjoy boozing, fighting, axe throwing, knife tricks, and taking on dares and activities that would make well behaved citizens shiver. Some of the gang members start pimping their girls; they call it "Waggel." This results in arrests, and many nights are spent at the Lohnhof Police Station. The Blizzards have very strict gang rules in these days, which are handwritten by leader Marcel Zimmerli right on their membership cards: "Do what the leader tells you to do! Drinking is only permitted when the majority of the gang is ok with it! No women at gang meetings! Weekly membership fee is two Swiss Francs! The gang will only be disbanded when the legal authorities say so!" Each gang rules document was signed by Marcel Zimmerli.

As the teenage gangs evolve, members head in different directions. Some end up in middle-class artisan jobs, some end up on skid row, some die early. Mecki, better known as Zack Zack, was often at the Café Oasis for some time. He would die in a motorcycle accident. Others disappear from one day to another without leaving traces and we don't know where they went.

START FOR HELLS ANGELS SWITZERLAND

The first leader of the Swiss Hells Angels was Tino (Martin Schippert), who was born in 1946 to an inland navigator. He ran first with the Blizzards, and then the Rächer (who we will cover later on). In 1970 he would go on to establish the Swiss charter of the Hells Angels. Some years later, Raymond Christen of the Strangers Gang Vampir Basel was asked if he want to join the Hells Angels Switzerland because he knows how to run a gang and rides a big bike. But he refused.

The foundation for the Hells Angels came from the Lone Stars from Zurich, lead by Romeo (Werner Berger) and his pack. This original MC gang was made up of different smaller gangs from Zurich and its suburbs. The toughest members of the early Zurich street gang scene and also some guys from other swiss cities would follow a path directly into the ferocious biker gangs of the Seventies.

TEENAGE GANGS IN THE COUNTRYSIDE: THE PUMAS

Between 1962 and 1965, the Pumas from Aesch are at constant odds with the local police. Founded by Erwin Häring (who later moved to the Philippines) and Peter Halbeisen, the pair would attract a highly dedicated group. Extra mention must go to the formidable Stauffer brothers: Erwin, Horst and Willi, and to Ruedi Racine, Willi Alder and Beat Bucher (who was also a member in the Vampires). The Pumas were known to ride their bikes and pick fights with everyone. They were dangerous and reckless and kept the coppers busy on weekends. What became of them is unknown to this day.

GIRLS, GIRLS, GIRLS!

Young girls are attracted to these teenage mobsters like moths to the light. Many come from tough backgrounds, a few from good families. Parents tell them to stay away from gangs because of the way they dress and behave and because of the music that inspires them. Their café clubhouses are poorly regarded by the adult world. These establishments are ridiculed in the press for twist shags. Vreni Marti and Vreni Ott, two girls who were attracted to the gangs, still recall

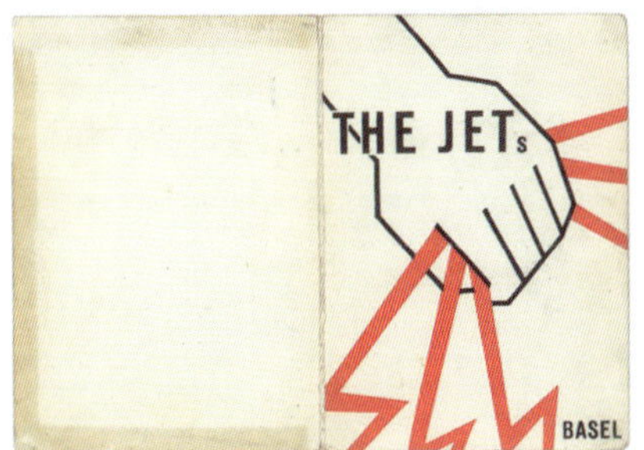

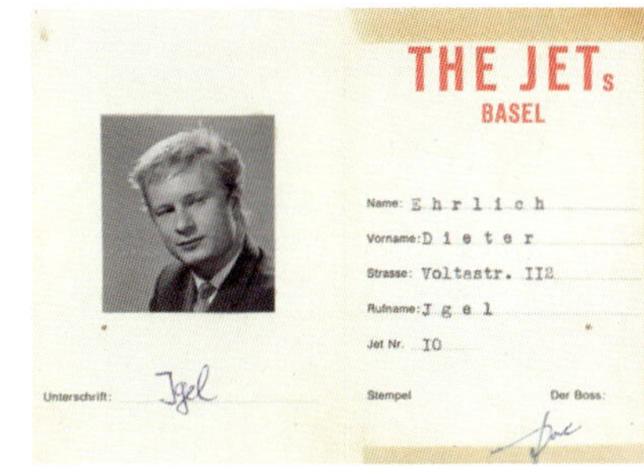

how their parents dictated to them what to wear, or rather what not to wear. Tight jeans and mini-skirts were forbidden, but there were ways to go around those rules, and the more enamored with the gangs they became, the more they disobeyed the family rules. Jeans got tighter and skirts got shorter. Vreni Marti, at one time the girlfriend of notorious Kid from the Vampires, later married and settled down as a housewife and mother with a nine-to-five job. But by 1999, she was working at the bar Erika's Oldies Corner in Dreispitz and was in a relationship with former gang leader Raymond Christen, whom she had known since the early sixties. Generally speaking though, it can be assumed that many underage girls were attracted to the gangs because they had difficulties at home or at their jobs. The boys with their Western boots were magnets for these young girls. Some of them started going out with them as early as fourteen because they were curious and adventurous. Not many of them were allowed to wear gang patches on their denim jackets. Two of these girls were Astrid Bieri and Priska Sonderegger, or Jenny and Rumy as they were known. Both were very dedicated to the gangs and went all in. Rumy wore a highly recognizable coal black beehive. Both girls were under the direct protection of gang leaders. Other girls were more opportunistic, like Esthy, also known as Angie, who used different surnames from time to time. Esthy later got into the Beat scene, but was first spotted in biker gangs. She worked as a waitress in different restaurants later on, as did Joyce Buxtorf, who had originally tended bar at the Café Oasis. Gang members picked up girls everywhere they went. According to Igel, the girls themselves actively flirted and took the initiative to get closer to the gangs. Fifi (Heidi Widmer) a voluptuous blonde was one of the more active girls. Boom! Pow! And off she went. Later the likeable lass worked as barmaid at the White Horse, the Moulin Rouge, Restaurant Adler and other seedy establishments.

INTRODUCING FROM BASEL: THE JETS AND THE LIONS

The Jets grabbed their handle from the movie gang in *West Side Story*, and did their hanging out around 1962 at a joint called Restaurant Krug, operated by the parents of their first leader, Doc (Paul Marggraff). Other Jets included vice boss Jacky Jacquiéry, Igel, Slim, Sunny (Erwin Metzger), Cliff a/k/a Elvis von Muttenz (Manfred Schmid), Tommy, Terry, and Pecos (Rudi Stücklin). In a photo from the St.Petersinsel at Bielersee, Pecos is clearly seen with a Colt .45 and a cartridge belt. This colt wasn't loaded, told us some eyewitnesses. But The Jets meant business.

Igel reports as to why he joined the Jets: "I can only speak for myself. My time with the Express Killers had come to an end in the winter of 1962. My buddies were either behind bars or dead. I was still looking for something. When Doc formed the Jets, I liked their style and the way they acted in public. You see, a gang gives you stability and security. I got the Jets logo, a fist with lightning bolts, tattooed on my right arm. I was in. My parents didn't care. I still have the membership card. And the tattoo."

The Jets's gang emblem showed a fisted hand with three lightnings. The jackets were painted by Paul Doc Marggraff. The Jets were contemporaries of the Vampires and Blizzards. They would roar all across Switzerland on their motorcycles. The goal was a good time wherever they went, and a good time was all about meeting up with the other gangs, drinking, and girls. And girls were everywhere they went, surrounding them as soon as they sped into town. Sylvia, Priska, Sibylle and Liane and others were always there to greet the gangs.

Boy gangs in Switzerland at that time included the Flaming Stars, the Jaguars and the Timbers, plus there were gangs in Basel's German neighbourhood. There were gangs in Weil am Rhein and Grenzach that also used the Jets name. But in these groups there were just a few persons.

In the summer of 1963 the Lions came along, with founding members including Sonny (Anton Späni from Zurich), Johnny (Fritz Wasser) and Macky Althaus (son of the famous painter Oskar Althaus). Macky's brother Lucky (Lukas Althaus) used to hang around with the crew. Their gang logo was a crouching lion with a raised paw and a snarling jaw. Sonny used Hells Angels jackets that he saw in *Time Magazine* the year before as an inspiration when he designed the Lions jackets. "I only used orange, silver and gold as colors and strong cardboard for the stencil," he

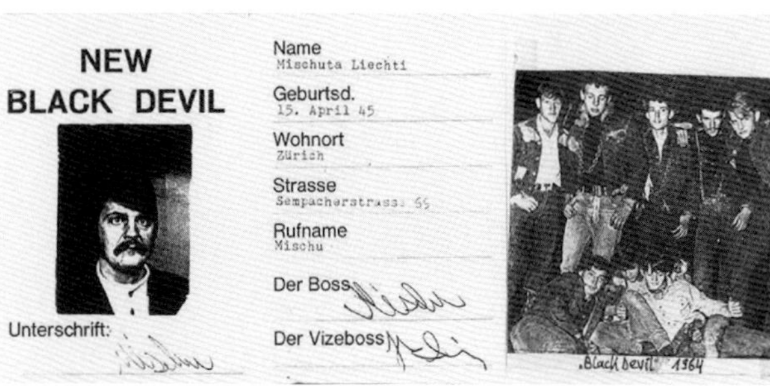

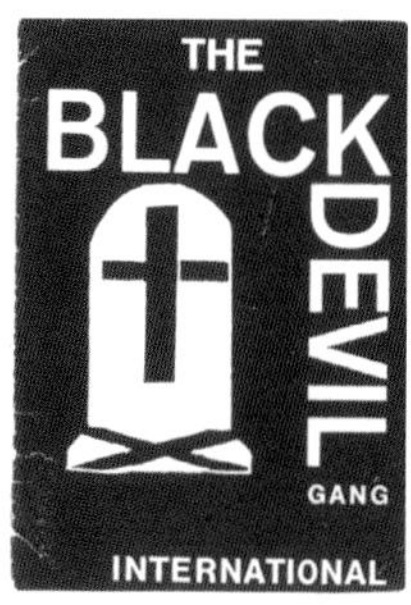

recalls. Every Lions jacket had a star on the left arm and a number on the right arm. Igel wore number 2. The early days of the Lions somehow remain a mystery. But what can be pieced together is that their first leader was Cliff, a Zurich character who is always identified as "Cliff ZH" (ZH = Zurich car plate) in Igels photo albums. Cliff had come from the Davies Gang from Rorschach, in St Gallen, and Igel delivered him to Basel. After Cliff left, Zorro (Billy Bickel) became the boss for a short spell, and finally, at the end, hunk-like Sumo (Hans Breitenstein) took the reigns. By that time, Igel, Conny (Conrad Ferdinand Thudium), Blacky, Billy, Pat, Joe and Sigi Michel (who later became famous as Trompetenmichi, playing his trumpet at the Swiss national soccerteam games) formed the core of the gang. Sigi was the last one to join just before the Basel autumn fair in 1963. The Lions stomping grounds were in the old town Kleinbasel, and some places in Kleinhüningen. Members enjoyed the Himalaya and Cortina Bob joy rides at the fair grounds, and had their suicidal kind of funstanding in the roadways of the city tunnels — today you can't live this particular kind of fun at swiss fairgrounds. The Lions lasted another year until fall of 1964. Some members would join the Rächer (Revengers) others, like Sigi, went to the Hells Angels.

THE DEMISE OF THE TEENAGE GANGS: BLACK DEVIL AND RÄCHER

In 1964 there was a final flare up of the Swiss Teenage Gangs boom. At the Basel Autumn Fair, the sinister looking Black Devils with their leader Micuta (19 year old Mischuta Liechti) entered the scene. They wore long metal chains over denim shirts. Their main hunting ground was the Rheingasse; their dressing style was aggressive like that of a biker gang. Very soon Micuta and Tino clashed over the structure of the gang and Tino split for Zurich after a bitter disagreement. Very soon Tino got the official go-ahead to form the Swiss charter of the Hells Angels, and soon afterwards, Micuta formed a new gang called Rächer (Paybacks). He was joined by Odin (Peter Freund), Puma, Jet (Hanspeter Siegrist) and some likeminded guys. Tino worked hard at Rhine port in these days. The guys of Rächer were real outlaws. They wore repainted Lions jackets, with a newly designed fox emblem on the back. Former Lions members supplied them with the used jackets. The Rächer gang was mainly active in the suburb of Kleinbasel. They liked to pose for mean looking pictures at the Rheingasse takeout. Micuta later on lived in Germany and was active in the red-light district of Munich. He always had a gun close by. Even years later, his girls who worked as prostitutes for him still wore their Black Devil tattoos.

BASEL BIKER GANGS: SKY DEVILS

At the end of the Sixties, a couple of tough, long haired, leather wearing bikers from Basel formed the Sky Devils, inspired by the US biker movies from that era. They rode the biggest and meanest bikes in the country and formed the gang out of necessity — the gang was family unit to those who didn't have a home or any social contacts. They lived with strippers, hookers, and tramps in vacant buildings. They took any job that was offered to them, working in construction or as stage hands and roadies at rock concerts. Sometimes they pimped their own girlfriends or ended up on the skids selling drugs. The Sky Devils had more than thirty members, and according to James (Harry Blind), only a handful are still alive today. Their personal fates would shock even the toughest guys. The grim reaper made the rounds — drugs, alcohol, stabbings, gun fights, deadly diseases and accidents at unsafe construction sites took their toll on the Sky Devils over the years. Harry Blind and former gang leader Thomas Lindenmaier are among the surviving members from that era. Bruno and Zuggi, two other members from the inner circle, are no longer alive. To put it into perspective how dangerous the early Seventies really were, here's a story:

In January 1972 a couple of biker gangs got 30 to 40 of its members to raid the Spectromachie Bar at Claragraben 123. They wanted 150 Swiss Francs that was owed to them. When the owners refused, the bikers wrecked the place. A juke box, a DJ equipment, a pinball machine and a football game table were smashed to bits. Total damage: 44.000 Swiss Francs. The police found out that the Sky Devils were the mainculprits. Policemen then cleared the emergency shelter at a cellar at Spalenring Basel. Eighteen rockers were detained.

GANGS IN ZURICH AND ELSEWHERE

Not only in the city of Basel and in the suburbs, but also in the whole Switzerland and in the German region near the Swiss frontier to Basel there were quite a lot of gangs with written jeans jackets on their way. The big city lights of Zurich attracted many men. For instants some bars and restaurants at Zurich Niederdorf (Schwarzer Ring, Café Mary and Hirschen) were hotspots for mopsters, so tell us Rocky (Peter Geissbühler) and Sonny (Anton Späni, who have furnished us some important informations about this time. In Zurich, there were often arguments and brawls with police presence in this hot zone. But there were no real gunfights, as Igel (Dieter Ehrlich) resumes.

In Zurich, there were some well-known groups of mopsters. They were the legendary notorious Totenkopf Gang with boss Al Capone (Peter Michel), founded around 1958/1959, and the also notorious Rächer, later Revengers with boss Romeo (Werner Berger), founded in 1959. By the way: The gang called Rächer consisted in two groups. A group in Zurich and also a smaller group in Basel, which was led by Tino (Martin Schippert). After serious troubles with the Basel police, Tino and a part of this group went to Zurich, where they had their headquarter in the bin at Helvetiaplatz. They did then a sort of a fusion with the Rächer from Zurich. Some weeks later they changed their names to Revengers. Romeo then had to go in jail for a while. So Tino founded the Lone Star Gang. He became boss of the Lone Stars in 1966. The Lone Star Gang was at that time sort of a link between mopster gangs and and the real motorbike gangs. 1968 the jackets of this Lone Stars were named "Hells Angels Lone Star" — without permission of the Hells Angels international. After the Swiss charter of Hells Angels was accepted by the Hells Angels family (1970), the name Lone Stars had to be given up on the jackets. Since then exist the Hells Angels Switzerland. Their first boss was Tino (Martin Schippert).

The name of 4 Star Gang comes from the four founder members. This quartet is formed by the boss Tom (Walter Grolimund) and the three Weidmann Brothers. At the beginning, they wear black shirts with four stars from officers uniforms. This gang counted several generations of mopsters. Another group from Zurich is called Tiger Gang, with boss Claude (Claude Saugy). It was formed in 1959. They used to be a part of Al Capone's Syndikat (the syndicate). Then in Igels photo scrapbooks at Basel state archive we also find some members of Black Stars, Jaguar, Panther and Flaming Stars. In the city of Winterthur we have The Rockers with boss Rocky (Peter Geissbühler), this group was founded in 1965. Rocky's girlfriend Sybille was from Basel, so Rocky lived for a certain time between the two places Basel and Winterthur. Another well-known gang is The Golden Star with boss Teddy (Fritz Gut), founded in 1964. In Aarau we have Telstar in the early sixties, with Elvis, Jimmy, Douglas and Billy. Last but not least there is also the Davis-Gang in action at small swiss town Rorschach. It was founded around 1961. They had a reputation as real diehards. Cliff, who also led the Basel gang The Lions for some months, came from this Davis-Gang in Rorschach. It was Igel who brought him to Basel.

For further informations about all these gangs you can consult the compilation of swiss gangs and groups on the next pages.

SO THEN, THANK YOU . . .

The show is over, the curtain has fallen. The chronicle of the teenage street gangs of Switzerland is closed.

It's time to say thank you. We want to thank the dozens of protagonists for the interviews they've given us in the last years at numerous bars in Gundeldingen and Kleinbasel. Some of them have died since, others are still with us. These contemporaries have lifted the curtain to look at the history of the teenage street gangs in Basel from all angles. We pay them our respects for the trust that they had in us that we would get their history right. Special thanks to Raymond, Vreni, Jess, Kid, Rumy, Blacky, Muus, Clochard, Rio, Doc, Jacky, Micuta, Rita, Esthy, Joyce and James. But also to René, Hans and the local statistics bureau of Basel. Further thanks to Erich, Ernesto, Fredi, Richard, Birgit and all the others who supported our research in one way or another. They know who they are.

Halbstark, Baby-Baby, Halbstark. Keep On Rocking!

—Lukas Müller and Dieter "Igel" Ehrlich

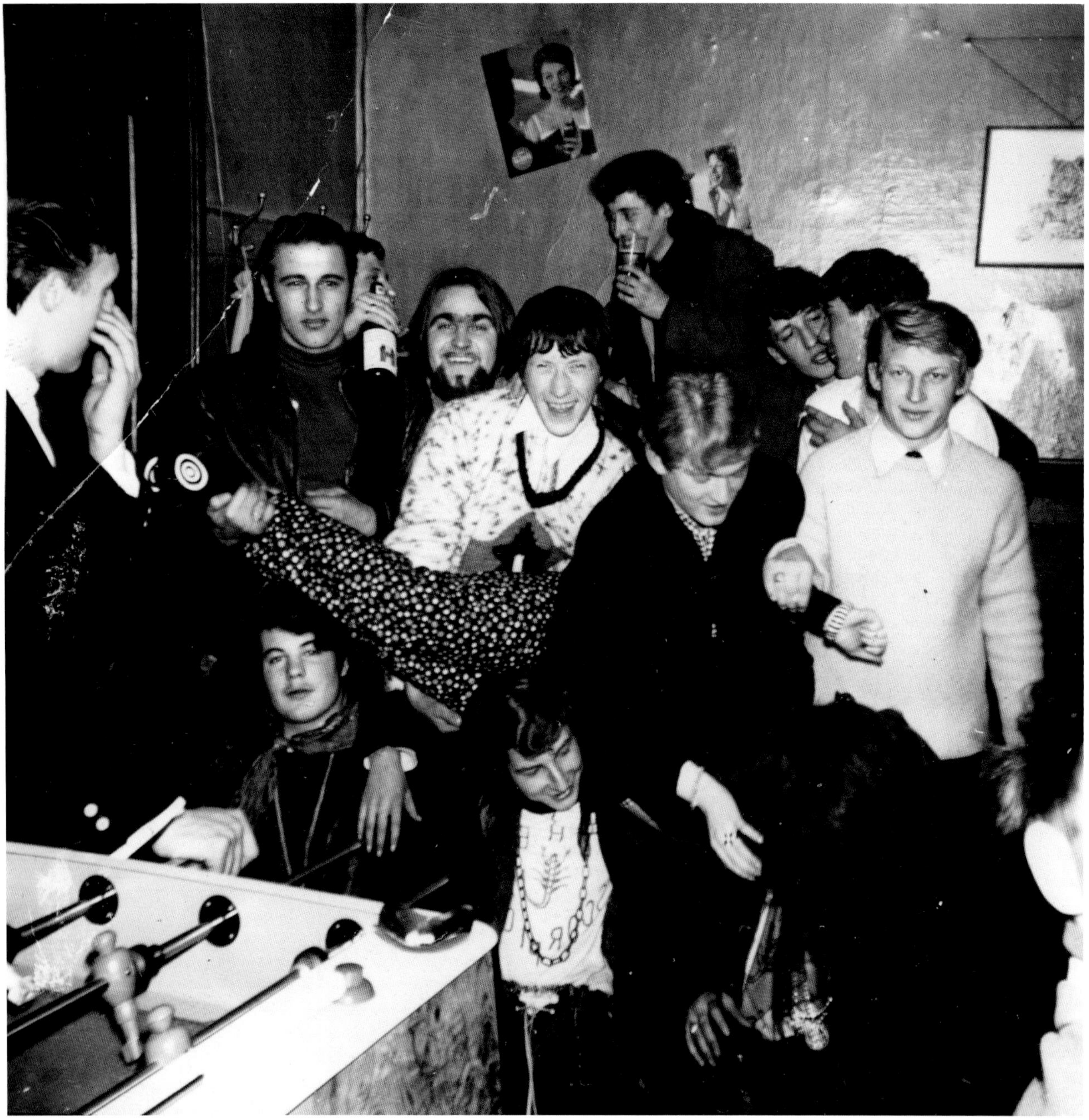

Members of the Black Star gang, Basel and other Basel gangs are having a drink at some unknown bar back in the mid 60s.

list of swiss gangs

BASEL

RED DEVIL, BASEL

Formed: late 1950s. Bosses: Urs Meier and Eugen Muff. This was the oldest and largest gang from Basel. Bruno Meier claims to have joined in 1958, while other sources suggest that they did not form until 1959 or 1960. At one point, they included up to forty members, many with motorcycles. Gang members included Eugen Muff, Urs Meier, Freddy Madörin and his brother, Jörg Ebi (who died in Ireland), Freddy Koch, Franz Lang, Bruno Meier, Peter Mai, Herbert Häuptli, Tullio, Schmuddle, Max Wasser, Ruth Bechtel, the Schellenbaum-sisters, and Margrit von Arx.

BROADWAY TRAMPERS

Formed: 1959; active through 1962. Formed at Café Broadway, located at Steinenvorstadt in Basel, the Broadway Trampers were a small gang of five teenagers. Dieter "Igel" Ehrlich joined them in 1960.

VAMPIR CLUB, BASEL

Formed: around 1960; active through 1967. Boss: Raymond "Killer" Christen, vice: Ruedi "Red" Schmid. The Vampirs originally formed as the Vampir Club, Basel, with founding members Raymond Christen, Jess, and Red. Their first Vampir Club Basel emblem was a spider, luridly emblazoned on the back of their jackets. By February 1963, their emblem had evolved into a bat, and the name became, "Strangers Gang Vampir, Basel". Despite the new moniker, they were still simply known as the "Vampir" (vampire) gang to all concerned. Members were Raymond "Killer" Christen, Ruedi "Red" Schmid, Max "Jess" Gass, Mucky, Werner "Cliff" Kesselring, Ronny Ort, Mexican Joe (from Mexico),Tscheito, Marcel "Jacky" Zimmerly (for almost half a year during 1962), Billy, Arnoldo "Kid" Steiner (who was the second vice boss for a short time in October 1963, until Red took over again), Beat "Ted" Bucher, Francois "Dracula" Jilly, Roger "Muus" Frech, Peter "Whisky" Frech, Peter "Elefant" Flach (who would become the bass player of The Dynamites in 1966), Arrigo "Johnny" Prestini, Bob, James, Priska "Rumy" Sonderegger, Astrid "Jenny" Bieri, Ferdinand "Ricky" Schäfer (ex-Venom and ex-Blizzard), René "Blacky" Schwarz, Hanspeter "Rio" Rütti, and René "Clochard" Rütti, who joined in November 1964. Dieter "Igel" Ehrlich has also received a Vampir membership passport, but he never ended up wearing their jacket.

BLACK STAR GANG, BASEL

Formed: 1961; active through 1968. First boss: Beat "Ted" Bucher, 2nd boss from 1962 on: Mecky (also known as Zack-Zack). Formed by Beat "Ted" Bucher (born 1944), this gang's emblem was a black star and one cowboy boot. Early members, aside from Boss Beat "Ted" Bucher were Mecky (Zack-Zack), a German from across the border in Loerrach, Mille Amman, Johnny, and the Oettli brothers. By the time when Hanspeter "Rio" Rütti joined them in 1962, Mecky (Zack-Zack) already used to rate as their boss. Their old boss Ted basically left (to join the more harmless Vampir, Basel) due to too many fights, and small crimes that he did not want to become part of. The final lineup of the Black Star Gang, Basel included a few beatnicks, and even some girls. At that point, their tough Halbstarken – gang stand was over. Hans "Boy" Wilhelm, a photographer and a member of the local Basel 60s garage rock band The Hell Hounds, was vice-boss during their final beatniks-and-girls-tolerating line up.

EXPRESS KILLER CLUB, also known as EXPRESS KILLERS, BASEL

Formed: 1962. Boss: René Bösiger. The ten-member EKC was Dieter "Igel" Ehrlich's second gang. Igel's nickname at this time was The Rebell. The back of his jacket flashed THE REBELL EKC BASEL in studs and silver rivets.

VENOM, BASEL, also known as VENOM CLUB, BASEL

Formed: 1962; active through end of February 1963. Boss: Marcel "Jacky" Zimmerli. Formed by ex Vampir Club, Basel member Marcel "Jacky" Zimmerli (who got kicked out of the Vampir Club after getting into a fight with their vice-boss), and Schlangepfiff, famous for his brutal head butts. The emblem on the back of their jackets was a golden bronze-colored print of their boss Jacky's hand, along with the hand painted club name Venom and the name of the town Basel. Members also wore small black sleeve patches bearing a yellow skull and crossbones, with the name VENOM printed on them. They broke up in March of 1963, with most members moving on to The Blizzard Club, Basel. Members included Marcel "Jacky" Zimmerli, Schlangenpfiff, Ferdinand "Ricky" Schäfer, Hans-Peter "Jet" Siegrist, Michel "Mario" Clemens, Conrad "Conny" Thudium, Mike, Trinker-Raymond, Max "Jess" Gass, Choya, and Jimmy.

THE BLIZZARD CLUB, BASEL
Formed: March 1963; active through 1968. Boss: Marcel "Jacky" Zimmerli; Vice-Boss: Ferdinand "Ricky" Schäfer.One of the most important gangs from Basel, The Blizzard Club was formed out of the ashes of the Venom gang by Marcel "Jacky" Zimmerli (born: 1947), who named the gang, whose tag appears misspelled as The Blitzard Club Basel on the very first version of their jackets. Ricky created the round metal buckle belts bearing a lightning bolt, with "The Blizzard" inscribed on them. They were the first gang for Martin "Tino" Shippert, who later took over Romeo's action, to first become the boss of the Rächer, Basel in Autumn of 1964, and then by January 1965, of the Lone-Star Gang, Zürich. The Blizzard Club, Basel were never including more than 12 members at once. Members at one point or the other were including Marcel "Jacky" Zimmerli, Ferdinand "Ricky" Schäfer, Schlangenpfiff, Martin "Tino" Schippert, Martin "Mischuta" Liechti, Johnny, René "Blacky" Schwarz, René "Clochard" Rütti, Hanspeter "Rio" Rütti, Michel "Mario" Cle https://www.alamy.com/stock-image-switzerland-map-grey-169140405.html mens, Bruno "Nilsen" Sutter, Otti "Blondy" Bucher, Cliff, René "Lee" Schmassmann, Ferdinand "Ricky" Schäfer, Jimmy, Robert "Joe" Amm, and Choya

THE PUMAS
Formed: 1962; active through 1965. Bosses: brothers Erwin "Schwynli" Stauffer, Horst "Hotte" Stauffer, Willi Stauffer. Formed by Erwin Häring, and Peter Halbeisen, The Pumas were a tough gang consisting of ten delinquents from the Aesch suburb of Basel. Members included the Stauffer brothers Schwynli, Hotte, and Willi, founders Erwin Häring and Peter Halbeisen, and Ruedi Racine, Willi Alder, and Beat "Ted" Bucher (ex-Black Star and ex-Vampir). Ted stayed with The Pumas for about six months before returning to The Vampir, Basel.

THE JETS, BASEL
Formed: 1962; active through 1965. Boss: Paul "Doc" Marggraff, vice boss: Jacky Jacquiéry, 2nd vice boss: Arrigo "Johnny" Prestini. Formed by Paul "Doc" Marggraff (born June 16, 1946), who earned his nickname with his ability to pull a pistol as fast as famous western gunslinger Doc Holliday. Their emblem was three lightning bolts clenched in a fist, which was hand painted onto the back of each gang members jacket by their boss, Paul "Doc" Marggraff. Jacky Jacuiery exited the gang when he was drafted into the Swiss army in 1964. He would go on to marry Eveline, the sister of The Dynamites lead guitarist Rolf Antener. By 1965, Doc, who used to work as a photographer, quit the gangs to open the "Beat-Club" at his parents' Restaurant Krug in Basel. It became an instant hot spot for local Swiss beat/garage bands to play. In 1973, Doc moved to Ecuador, South America, where he worked as a fashion photographer, as well as the official distributor for Harley-Davidson motorcycles, and gained international fame as an Olympian and the Pan American Champion in pistol shooting. Jets members were: Dieter "Igel" Ehrlich, Slim, Conrad "Conny" Thudium, Jerry, Arrigo "Johnny" Prestini, Erwin "Sunny" Metzger, Terry, Tommy, Ted, Tiger, Jess, Jimmy, Alex, Manfred "Cliff" Schmid (also known as "Elvis" from Muttenz), Lexi, Rudi "Pecos" Stücklin, Vreni Ott, Jenny.

THE LIONS, BASEL
Formed: end of summer 1963; active through1966. First boss: "Cliff" (ex-Davis Gang, Rohrschach), later on Billy "Zorro" Bickel, and then finally Hans "Sumo" Breitenstein. The Lions were formed by Anton "Sonny" Spaeni, Fritz "Johnny" Wasser, and Markus "Macky" Althaus (son of artist Oskar Althaus) in 1963. Their jackets were handmade by Sonny. The club membership was limited to twelve, each with jackets that were numbered from 1 to 12. Zorro came up with the gang name which made their first public gang appearance (complete with their finished jackets) at Herbstmesse Basel, in October

of 1963. You had to be a tough, fearless fighter in order to join the Lions. Macky Althaus would end up as the rhythm guitarist of beat groups The Silverbeats and The Blue Sounds. Members were: Anton "Sonny" Spaeni, Markus "Macky" Althaus, Fritz "Johnny" Wasser, Lukas "Lucky" Althaus (brother of Markus), Dieter "Igel" Ehrlich (until May 17, 1964), Cliff (ex-Davis Gang, Rohrschach), Billy "Zorro" Bickel (and his dog), Hans "Sumo" Breitenstein, Conrad "Conny" Thudium, "Sigi" Michel, Jacky, Billy, Milly, Pat, Blacky, Spitzgi, Joe, and Kelly.

TIGER CLUB, BASEL
Formed: early 1960s. Nothing is known about this small, short-lived gang, photos taken by Karlheinz Weinberger do exist, showing their members wearing round chain medallions featuring the face of a tiger and name of their club.

PANTHER, BASEL
Formed: early 1960s. No details exist of this early gang from Allschwil, a suburb of Basel.

THE BLACK DEVIL GANG, BASEL
Formed: summer 1964; active through the end of 1964. Boss: Martin "Mischuta" Liechti (born: Zürich April 15. 1945) Vice boss: Jeff. Formed by ex-Blizzard Club, Basel member Martin "Mischuta" Liechti in summer of 1964. They were active a few short months, closing up shop before the end of the year. Mischuta reportedly got expelled from the city of Basel, and then moved to Winterthur to form the Black Devil Gang, Zürich in 1965. They included well over a dozen of members, including: Jeff, Mike, Ricky (from Winterthur), and possibly Terry.

RÄCHER, BASEL
Formed: 1964. Boss: Martin "Tino" Schippert. Second boss from 1965: Jet Siegrist. They were able to use the name of Romeo's early gang the Rächer, Zürich with Romeo's permission. By the end of 1964, Tino moved back to Zürich to take over Romeo's Lone Star Gang that eventually became known as the Hells Angels, Zürich on December 20, 1970. After Tino's departing the Rächer, Basel continued for about two years with Jet (ex-Venom, Basel) as the new boss. Members were: Martin "Tino" Schippert, Hans-Peter "Jet" Siegrist (ex Venom, Basel), Cliff, Johnny, Puma, Elvis, Schlangenpfiff, Little, and Kelly.

SKY DEVILS
Formed: May 1969, active for less than 10 years. First boss: Jacky, 2nd boss from 1972 on: Thomas Lindenmayer. This savage motorcycle gang from Basel was inspired by movies such as *The Wild Angels*. They formed in May 1969 at the Klagemauer (located at Barfüsserplatz) in Basel, and were including a total of 36 members over the years. Harry "James" Blind (who used to hang out with the Halbstarken back in 1963 already, rates as one of their last surviving members. Names of the known members included: Jacky, Harry "James" Blind, Thomas Lindenmaier, Bruno, and Zuggi.

BOA, BASEL
Formed: early 60s. This is the only gang in our listing that does not count as a true Halbstarken-Gang. They wore blue jeans, and could be identified by a cloth badges (bearing the name BOA BASEL) attached onto the upper arms of their jackets. They were a small club that hung out with the Halbstarken gangs. They were known to throw big parties. Members were: "Niggi" Tschopp (rhythm guitarist of the Tombstones / Cousins), Jacques André, Gilbert "Mozart" Hänni, and Wolfgang "Stägge" Stahli.

AARAU

TELSTAR-GANG, AARAU
The main gang from Aarau during the early 60s. Members included Elvis, Jimmy, Douglas, and Billy.

VAMPIR CLUB, AARAU
Details are unknown, but they used a spider emblem on their jackets, just like the one used by the Vampir Club Basel. One of their members went by the name of Blacky. Judging from their jackets, they must have been part of Raymond Christen's Vampir Club, Basel.

PARTISANEN GÄNG, AARAU
Details unknown

FRAUENFELD

SCHWARZ PANTHER, FRAUENFELD

They later on became known as the Black Panther.

LUCERNE

TORPEDO

This was the biggest and longest lasting gang from Lucerne, formed in the early 1960's. Known members were including Tello, and Jumbo.

ROHRSCHACH

DAVIS GANG

Formed 1961; active until 1963. Cliff, who would become boss of the Lions, Basel, came out of the Davis Gang.

WINTERTHUR

GOLDEN STAR, WINTERTHUR

Formed: end of 1963. Boss: Fritz "Tex" Gut. The first gang from Winterthur. Peter "Rocky" Geissbühler joined in June of 1964.

TODES BLITZAR

Formed: February 19, 1964. Boss: Peter "Rocky" Geissbühler. This was the short-lived first gang of Peter "Rocky " Geissbühler, composed of four boys who Rocky knew from school. Despite their youth and inexperience, they had professional looking Todes Blitzar membership cards made by February 19, 1964. After they broke up, Rocky joined the Davis Gang on April 13, 1964.

DAVIS GANG, WINTERTHUR

Formed: early 1964. Boss: Blacky. These gangsters took the name of the defunct Davis Gang out of Rohrschach. Members included Blacky, Jimmy, Johnny, Kooky, Liberty, Sharky, and Rocky, who by June 1964 had moved on to the Golden Star Gang, Winterthur.

THE ROCKERS, WINTERTHUR

Formed: January 30. 1965. Boss: Peter "Rocky" Geissbühler. The Rockers took their name from the British "Mods and Rockers" movement. The first incarnation of The Rockers shows the gang members with just the two (big) letters TR painted onto the back of their jackets. Due to unknown circumstances, The Rockers were not existing as a gang for a period of about eleven months, starting from June 1965, by which time Rocky had moved on to Tino's Lone-Star gang for about eleven months. By May '66 they were using their full name (The Rockers) for their colors. They were active for about six years. As Rocky was often seen in the streets of Basel, as his girlfriend Sybill lived there.

THE BLACK DEVIL, ZÜRICH

Formed: early 1965. Boss: Martin "Mischuta" Liechti. After Mischuta's move from Basel to Winterthur back in early 1965 he reformed his gang as The Black Devil, Zurich, this is even though they really came from, a suburb of Zurich.

THE TIGER, WINTERTHUR

Formed: 1965. This small gang from Winterthur had nothing in common with the much older Tiger Gang from the city of Zurich. Known members were Piggi, Blacky, Micke, Wiskhy, and Charly.

THE THUNDERBIRDS, WINTERTHUR

Formed: 1968; active through 1972/1973. Boss: Brian. Details unknown

THE DOGS, WINTERTHUR

Formed: 1968; active through 1971/1972. Details unknown.

ZURICH

4 STAR

Formed: end of summer 1958. Boss: Walter "Tom" Grolimund. The 4 Star gang was the first gang from Zurich, the name representing the four founding members: Tom (Walter Grolimund), and the three Weidmann brothers. They originally wore black shirts with four stars on them. The 4 Star gang used to be part of Al Capone's Syndikat during 1962 – 1965. They existed for several decades and are still celebrating their jubilees in form of events labeled as "Four Star Camp" (organized by their boss Tom, and late member Peter "Rocky" Geissbühler) all couple of years.

RÄCHER, ZÜRICH

Formed 1959; active through 1962. Boss: Werner "Romeo" Berger Rächer was one of the first and most notorious Swiss gangs. Rächer is German for Revenger. See also: The Revenger Gang, Zurich.

THE REVENGER GANG, ZÜRICH

Formed: 1962; active through 1963. Boss: Werner "Romeo" Berger. This was the same gang as Romeo's Rächer, Zurich, but under a new English name. Since Revenger stands for Rächer, various locals (including the police) still went on to call them by their German name, the "Rächer Gang." The backs of all of the gang members' jackets were hand-painted by their boss Romeo, bearing an emblem showing a sword with a snake, along with their name The Revenger Gang. Romeo's jacket was an exception. His bore a stunning handpainted portrait of an Indian chief, along with the line "BOSS" in big letters.

THE LONE-STAR

Formed: 1963. First boss: Werner "Romeo" Berger, second boss, from 1965 forward: Martin "Tino" Schippert. This was basically the same gang as Romeo's Revenger Gang, Zürich under a new name. They wore the same jackets as The Revenger Gang, Zürich (featuring the with a snake emblem), but with the new name of the Lone-Star painted over the old name. At the end of June '64, Romeo was arrested (girlfriend was a minor) and did jail time for seven months. He was released on conditional parole for five yars and could not rejoin the gangs. The Lone-Star torch was passed to Martin "Tino" Schippert directly after Romeo found out that he had to go to jail. Tino came up from The Blizzard, Basel to form The Racher, Basel, before moving to Zurich to form a new Lone Star gang in early 1965. They wore the same colors as the earlier gang (painted by Romeo). Some photos even show Tino wearing Romeo's Boss jacket with the Indian chief on the back. By 1968, they had begun to unofficially use "Hells Angels - Lone Star" for emblem on back of their jackets, which was noticed by the real Hells Angels. Tino was asked to travel to the USA for a test period of two months to become an official member of the Hells Angels and to form a Swiss franchise. By December 20, 1970 they became officially known as the Hells Angels, Zurich (with Tino as boss).

TOTENKOPF GANG

Formed: 1959; active through1964/65. Boss: Al Capone (Peter Michel); Vice-Boss: Peter Grob. Al Capone's main goal was to form an organization called the Syndikat (the syndicate) that would make him the boss of all the Swiss gangs. However, since because most of the gangs wanted to stay independent, only a few gangs (most of them from Zurich) eventually agreed to join the Syndikat, which existed 1962-65.

THE TIGER GANG, ZÜRICH

Formed: 1959. Boss: Claude Saugy. This was one of the earliest and most notorious gangs from Zurich, and part of Al Capone's Syndikat from 1962 forward.

F.L.J. ZÜRICH

Formed: early 1960s. Details unknown. No one recalls the significance of the acronym.

RED LIGHT, ZÜRICH

A later gang circa 1967-70.

THE DIABOLIC GANG, ZÜRICH

Formed in the late mid 1960s.

MISCELLANEOUS RELATED SWISS GANGS

JAGUAR

This classic Swiss gang is believed to have originated in Zurich in the early 60s early. Their members show up in many photos.

FLAMING STARS

Details unknown. The only known member was "Jessy".

EL DORADOS

Details unknown

STRANGERS

Details unknown

—Rolf Reiben

1962

01 / the express killer gang at the express bar, basel
july 1962

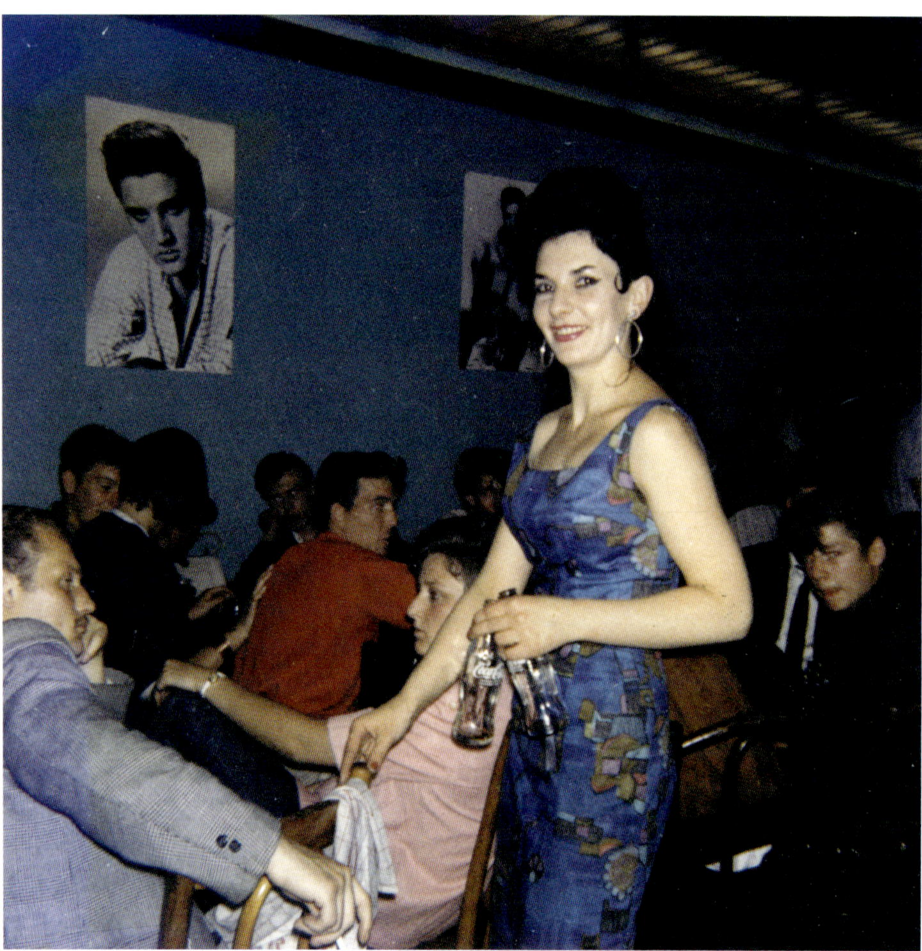

Barmaid Rita at the Express Bar, Basel, July 1962.

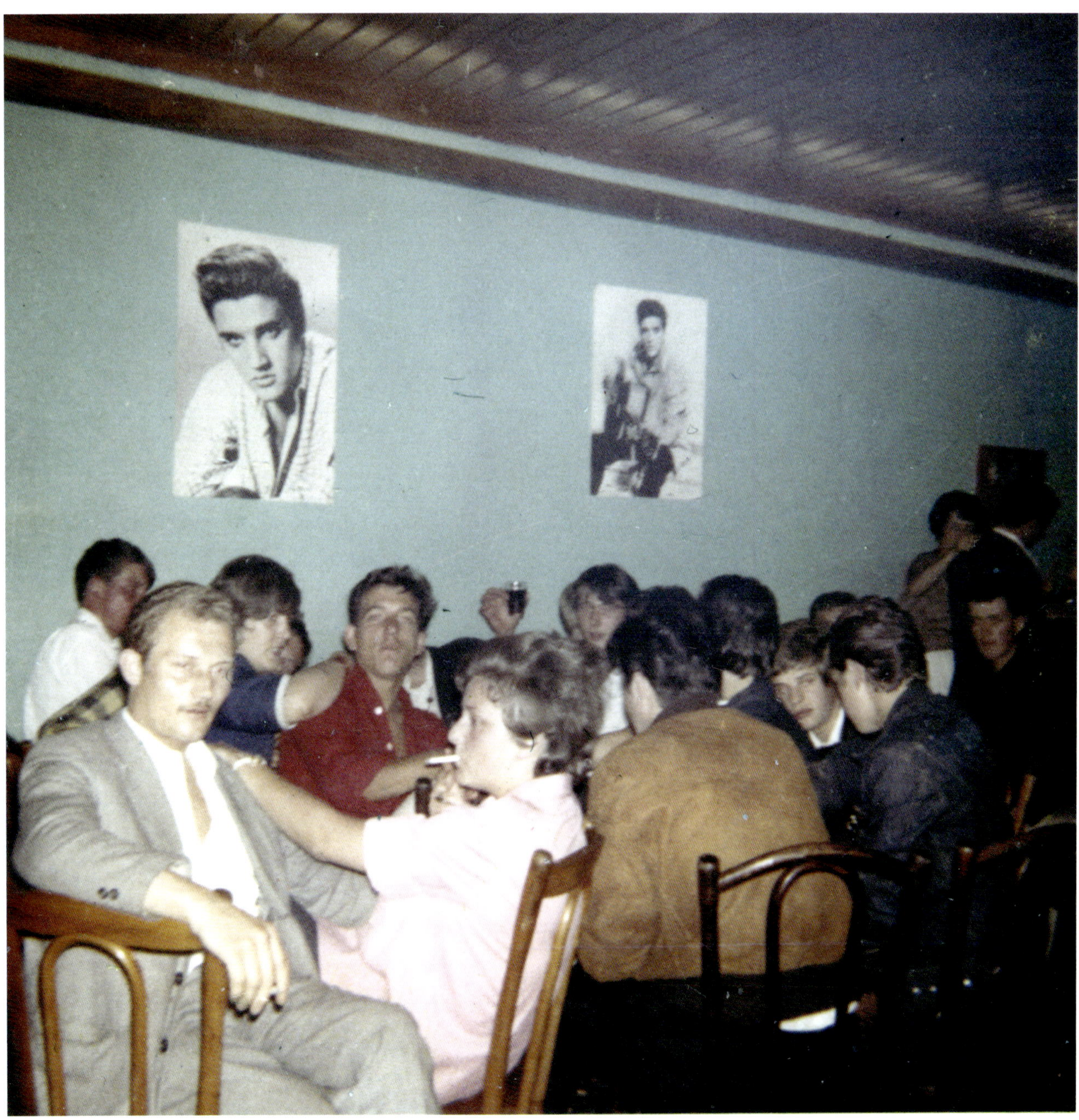

Hugo and Gipsy (with cigarette).

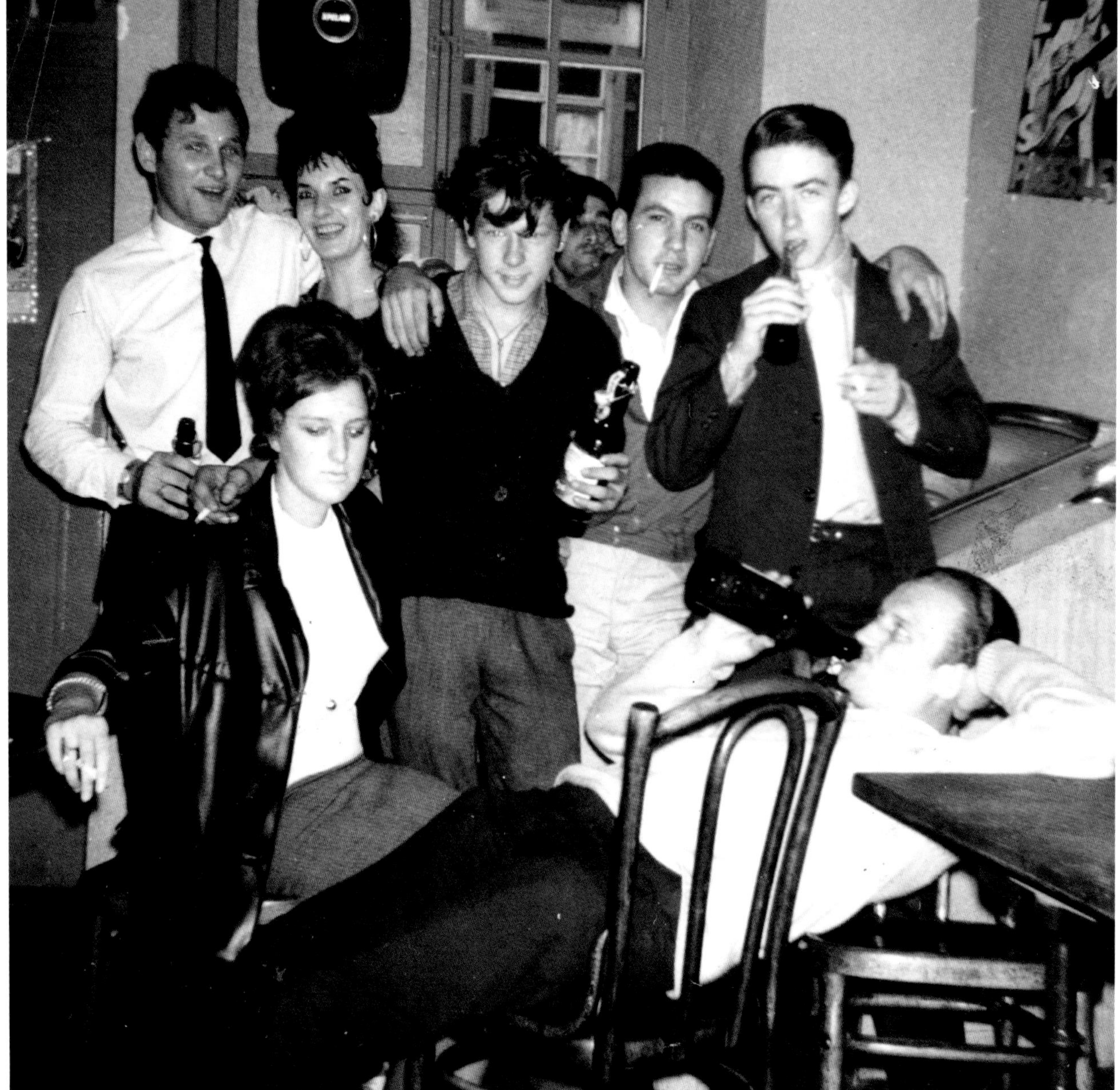

Front: Gipsy (smoking) and Hugo (drinking). Back: Tello and barmaid Rita with party boys.

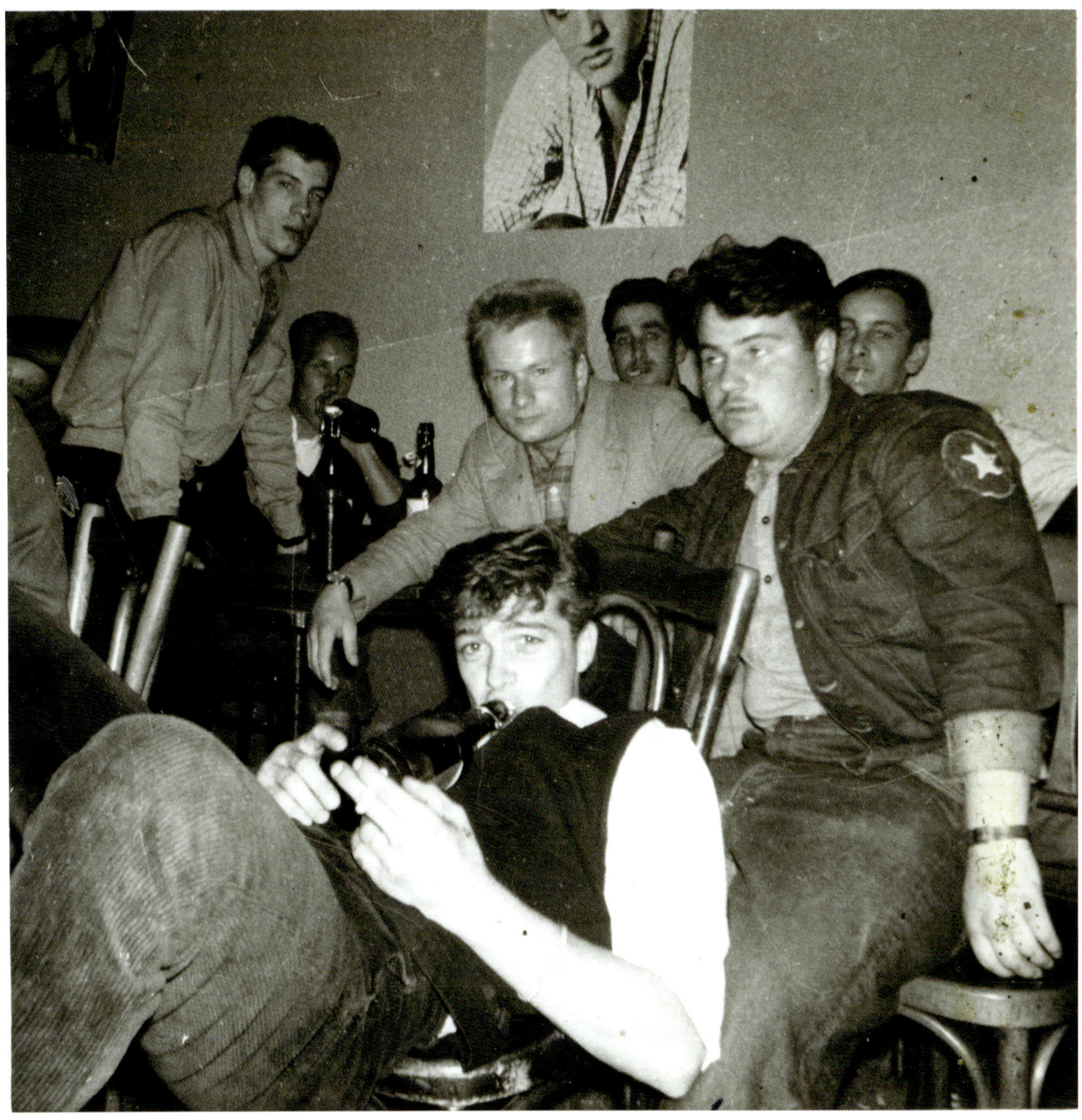

Igel (in sports coat) and friends.

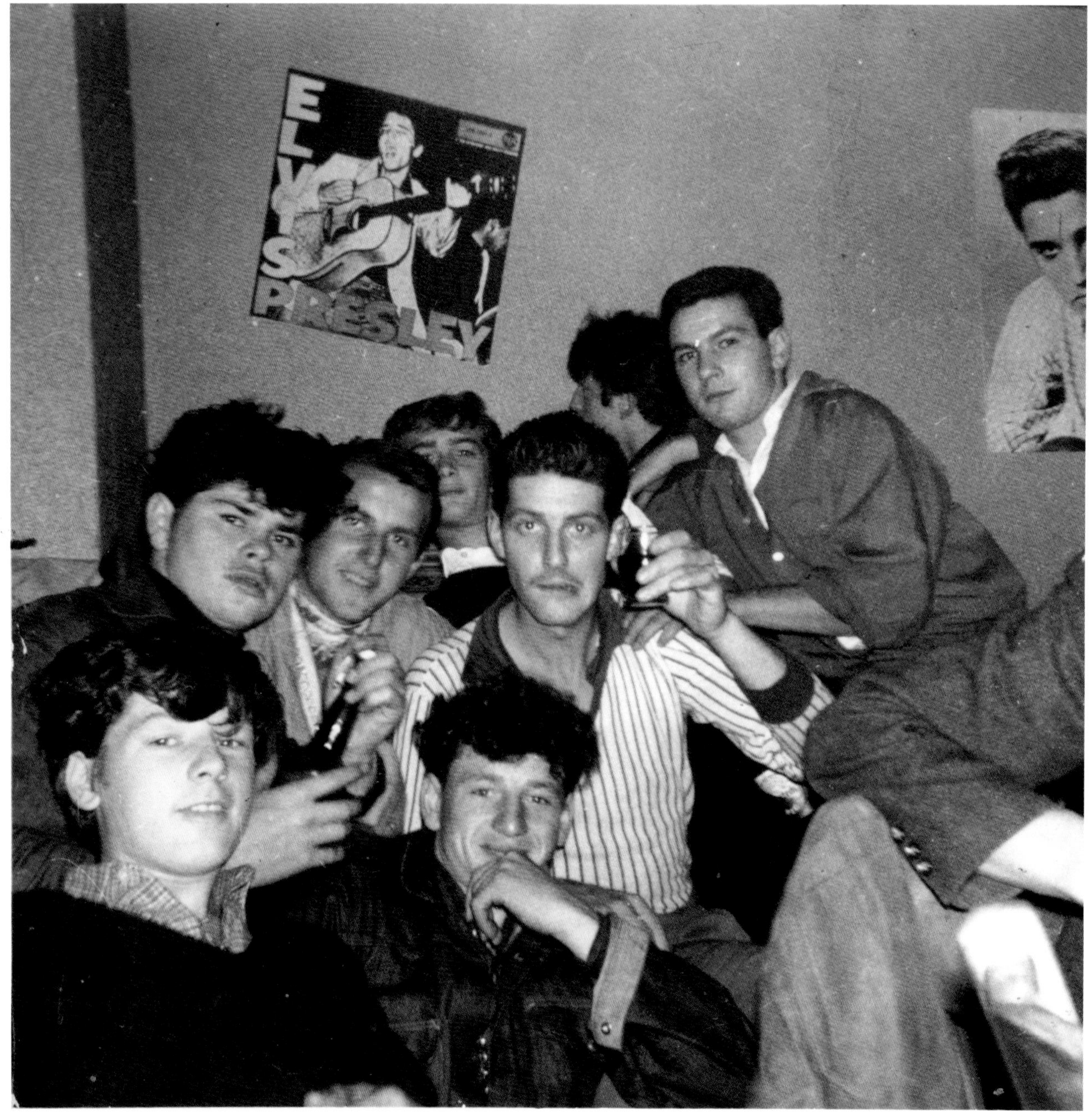

Mackey aka Zack-Zack (with bottle) and crew. Mackey was from Lorrach, Germany, and died young in a motorcycle crash.

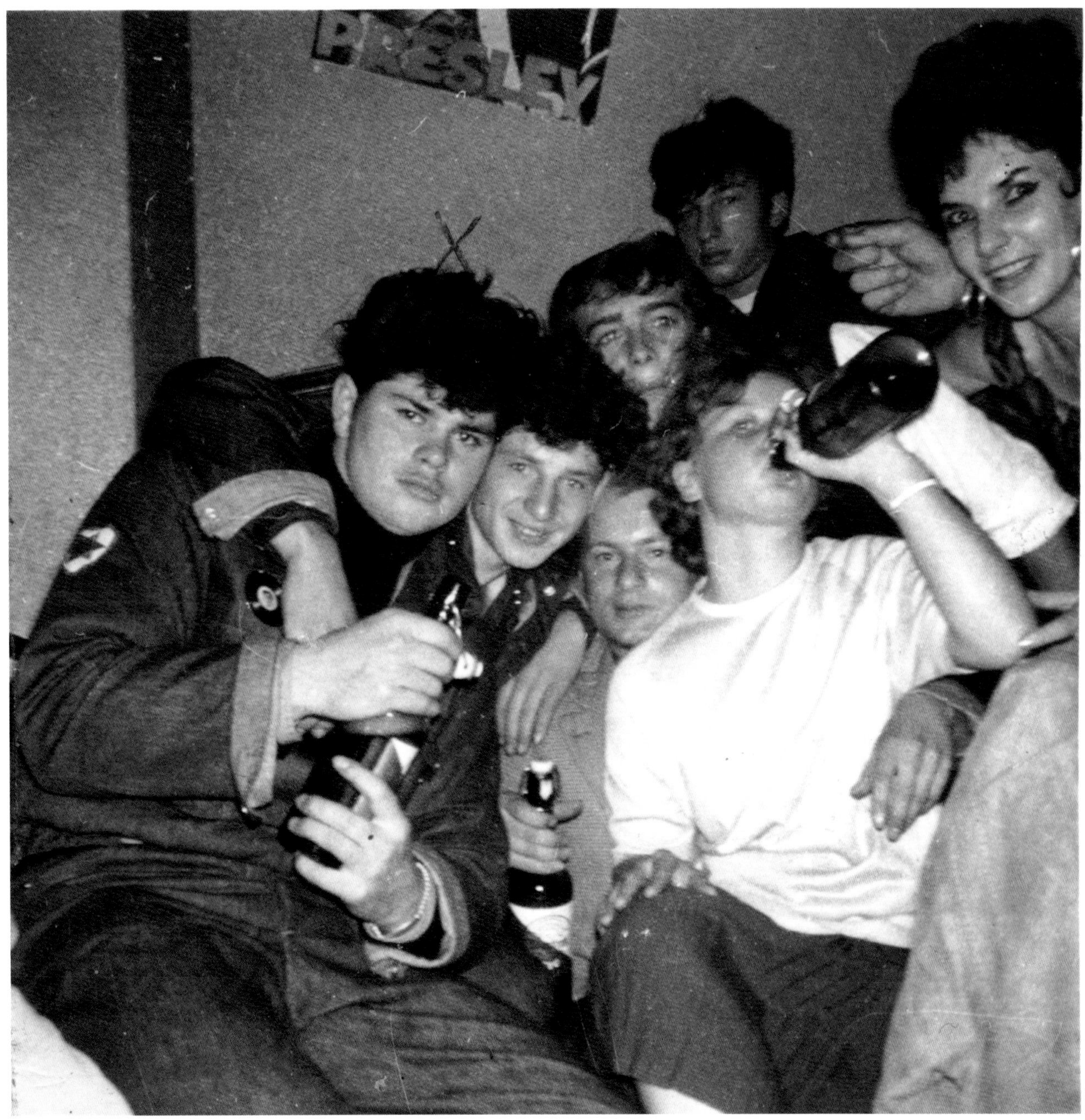

Zack-Zack with Igel and Angel and the gang. Rita at right.

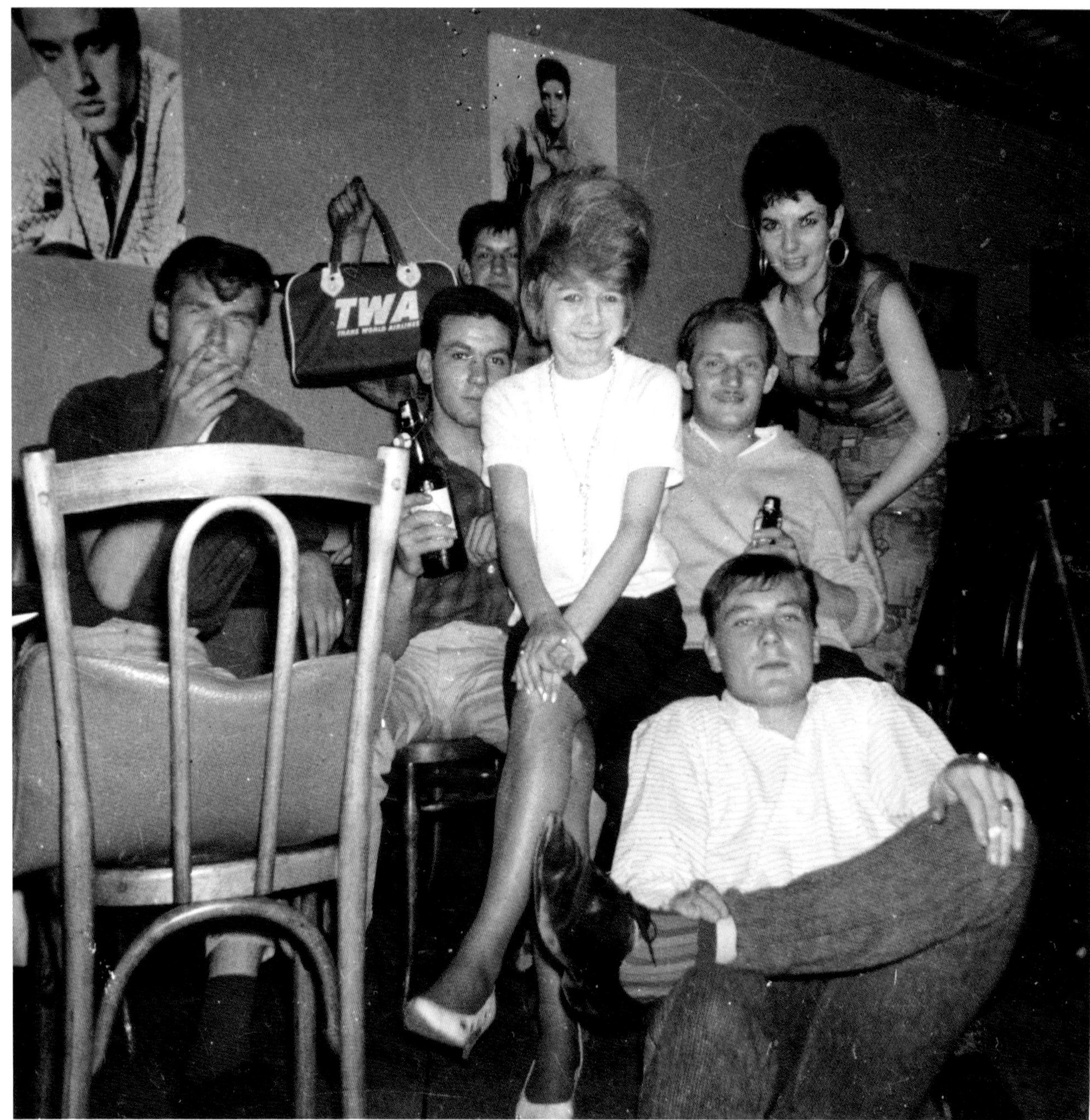

Leggy hairhopper with Fritz Breitenstein (bottom right), who was always looking for trouble. Hugo and Rita at right.

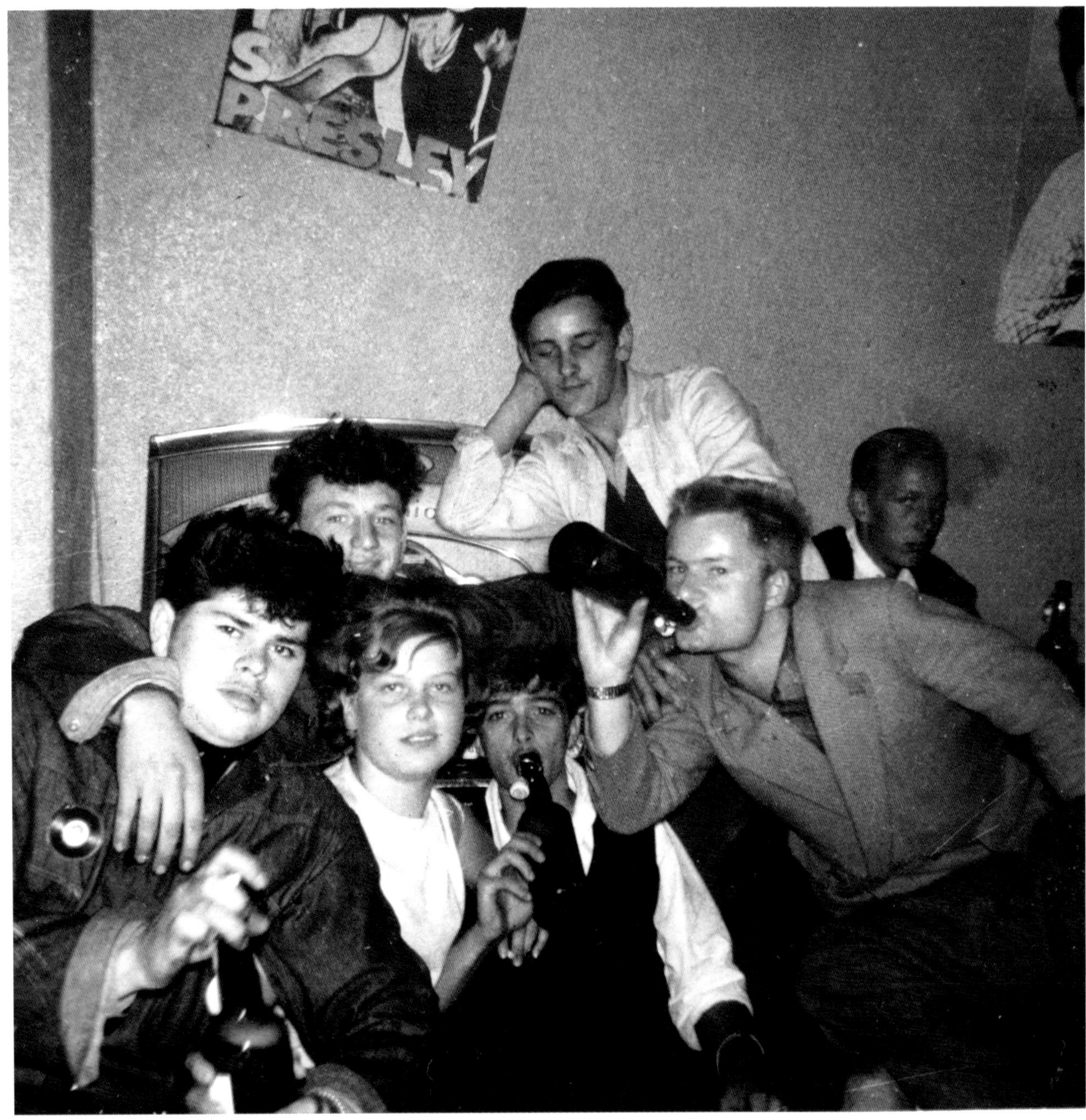

The Express Bar on Rheingasse was open every night. Zack-Zack and Angel; Igel with beer.

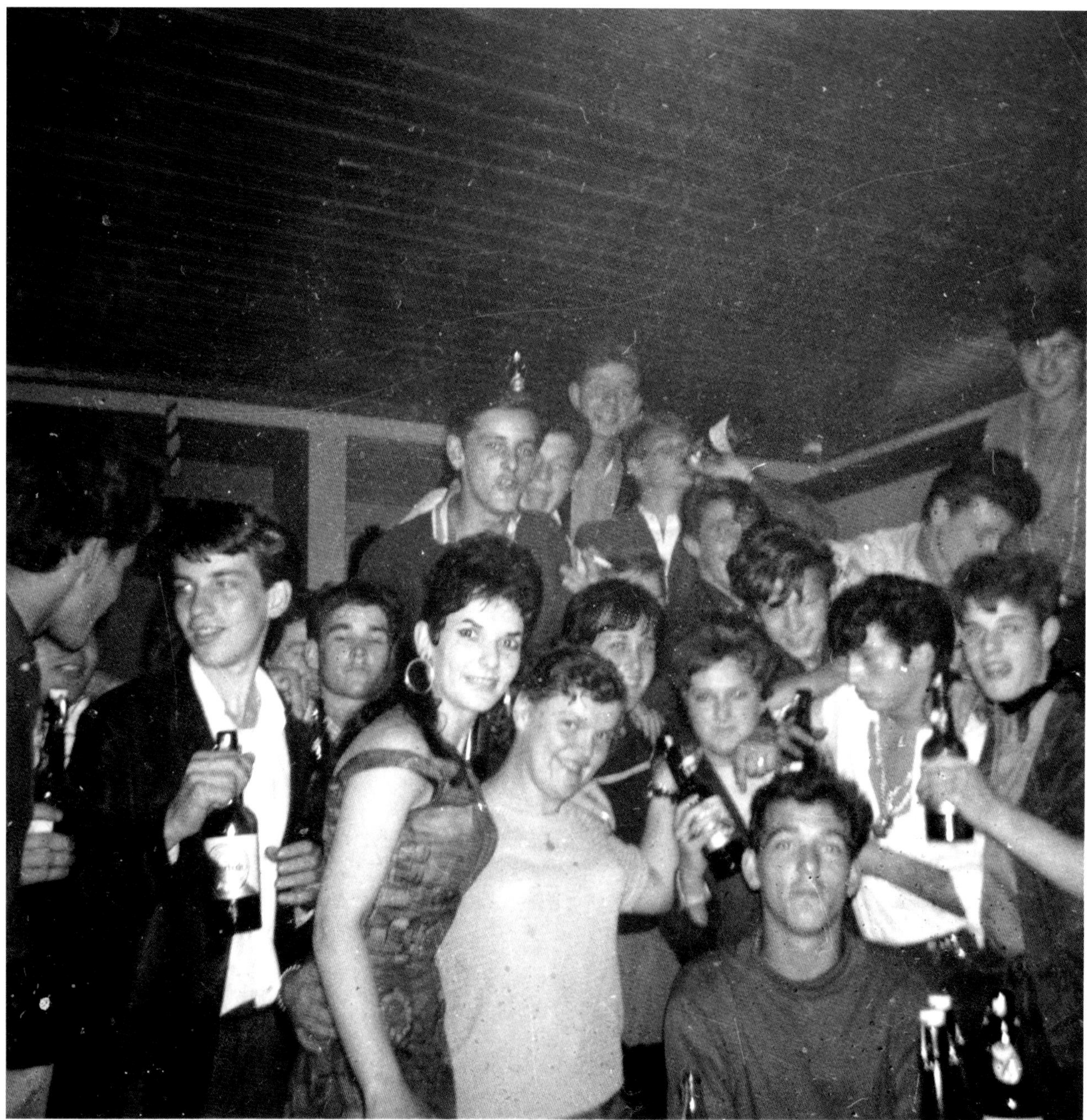

Barmaid Rita with the wild bunch at the Express Bar.

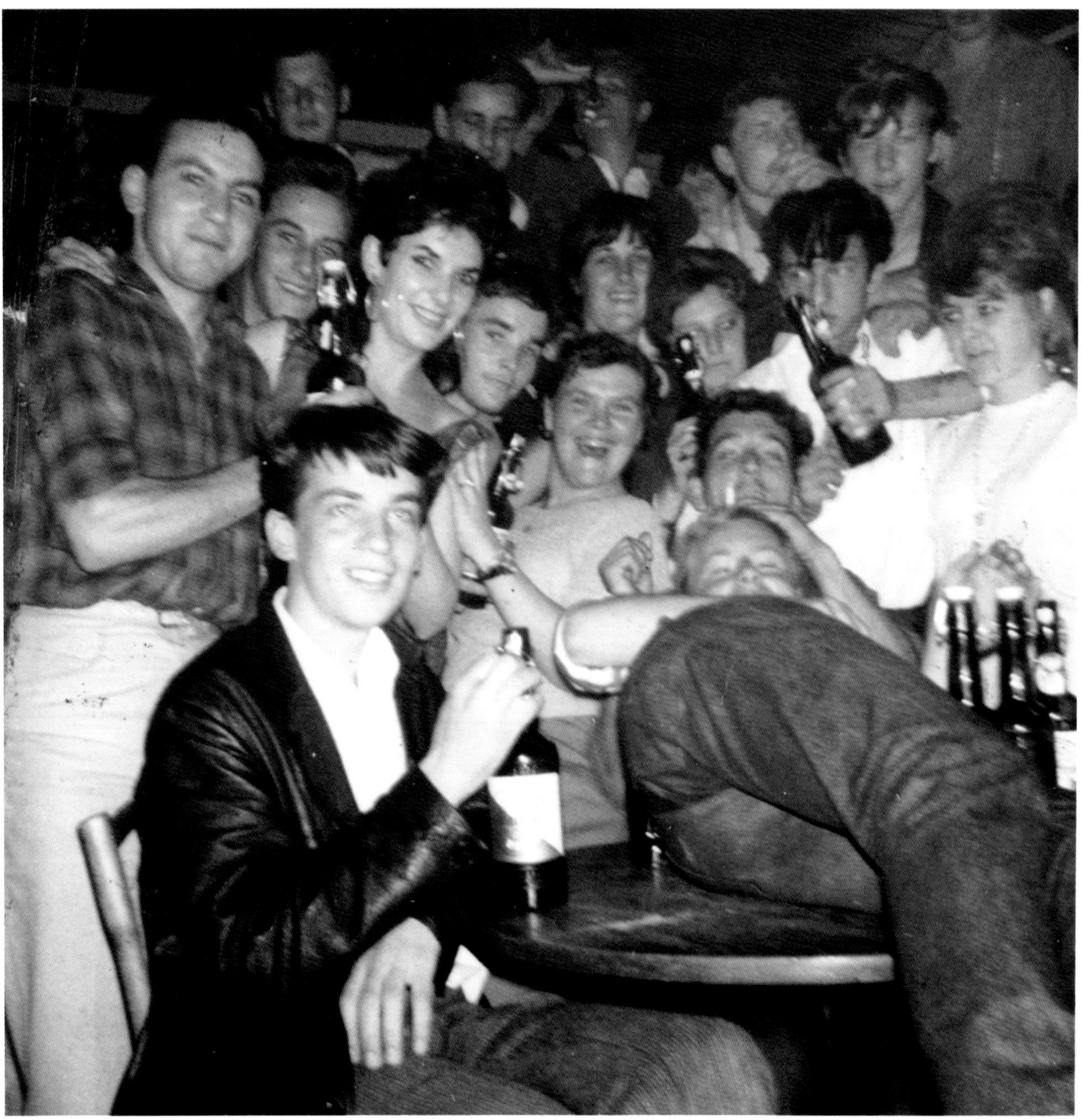

Another boozy night at the clubhouse. Igel on table, Rita and Johnny in crowd.

02/ out in the streets
summer 1962

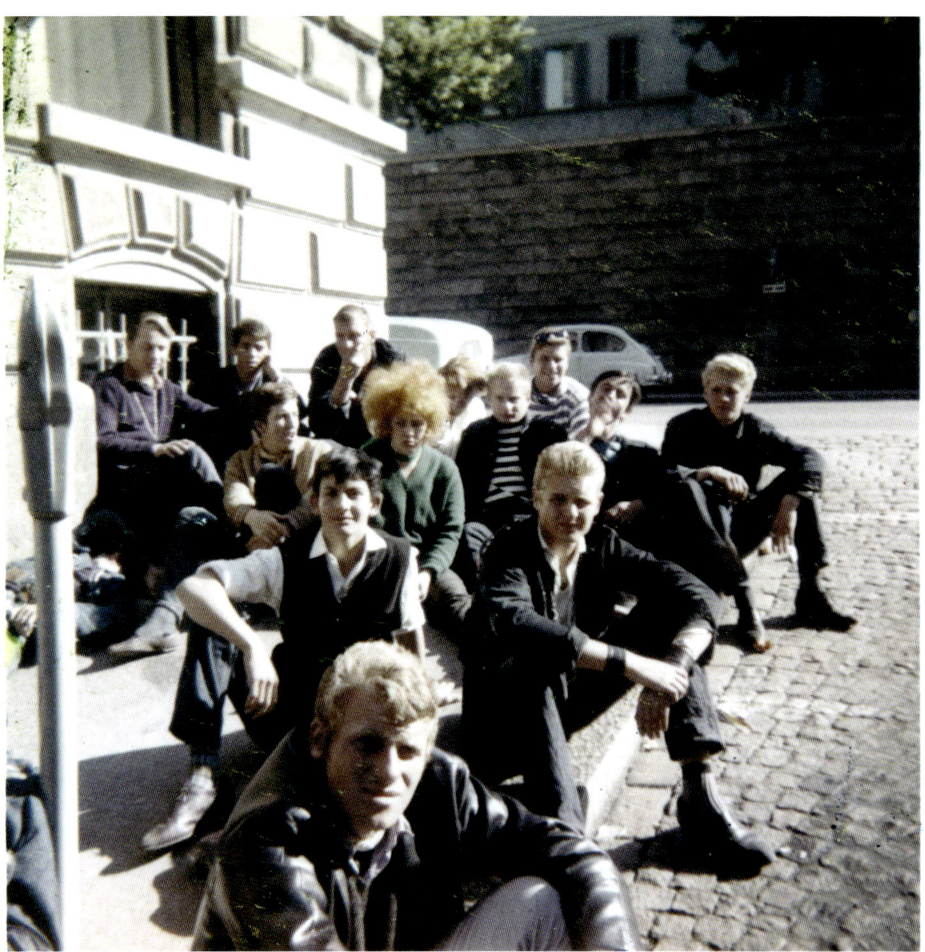

Zurich, Knabenschiessen. Igel and friends.

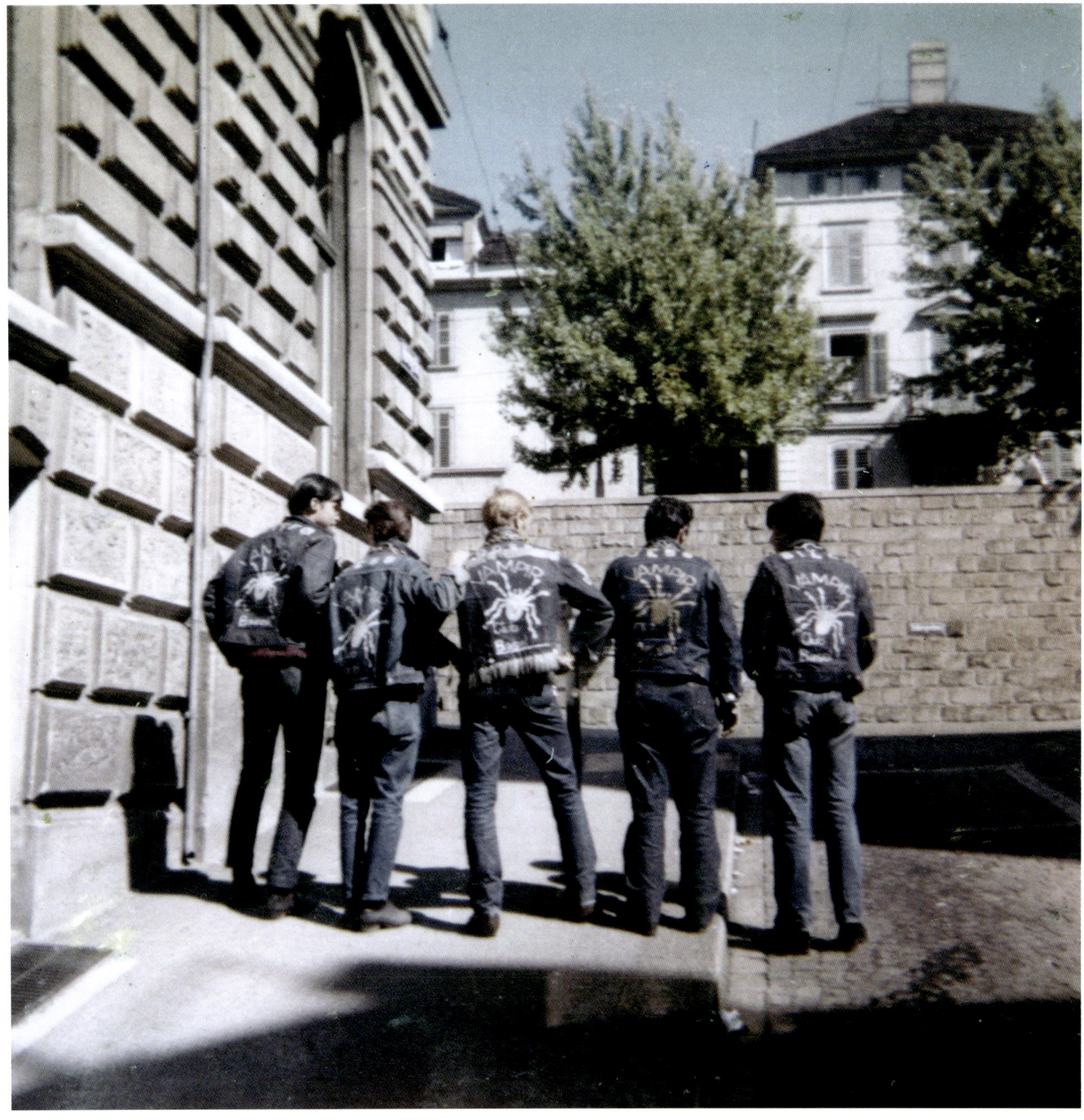

Strangers Gang Vampir Basel, 1962: Cliff, Jess, Boss Raymond, Mucki, Billy.

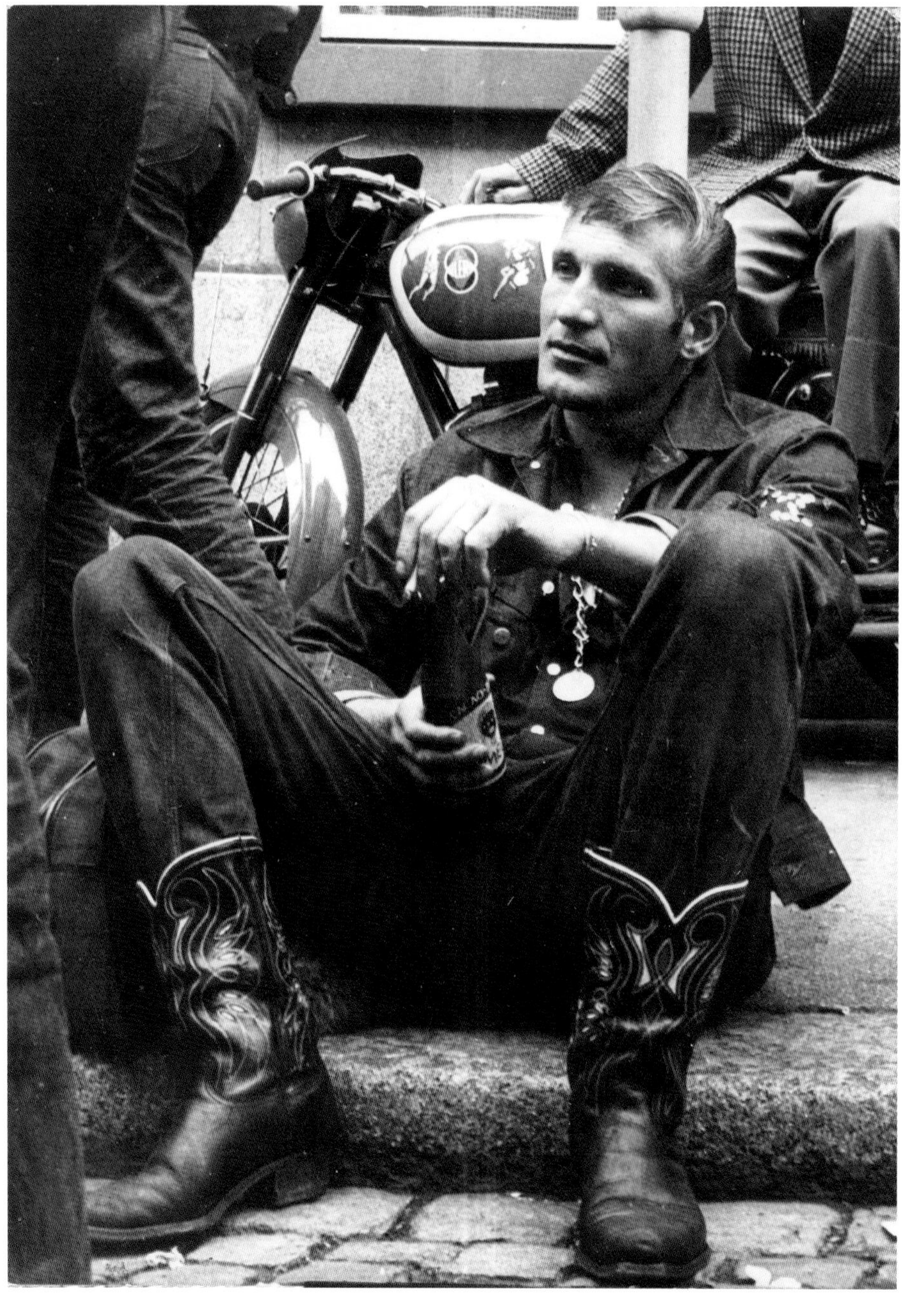

Rene Bosinger was a member of the EKC. No one messed with Rene. (News File photo)

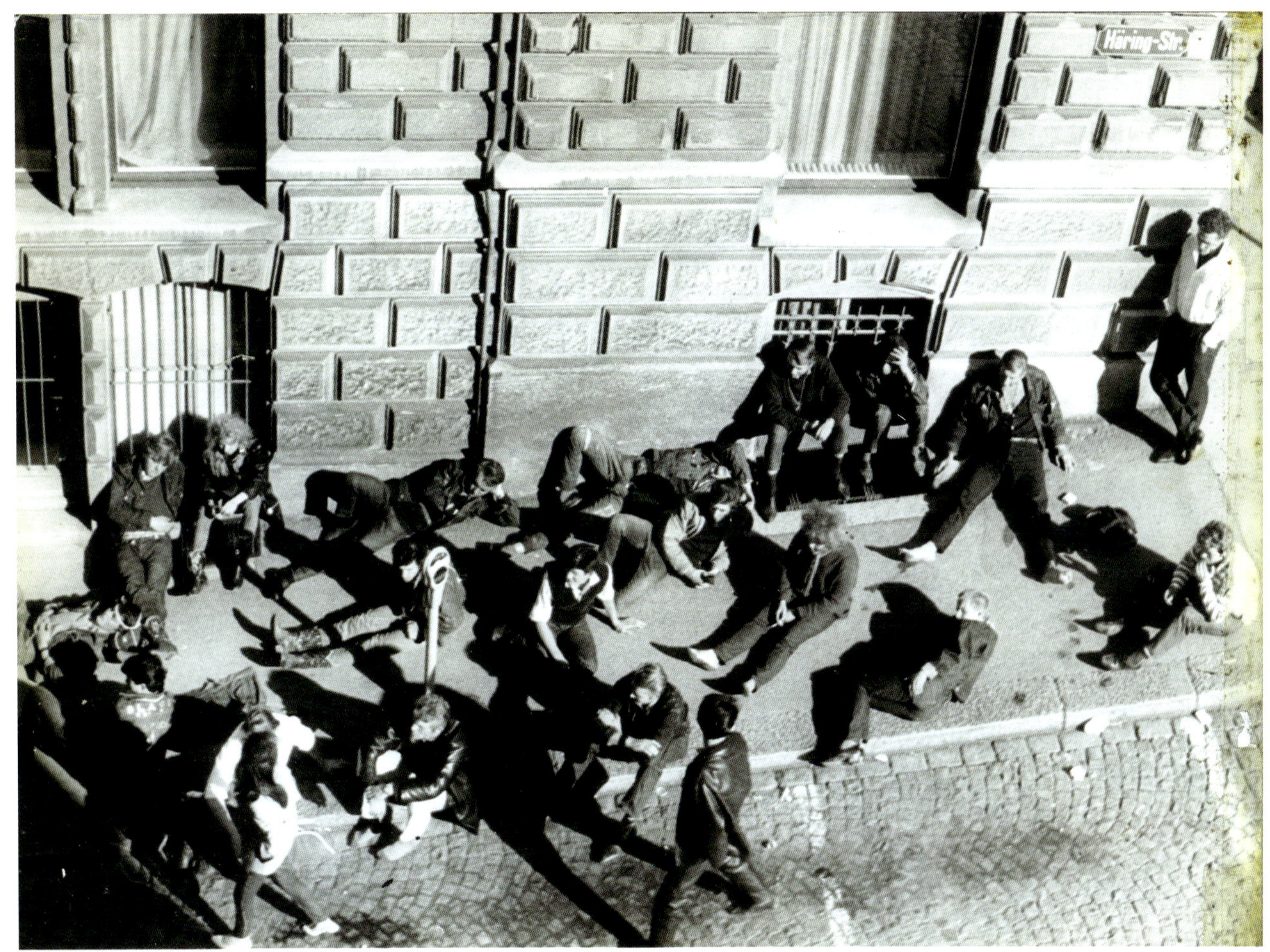

Hanging loose on Haring-Strasse, Zurich.

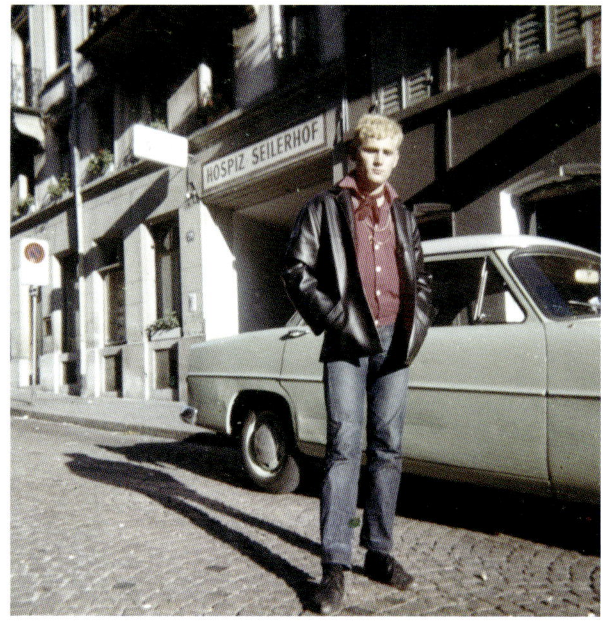

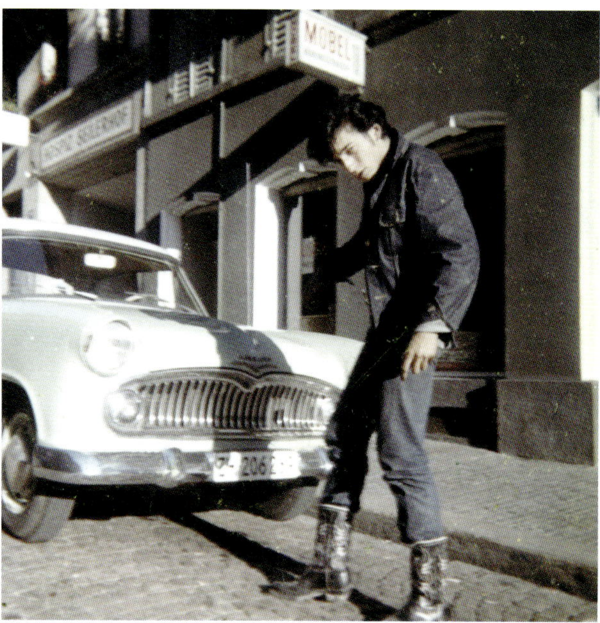

Left: Zurich, Hospiz Seilerhof: Tello, hangaround, didn't carry a club card. Right; Arrigo Prestini (Johnny), the Strangers Gang Vampir Basel.

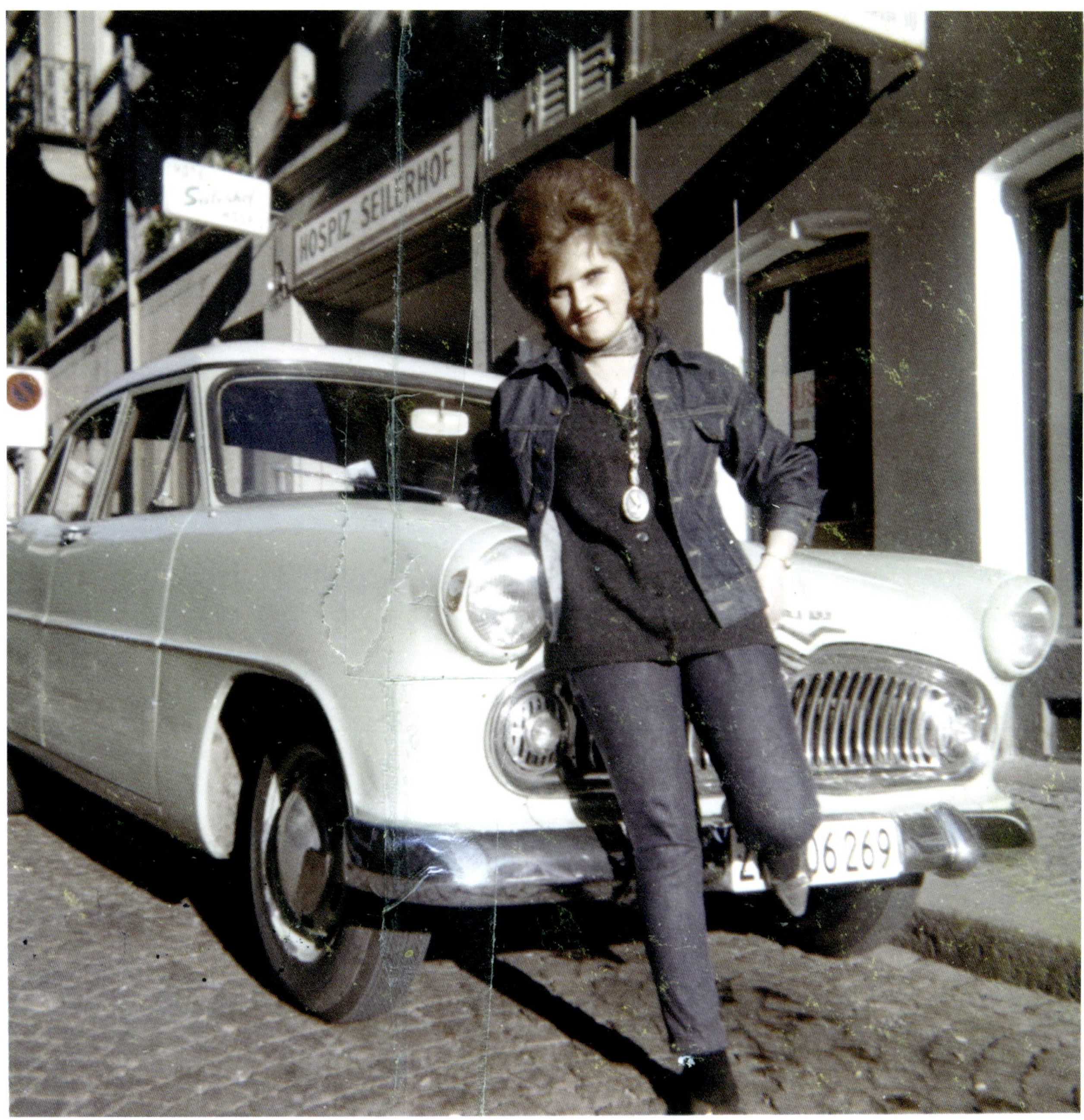

Priska (Rumy) Sonderegger from Basel.

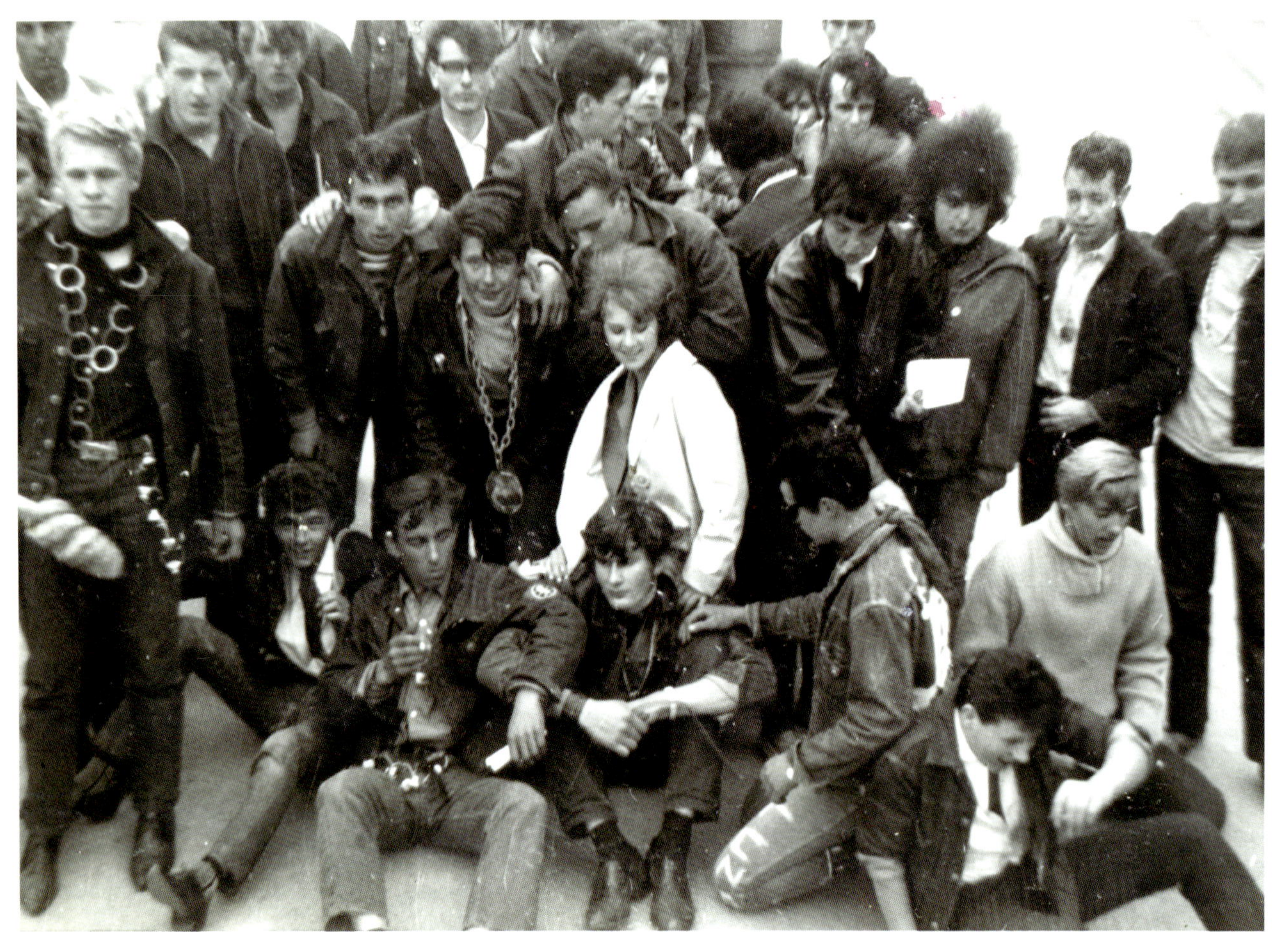

"Chain gang."

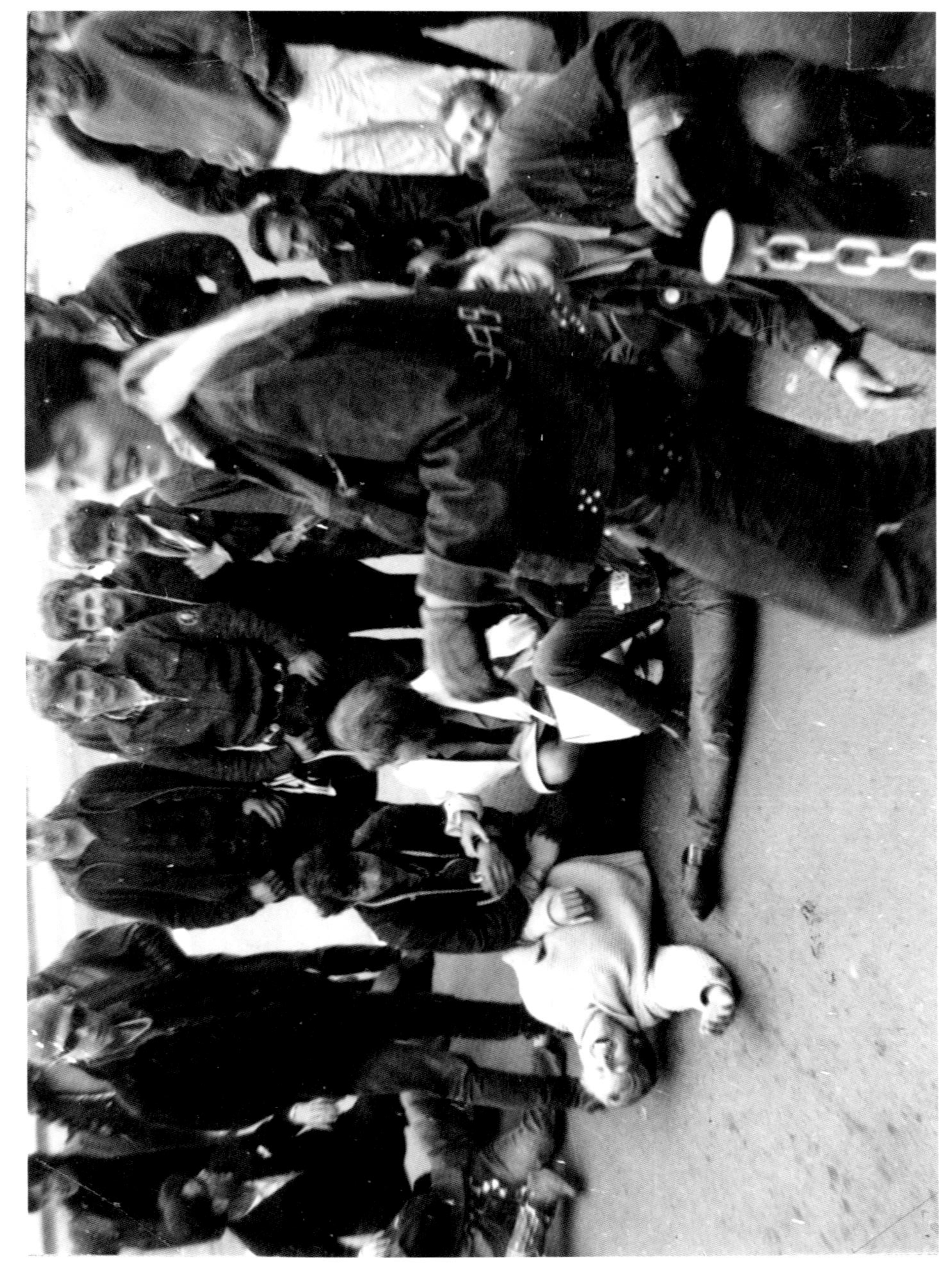

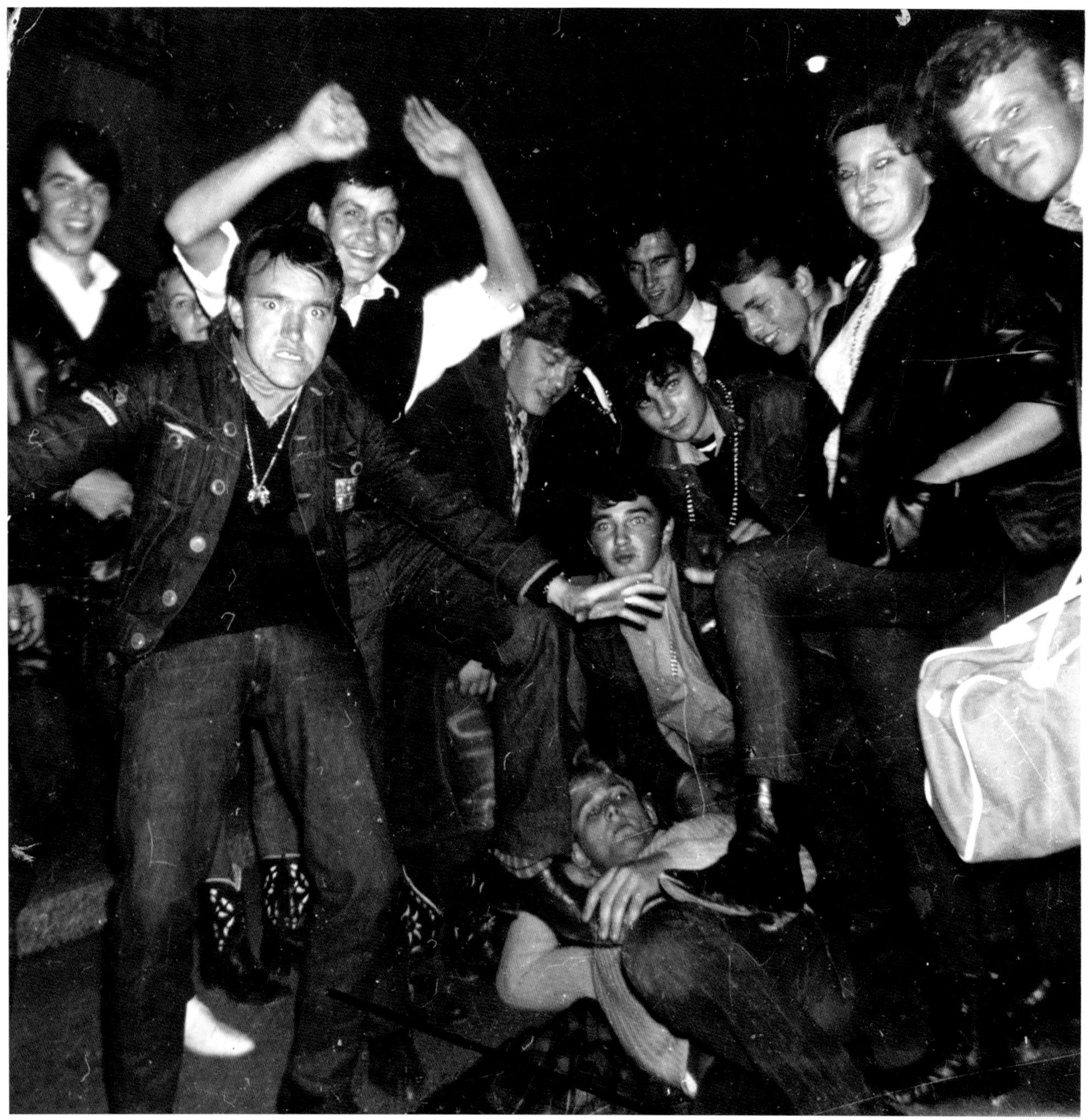

Johnsy (Walter Baumann) inspired Igel to take photographs.

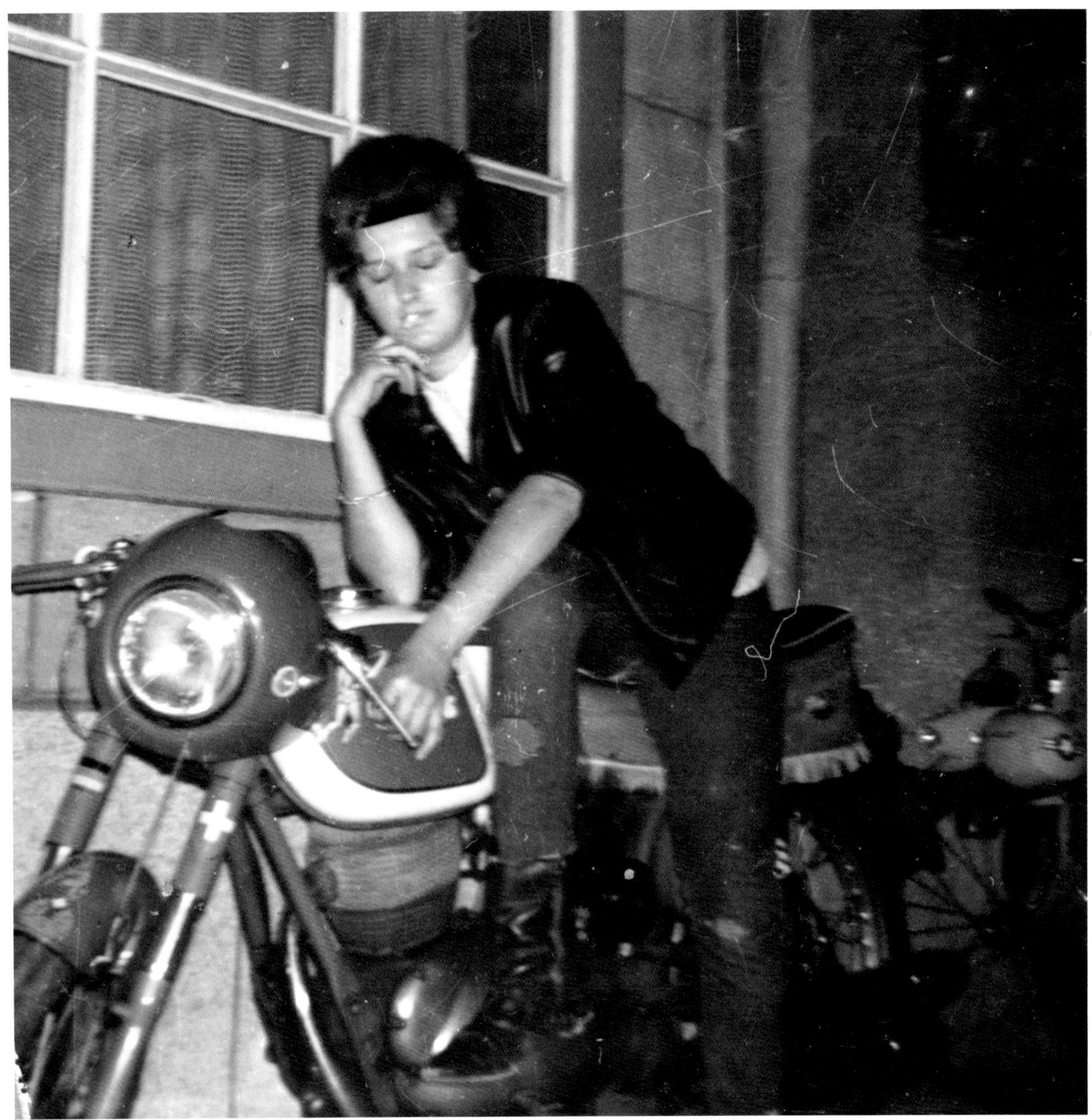

Gipsy posing.

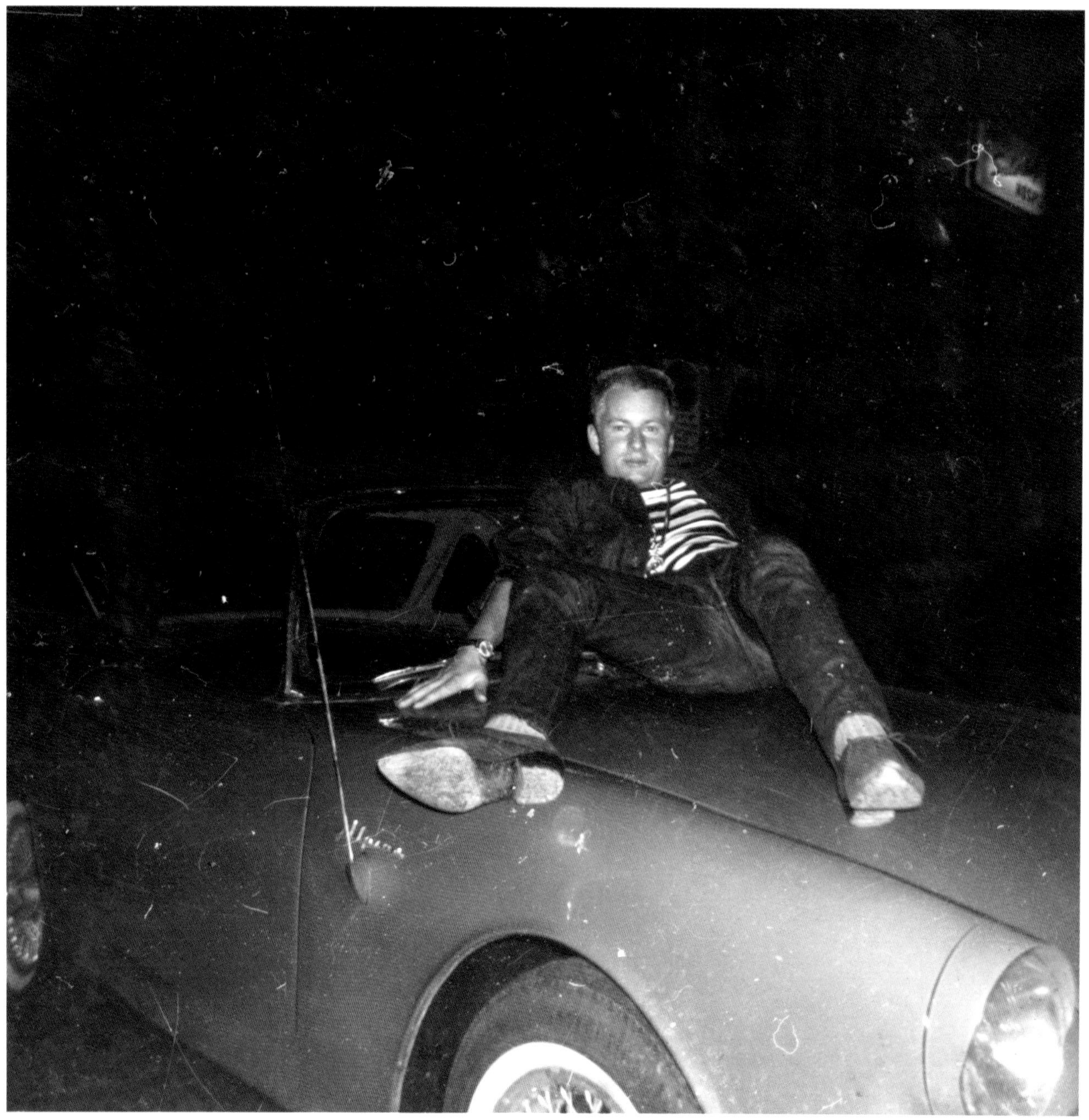

Igel.

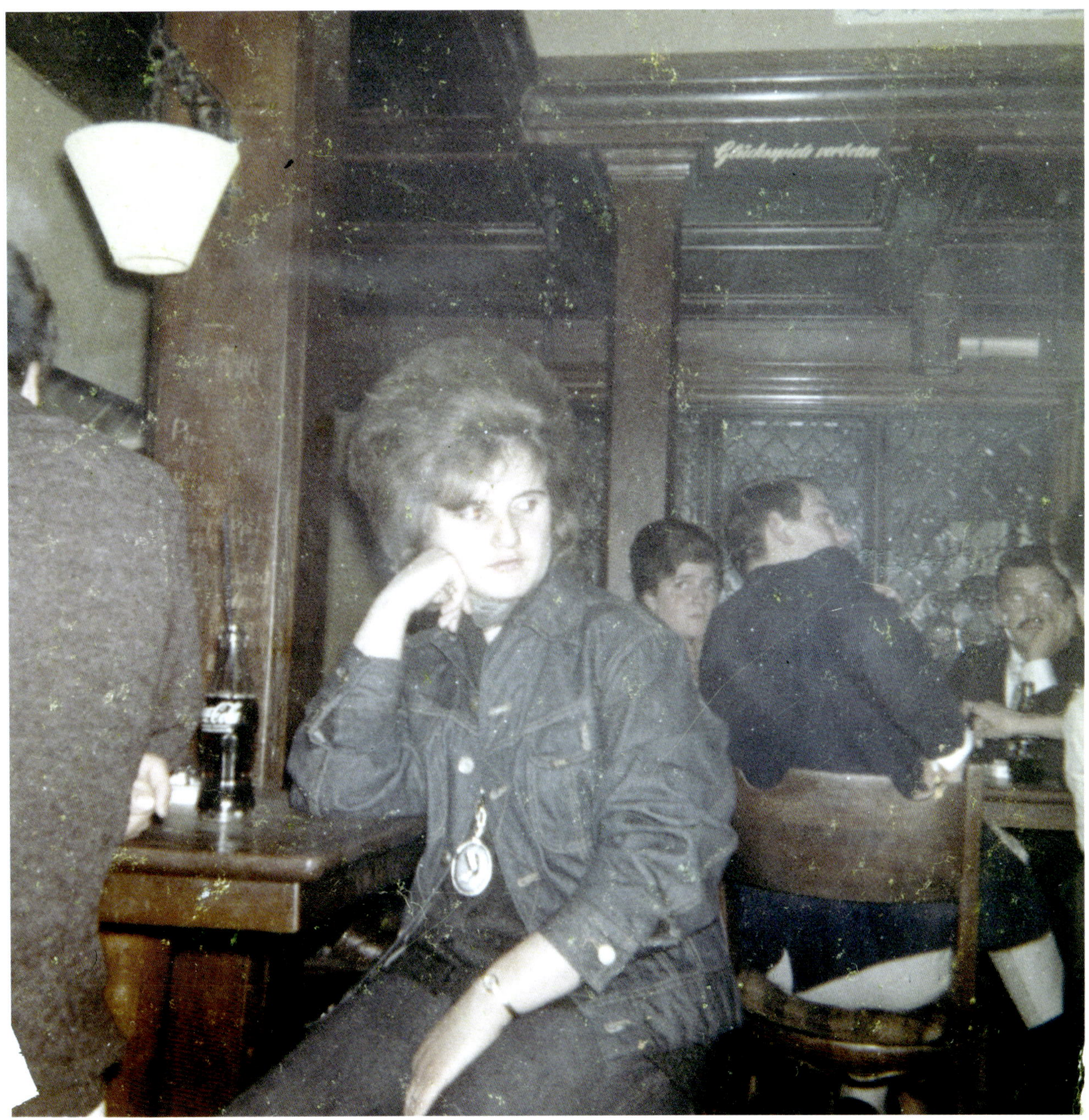

Priska at Schwarzer Ring, Zurich.

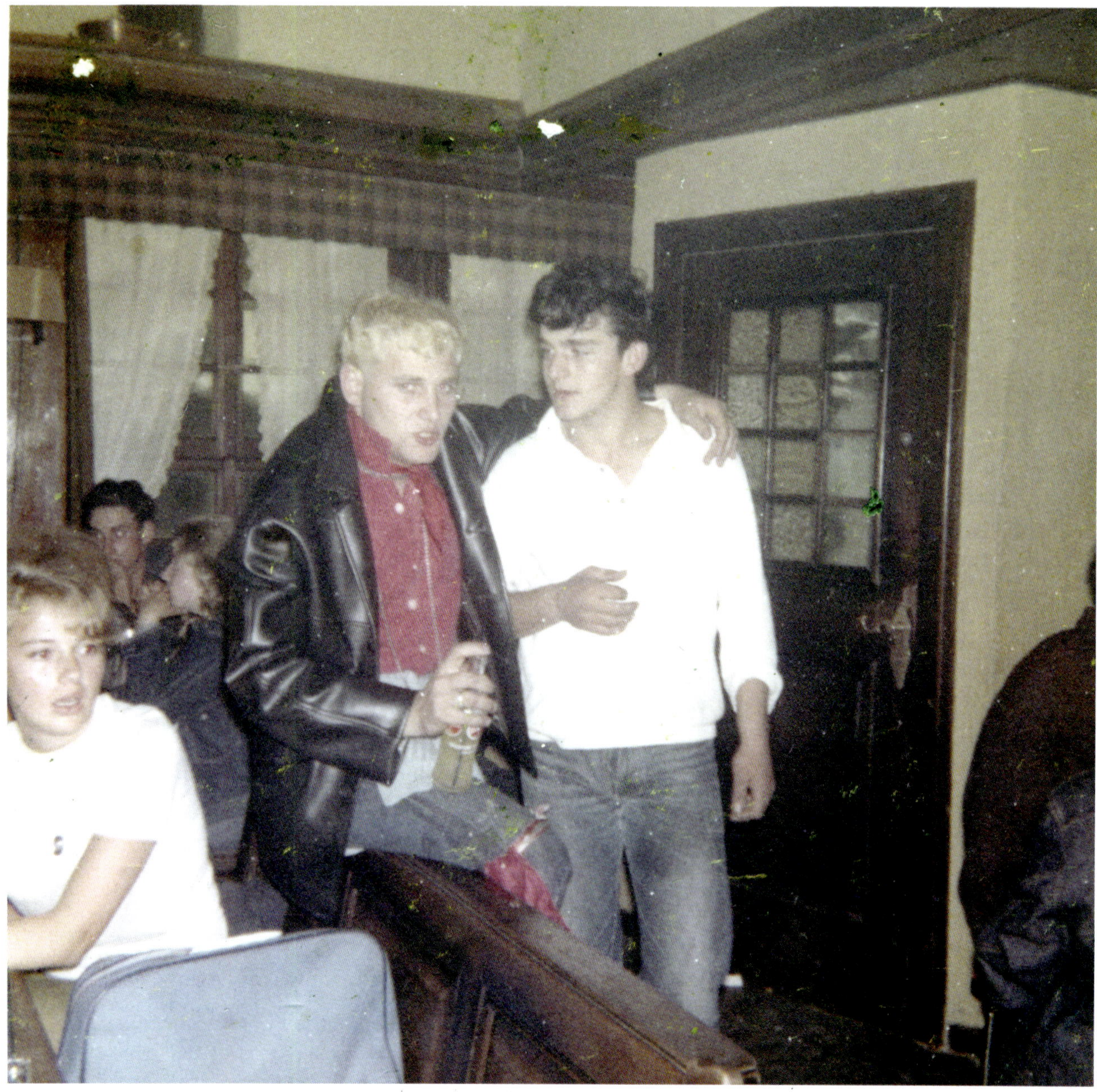

Tello and friends at Schwarzer Ring, a hot spot for young mobsters. It was the location for a film that warned teenagers about juvenile delinquency.

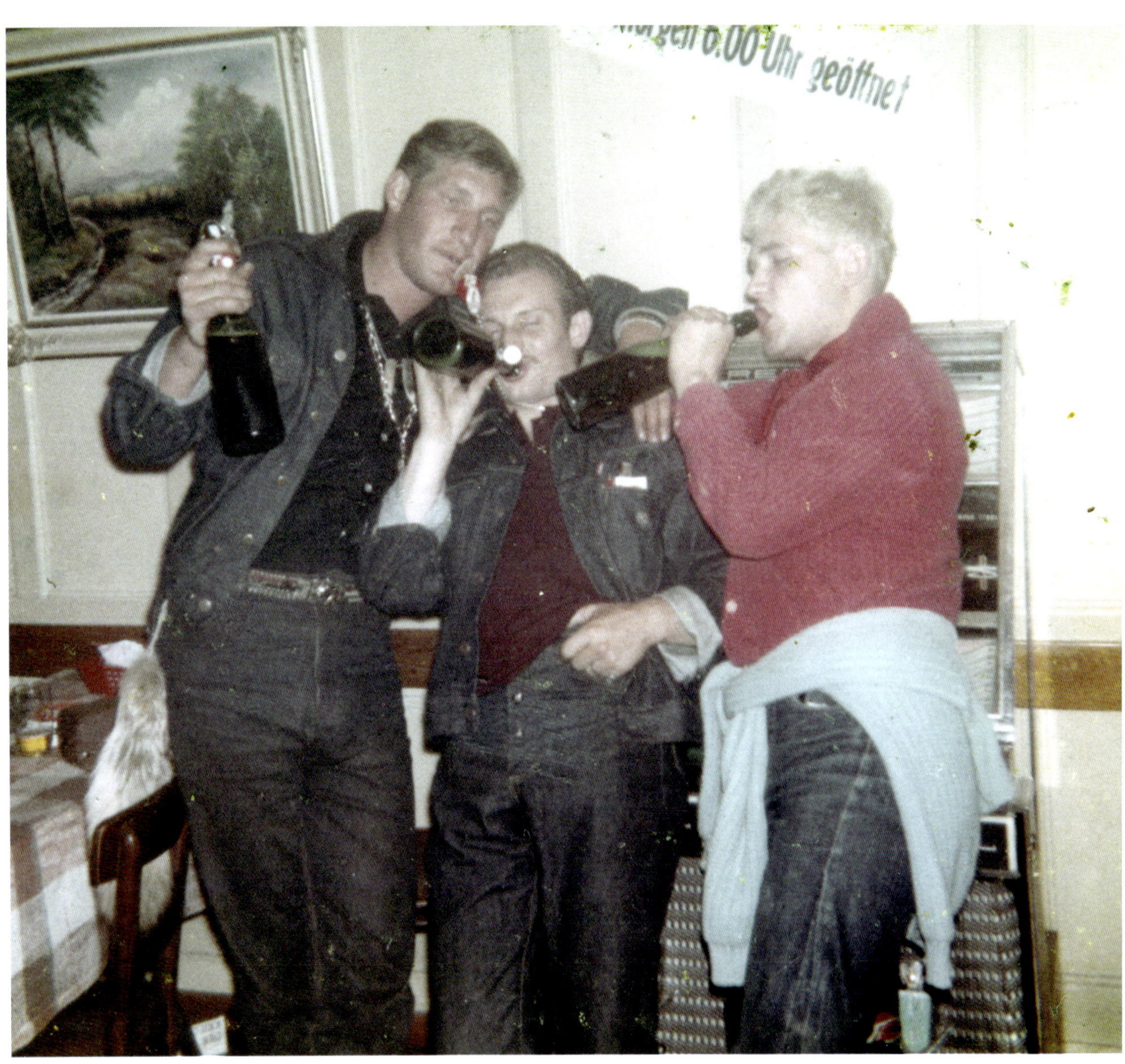

Rene and Tello flank Igel in Zurich.

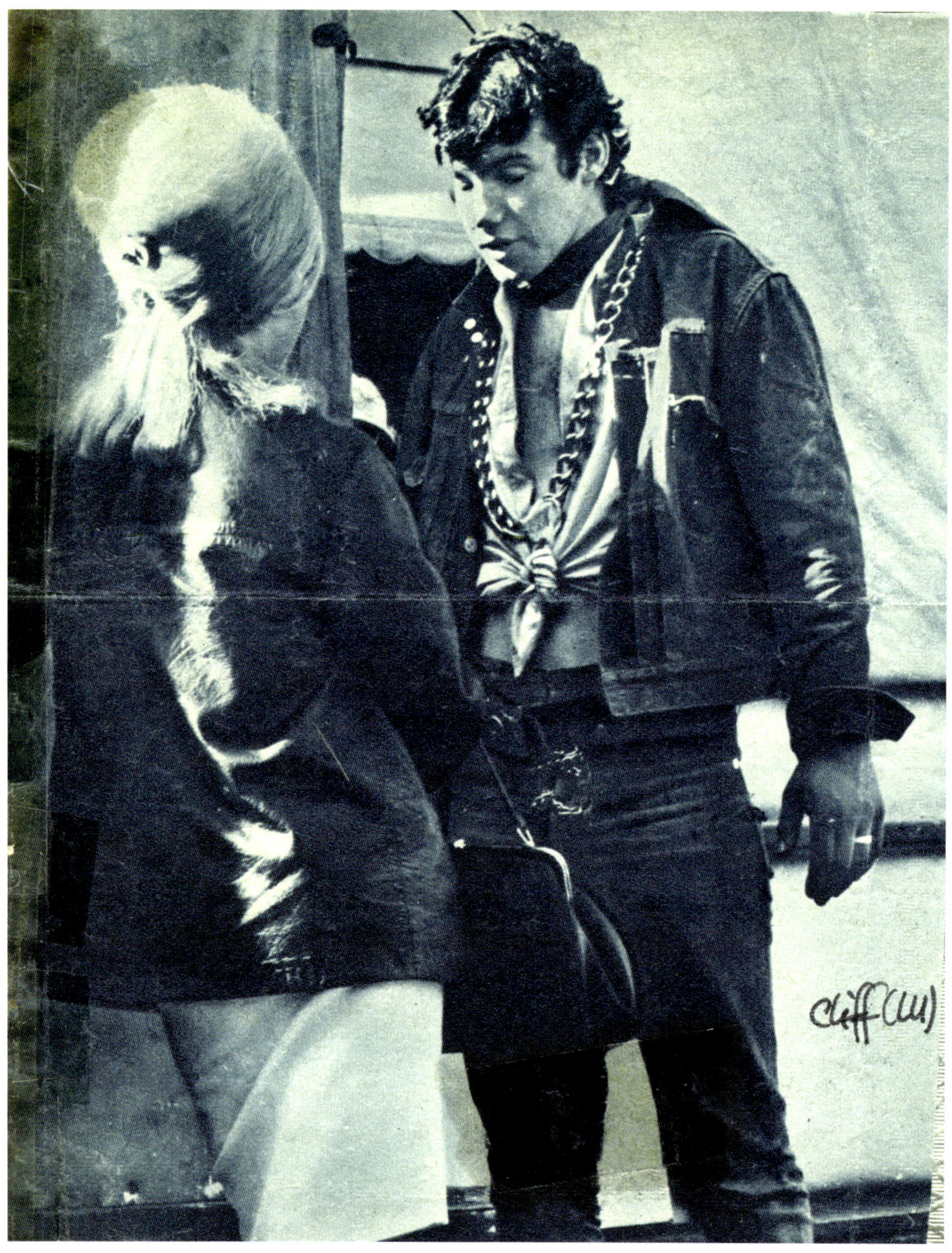

Cliff from Lucerne meets leather girl. Photo courtesy Swiss yellow press.

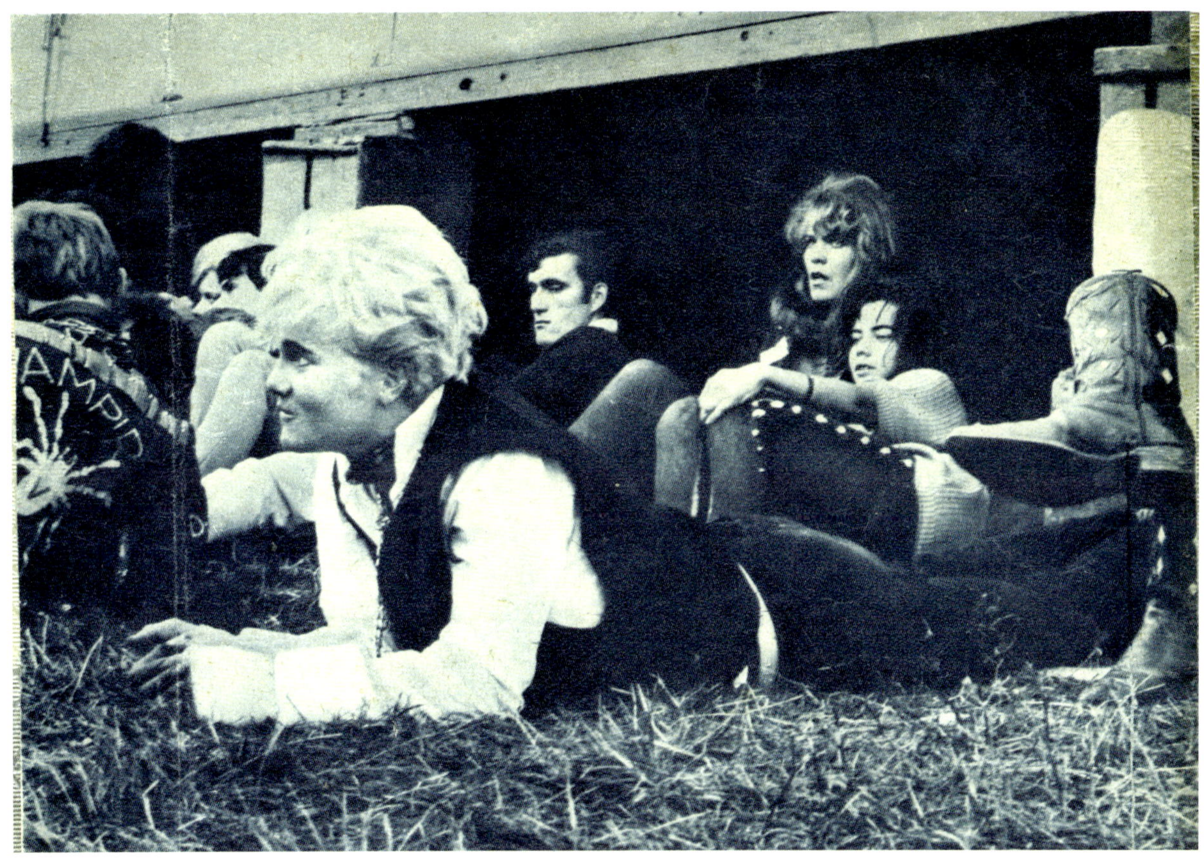

Blonde Tello, from the Vampir Club, Basel, lounges with boss Raymond (back). This photo predates the gang adding The Strangers Gang to their monicker.

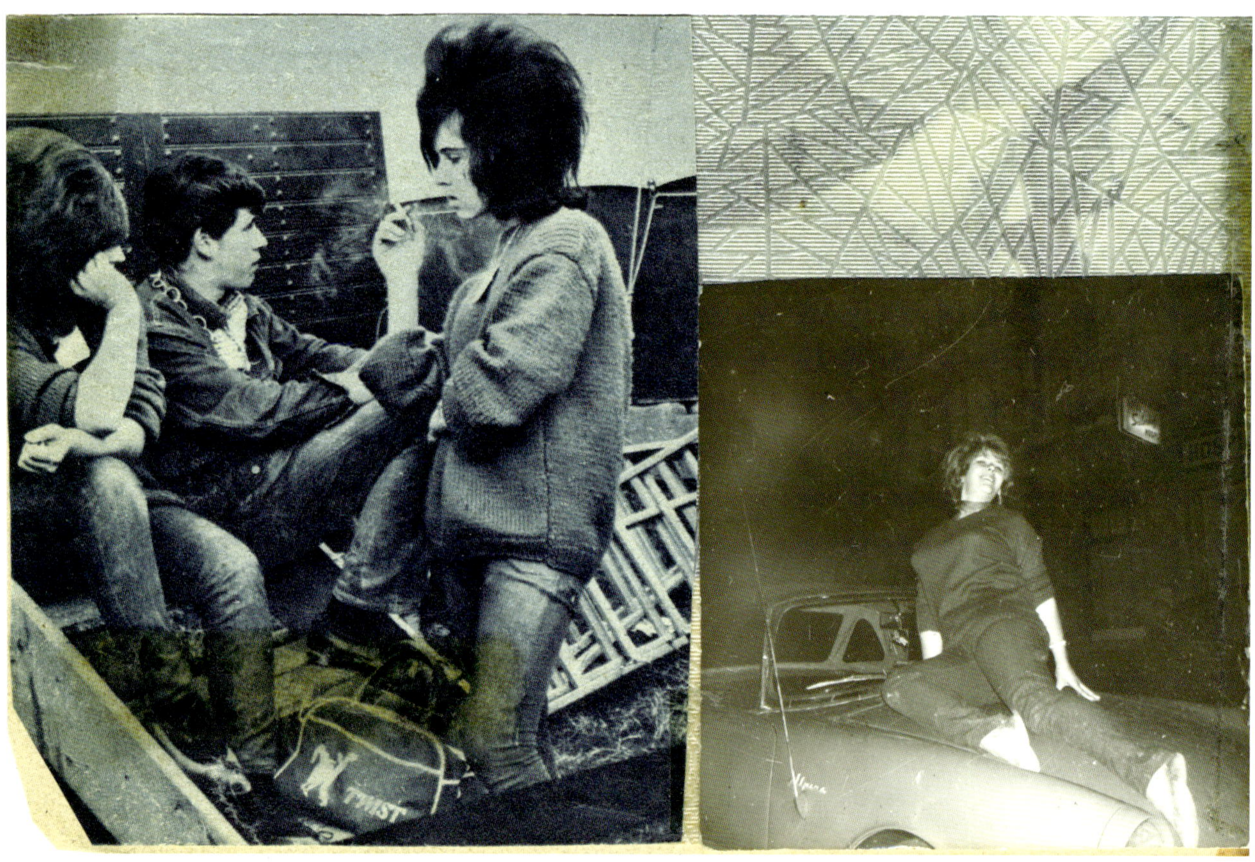

The girls.

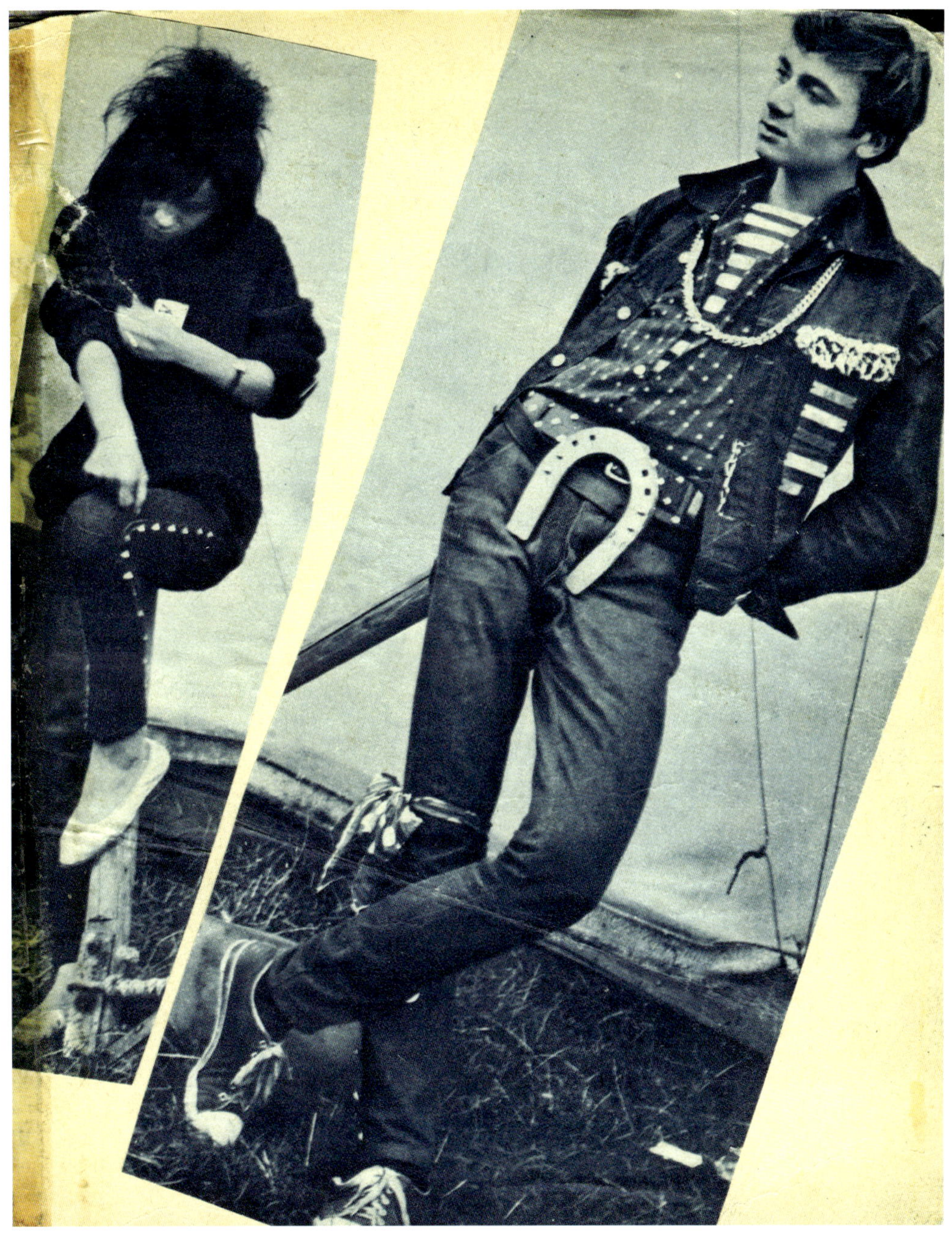

Studs, chains and horseshoes: gang fashion.

03/winzerfest (winemaker festival) in aesch
september 1962

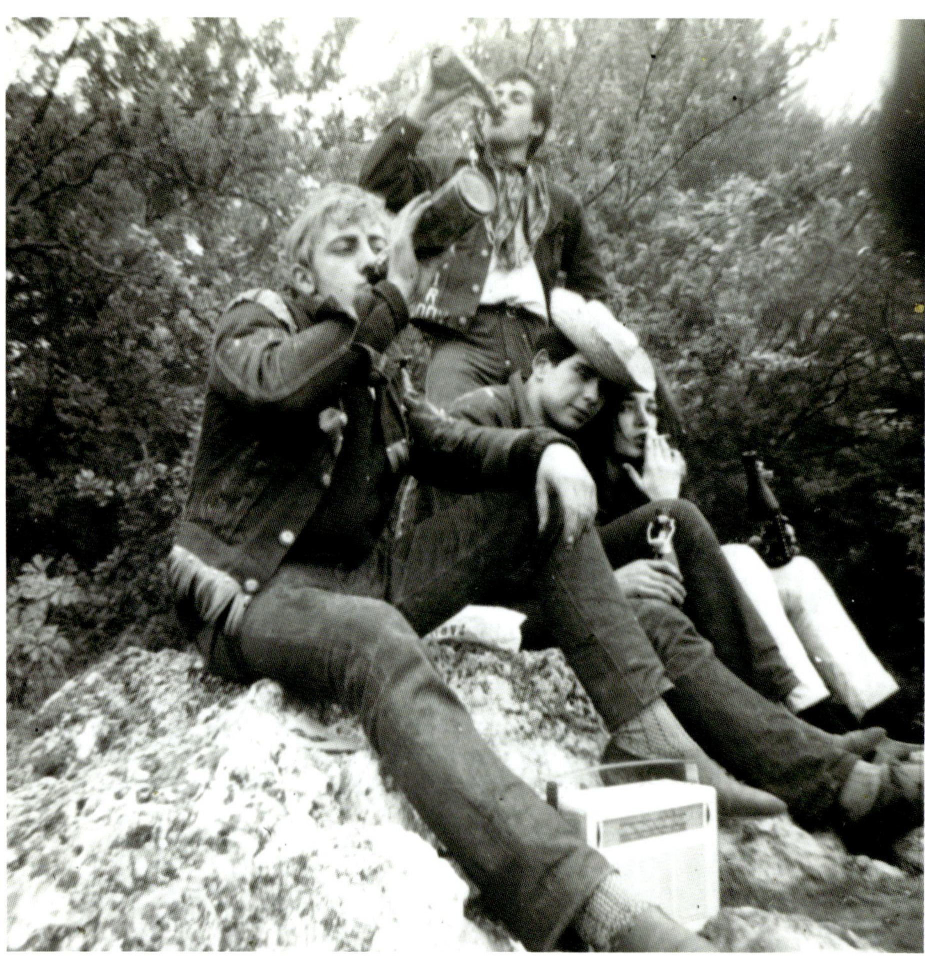

Vampirs boss Raymond Christen with thirsty friends and a radio.

04/lucerne
september 22–23, 1962

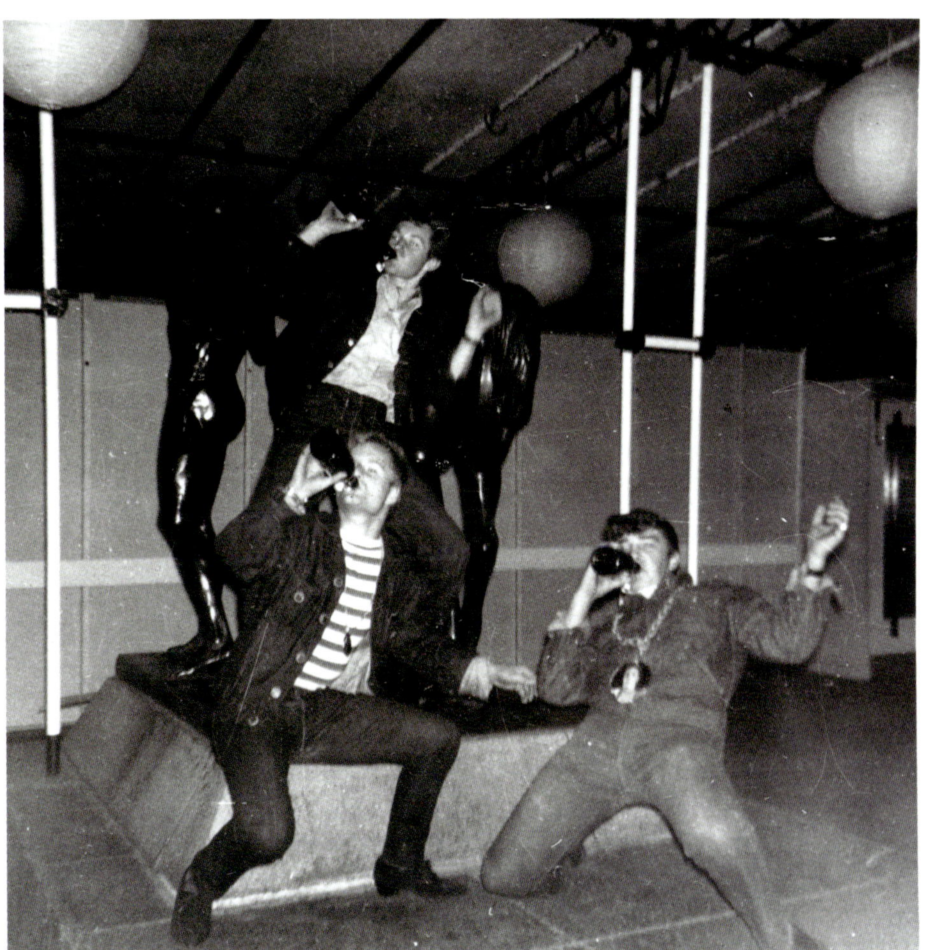

Igel with The Pumas, from Aesch.

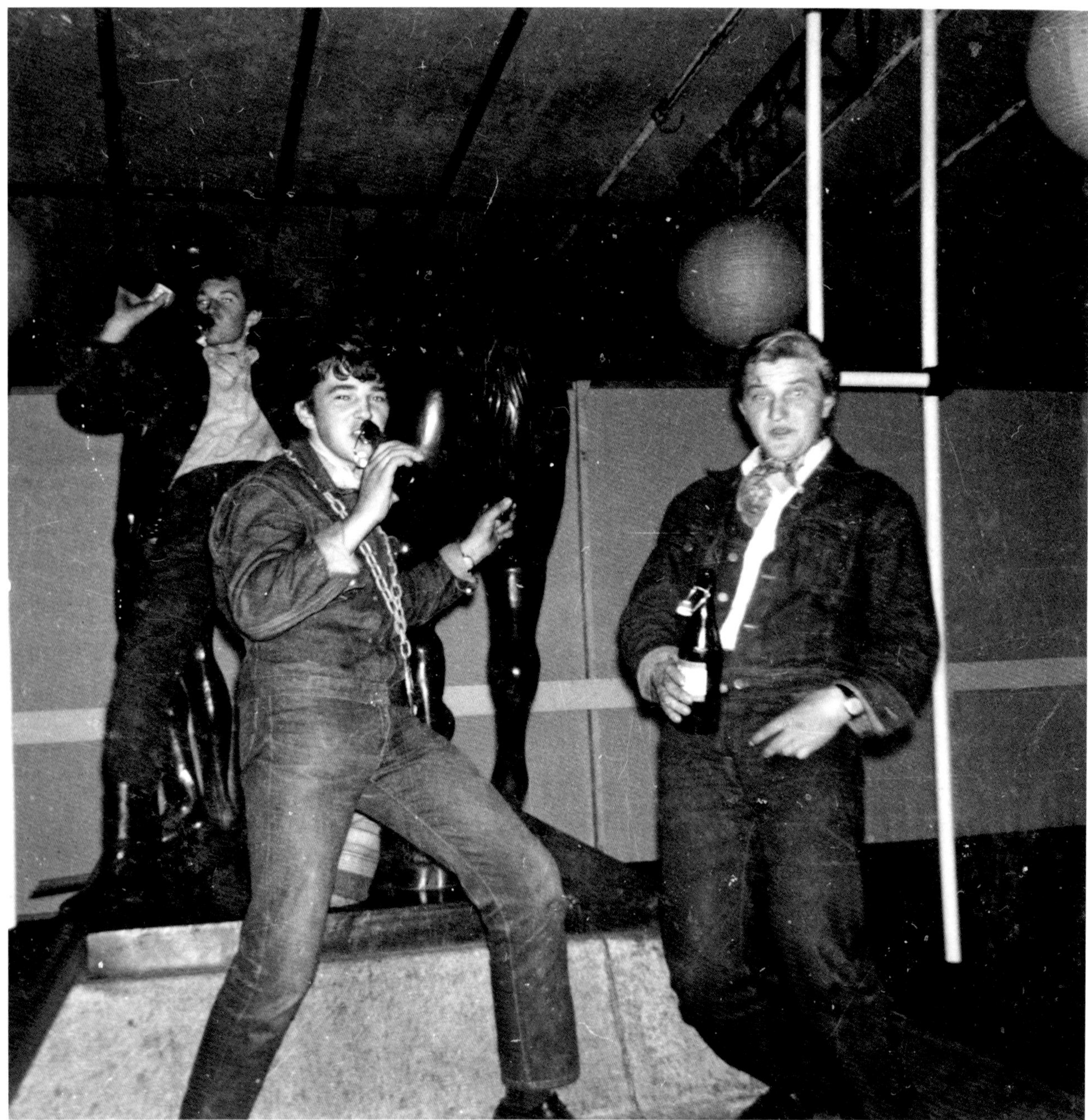

Front: Pumas Schwynli and Hott, and (back) friend.

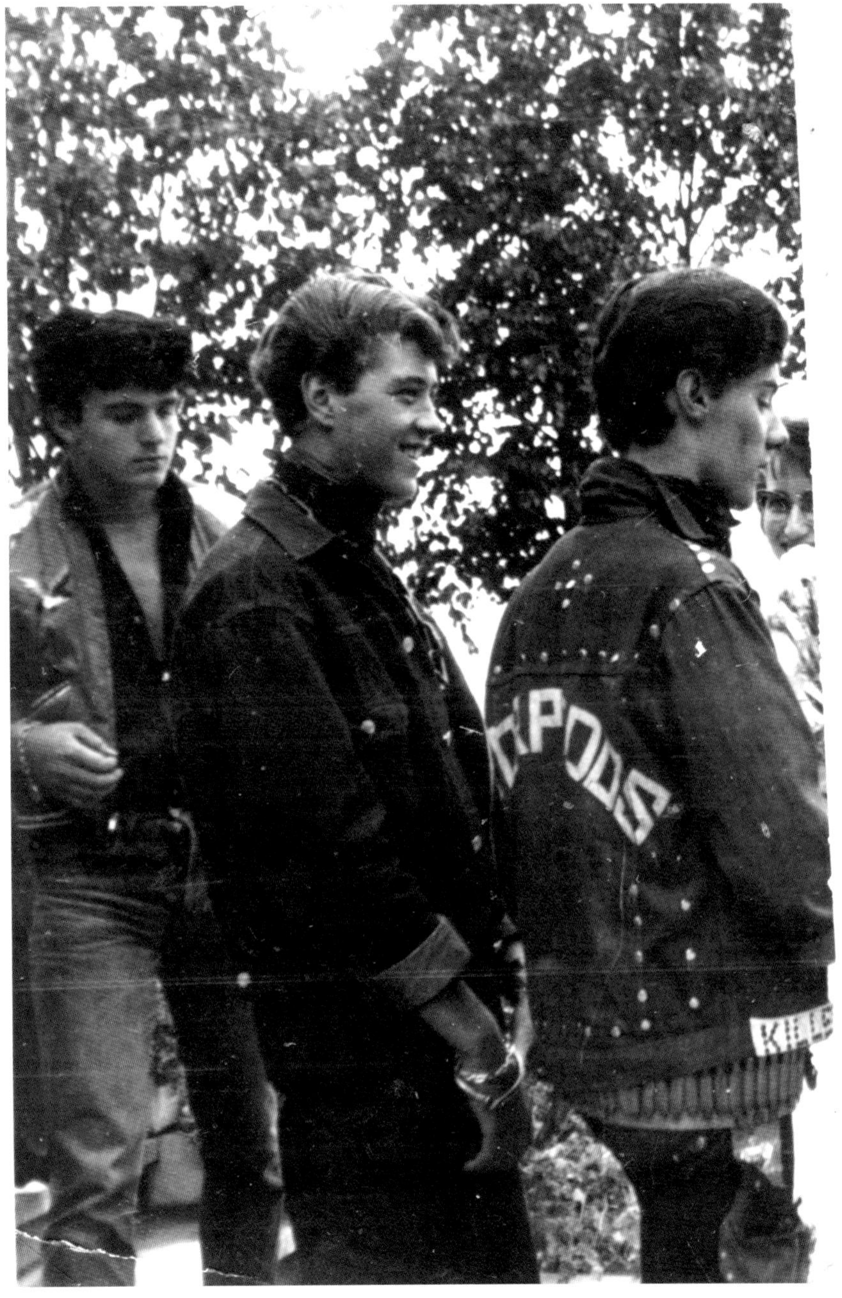

The Torpedos from Lucerne.

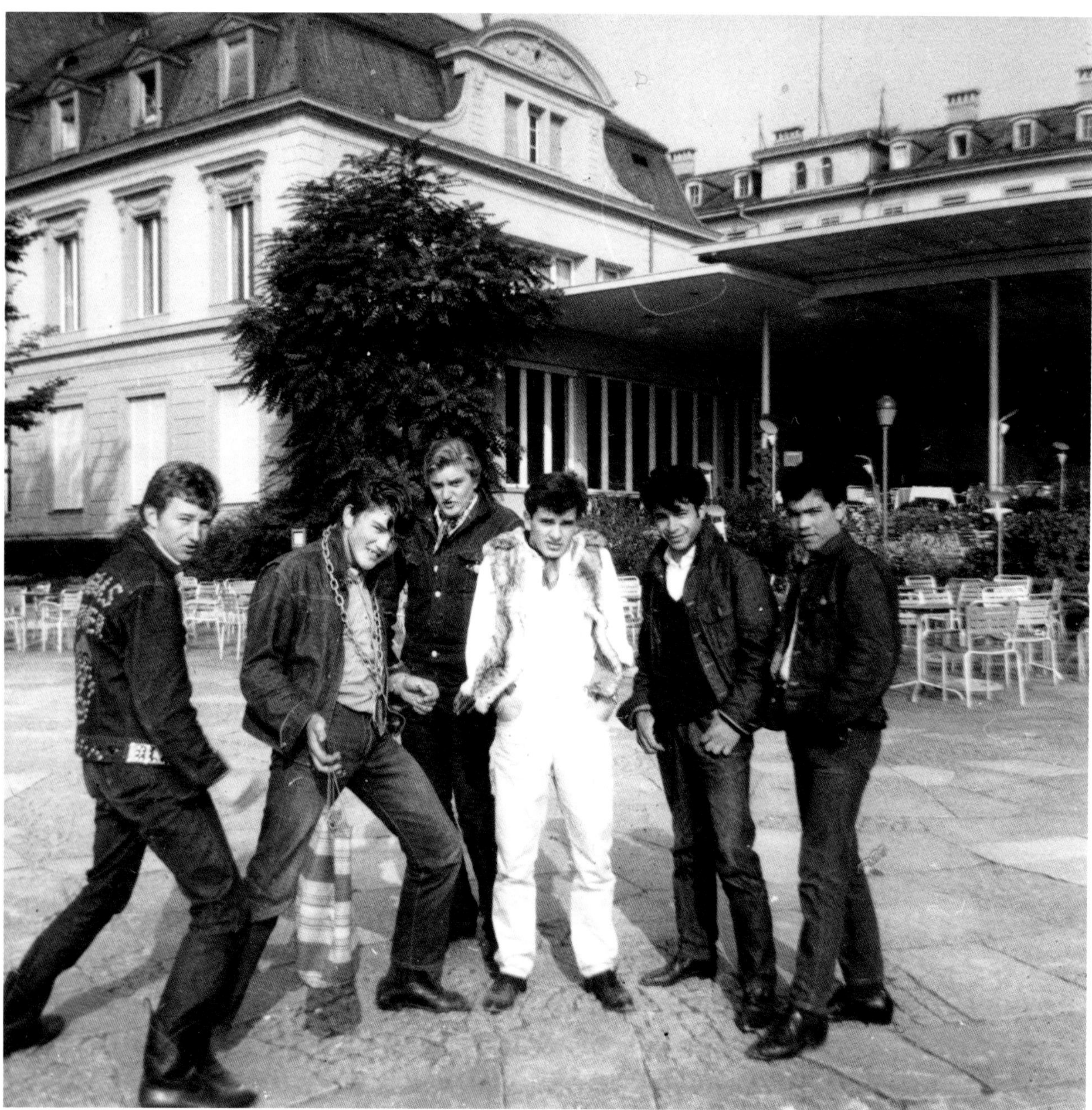

Hotte and Schwynli (second and third from right) haze new gang members.

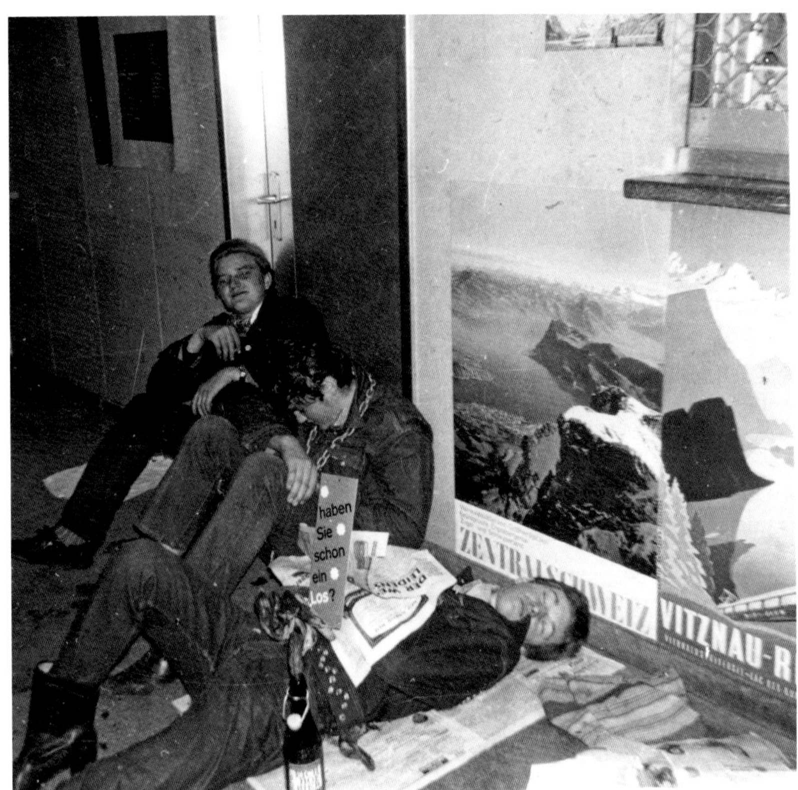

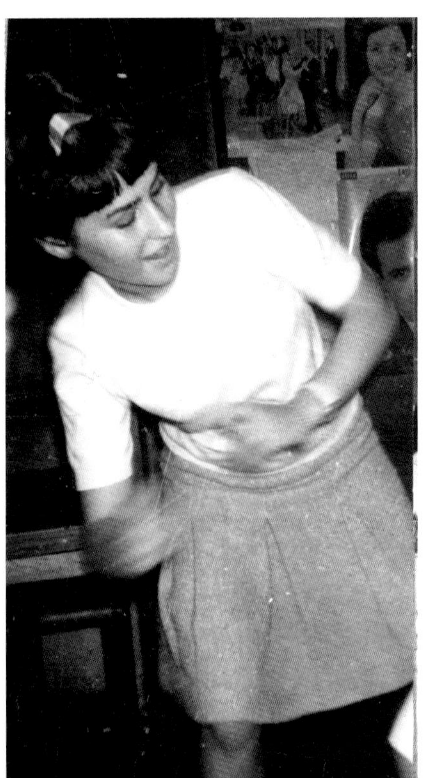

Midnight ramblers in Lucerne.

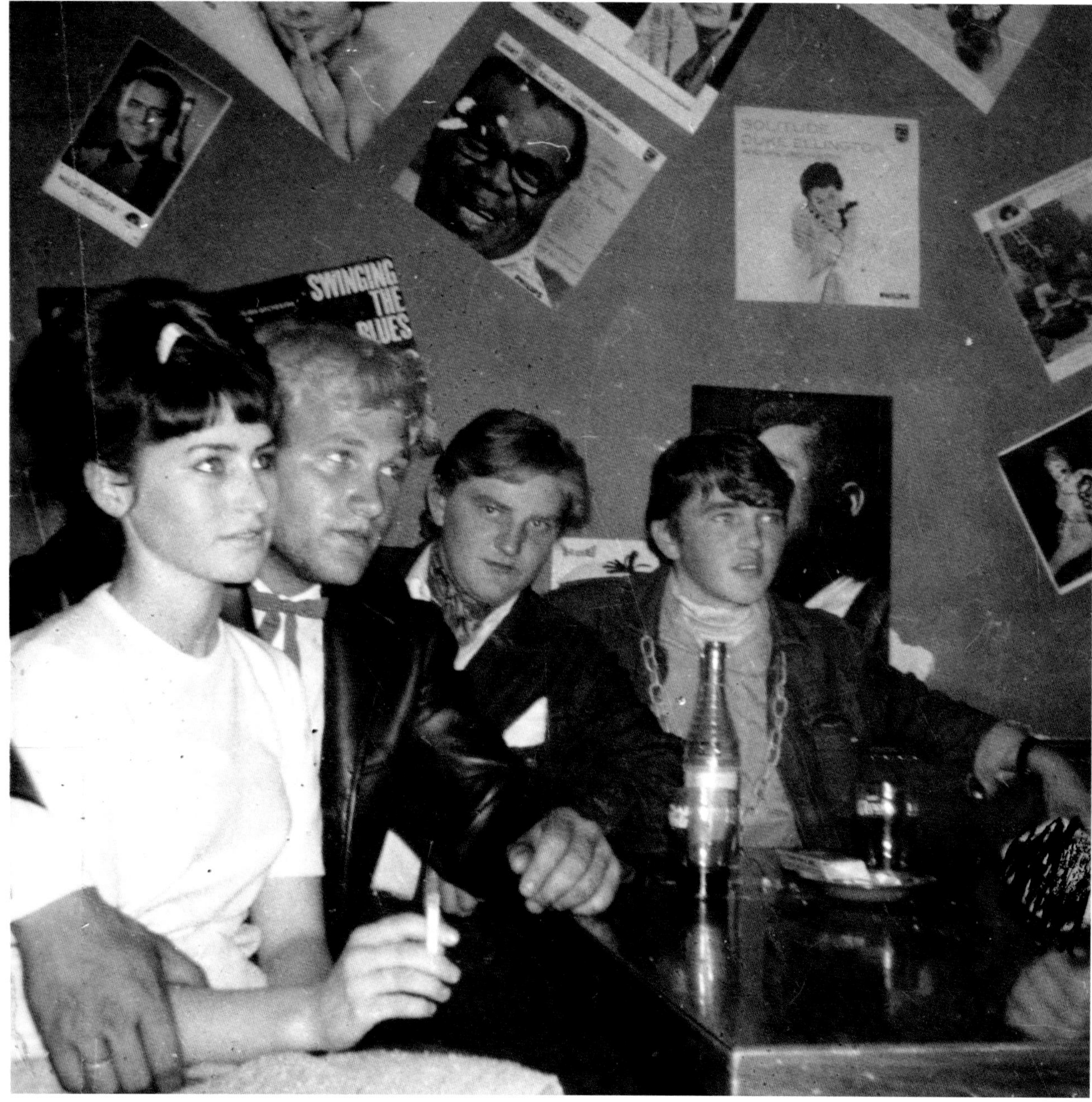

Café Nebelspalter Lucerne: Tello with unknown beauty, with Pumas, Aesch members Hotte and Schwynli. Aesch is a small town located on the countryside of Basel.

05/lucerne, at inselipark and cafe nebelspalter
november 6–7, 1962

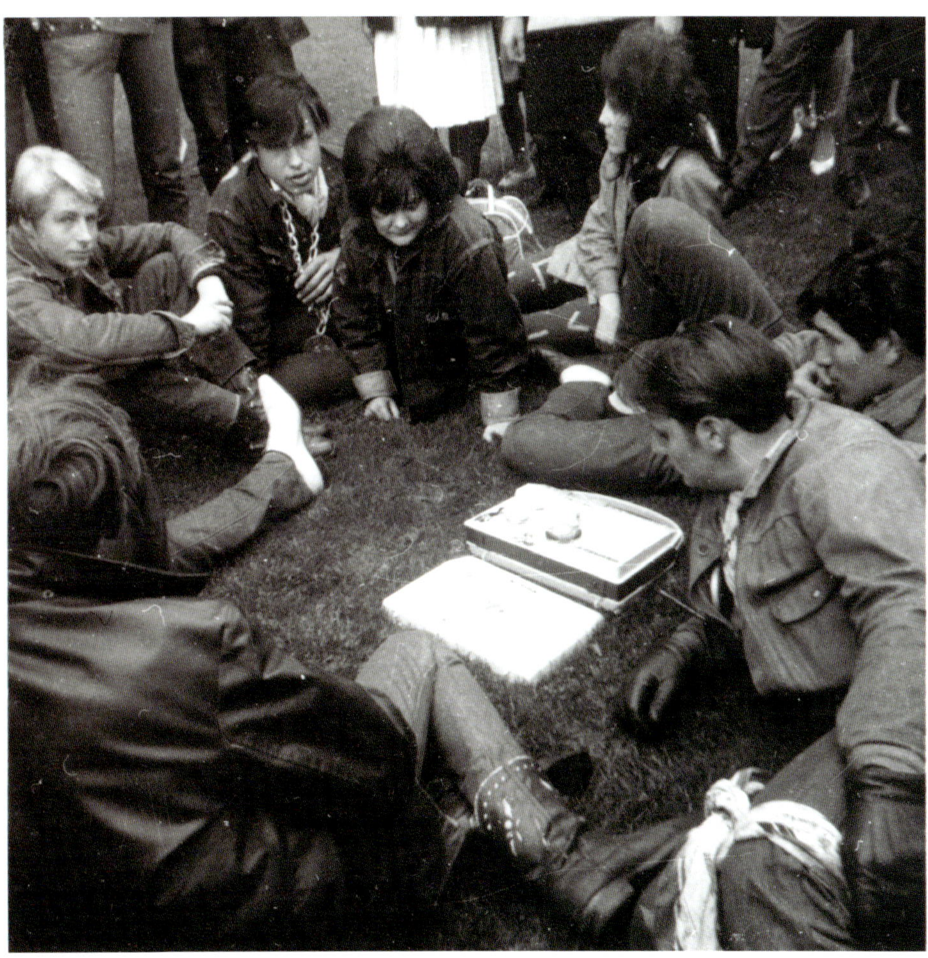

Blondie, Cliff (from Basel), Rumy (Priska), and gang surround a portable reel to reel tape recorder blasting their favorite Rock 'n Roll tunes in Lucerne.

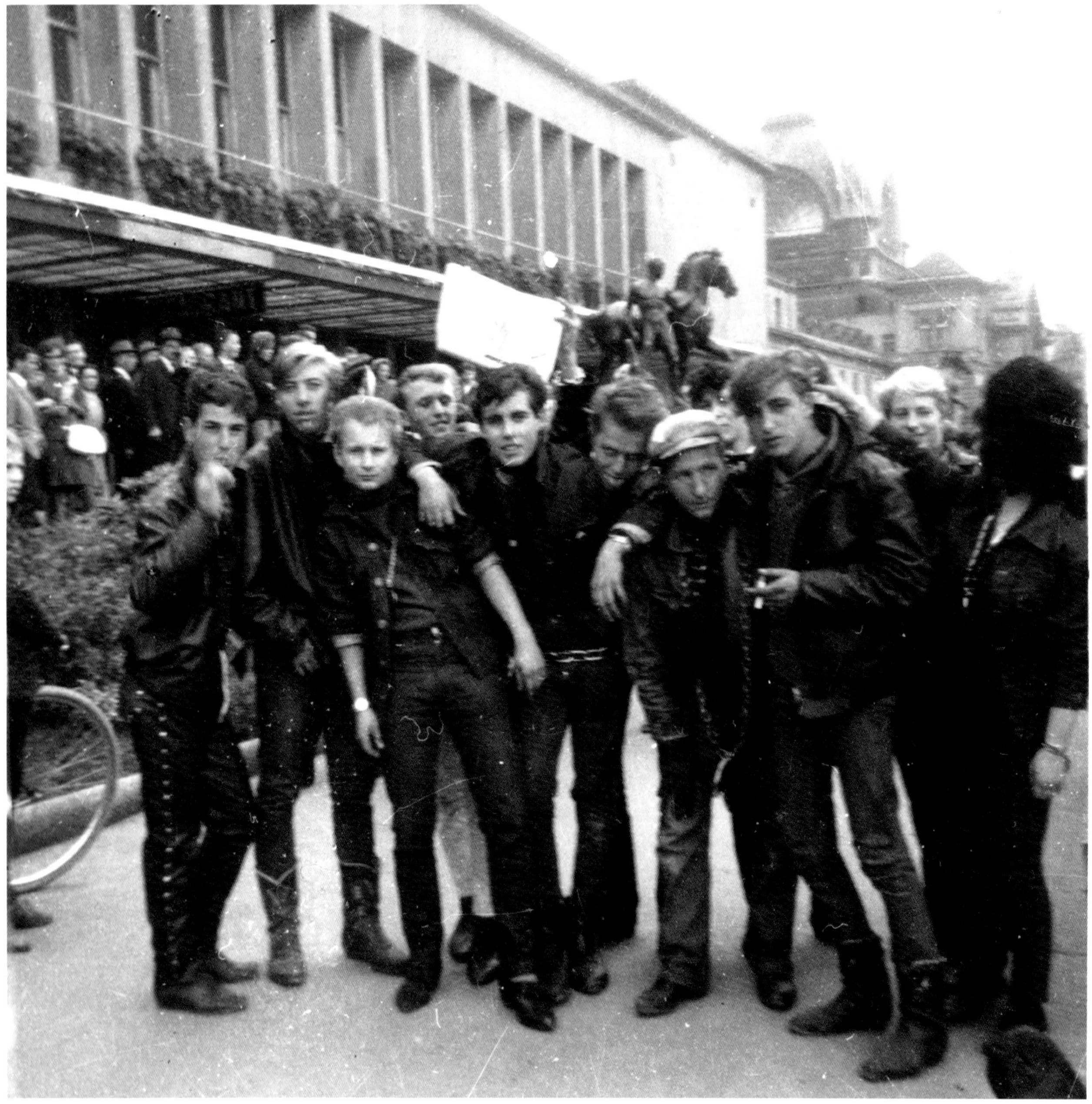

Lucerne railway station: Igel surrounded by other gang members and hangarounds. James (second from left), Igel (third from left), The Driver (fourth from right), Blondie (second from right) and Rumy (far right).

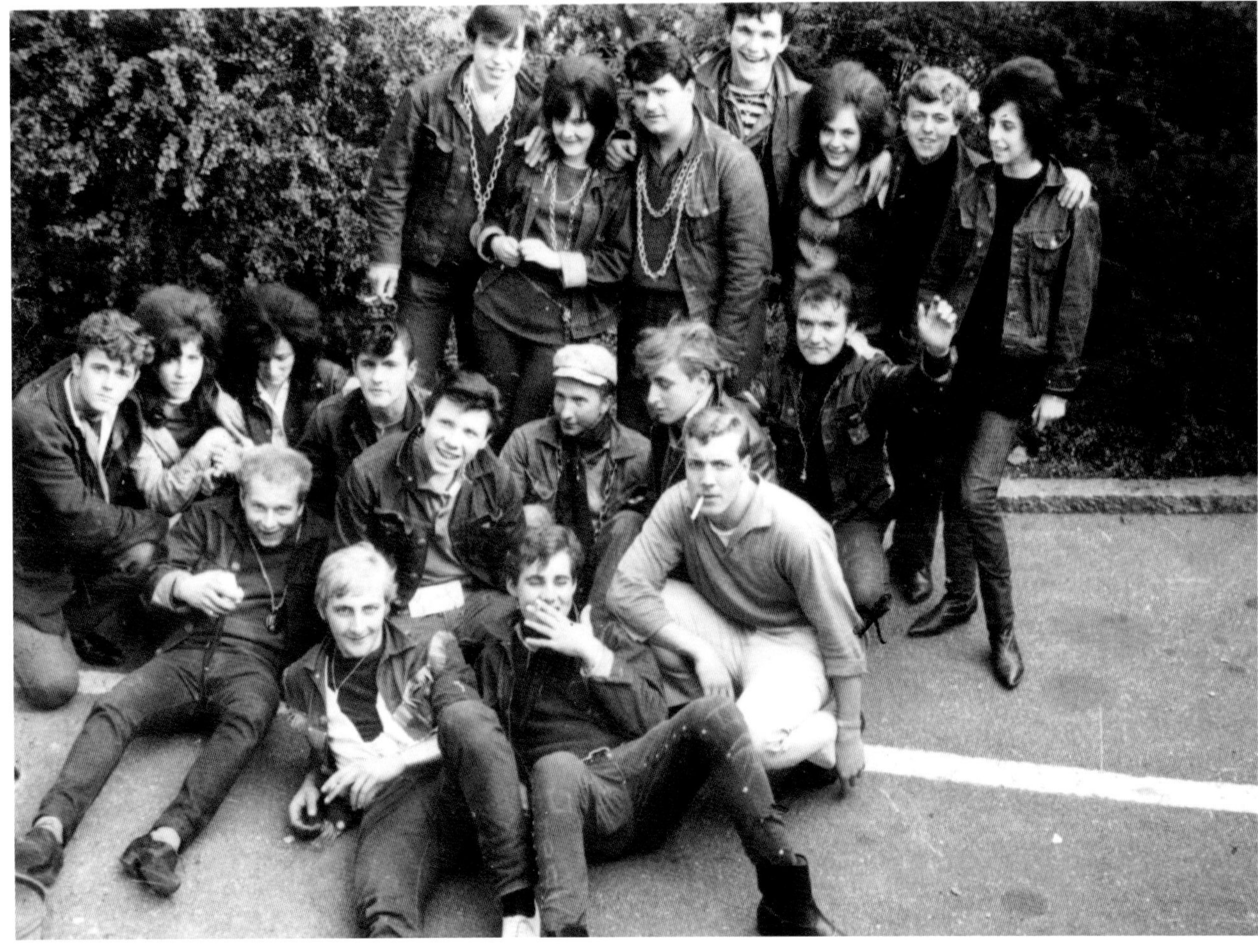

Gang meeting in Lucerne: Max “Jess” Gass, Dieter “Igel” Ehrlich and Vampir boss Raymond “Killer” Christen, together with wheel man (in the middle) who drove the Vampir, Basel all around Switzerland in these times. Pictured here are many others including Cliff, Zora and Mucki.

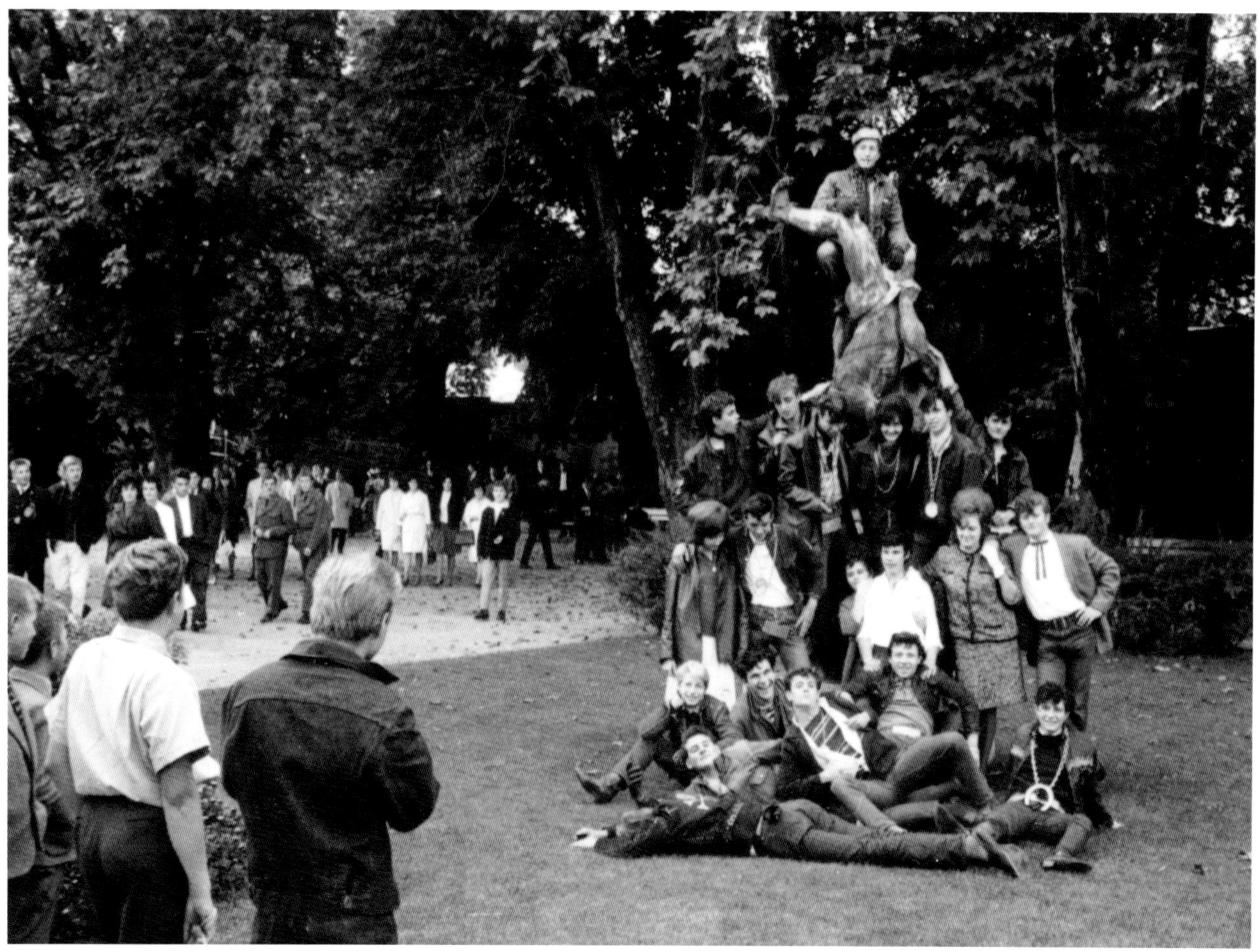

Lucerne: Gang members from Zurich and Basel form a pyramid. Igel (far left), Marcel Zimmerli aka Jacky (far right). To Left, Zora and Cliff (with medallion) and Jess from The Vampirs. Top: The Vampirs wheel man.

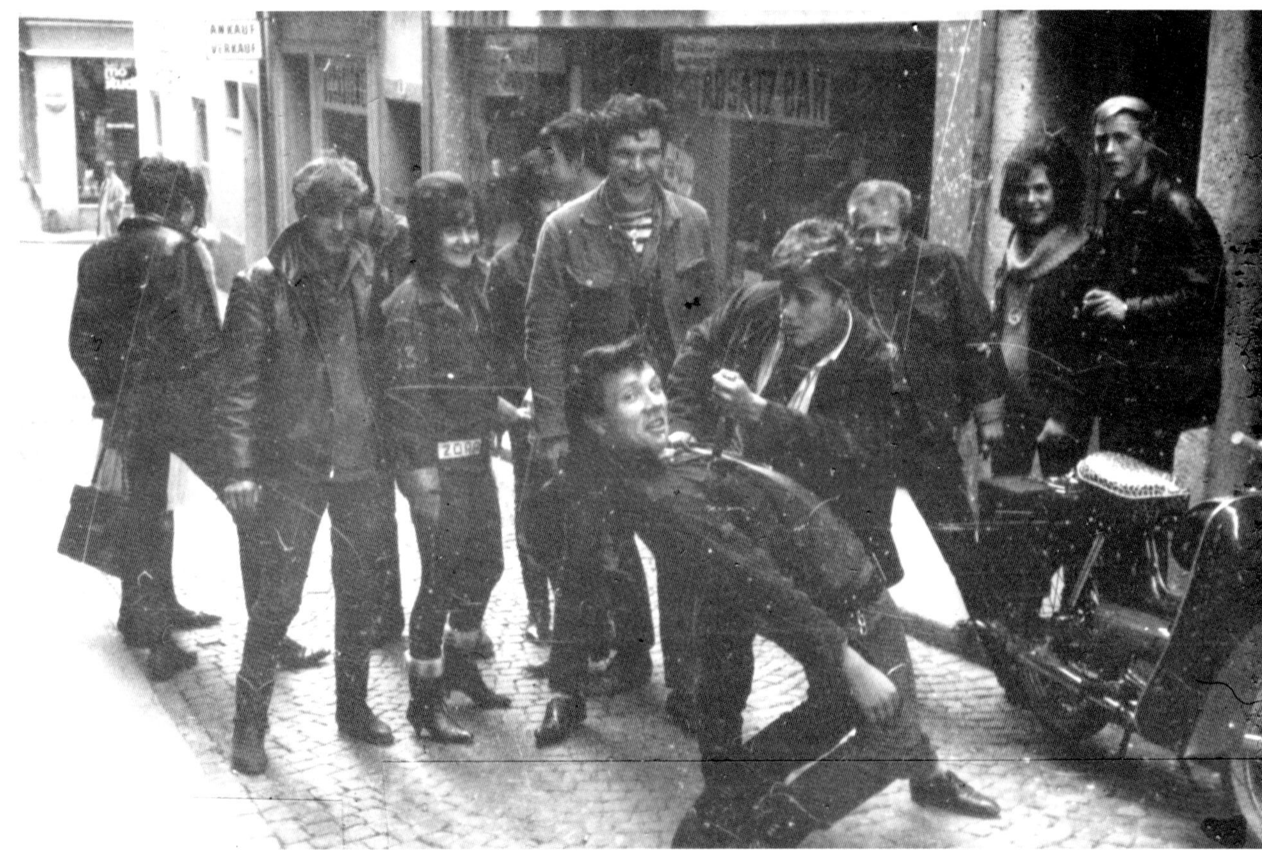

Jess, Raymond, Red and Igel with fellow mobsters.

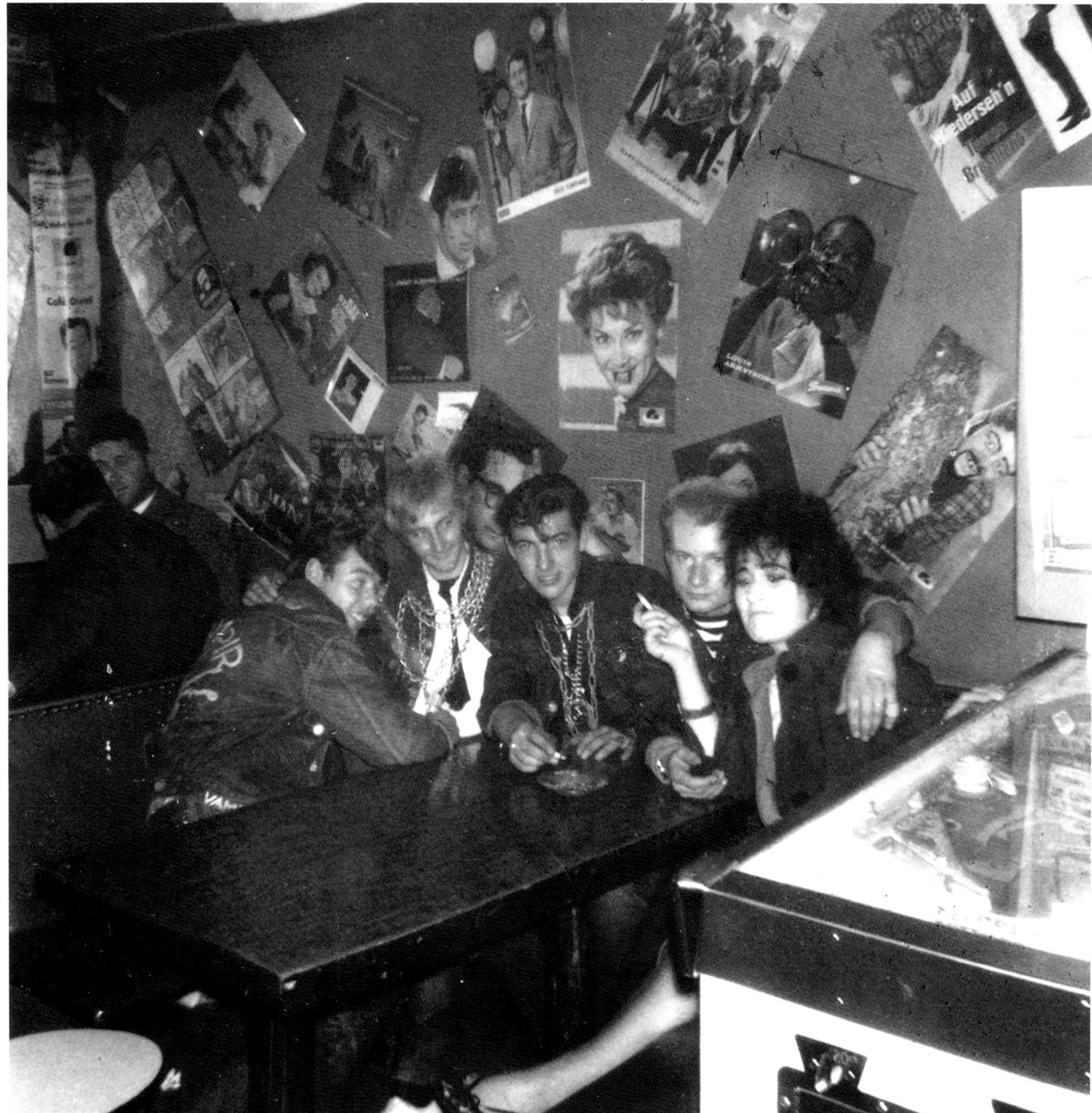

Igel and friends inside the famous Halbstarken-Hangout Cafe Nebelspalter in Lucerne.

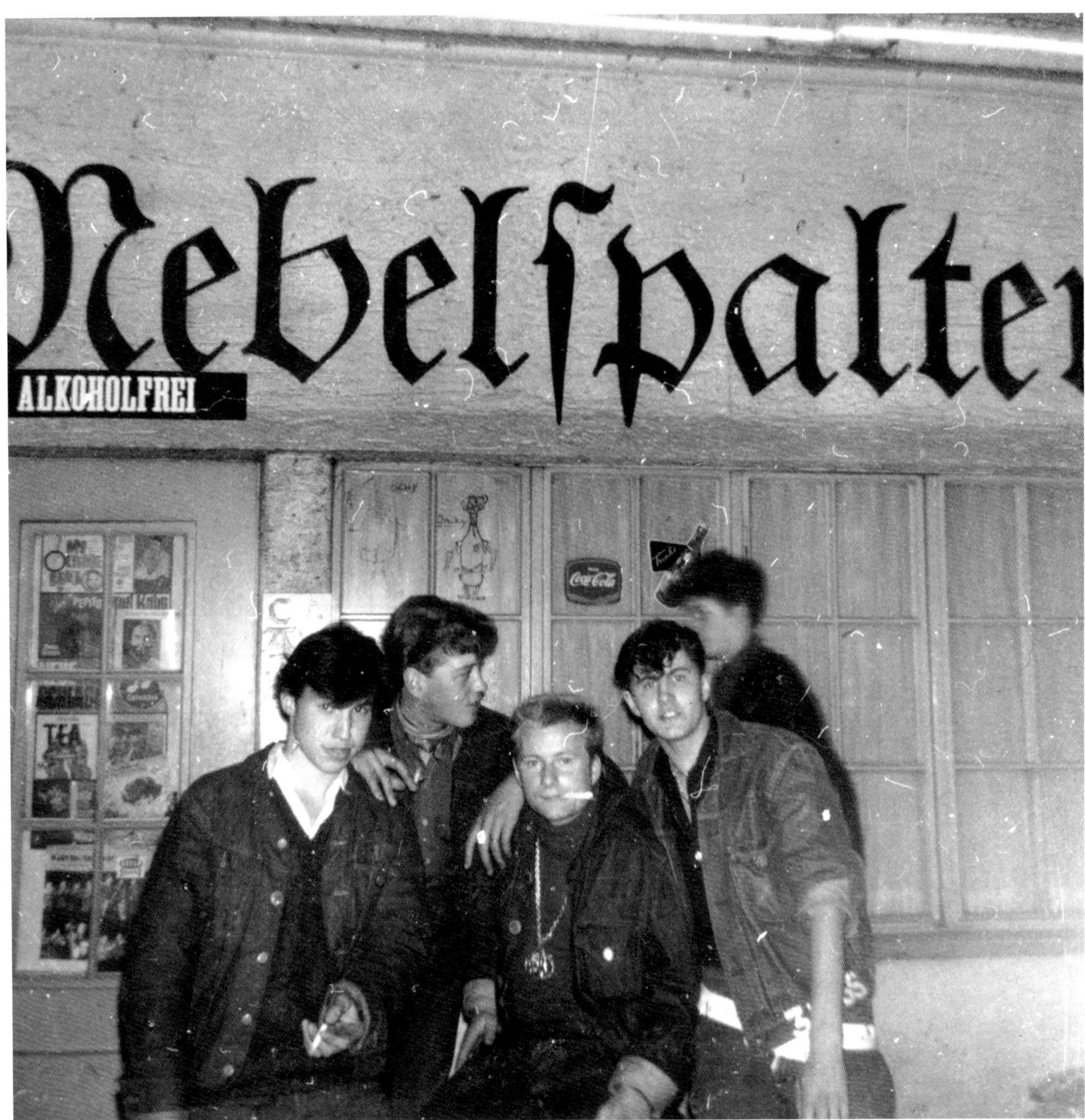

Standing in front of Café Nebelspalter, Lucerne. Cliff Igel and Jess in front row.

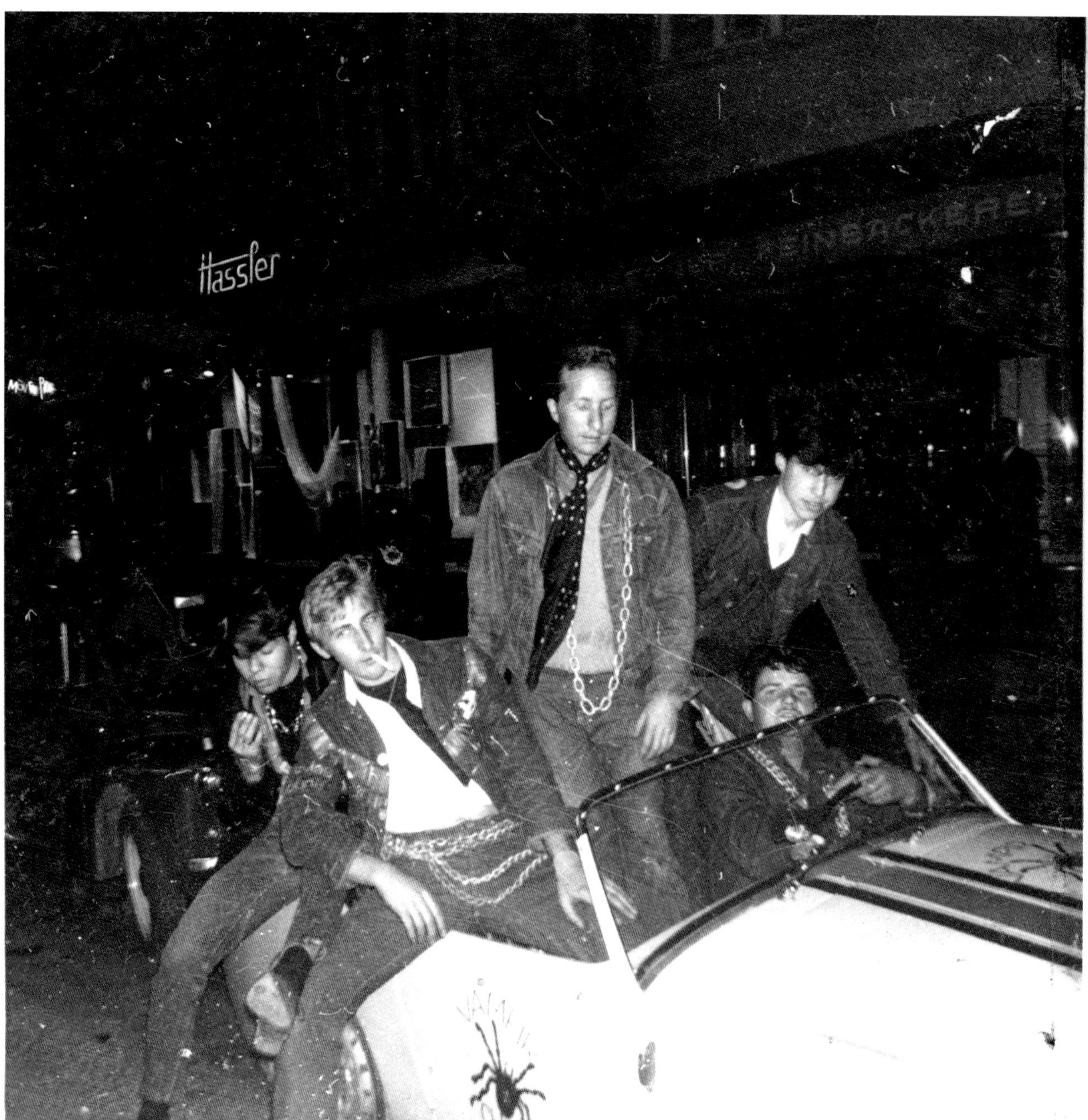

Vampir Boss Raymond, with cig, with Cliff and fellow chain swingers in their club Vampir club car MG.

06 / basler herbstmesse
october–november 1962

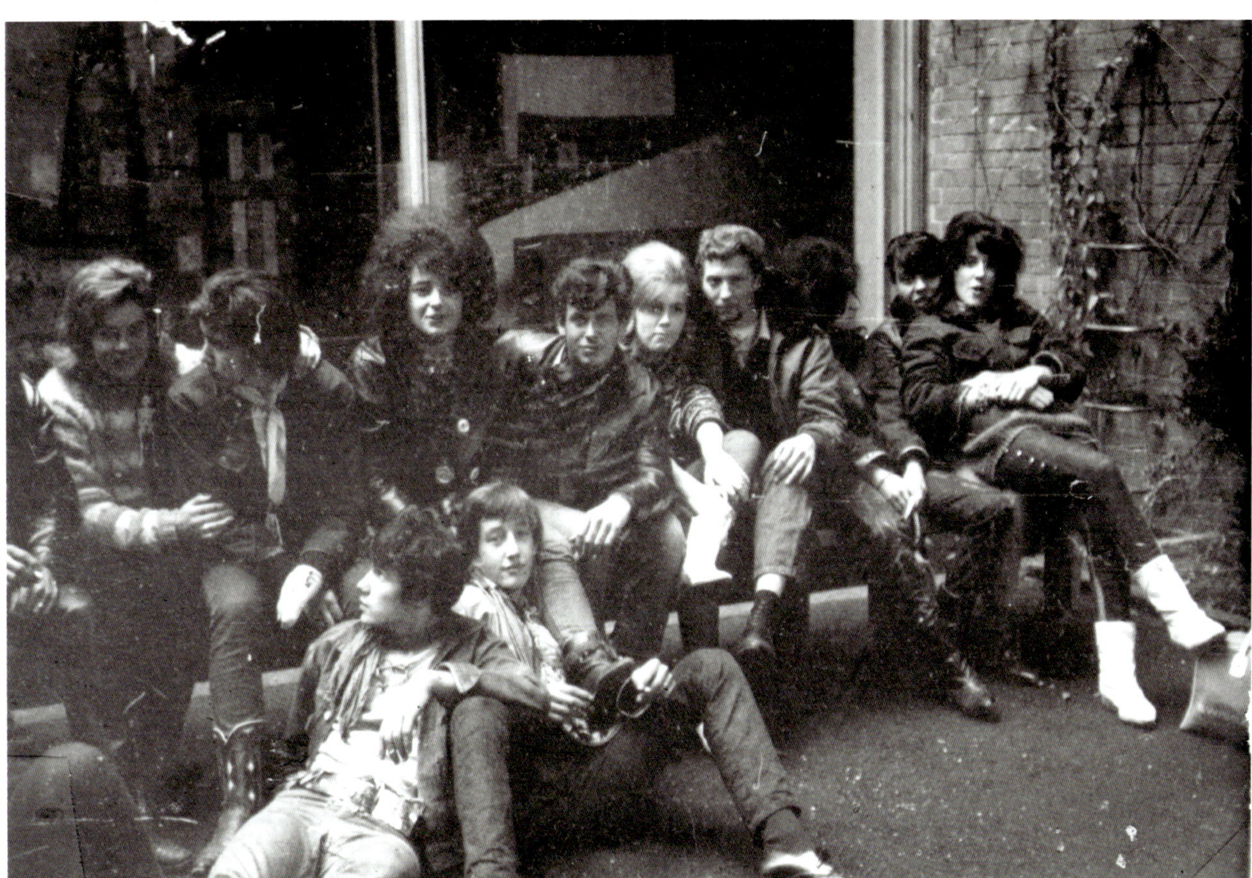

Young gang members at Herbstmesse, Basel.

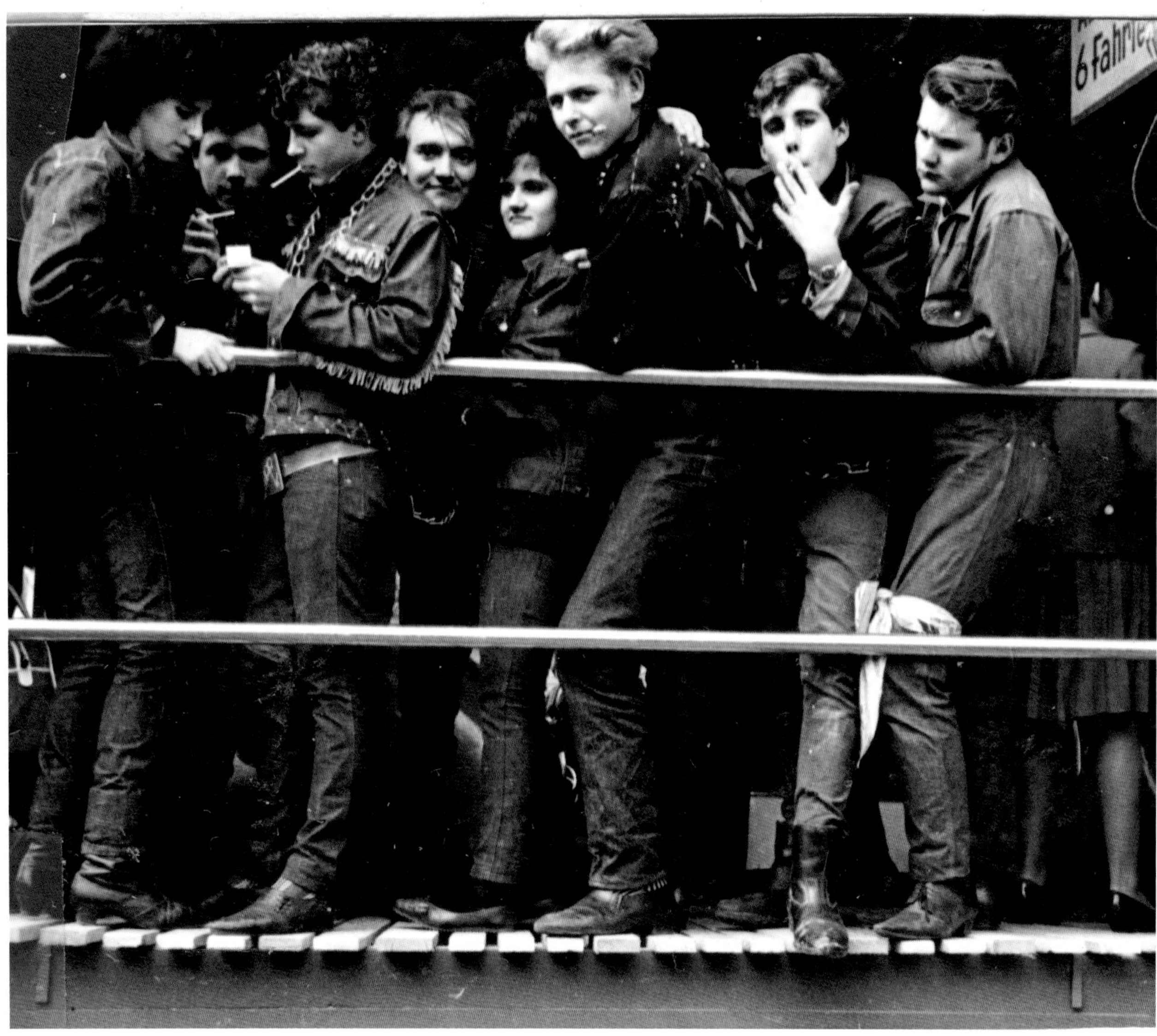

Marcel Zimmerli aka Jacky (third from left) with Johnsy, Rumy and Timber from Germany on a fairground attraction. A scarf tied at the knee was gang fashion.

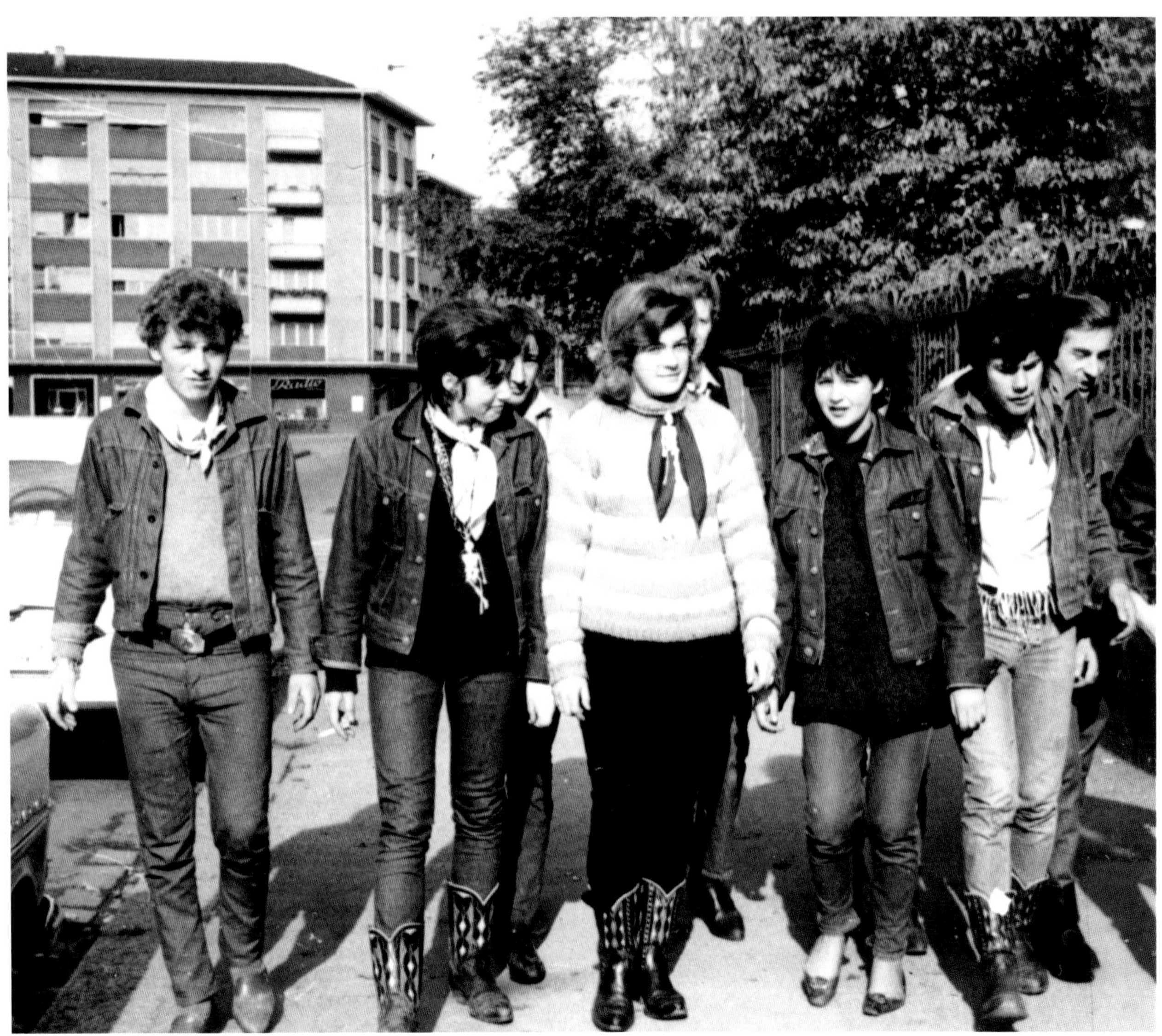

Halbstarke from Lucerne and Zurich join the Basel forces at Restaurant Old Sailor.

07 / cafe nebelspalter in lucerne
november 17, 1962

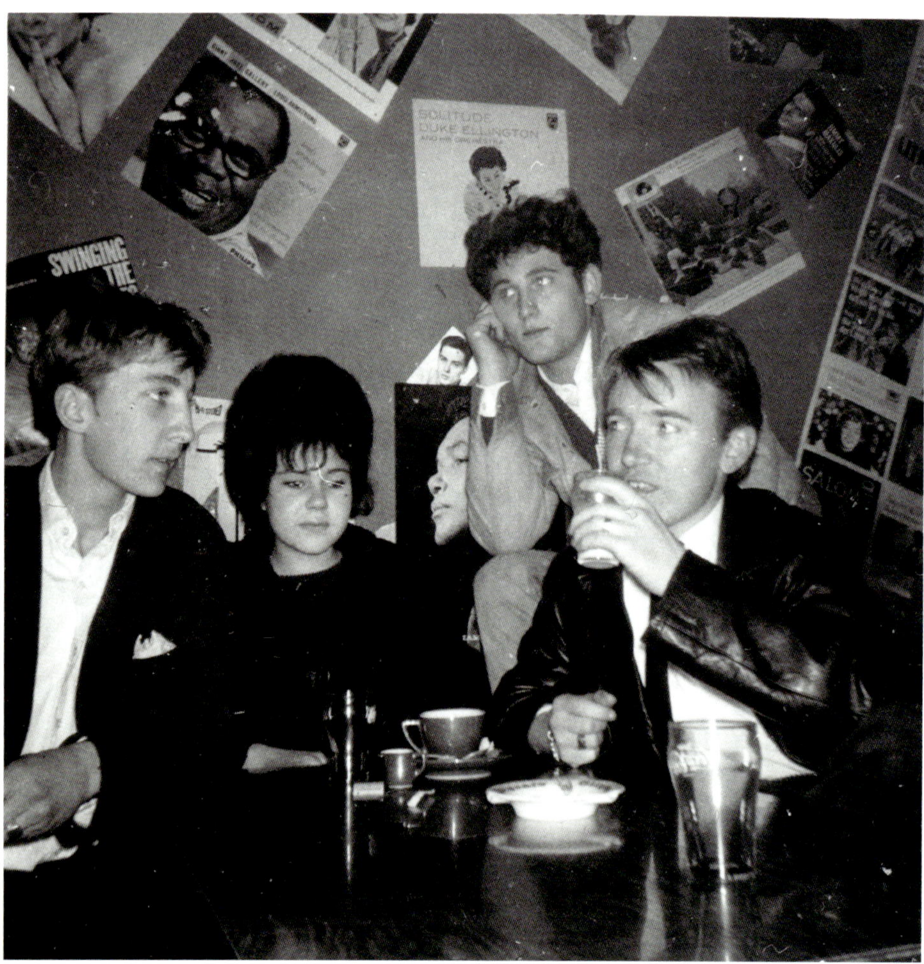

Cafe Nebelspalter, Lucerne. Tello and Johnsy (at right) with local gang couple.

08/restaurant magdalena in lucerne
november 24–25, 1962

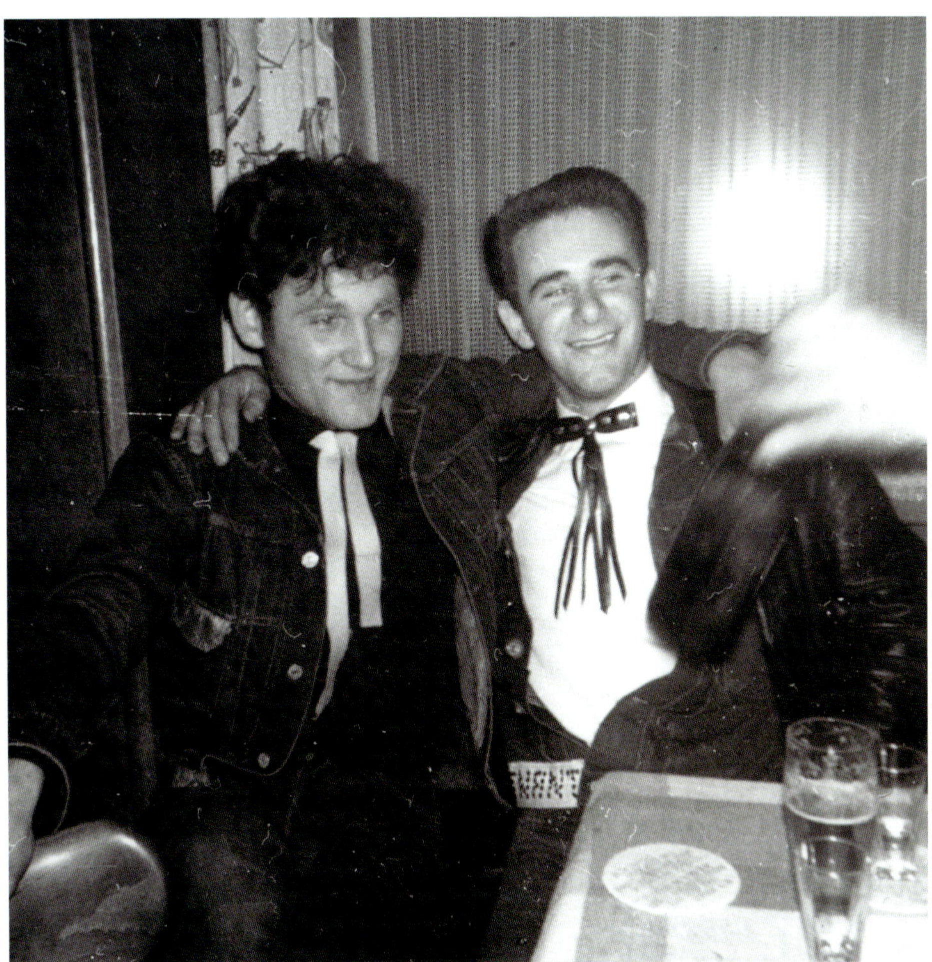

Tello with Leutnant.

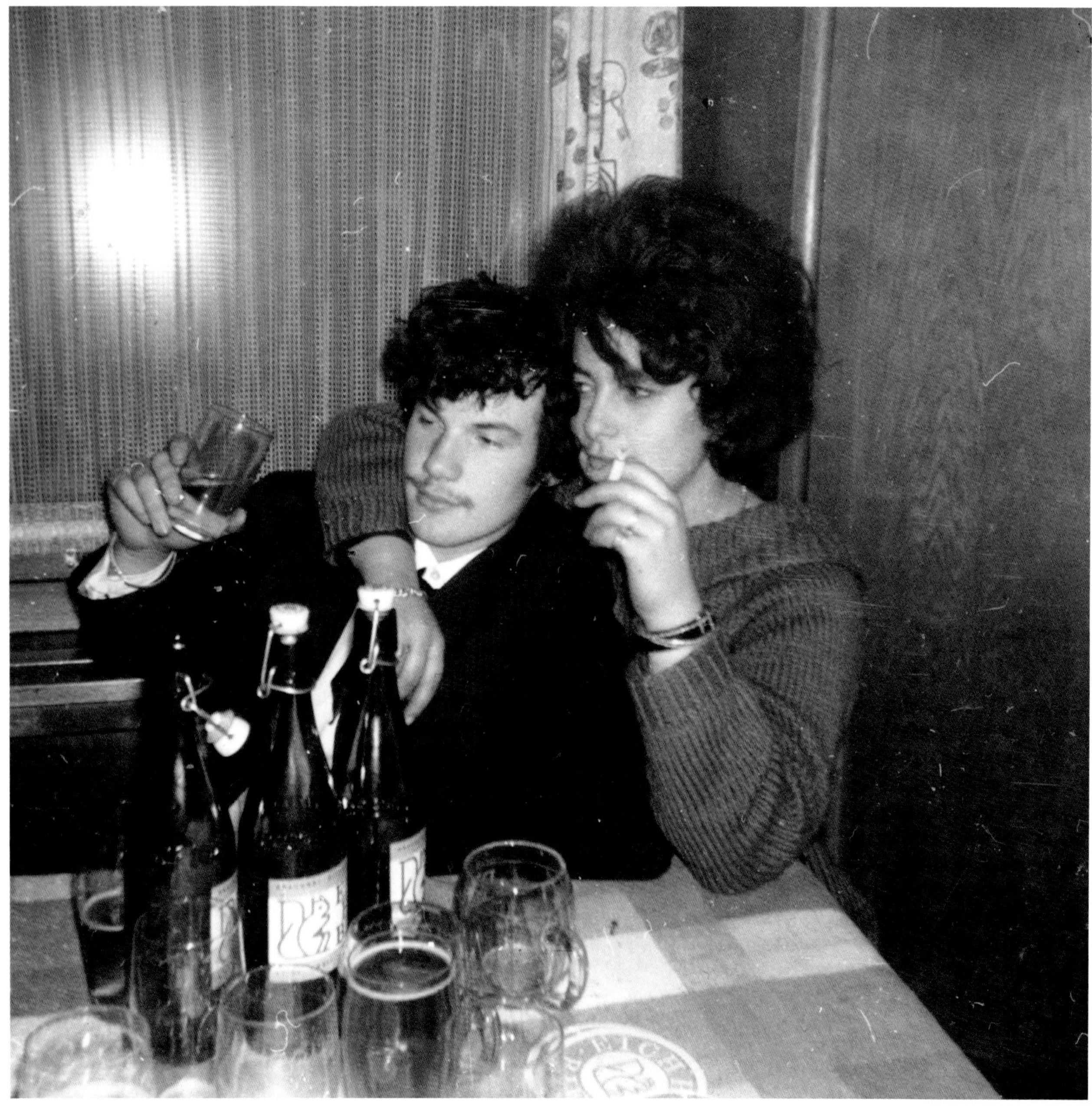

Cliff from Lucerne in a close situation with Margrit Risi aka Maggi at Restaurant Magdalena. There were umpteen Cliffs due to Cliff Richard's influence.

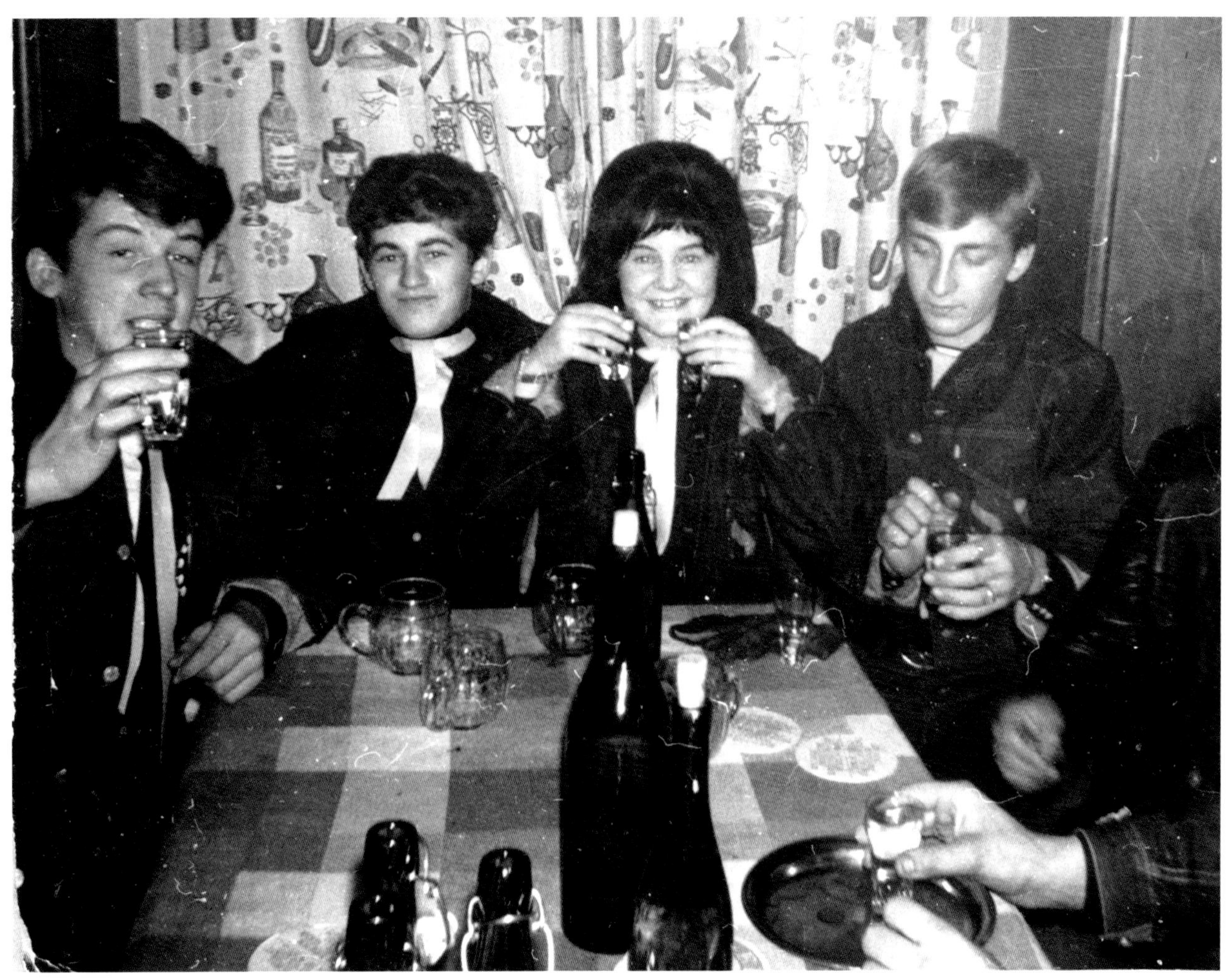

Let The Good Times Roll.

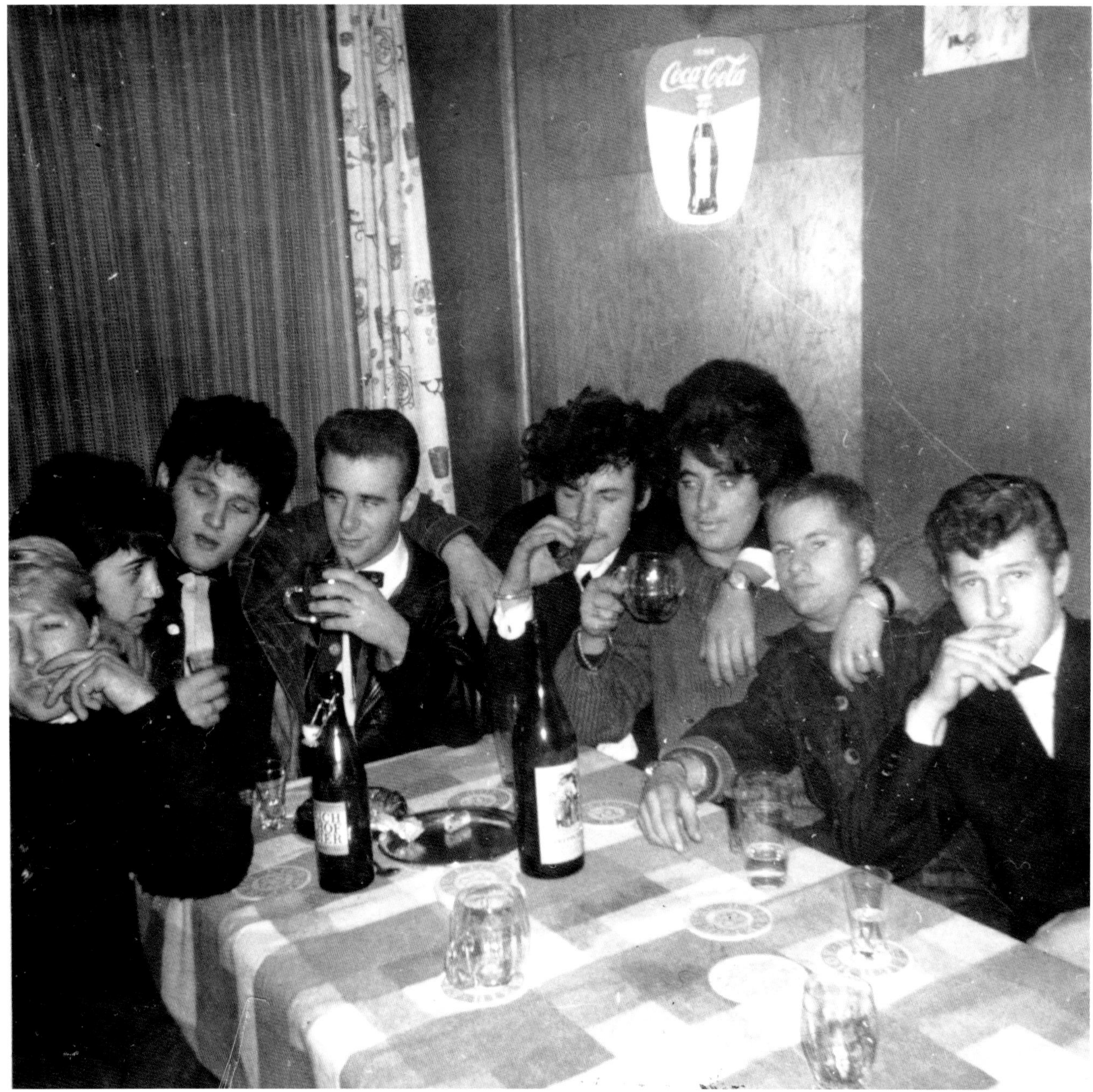

From left to right: Blondie, unknown gang member, Tello, Leutnant, Cliff Lucerne, Maggi, Igel and unknown smoker.

09/lucerne
december 1962

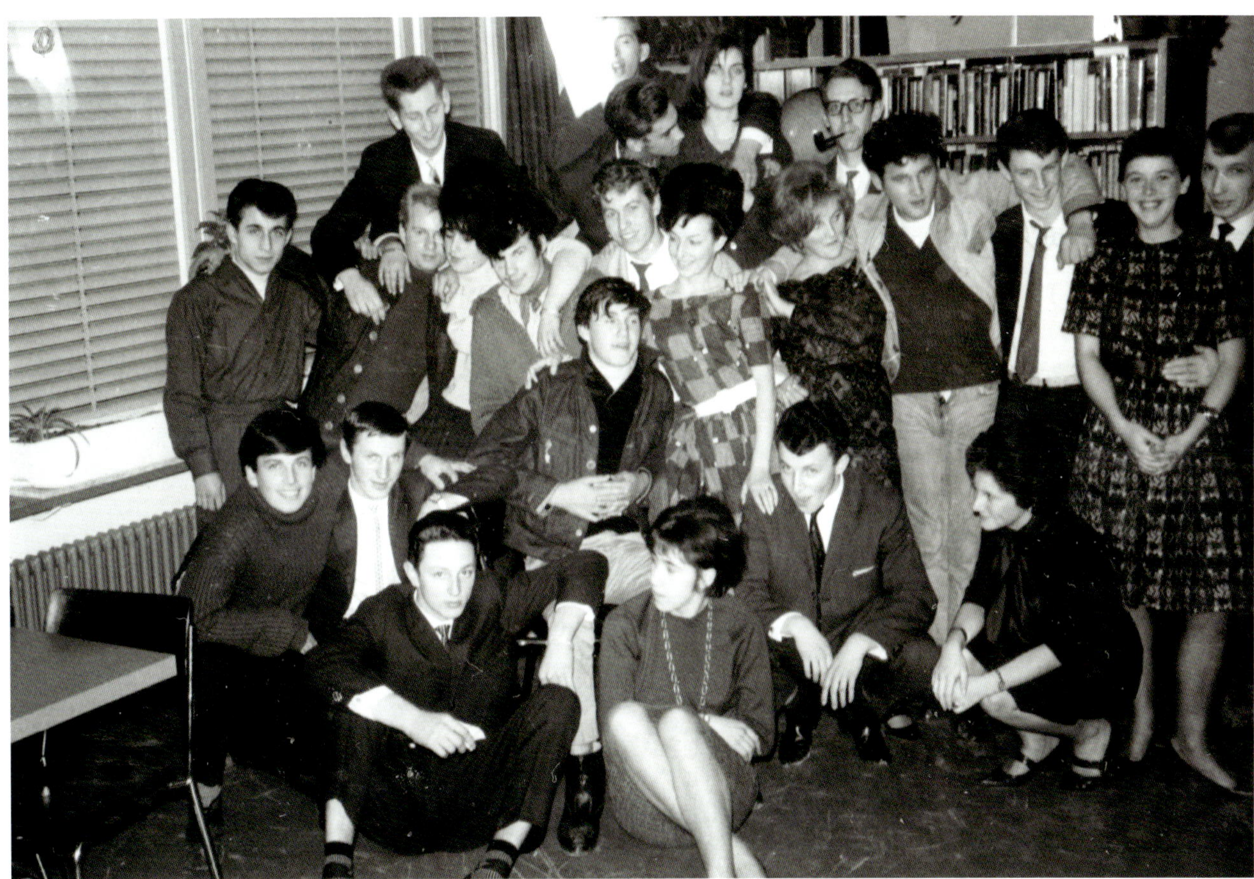

Igel, surrounded by various Halbstarke.

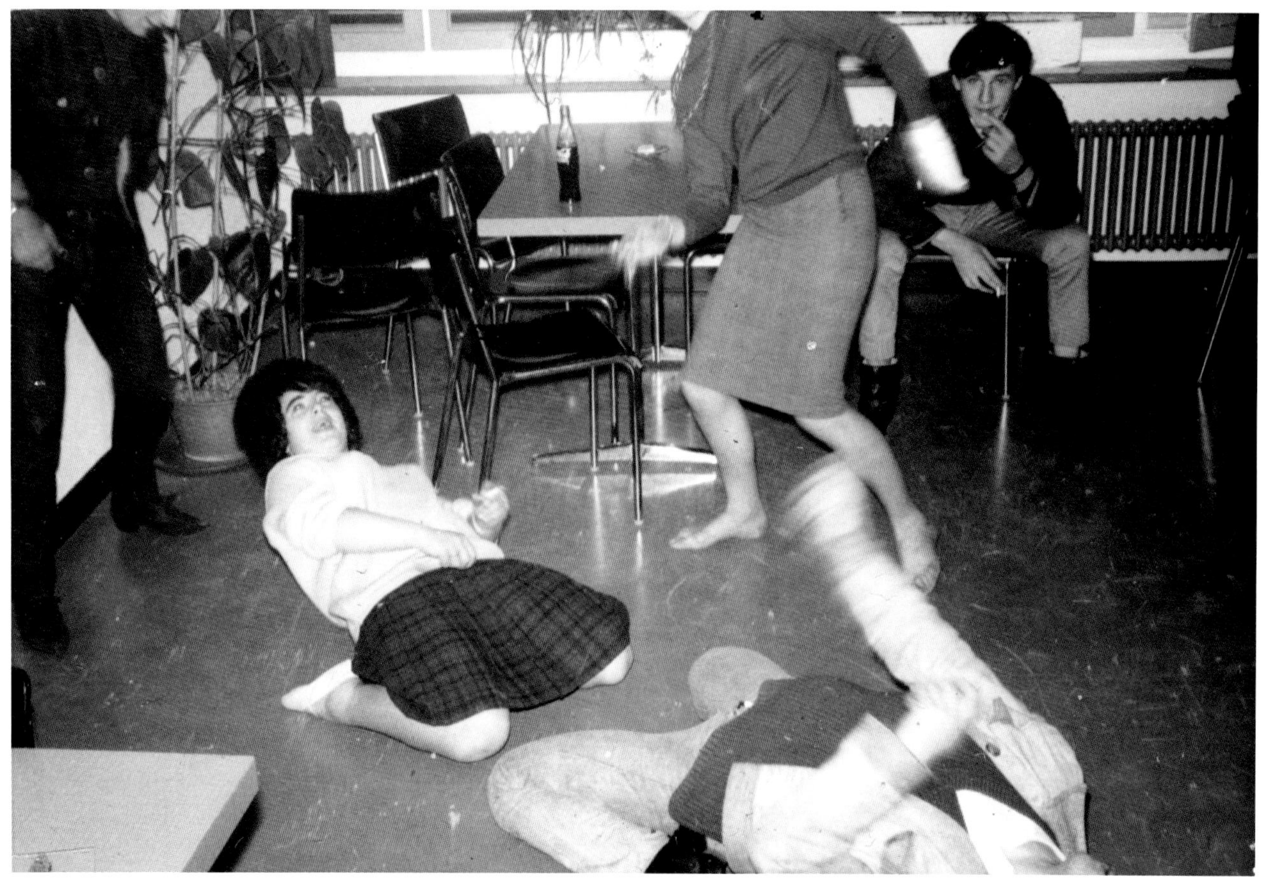

Margrit aka Maggi shows off the latest dance moves.

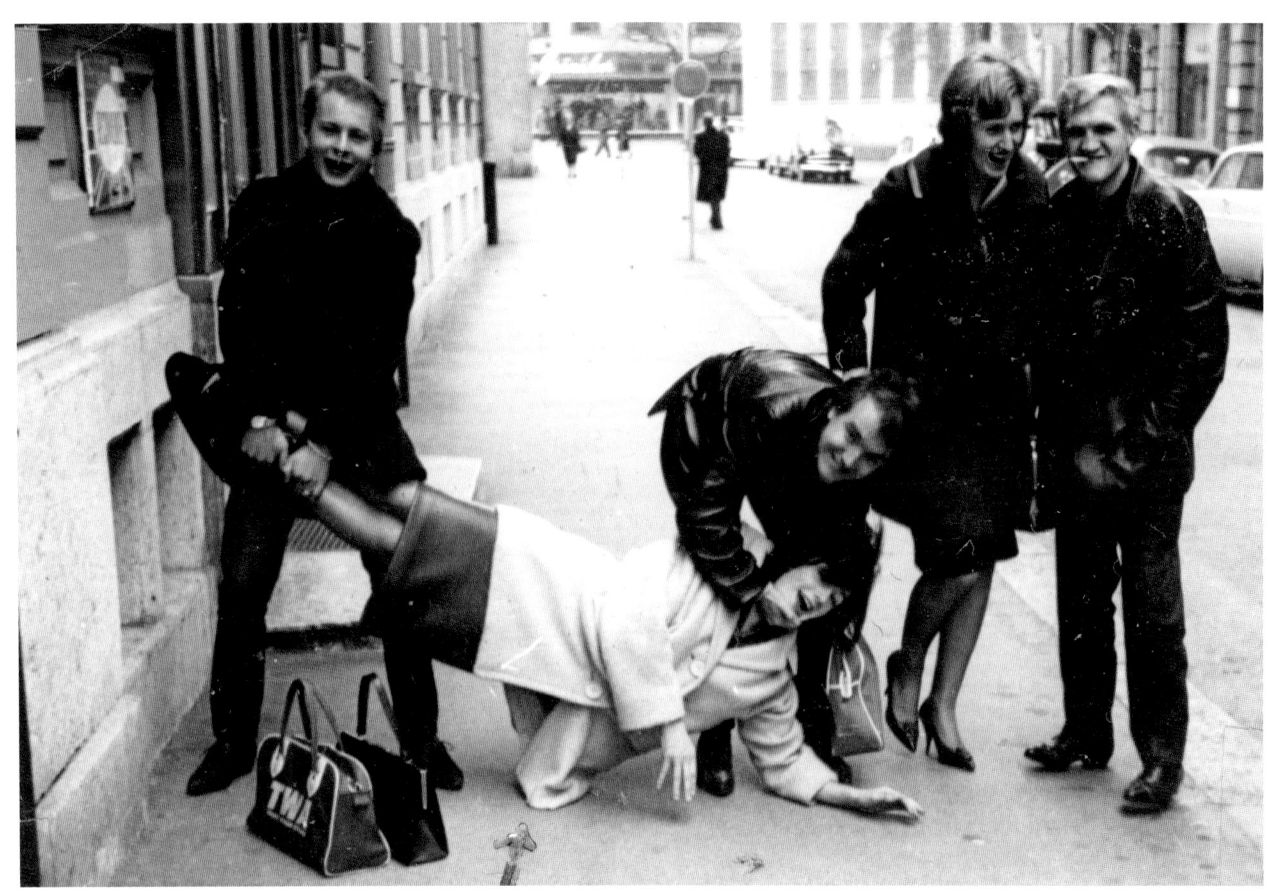

Igel and Johnsy have fun with Leather and Beatrice.

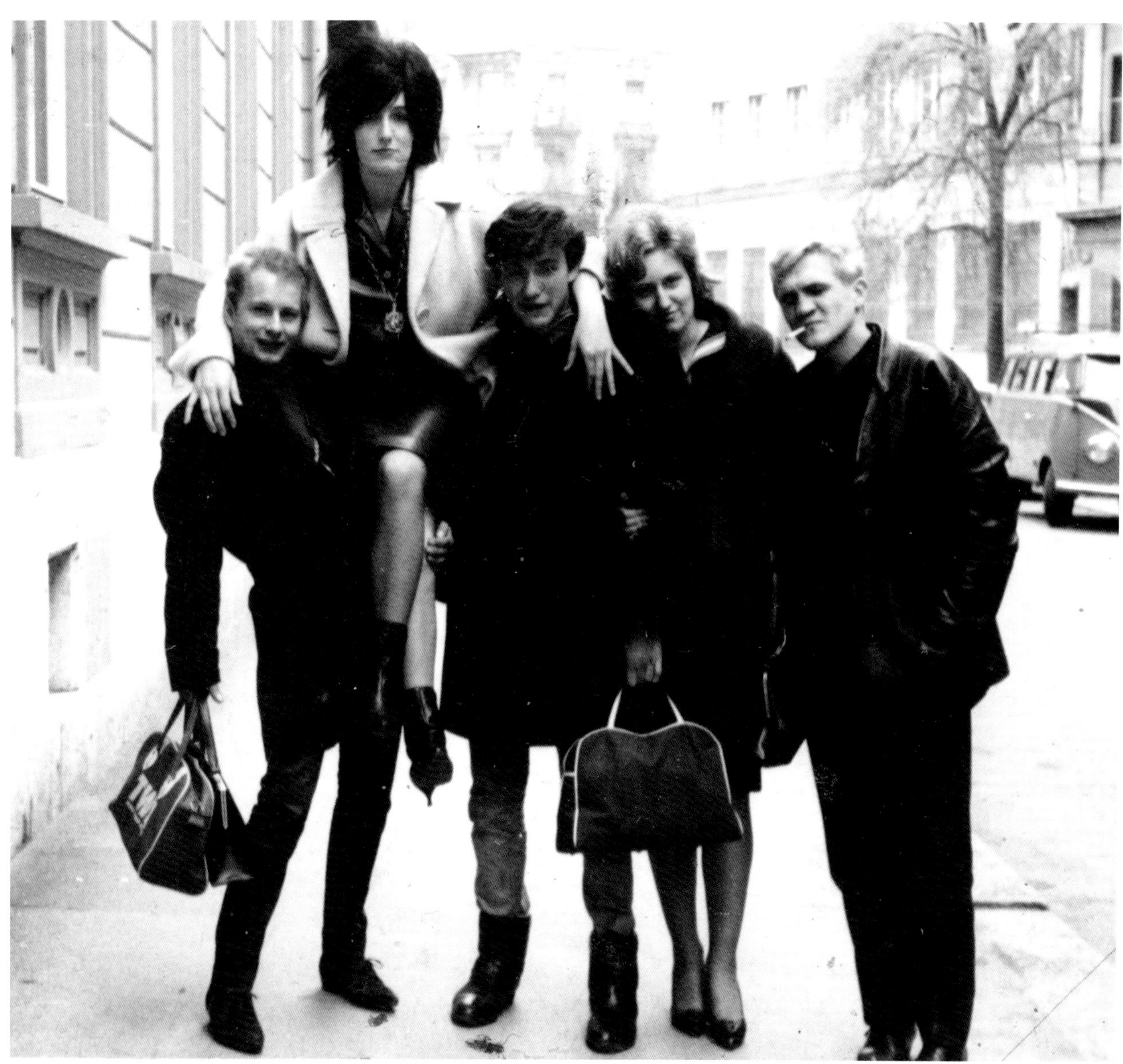

Leather (in Swiss German: Laader) held aloft by Igel, and her blonde sister Beatrice.

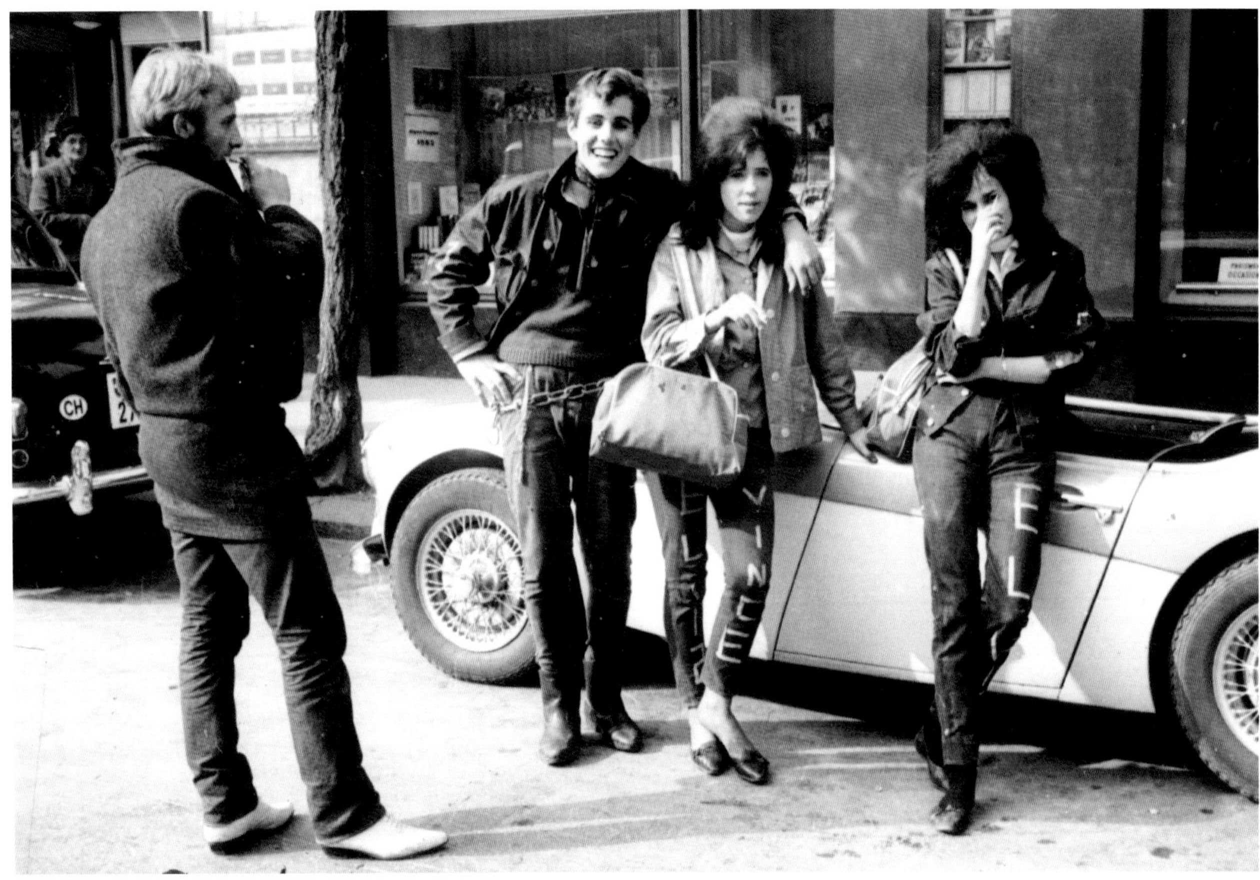

Boss Raymond Christen, in white cowboy boots, with trendy gangsters in Lucerne. Note girls' jeans bleached with the name of their fave stars, Vince (Taylor) and Elvis.

10/new year's eve party, münchner keller, lucerne
december 31, 1962–january 1, 1963

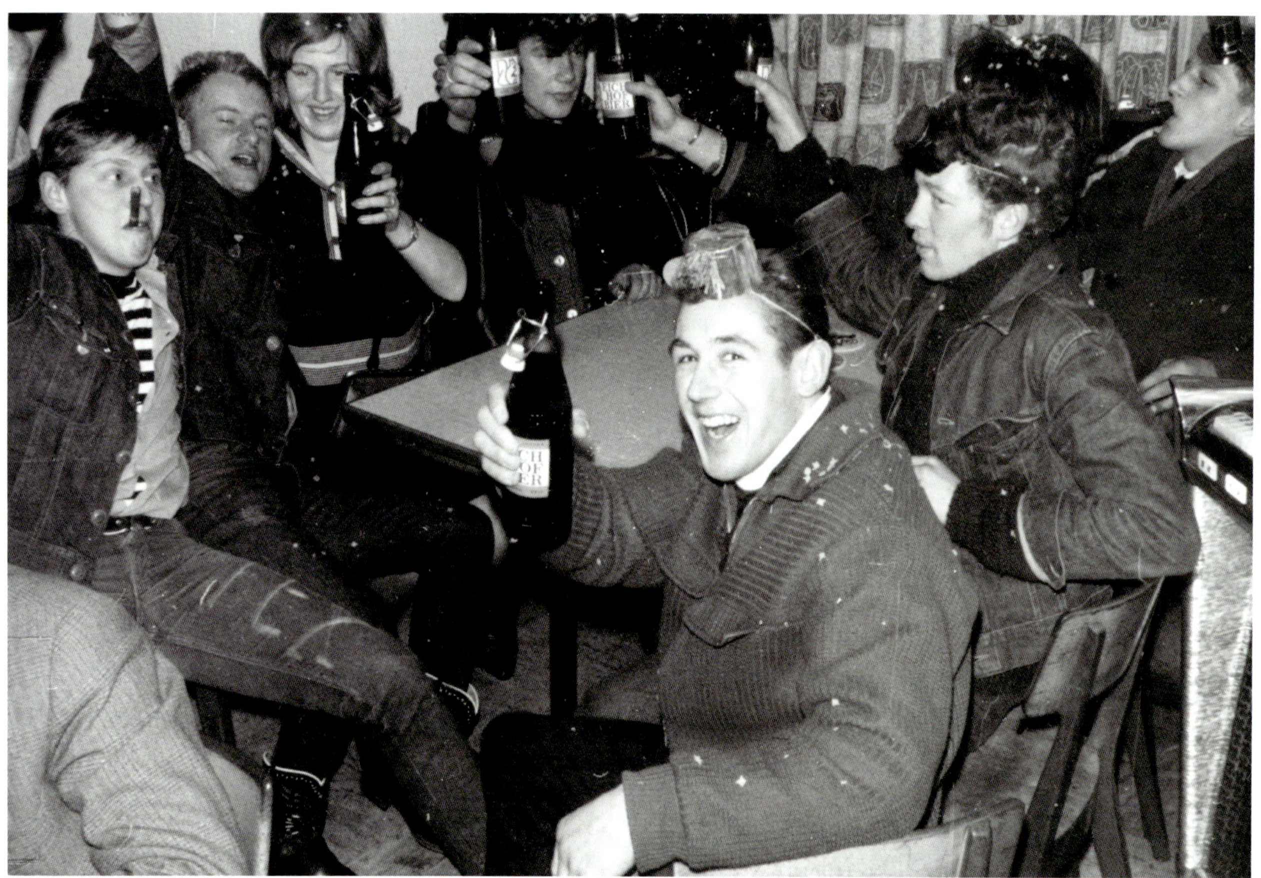

Munchner Keller, Lucerne. Igel, Beatrice and Cliff Lucerne (center back) with rabble rousers.

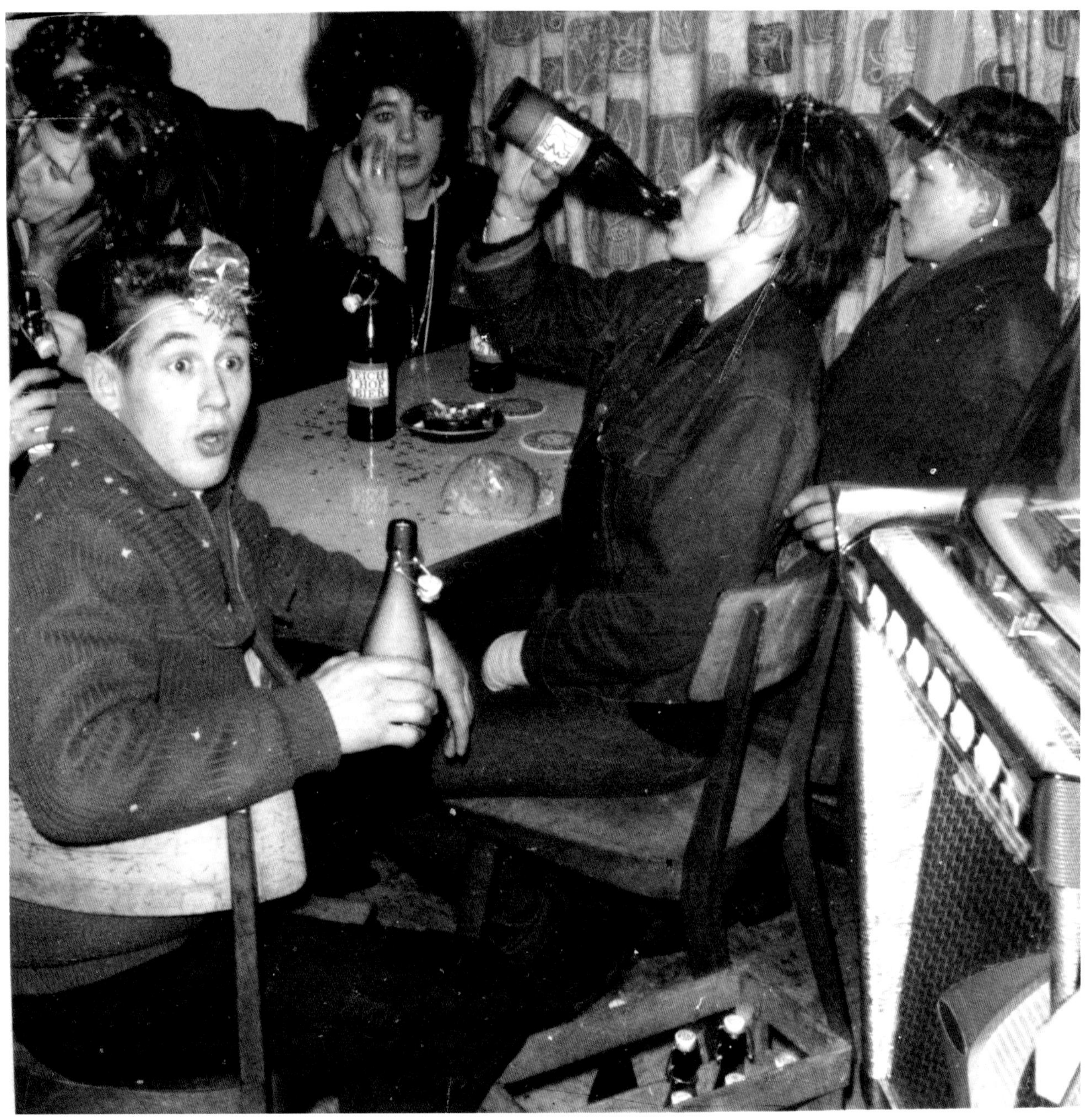

Party at Munchner Keller.

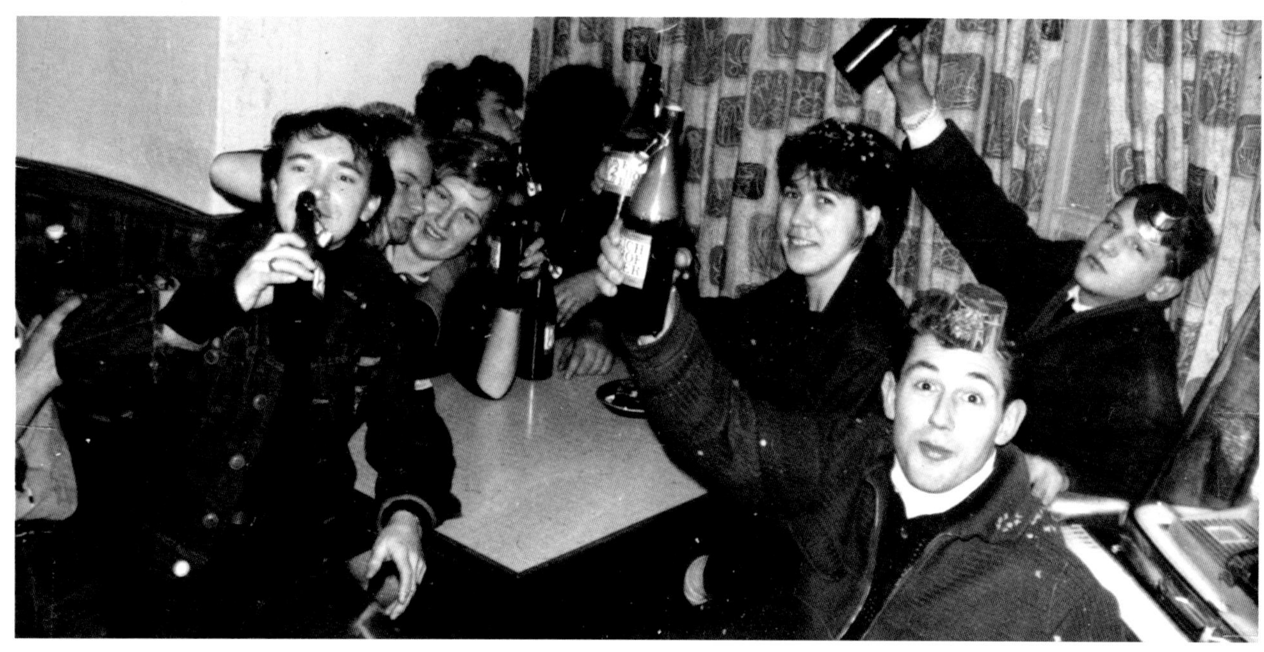

Bottoms up! Johnsy (left) joins the revellers.

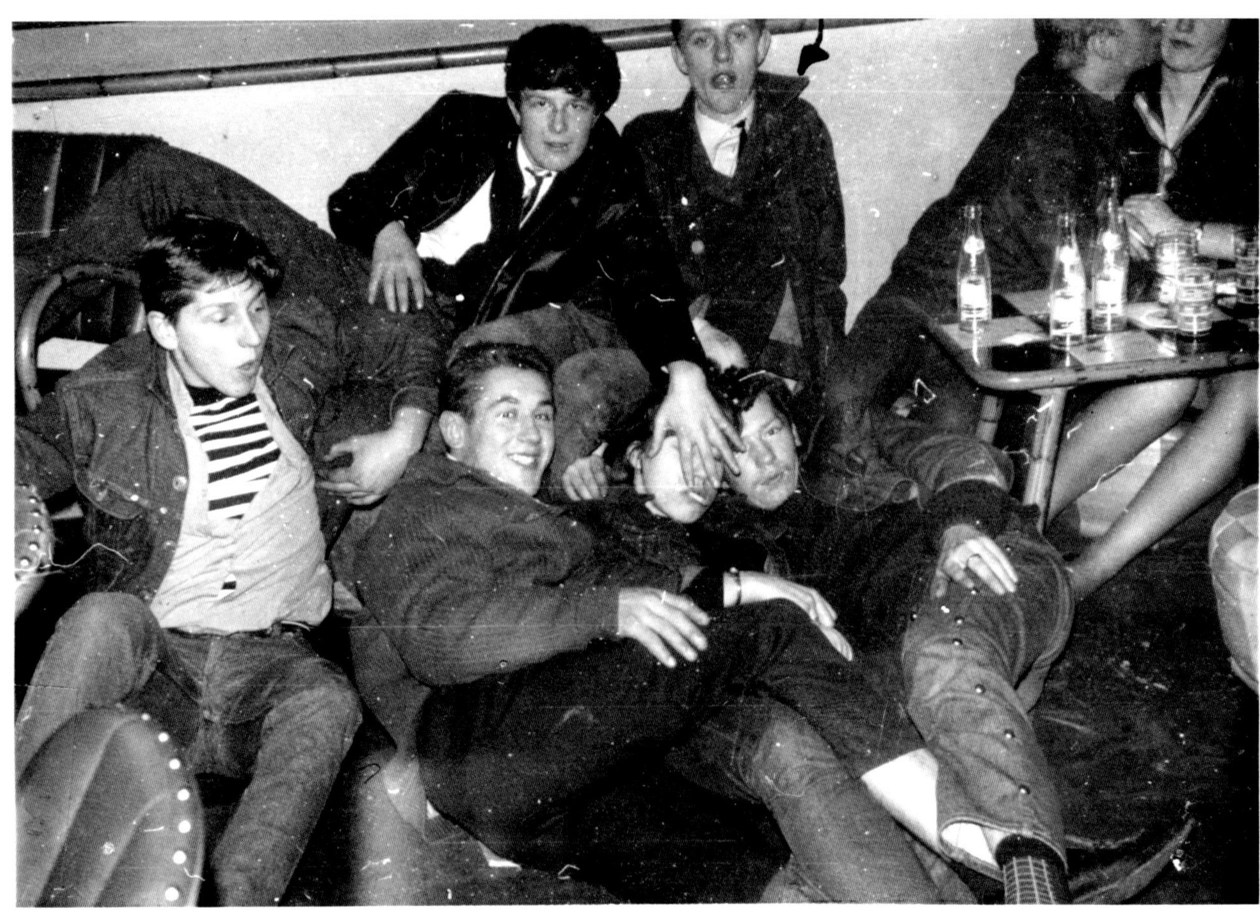

Halbstarke from Basel party in Lucerne.

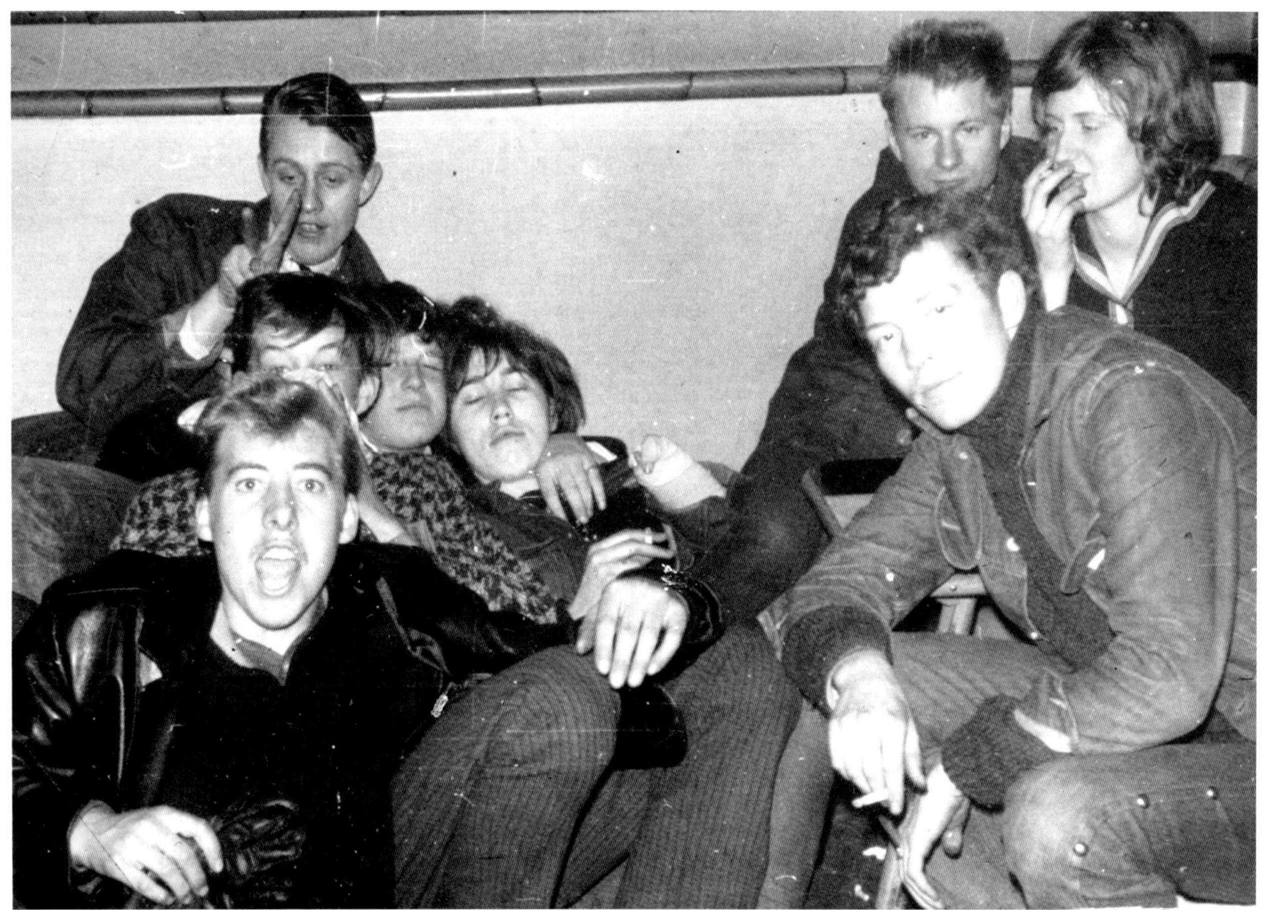

Toughs at Muenchner Keller.

1963

11 / allschwiler fasnacht (carnival in allschwil)
february 1963

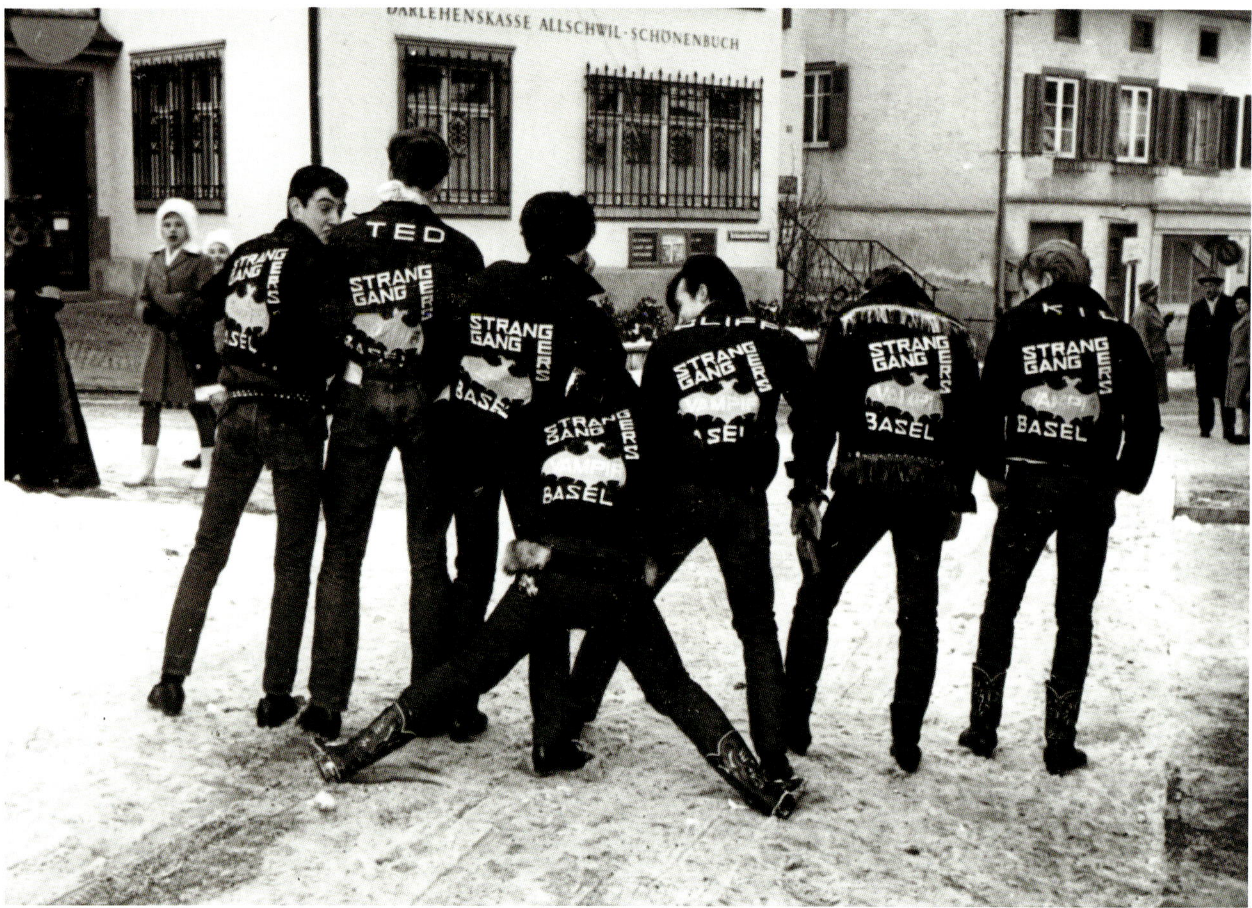

The Vampir Club, Basel display their new bat jackets. Their Vampir emblem added "Strangers Gang Basel", due to the fact that the Halbstarken were actually regarded as strangers by everyone. Left to right: Ruedi (Red) Schmid, Beat (Ted) Bucher, two unknown, Werner (Cliff) Kesselring, their boss Raymond (Killer) Christen, and vice-boss Arnoldo (Kid) Steiner.

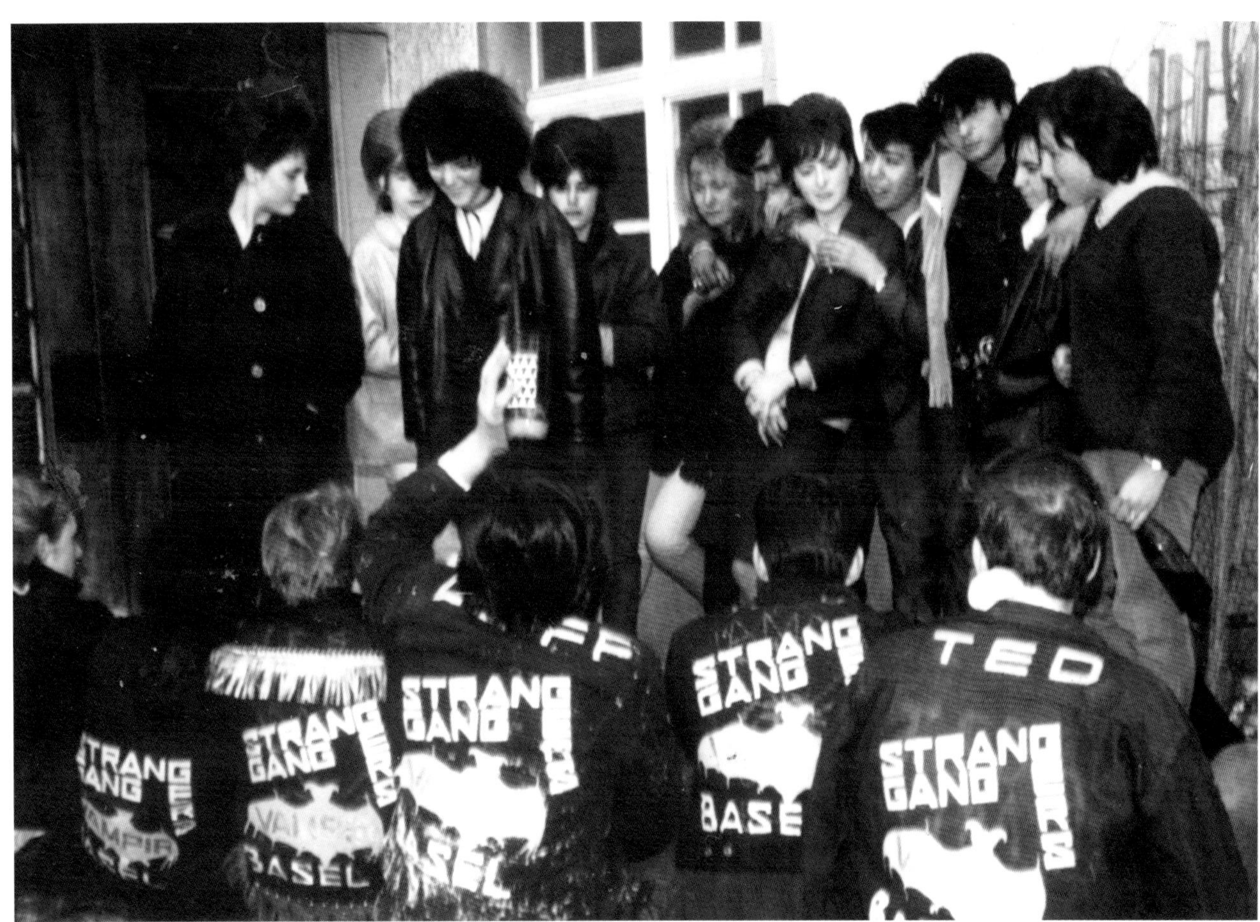

Front left: vice-boss Kid; boss Raymond, Cliff, unknown guy, Ted.

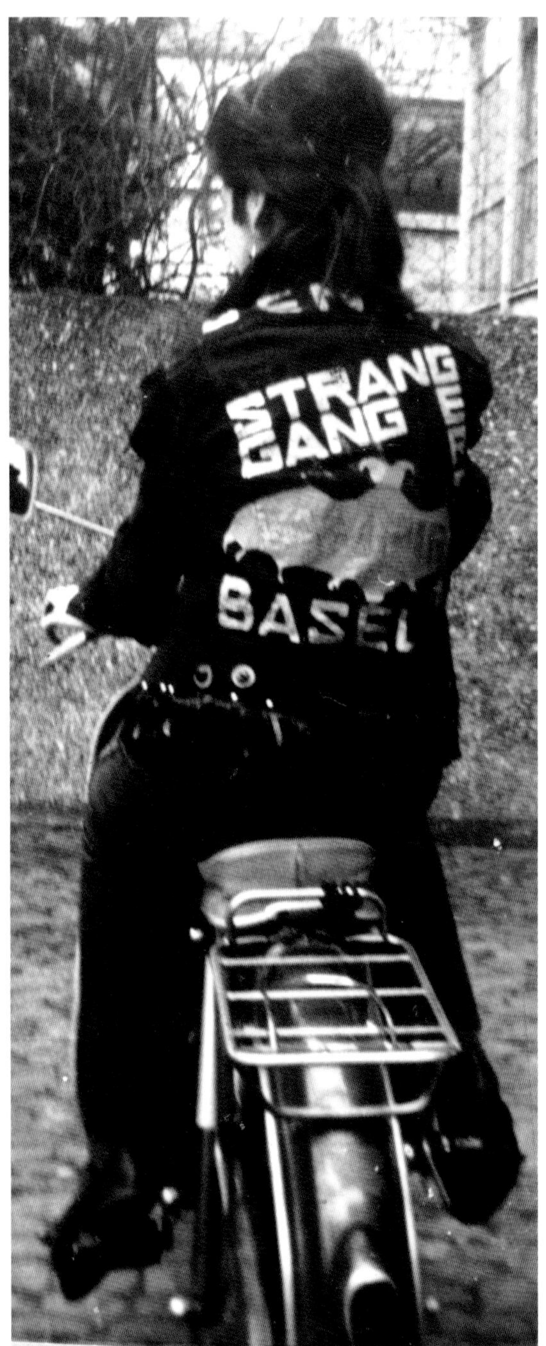

Jenny (Astrid Bieri) and her best friend Rumy (Priska Sonderegger) were the only girls in Basel who had permission to wear the Strangers Gang Vampir Basel gang jackets. Jenny died young; Rumy would later work in a kiosk at Schifflande in Basel.

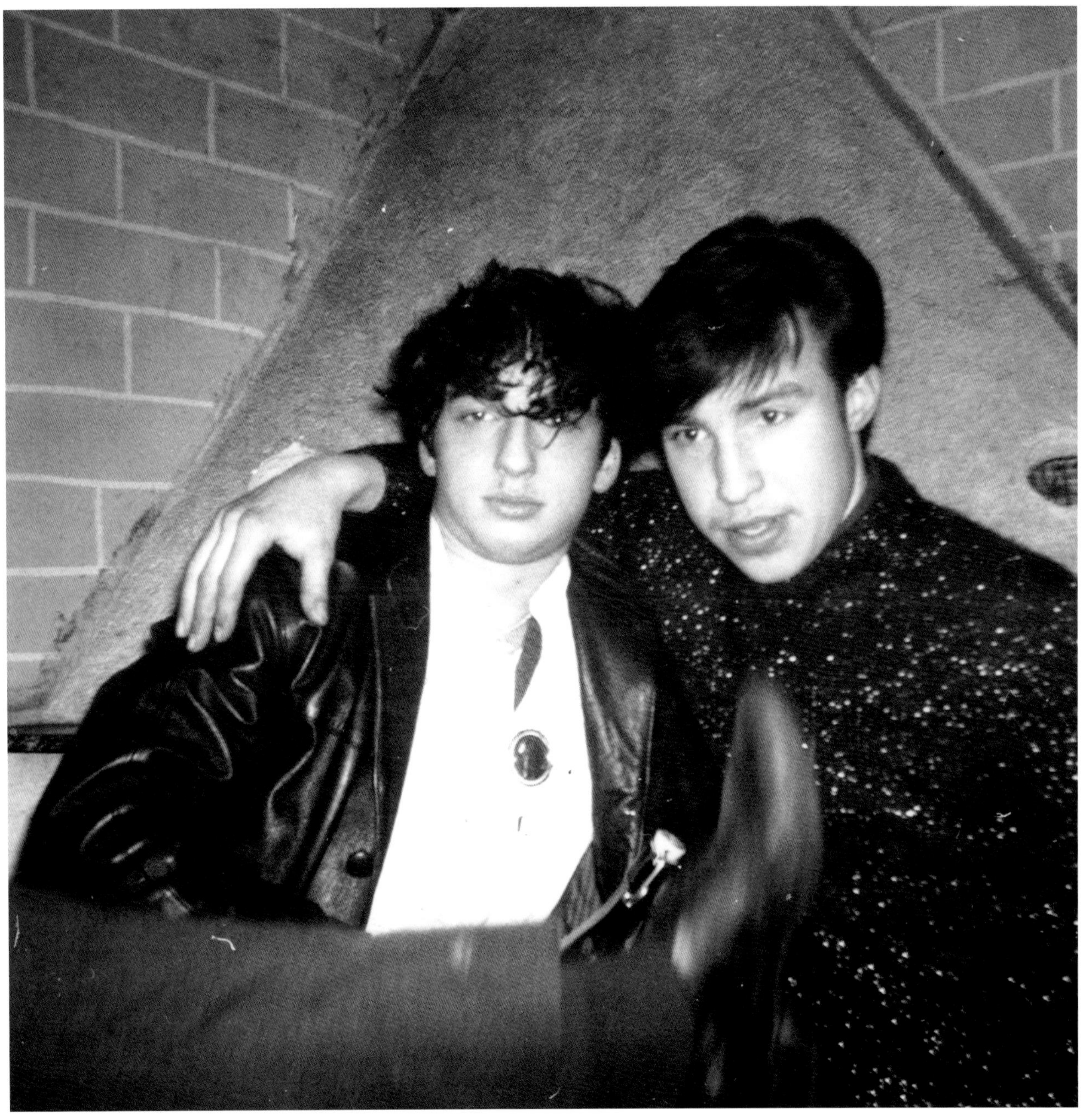

Johnny (Arrigo Prestini) and Cliff (Werner Kesselring), Restaurant Roessli, Allschwil.

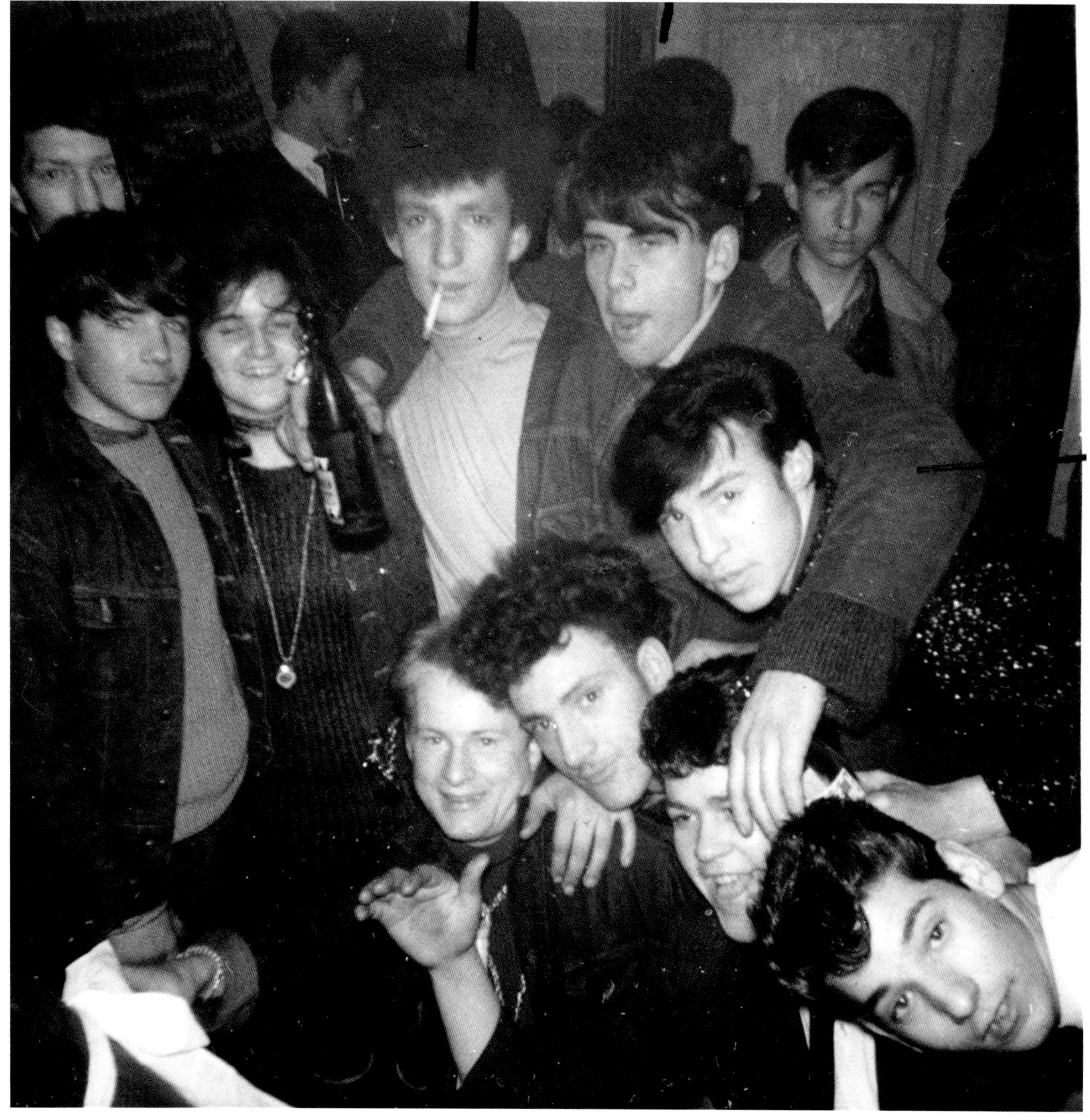

Gang girl Priska Sonderegger aka Rumy, with the boys.

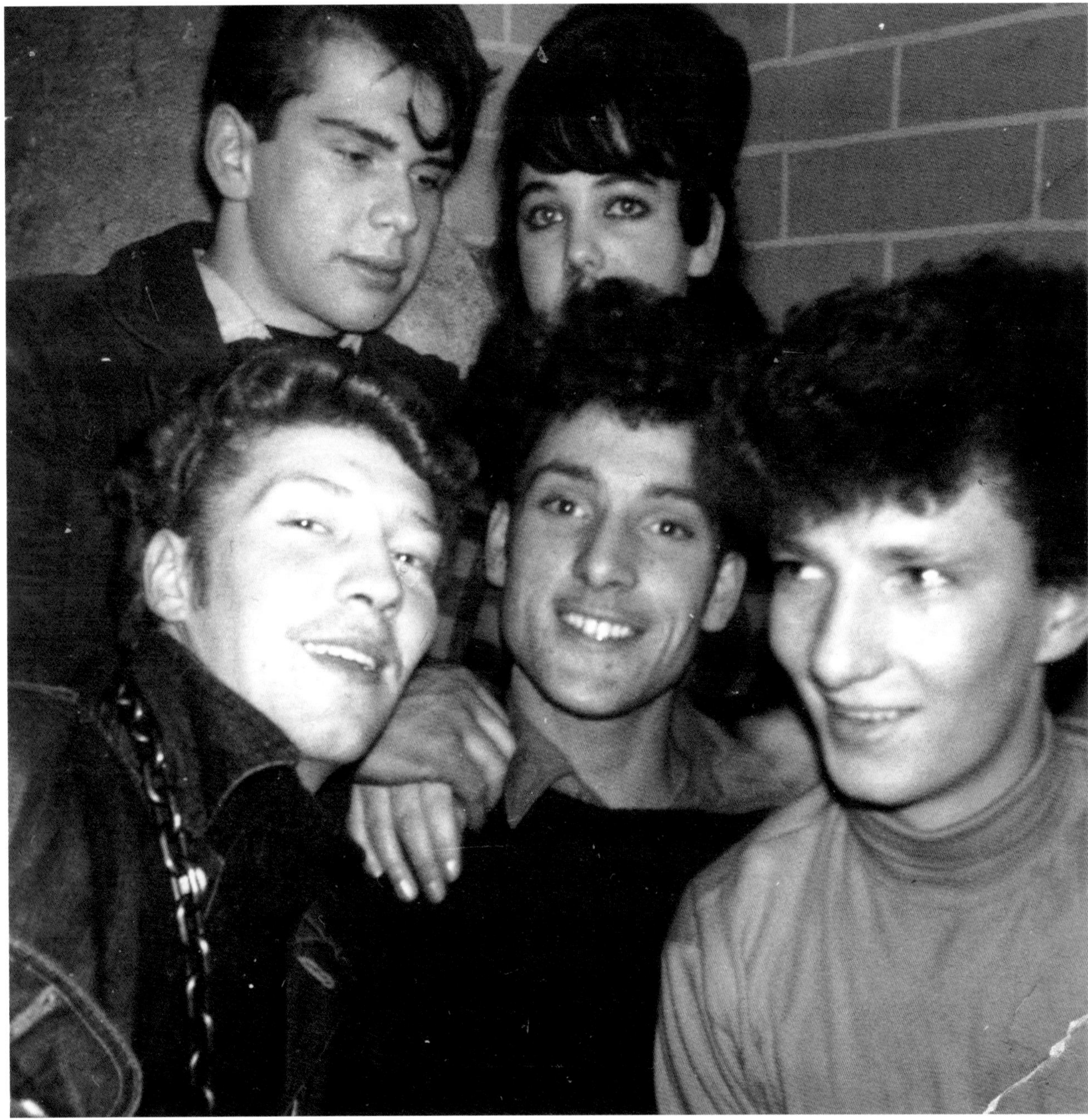

Freddy Madorin (top left) with unknown beauty; Gufekissi and Lexi at right with friend (with chain).

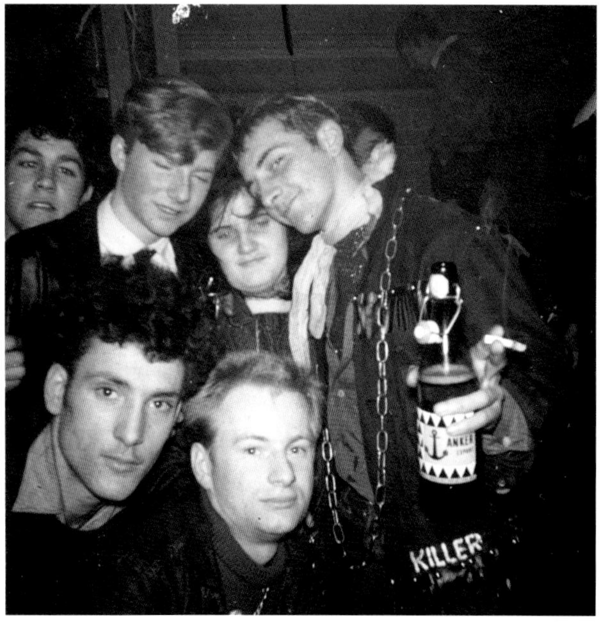

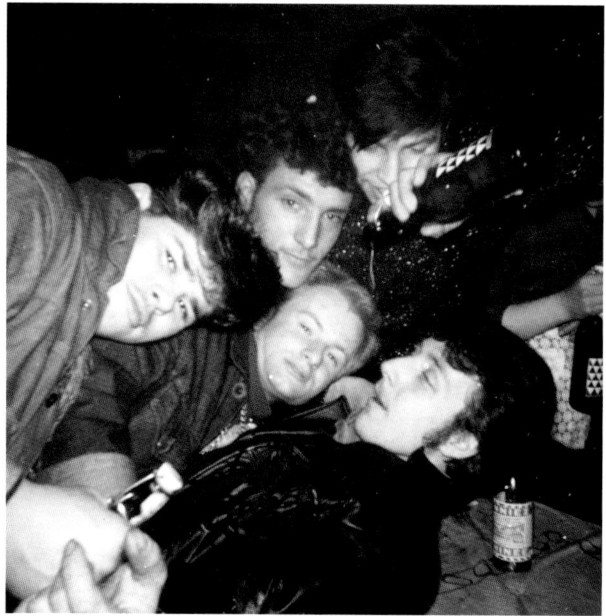

Left, front row: Gufekissi and Igel. Back row: Walti Fricker, Molotow, Rumy and Boss Raymond aka Killer (with chain) at Restaurant Roessli, Allschwil. Right: A legendary snap taken at Restaurant Rössli, Allschwil: Black Star Gang, Basel boss Mecky (aka Zack-Zack) is shown at left, Igel (middle), Mexicano Joe, Gufekissi, Lexi and Cliff (goofing with a bottle in the background, above).

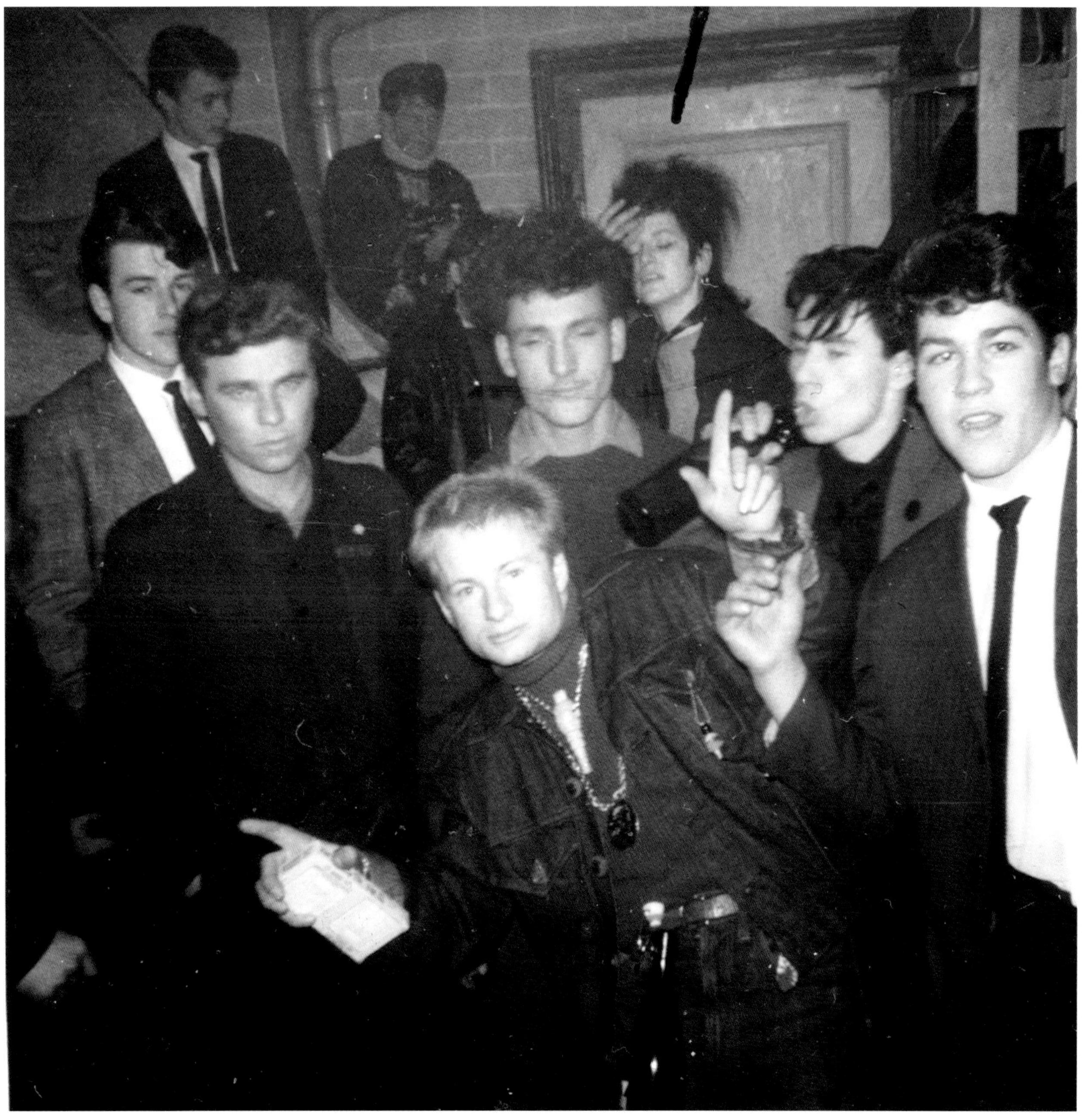

Igel and crew at Rössli, Allschwil, Feburary 1963. Igel appears with mementoes lifted from local pinball machines.

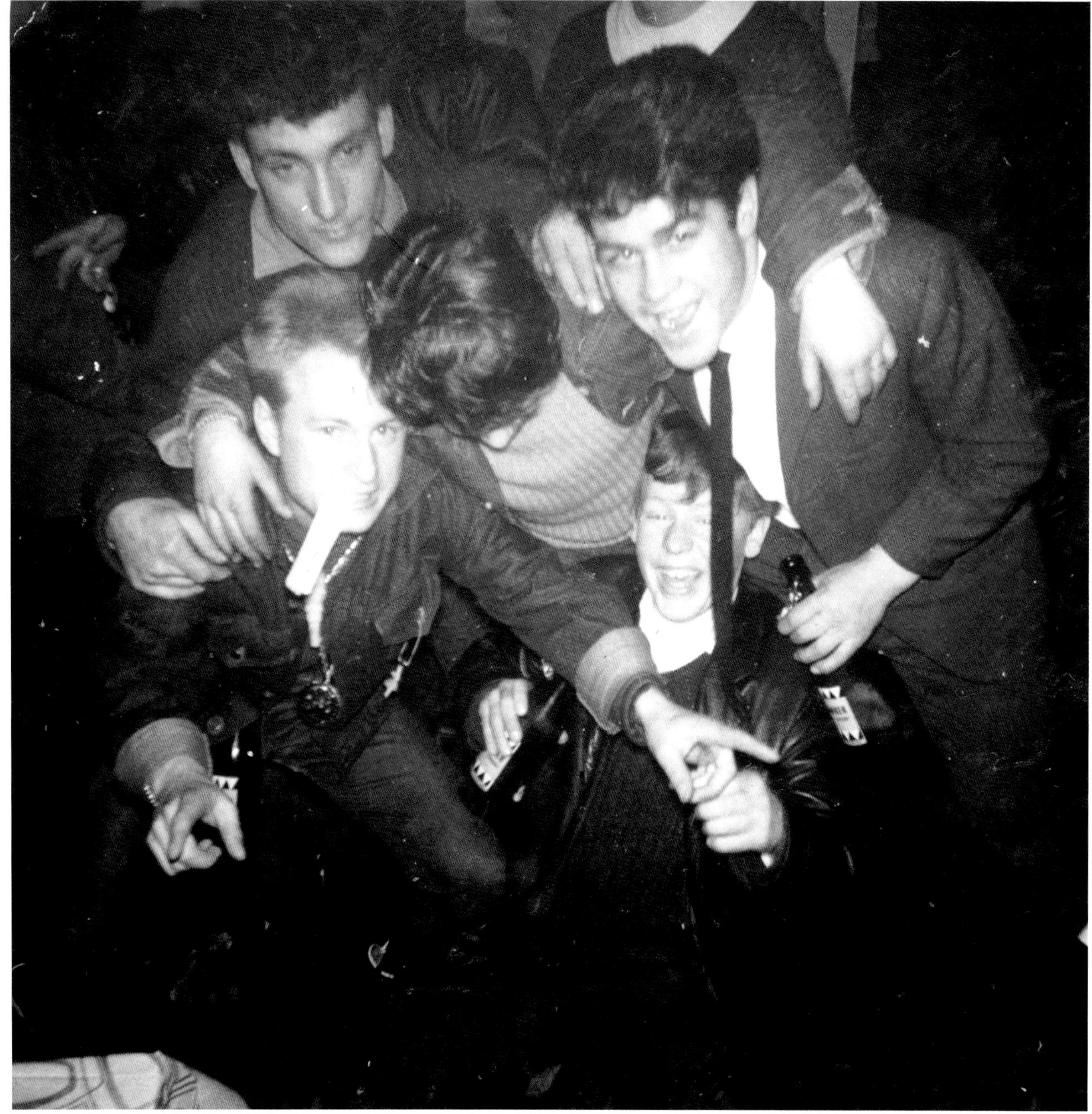

Igel, Gufekissi (above) and Walti Fricker (with tie), Restaurant Roessli, Allschwil.

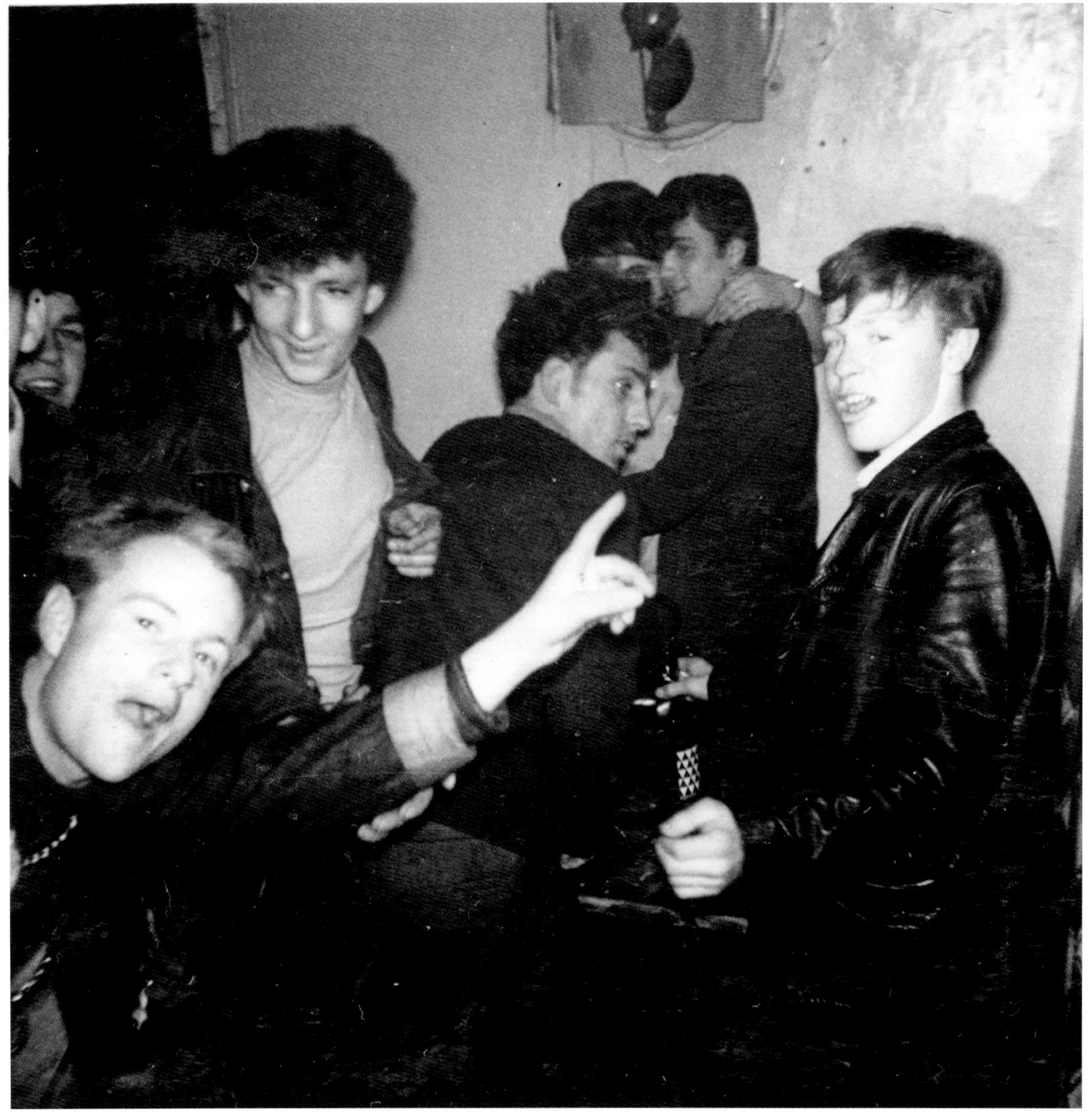

Igel, Lexi and Gufekissi with Max Gass (Jess) plus Vreni Sonderegger and Molotow, at Restaurant Roessli, Allschwil.

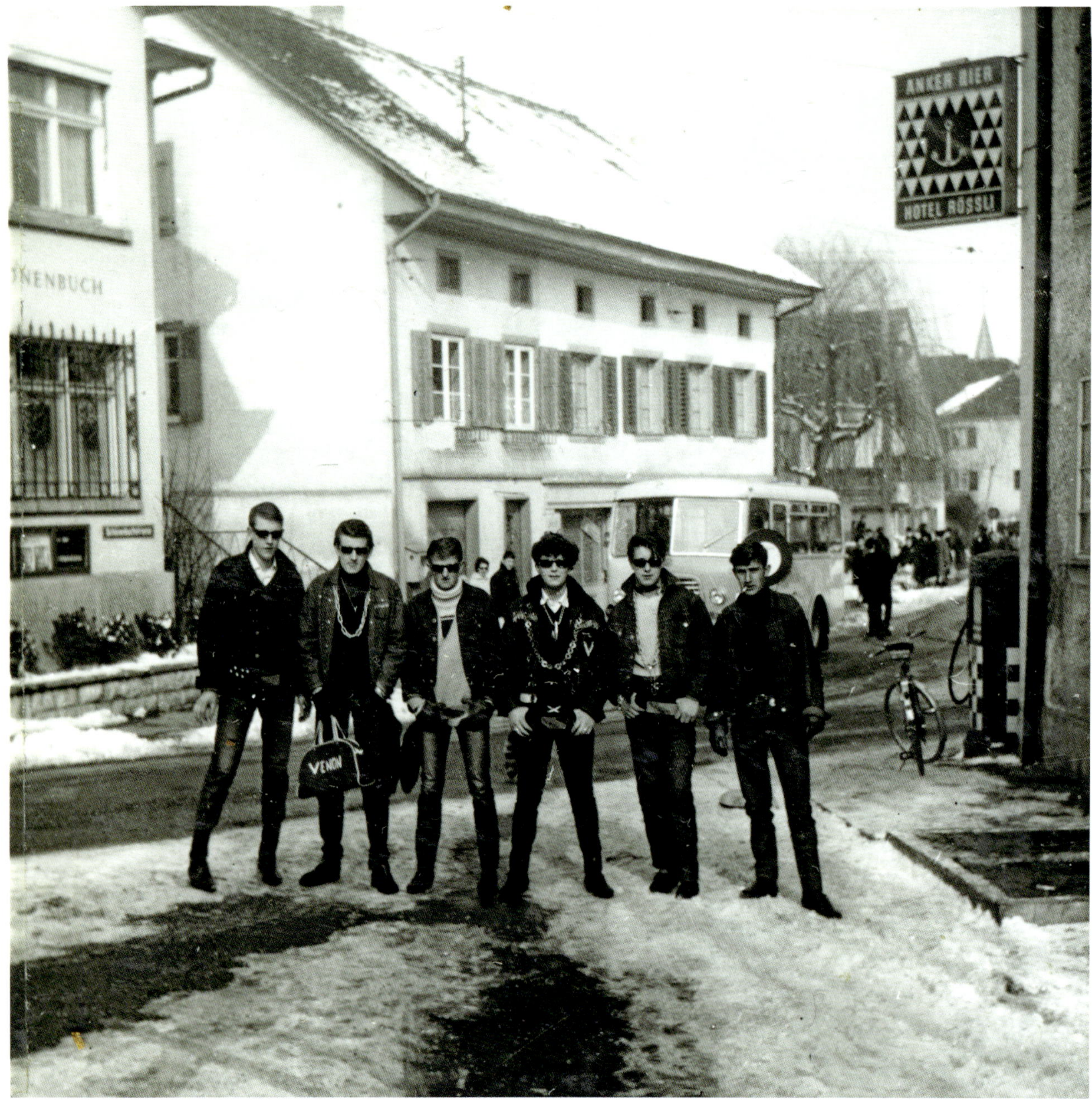

Venom at Restaurant Rössli, Allschwil, a small village located ten minutes from Basel. Left to right: Trinker-Raymond (Drinking Raymond), Schlangepfiff, Mario Clemens, Jacky, Jess and Choya.

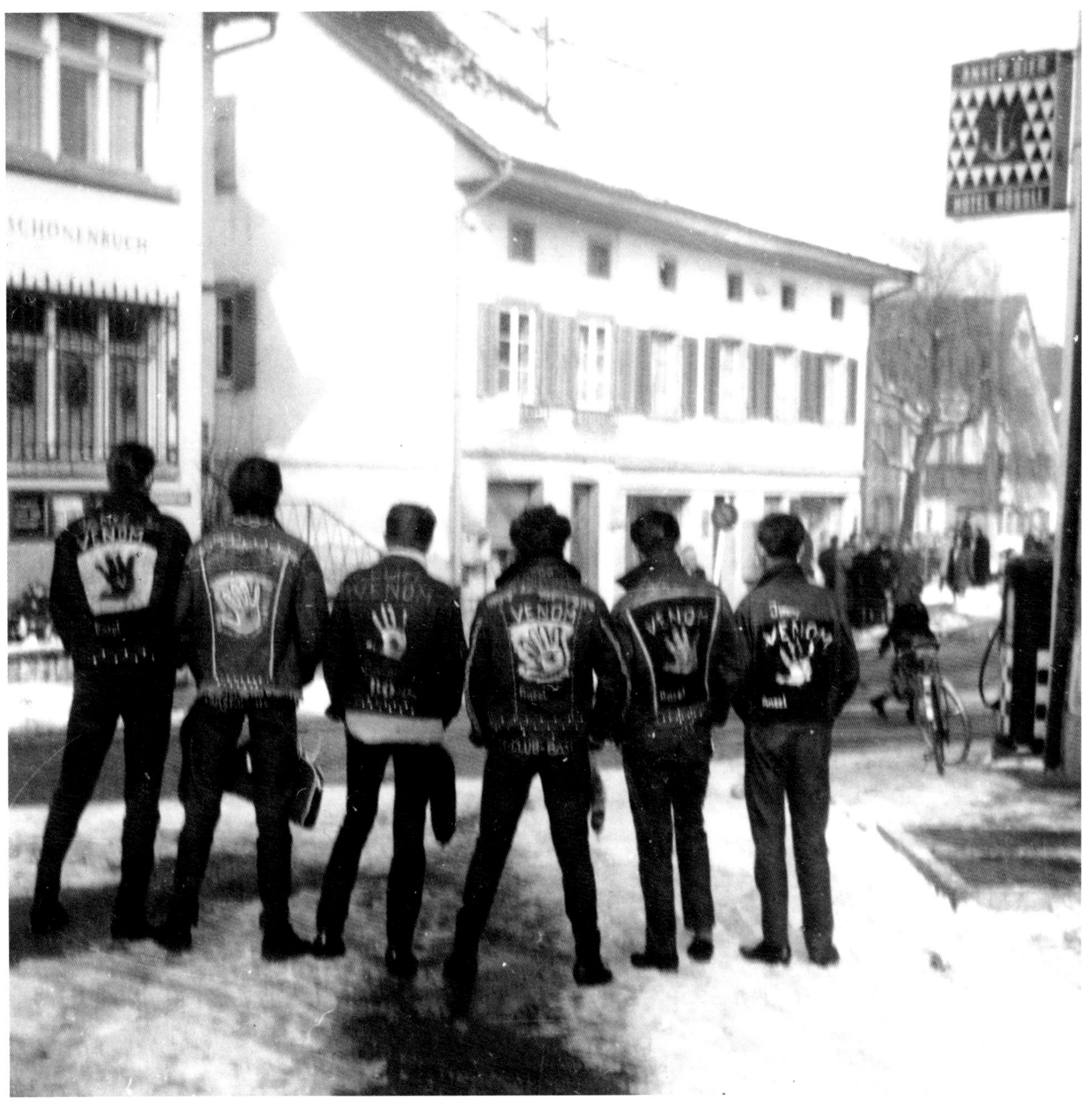

Venom in Allschwil near Basel in their gang jackets, which all bore a print of their boss Marcel "Jacky" Zimmerli's hand. Venom was the nucleus for a bigger and meaner gang to come: The Blizzards.

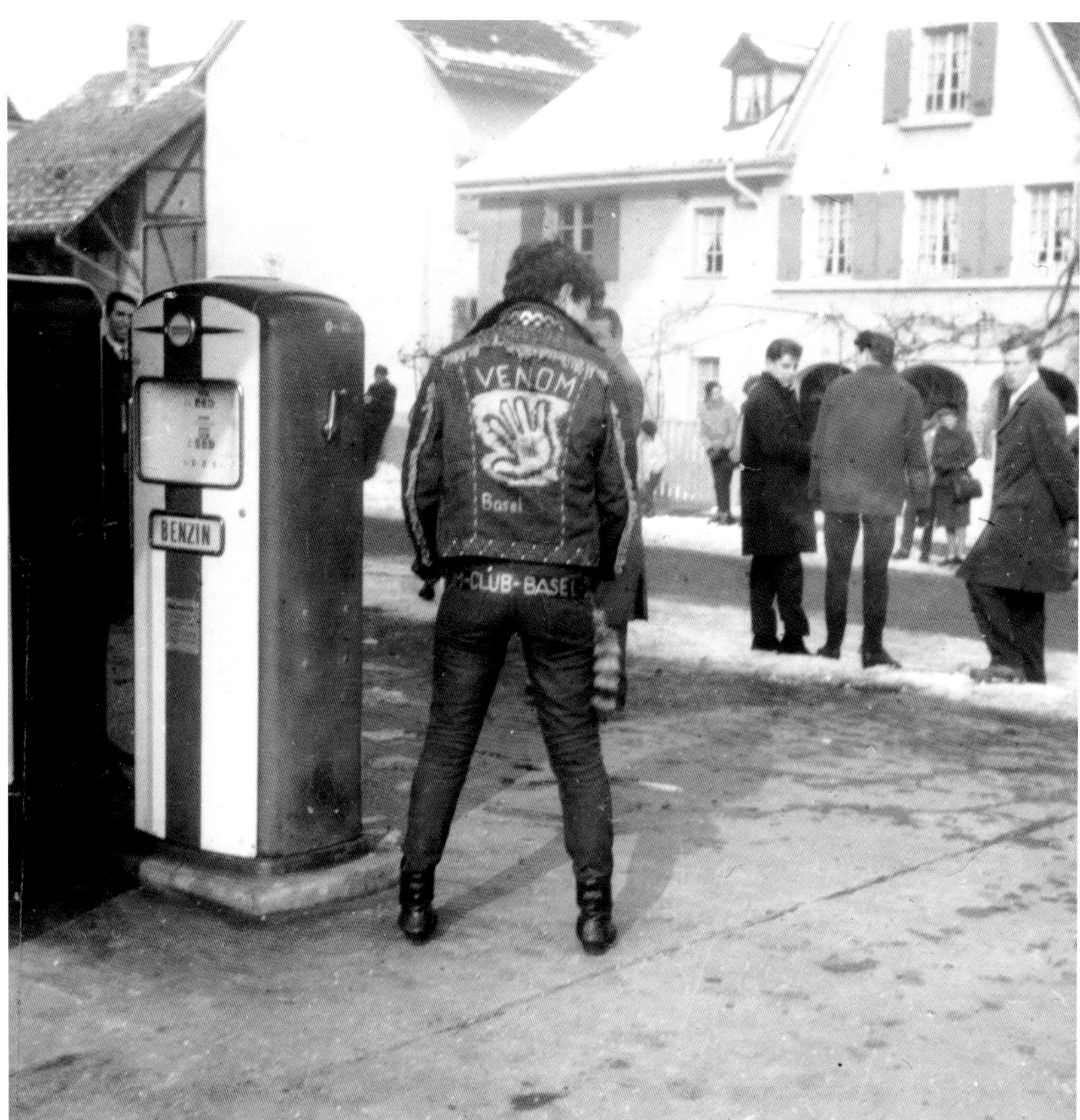

Venom boss Jacky in Allschwil.

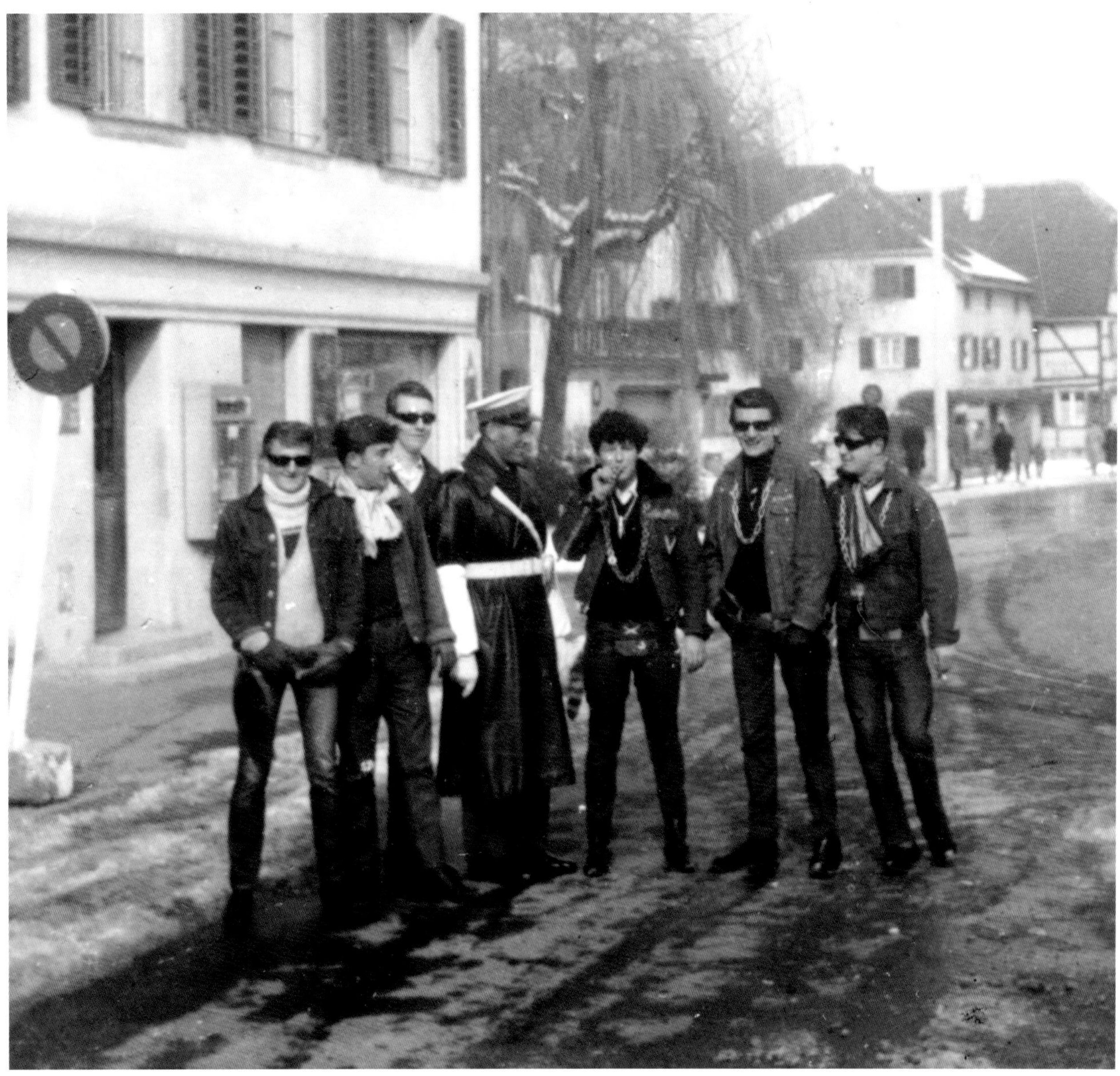

Venom: Mario and Trinker-Raymond in shades to left of cop and boss Jacky, Restaurant Roessli, Allschwil.

12/basler fasnacht (carnival in basel)
february 27, 1963

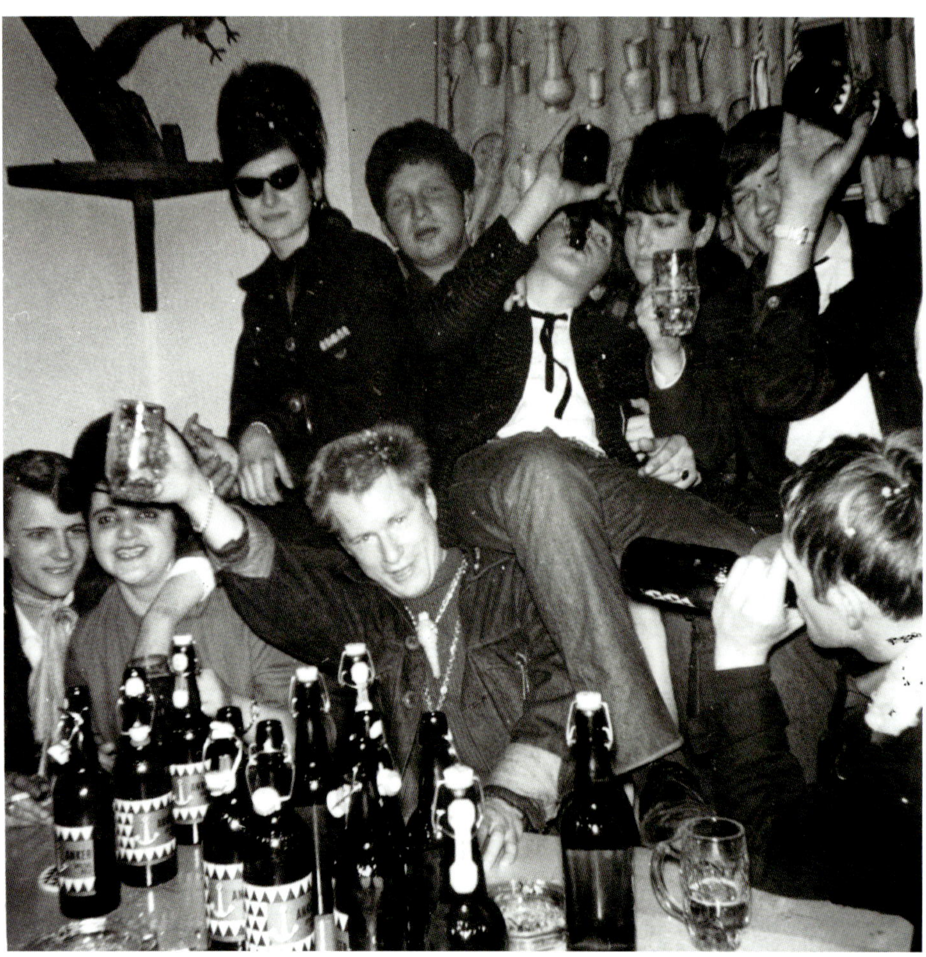

Restaurant Sonne, Basel: Igel and friends. Among others we have Vreni Sonderegger (second from left) and Asrid (Jenny) Bieri, with sunglasses.

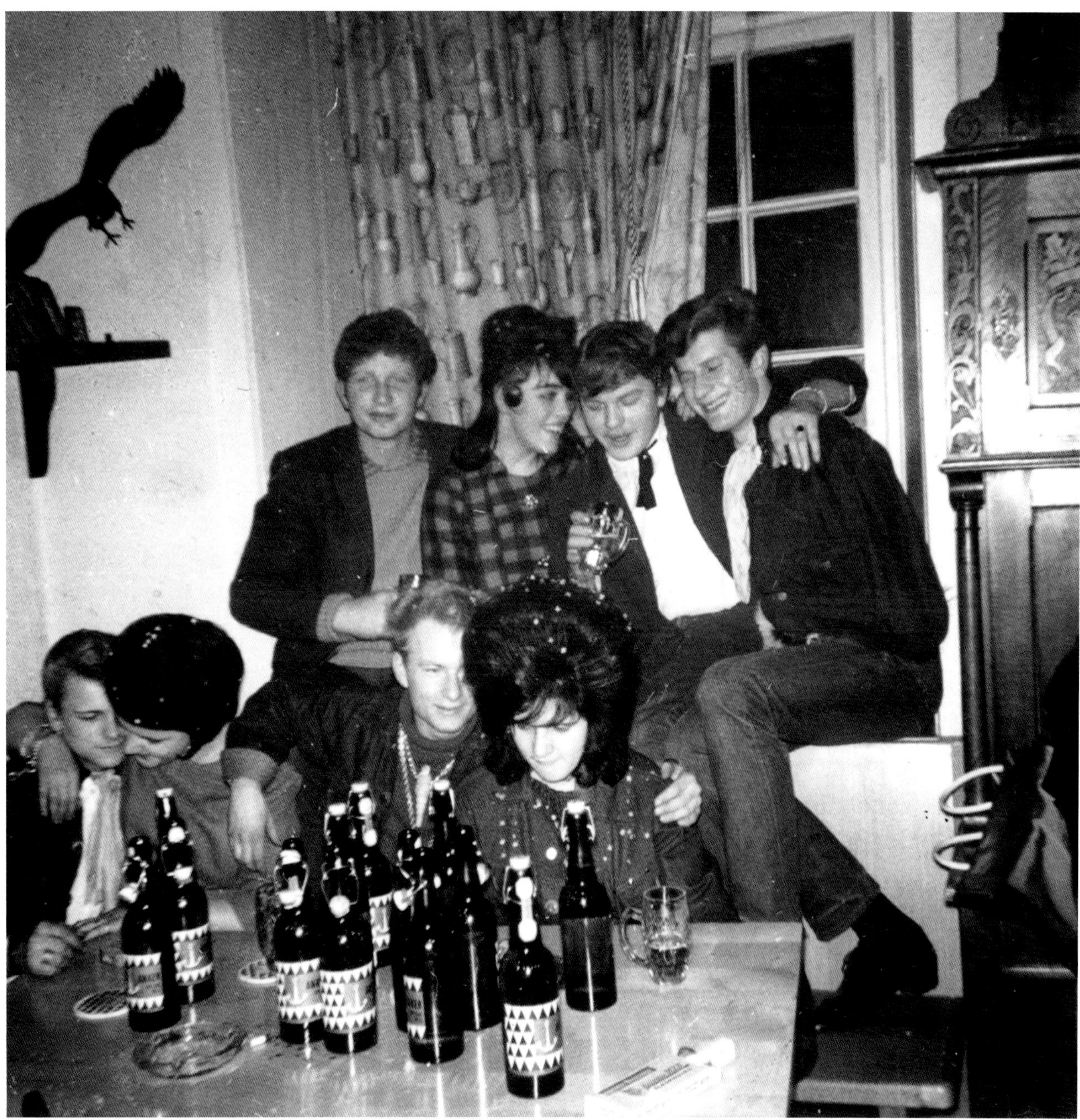

Igel hugs Priska (Rumy) Sonderegger.

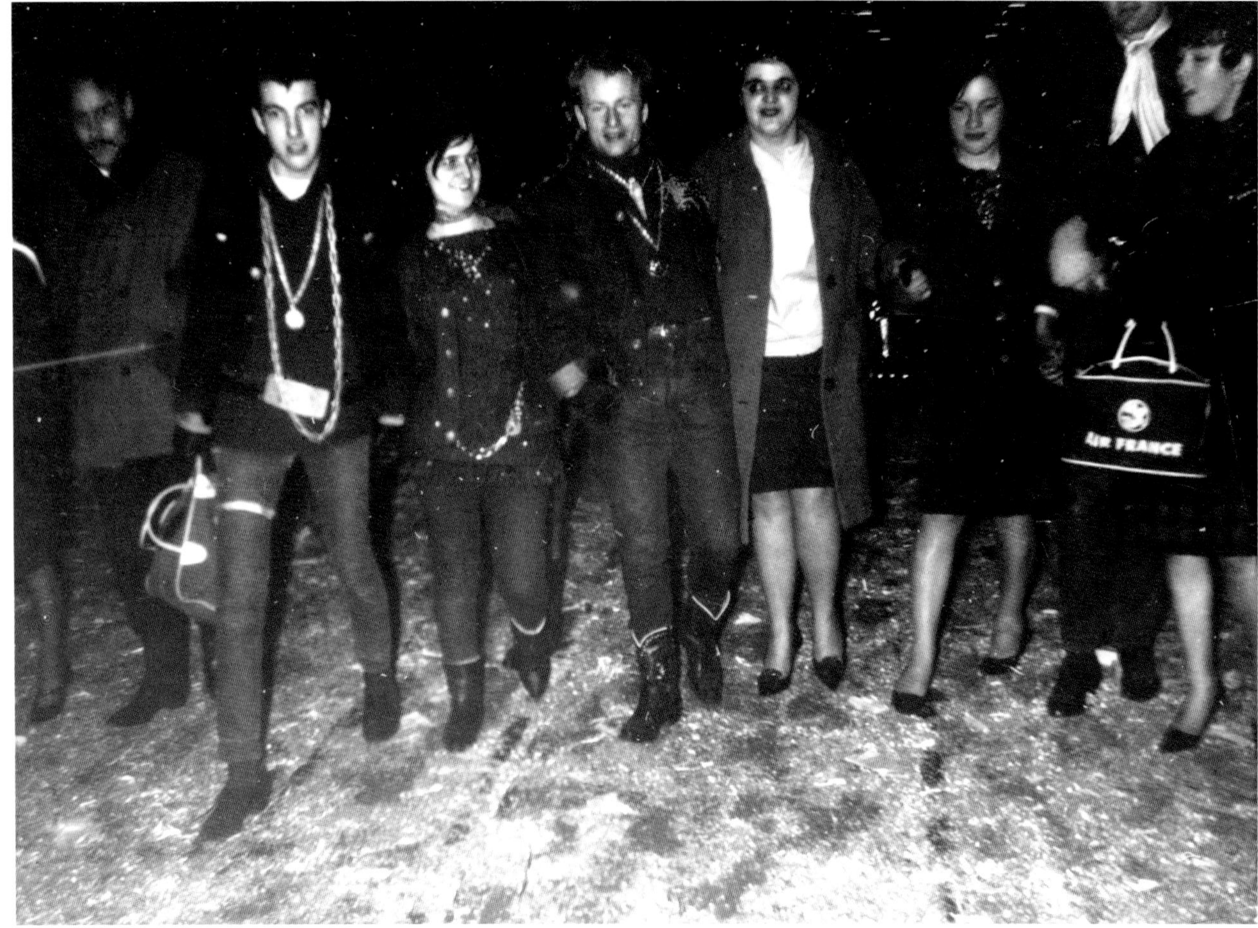

Basler Fasnacht (Basel Carnival) remains a big event today. Three Halbstarke (Red, Igel and Ted—with his white scarf) are joined by sisters Rumy and Vreni, and a couple of other high heel cuties. Airline bags were a popular accessory for Gang guys and girls.

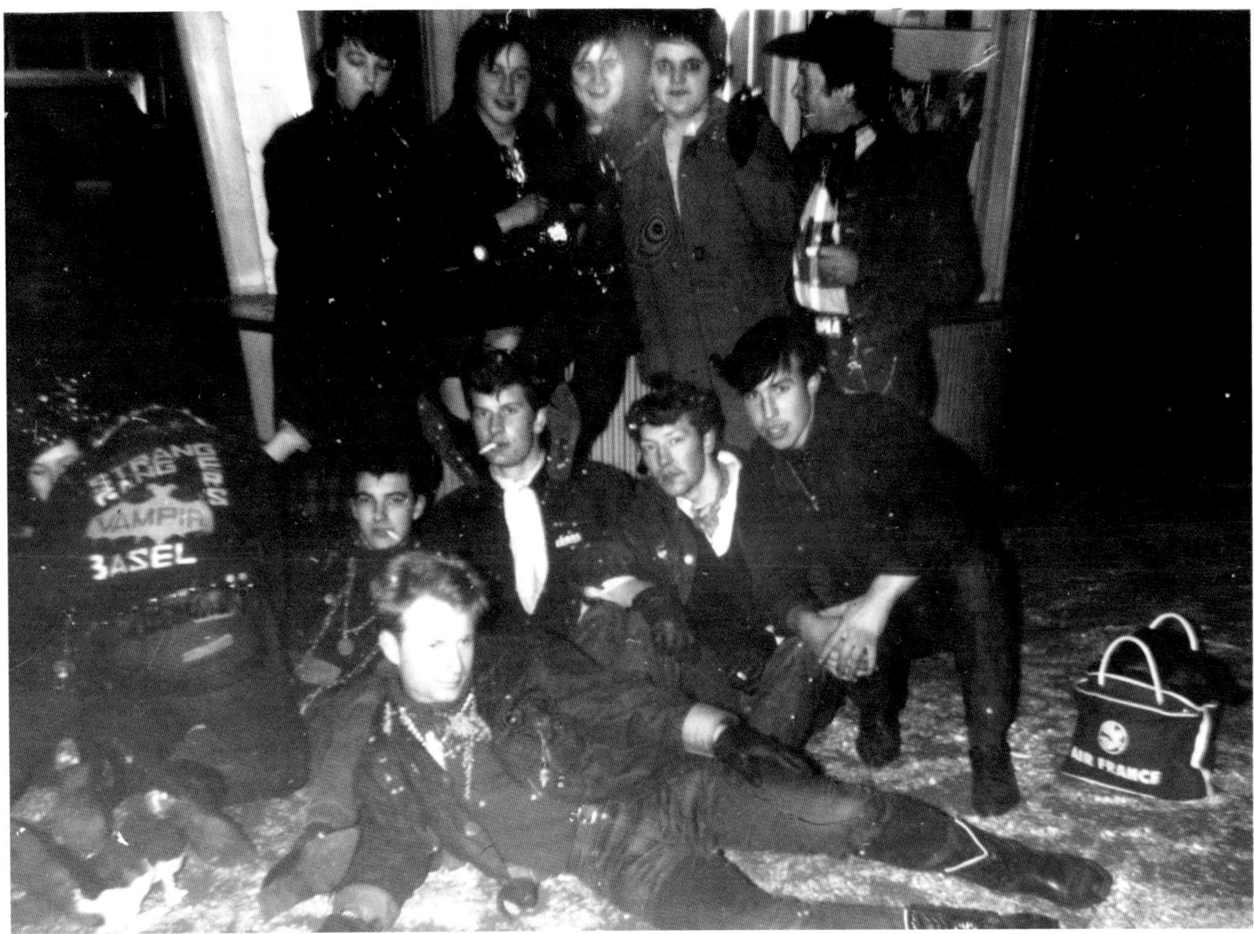

A historic shot taken during the Basler Fasnacht at Hautpost (main Post Office in Basel). Behind the pack, you see a small kiosk which was also part of a tramway stop.

13/café oasis, greifengasse 36, basel
march 1963

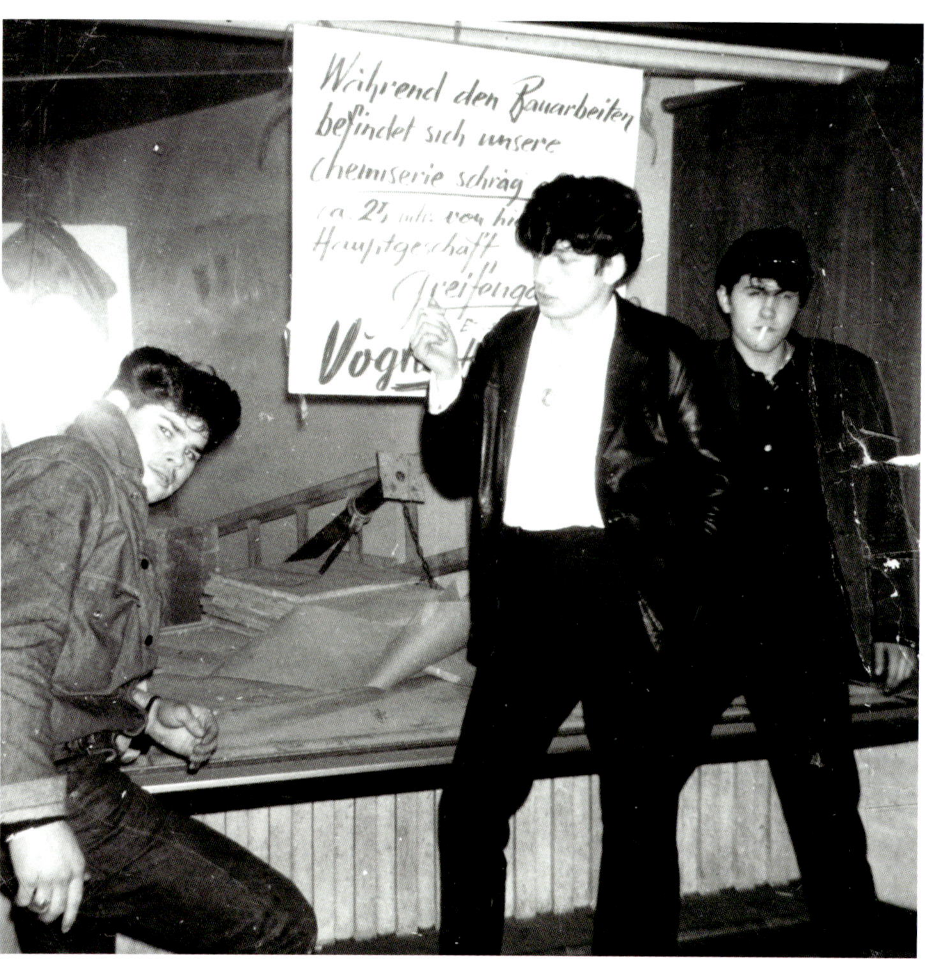

Mecky (Zack-Zack), with Arrigo (Johnny) Prestini, and Max (Jess) Gass at Cafe Oasis.

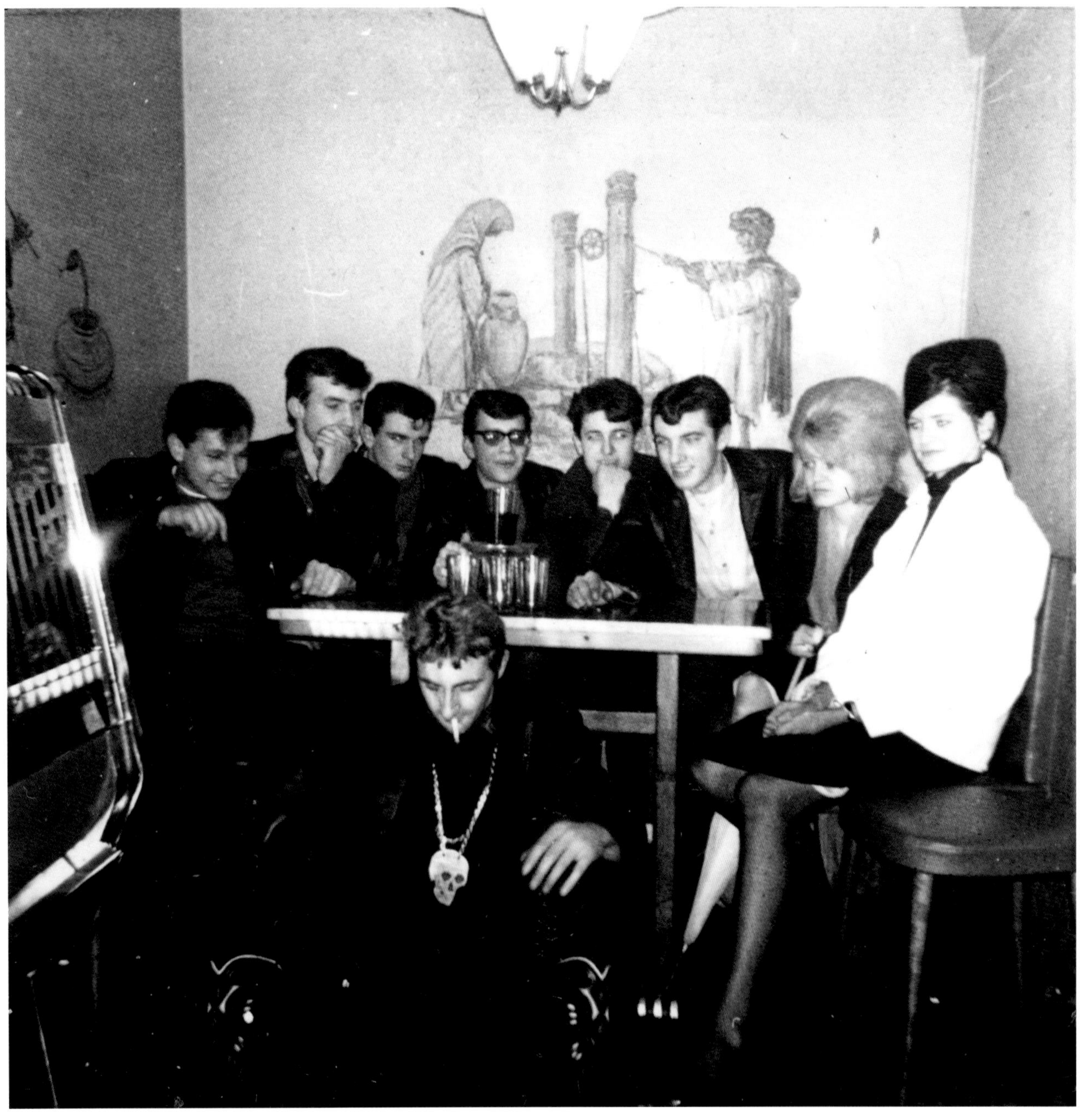

Cafe Oasis: Raymond Christen (front) with Werner (Cliff) Kesselring and friends. At right, unknown blonde with Red and Astrid (Jenny Bieri).

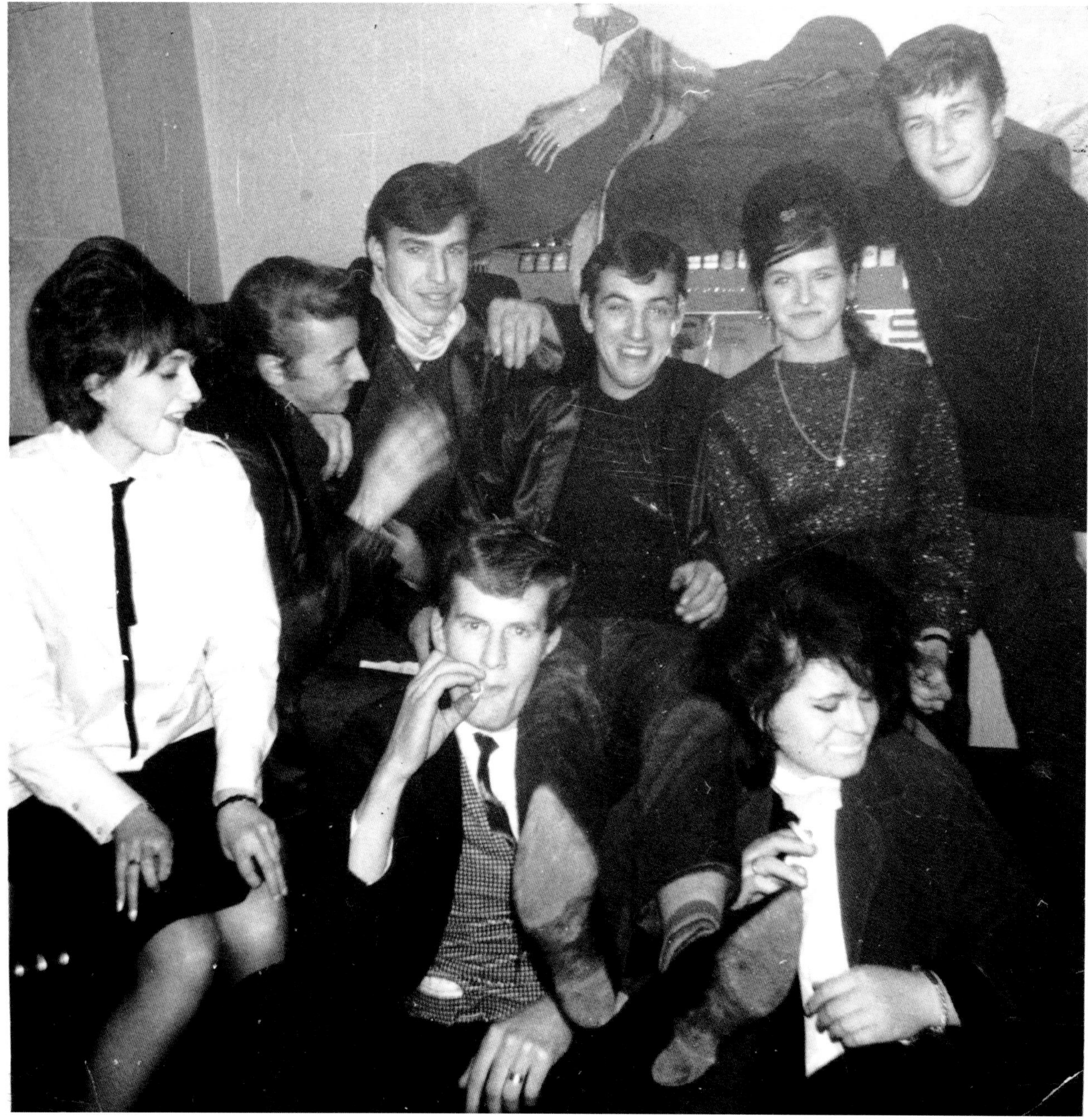

Cafe Oasis: Guys and dolls—Ted (front), Raymond, Cliff, Red, Astrid and friends.

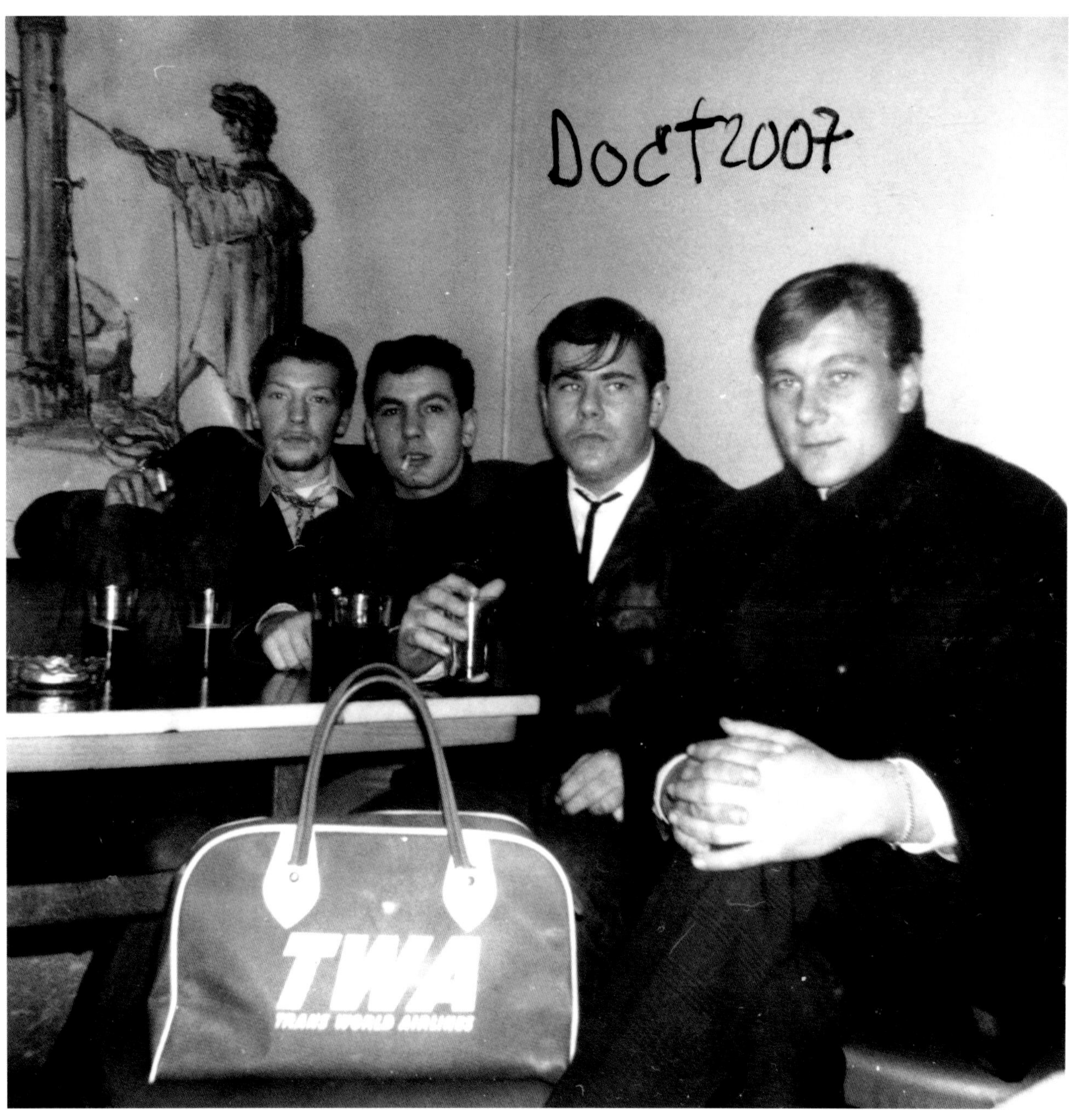

Cafe Oasis: Doc and Fritz Breitenstein, at right with friends. Fritz's brother Hans (Sumo) Breitenstein was the boss of The Lions.

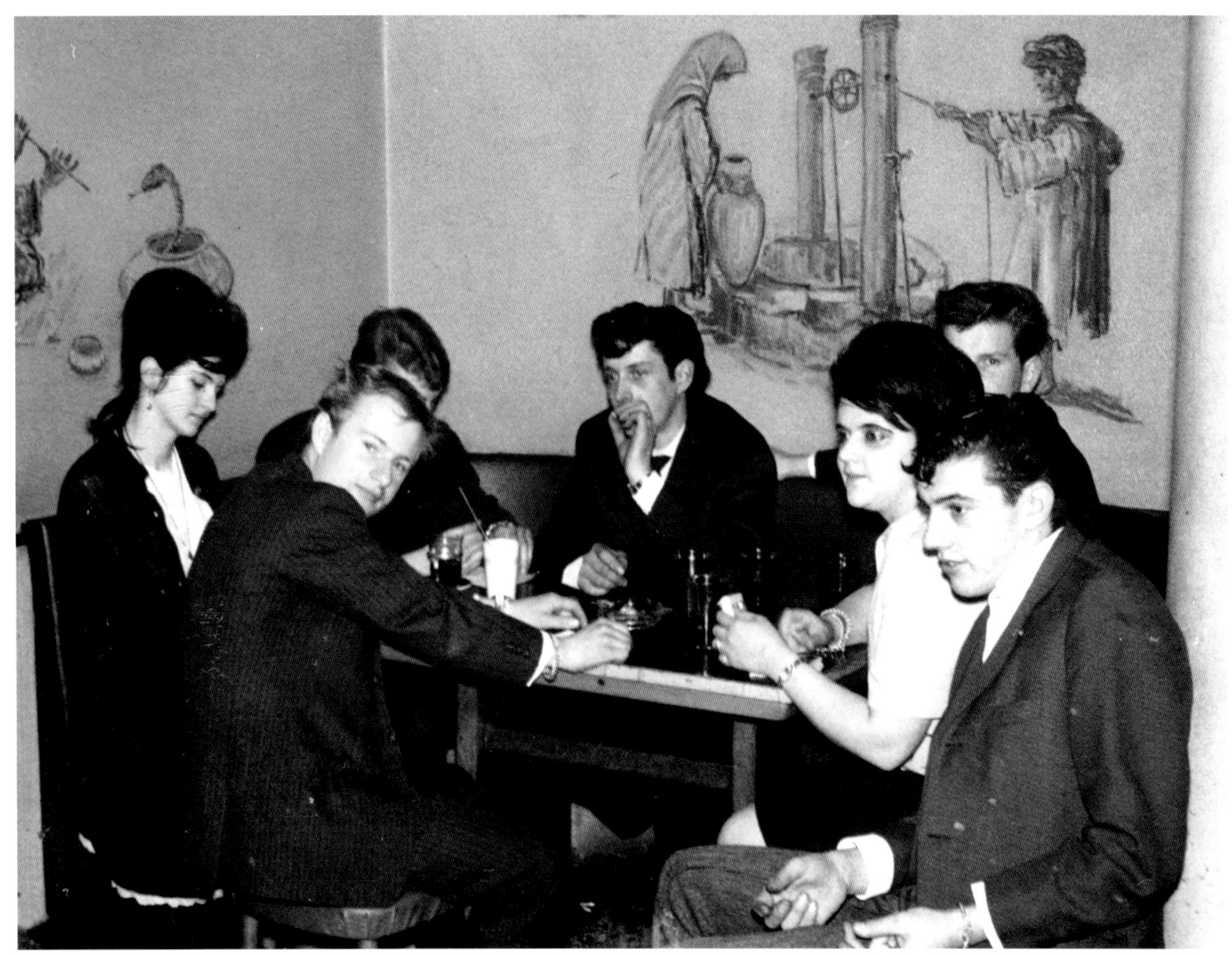

Jenny, Raymond, Igel, Ronny, Vreni, Ted (behind), and Red.

14/aarau
april 14–15, 1963

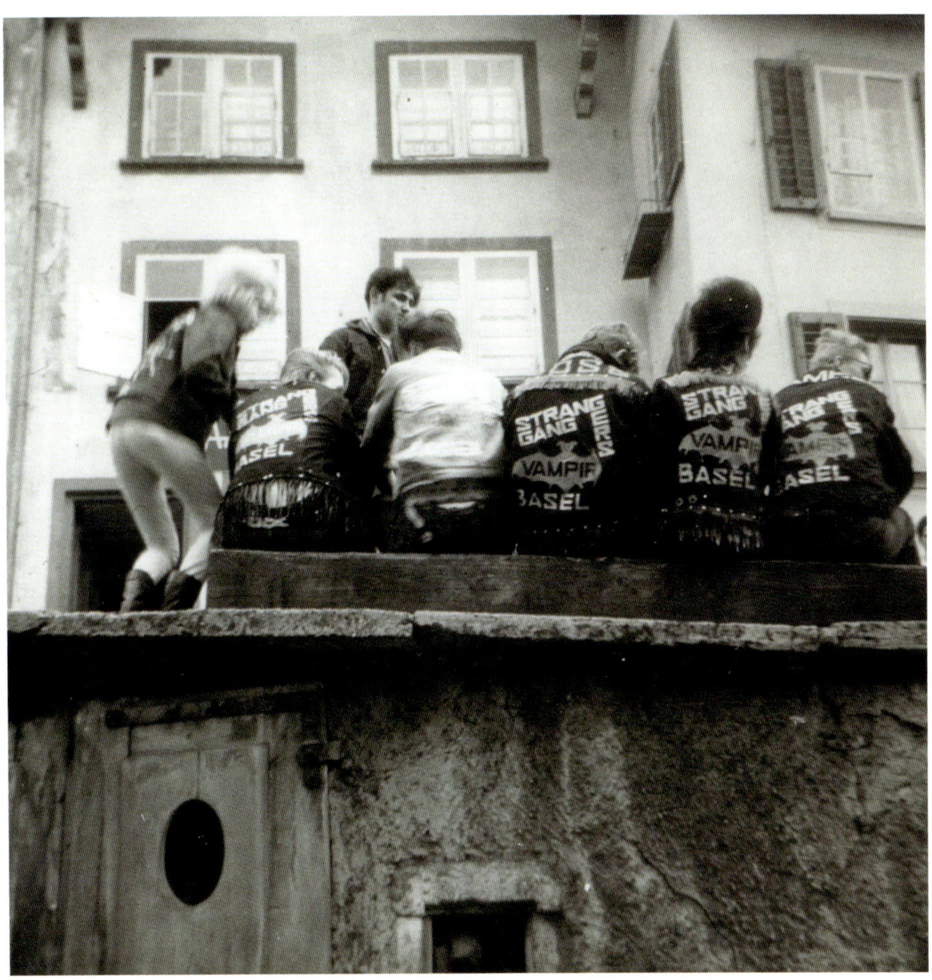

Gang bangers heading for Luna Park.

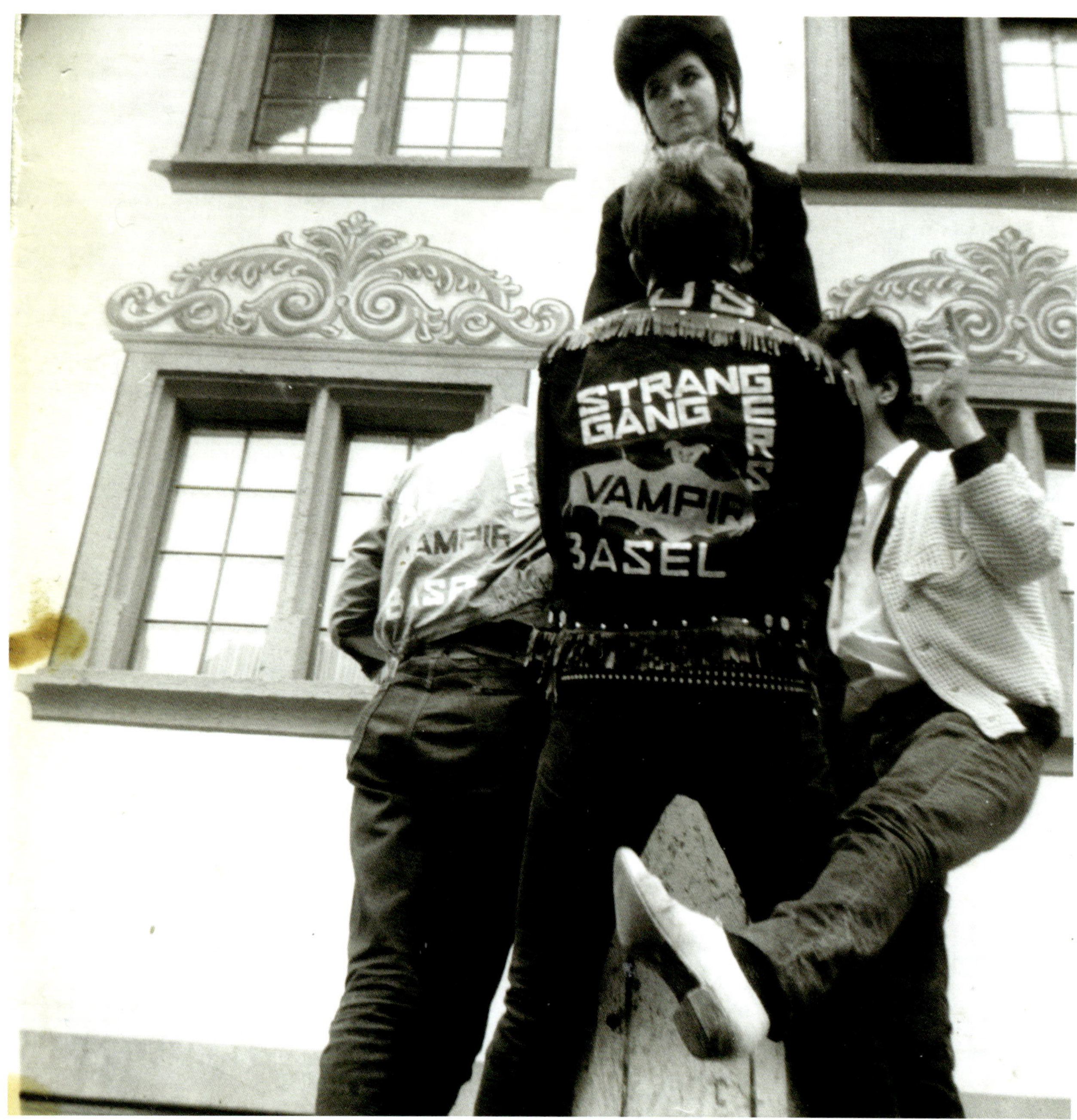

Rabble rousers.

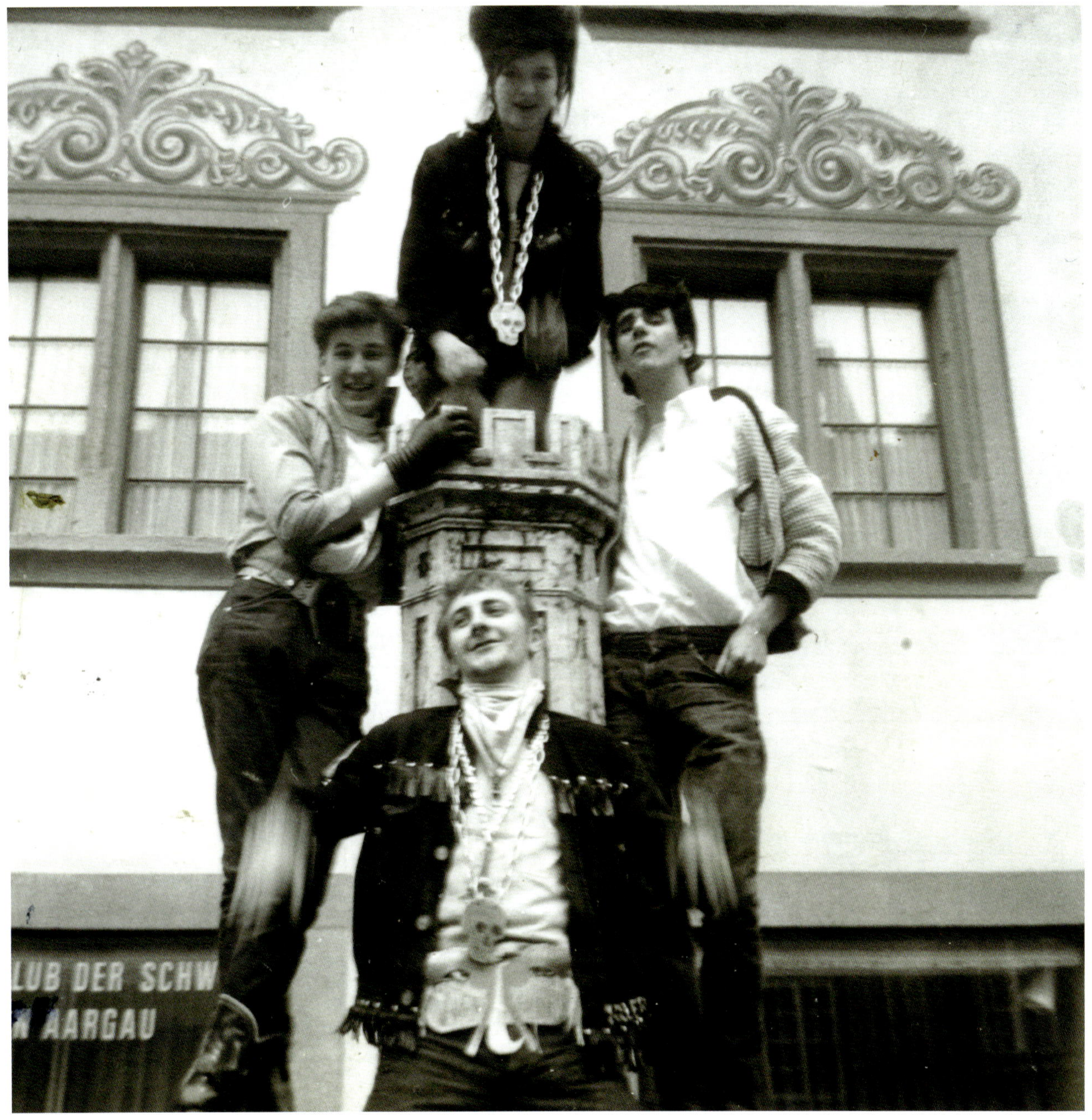

Jenny (top) and Raymond (bottom) with Polish guy who escaped the Holocaust as a child.

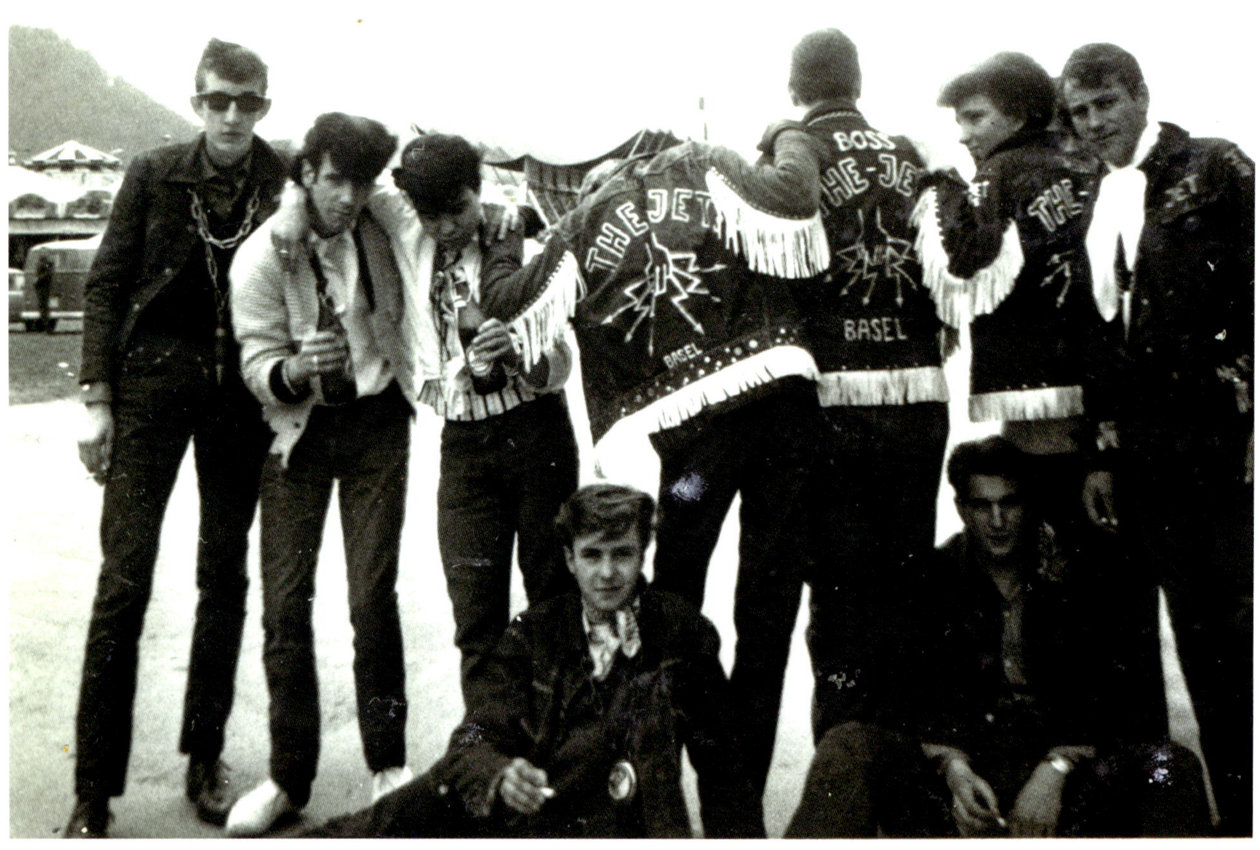

The Jets.

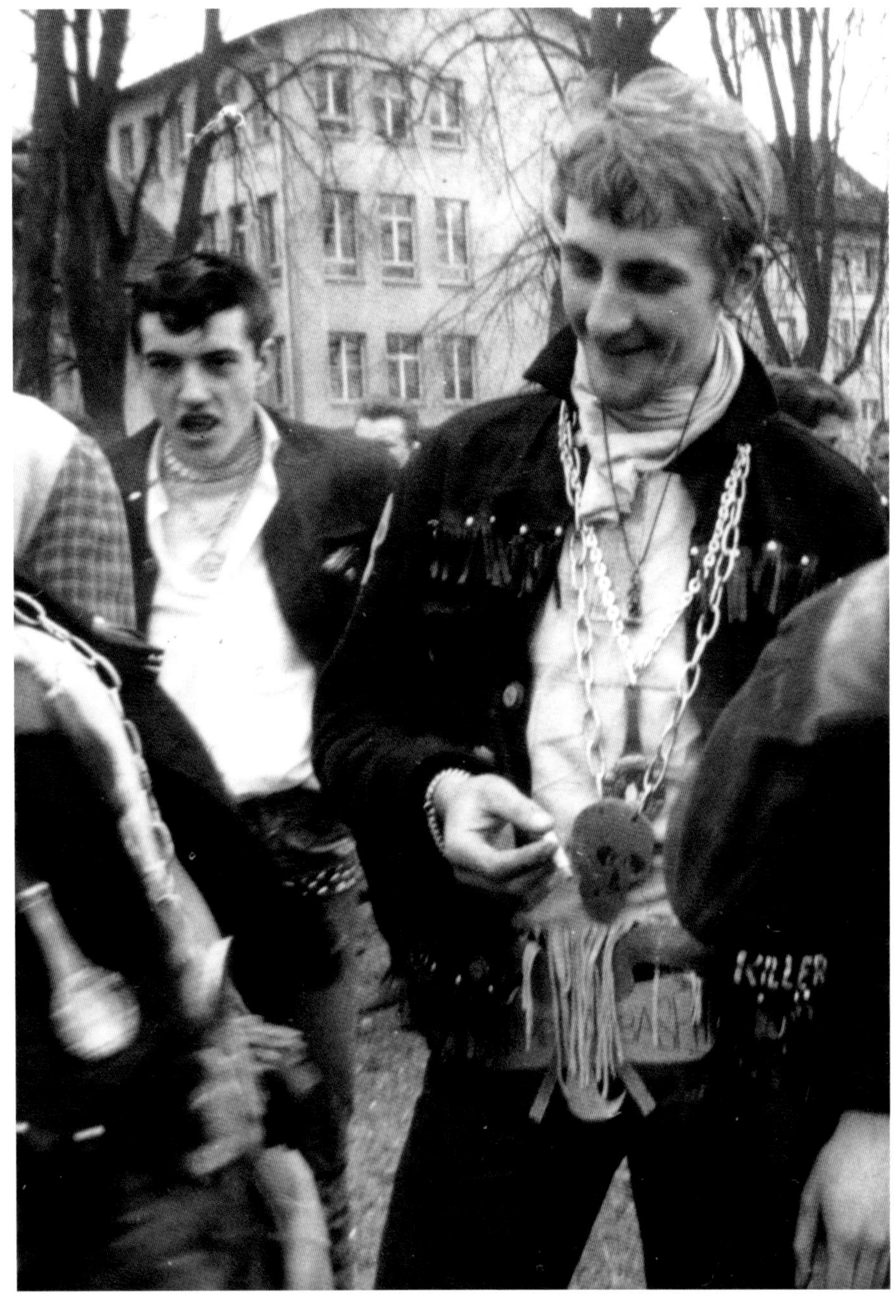

Raymond “Killer” Christen with the Totenkopf skull around his neck.

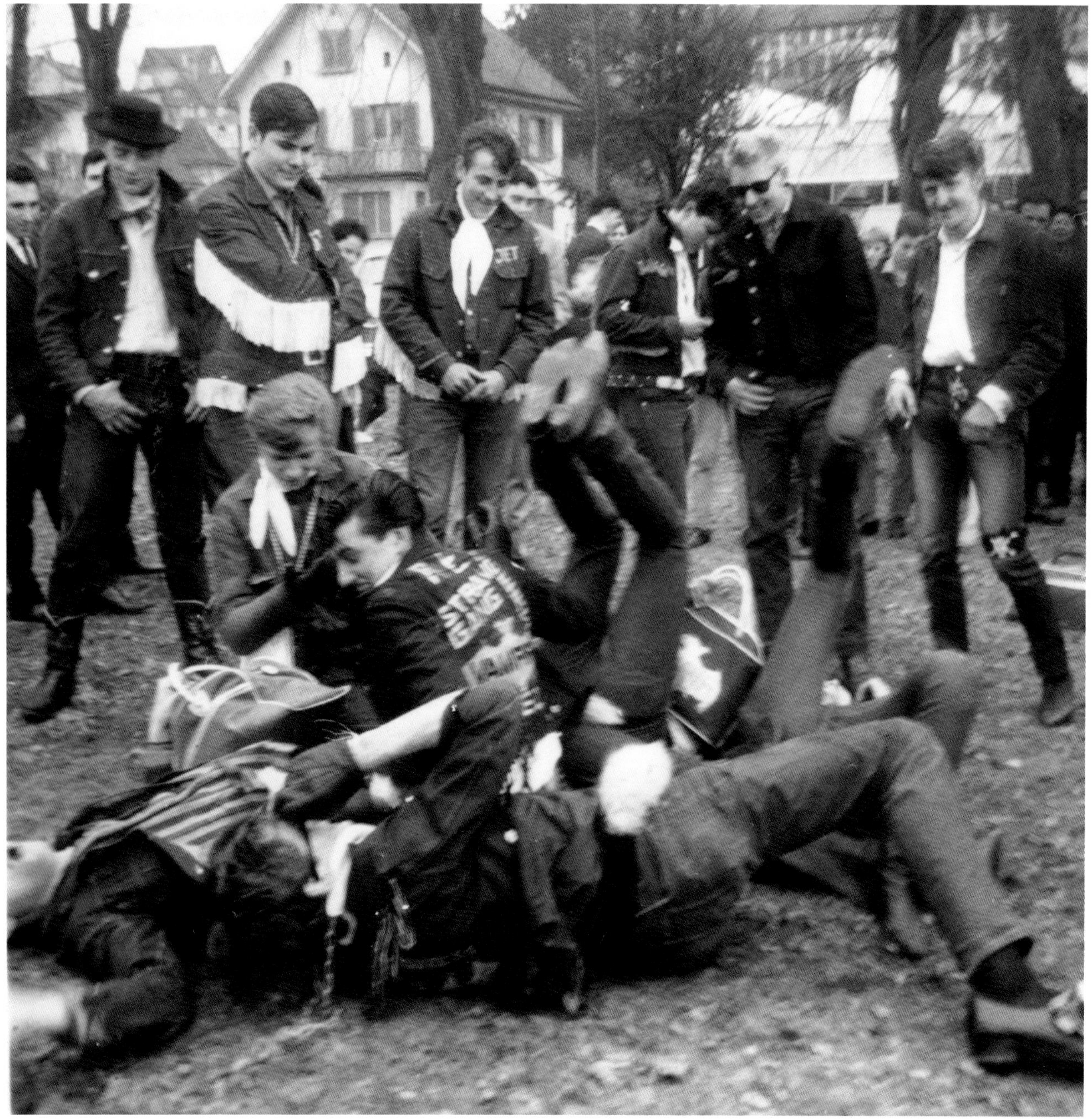

Tello and Red liked to brawl.

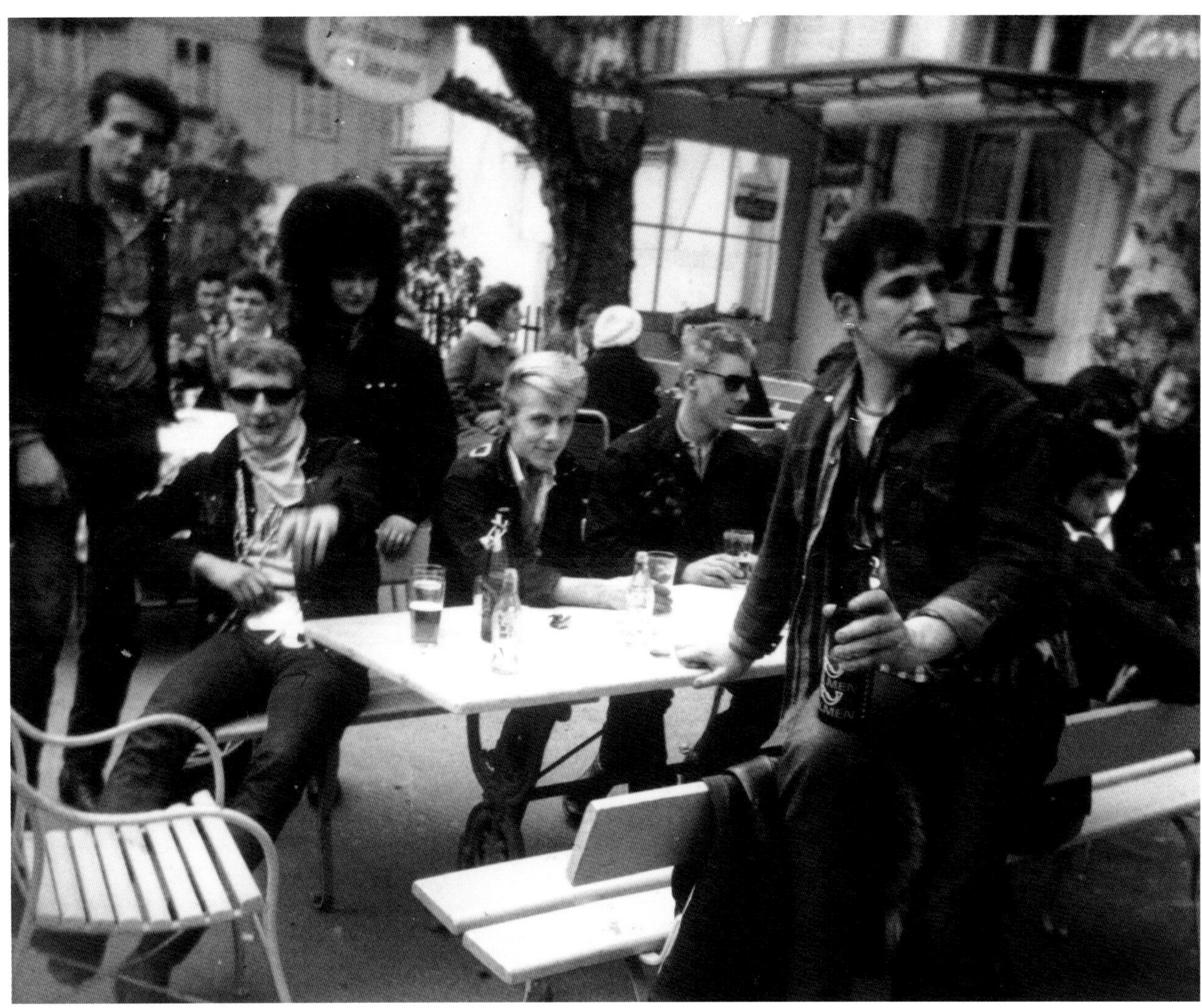

At Schachen in Aarau with cool shades Raymond (sitting), big hair Priska (standing), Kid, James and Tello.

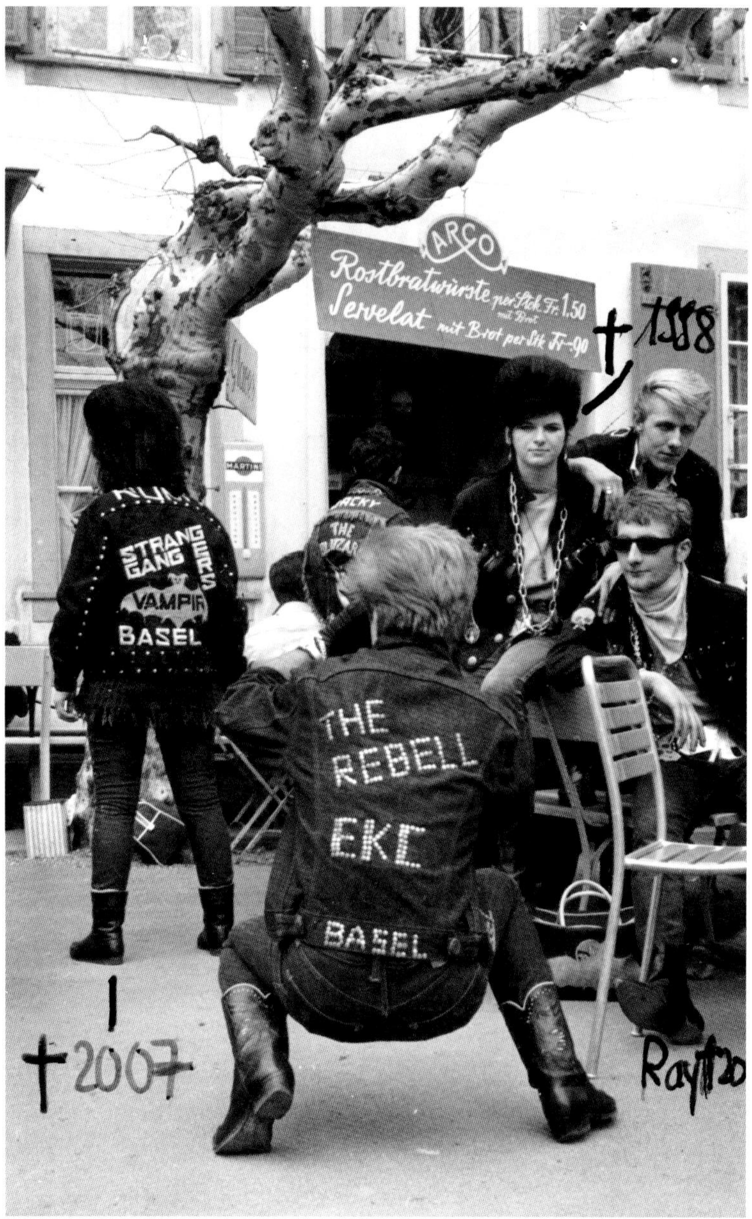

Schachen Amusement Park in Aarau (L-R): Priska "Rumy" Sonderegger, Dieter "Igel" Ehrlich (also known as "The Rebell", still wearing his Express Killer Club, Basel jacket), Blizzard boss Marcel "Jacky" Zimmerli (from behind), Astrid "Jenny" Bieri, Arnoldo "Kid" Steiner, and Raymond "Killer" Christen (sitting in the chair).

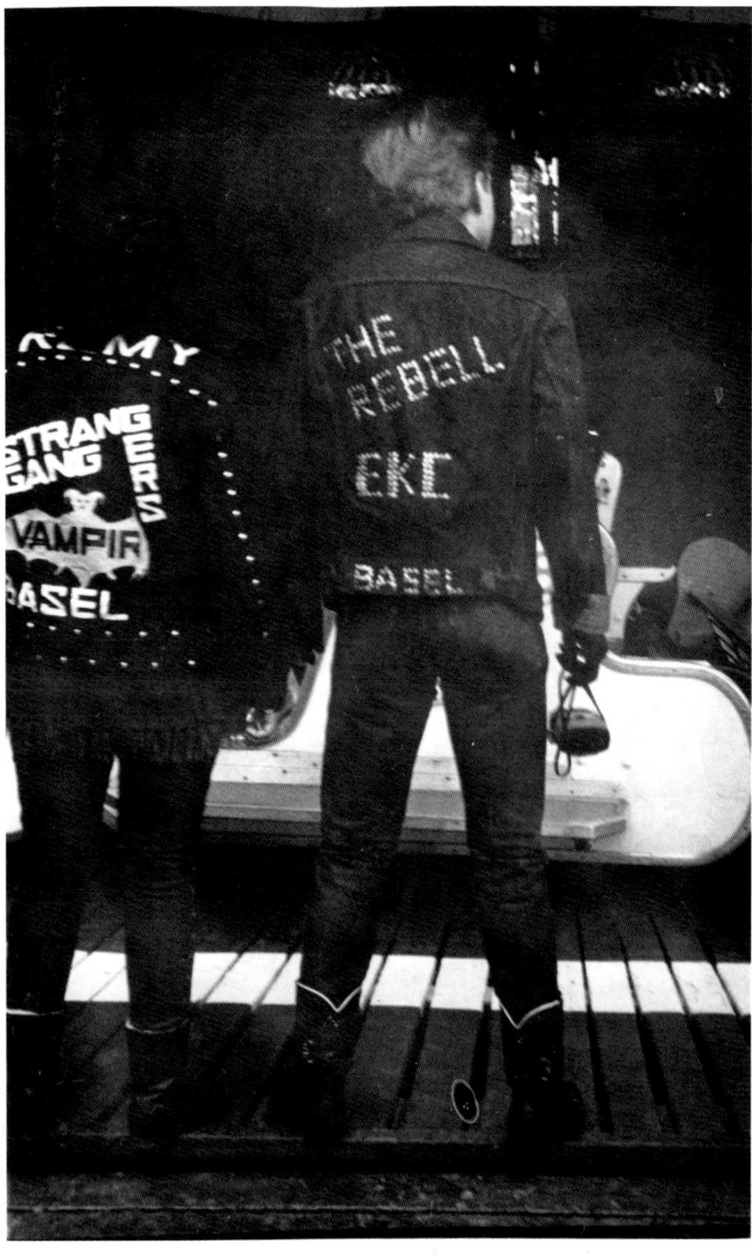

Rumy and Igel (The Rebell EKC—Express Killers Club Basel) are looking to ride the Himalaya at the fairgrounds. Igel has his pocket camera in his right hand. With this camera he made nearly all the photos which are in this book.

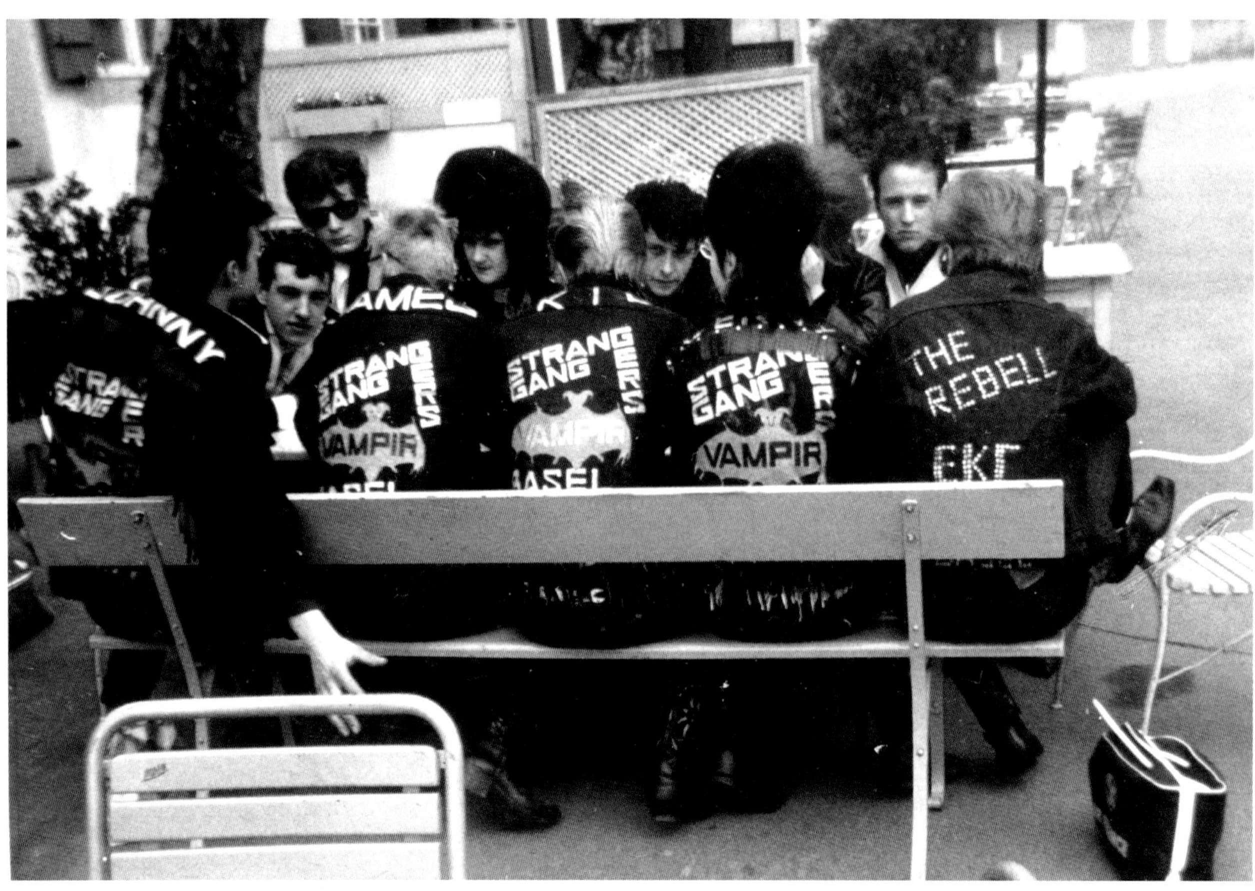

Gang meeting.

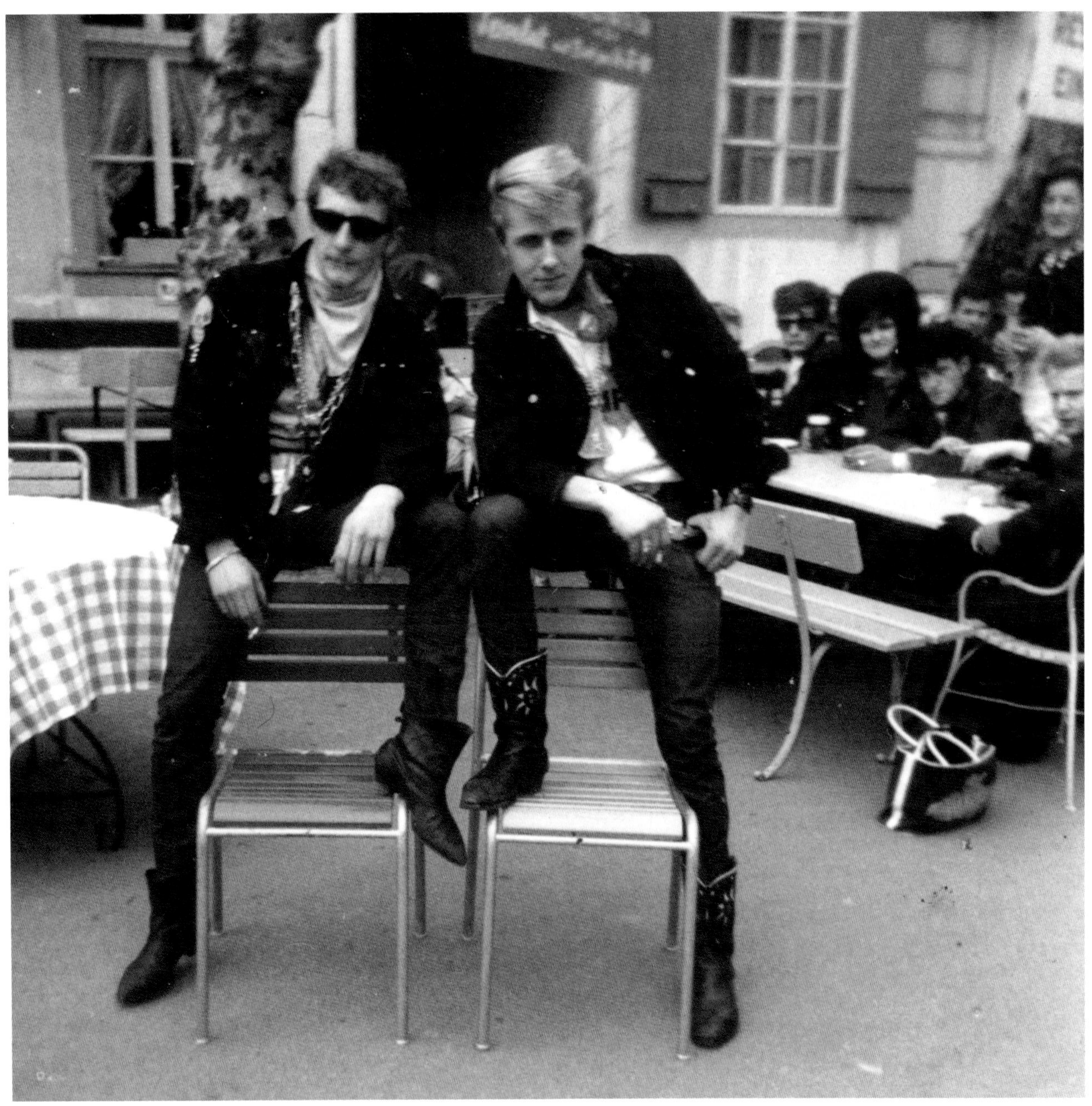

Vampir boss Raymond "Killer" Christen with vice-boss Arnoldo "Kid" Steiner. Kid would later move to England for a couple of years, returning to publish 20 issues of the Swiss punk fanzine *Pin-Up*, starting in 1978. He is still an active club DJ today.

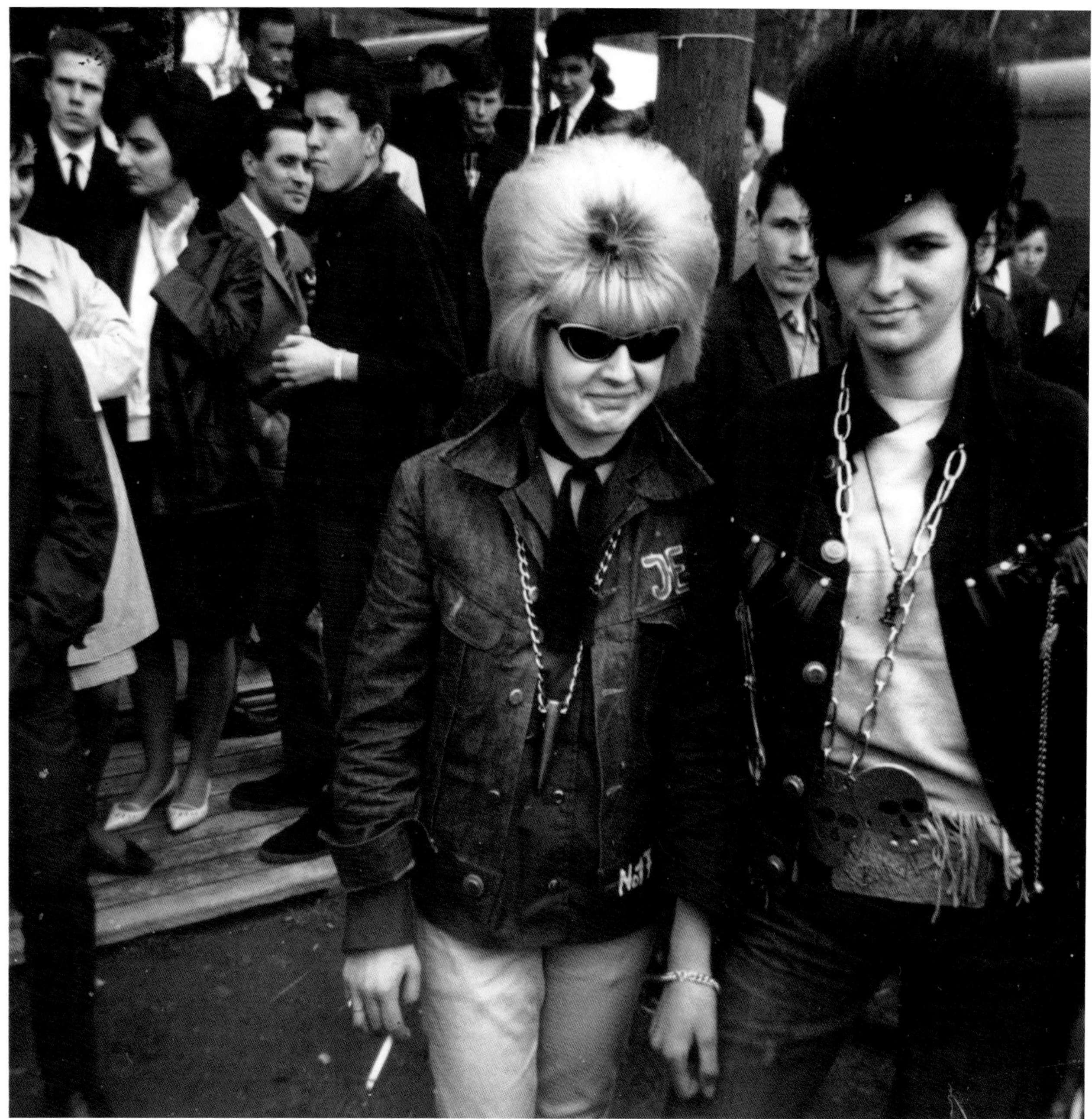

Blonde and Black: Vreni with Jenny.

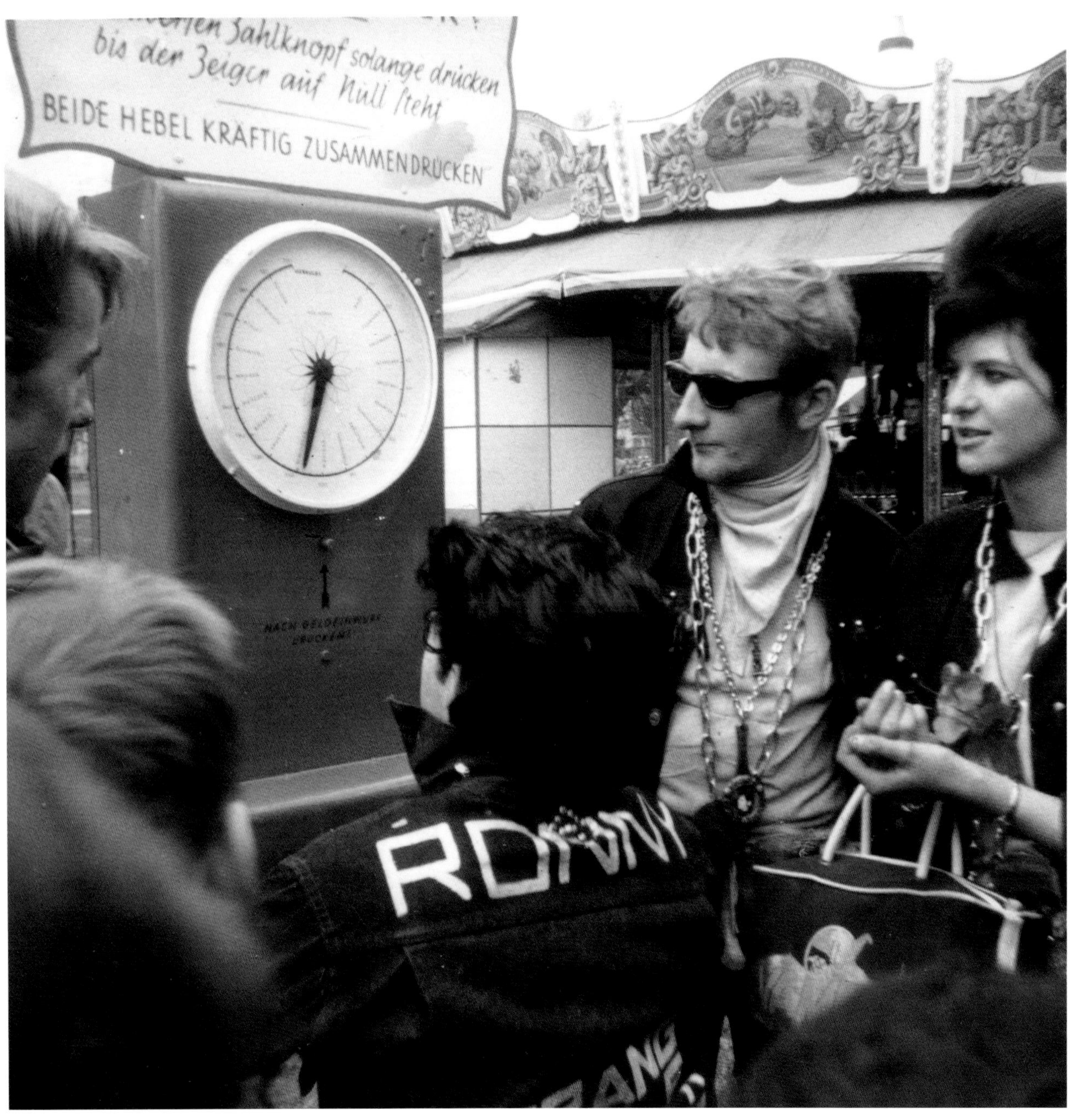

Ronny at the fair with Raymond and Jenny.

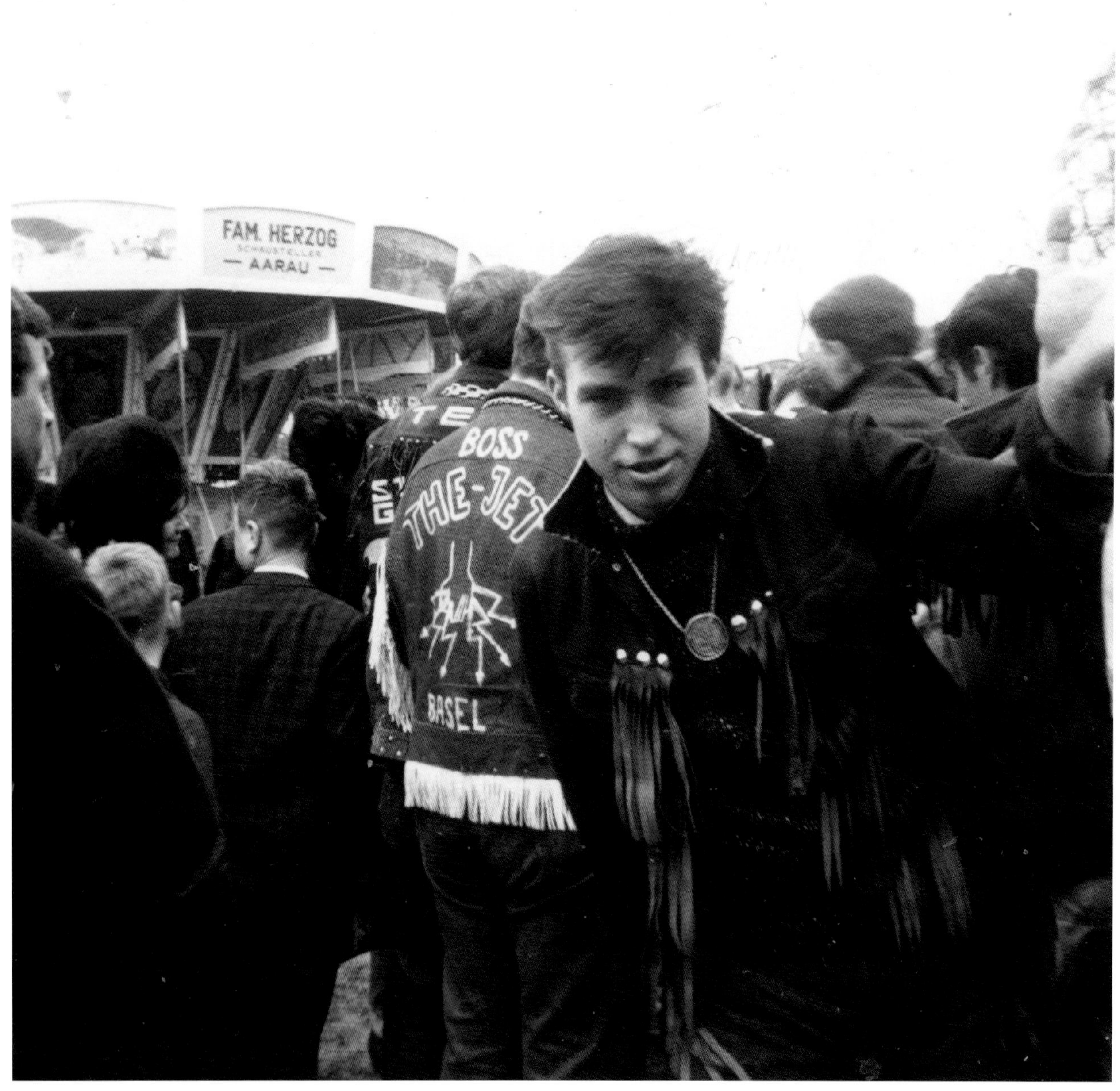

"Cliff" Kesselring shows off his wild west get up, Aarau.

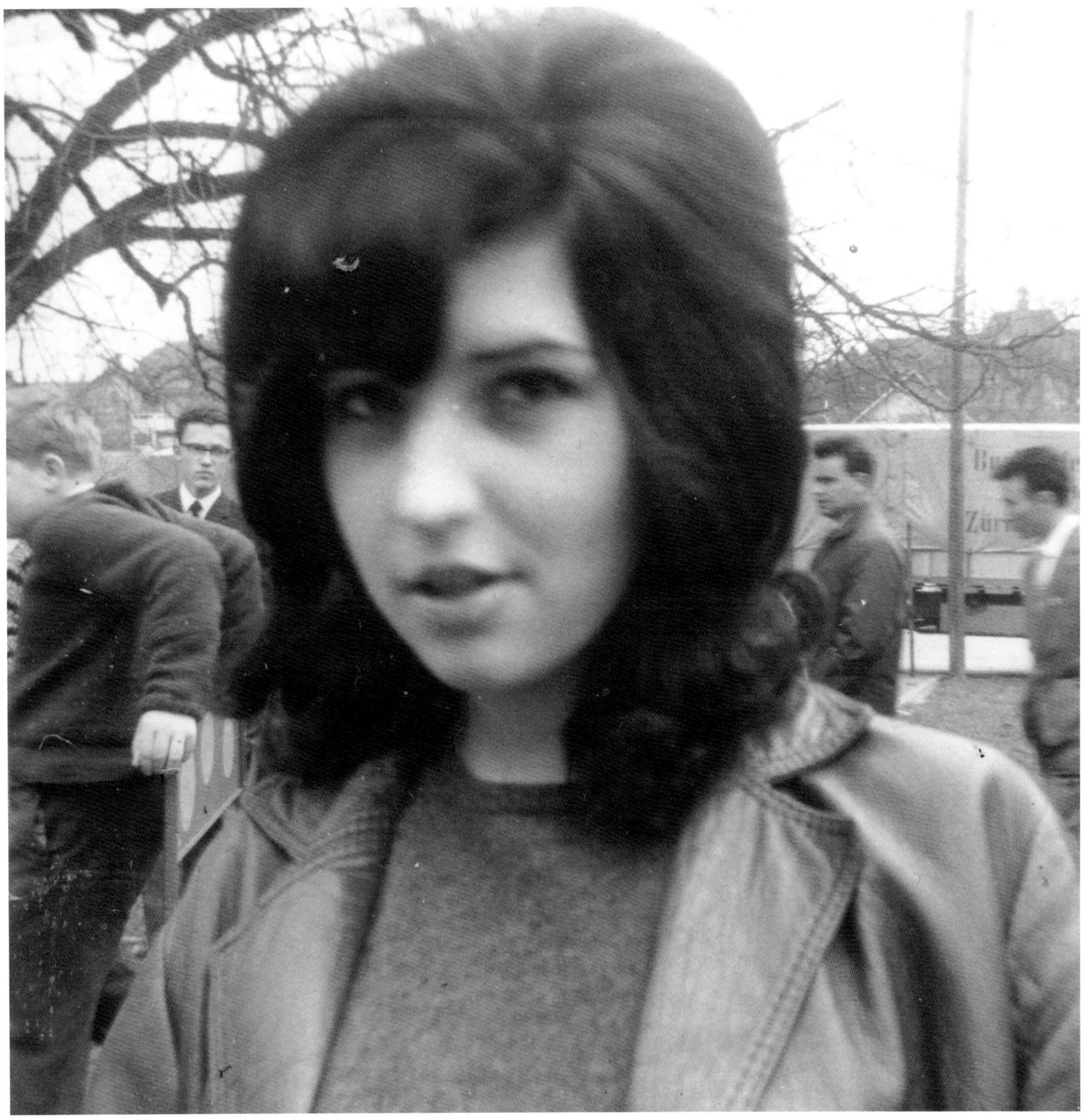

Dorli, the Halbstarke girl who was later engaged to Arrigo "Johnny" Prestini.

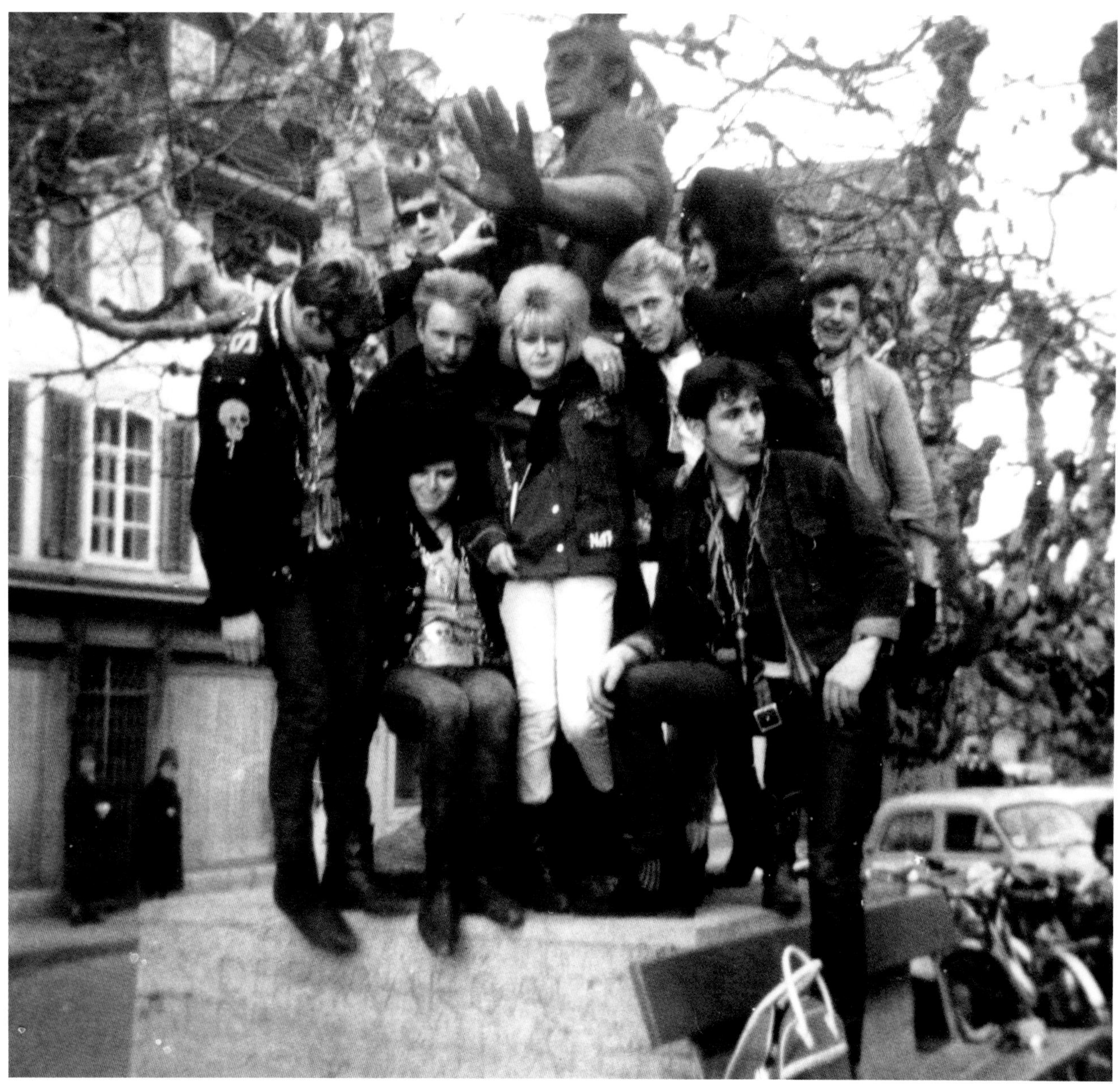

Family photo.

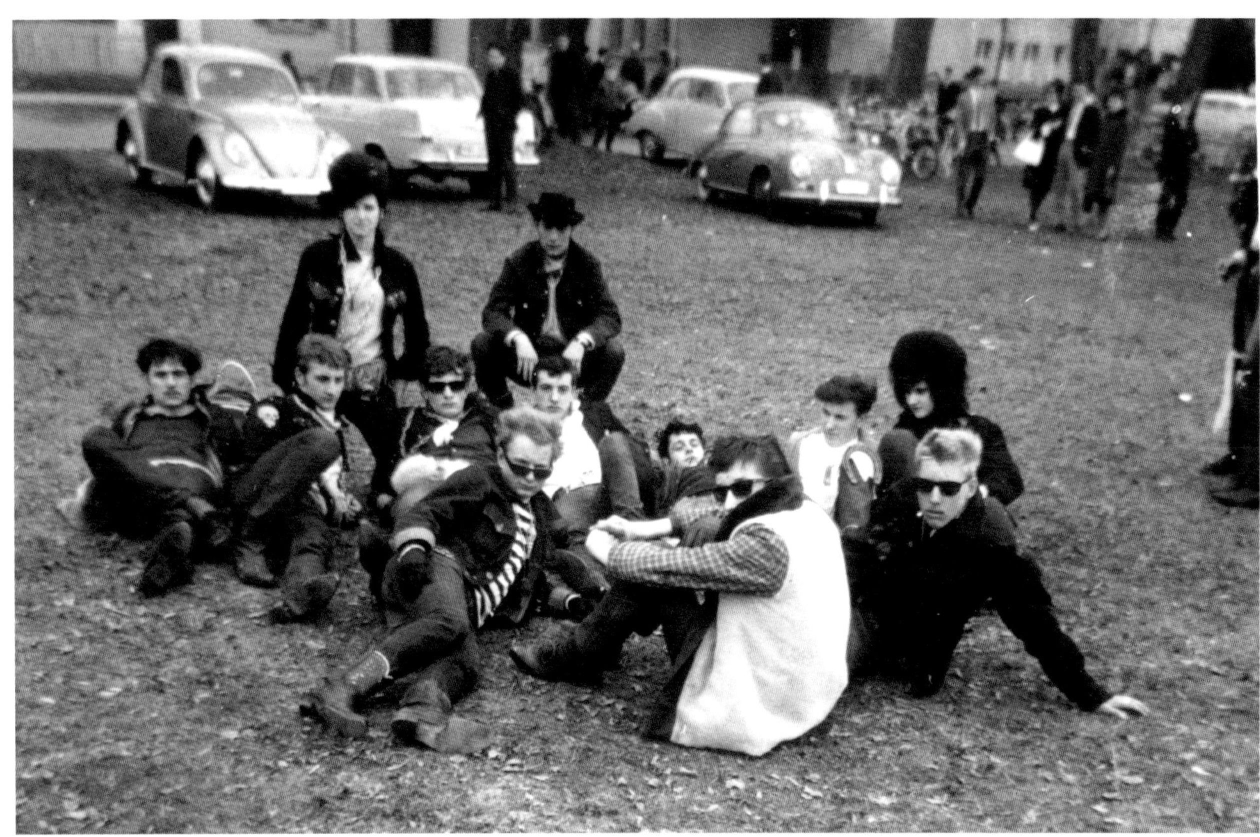

Break time.

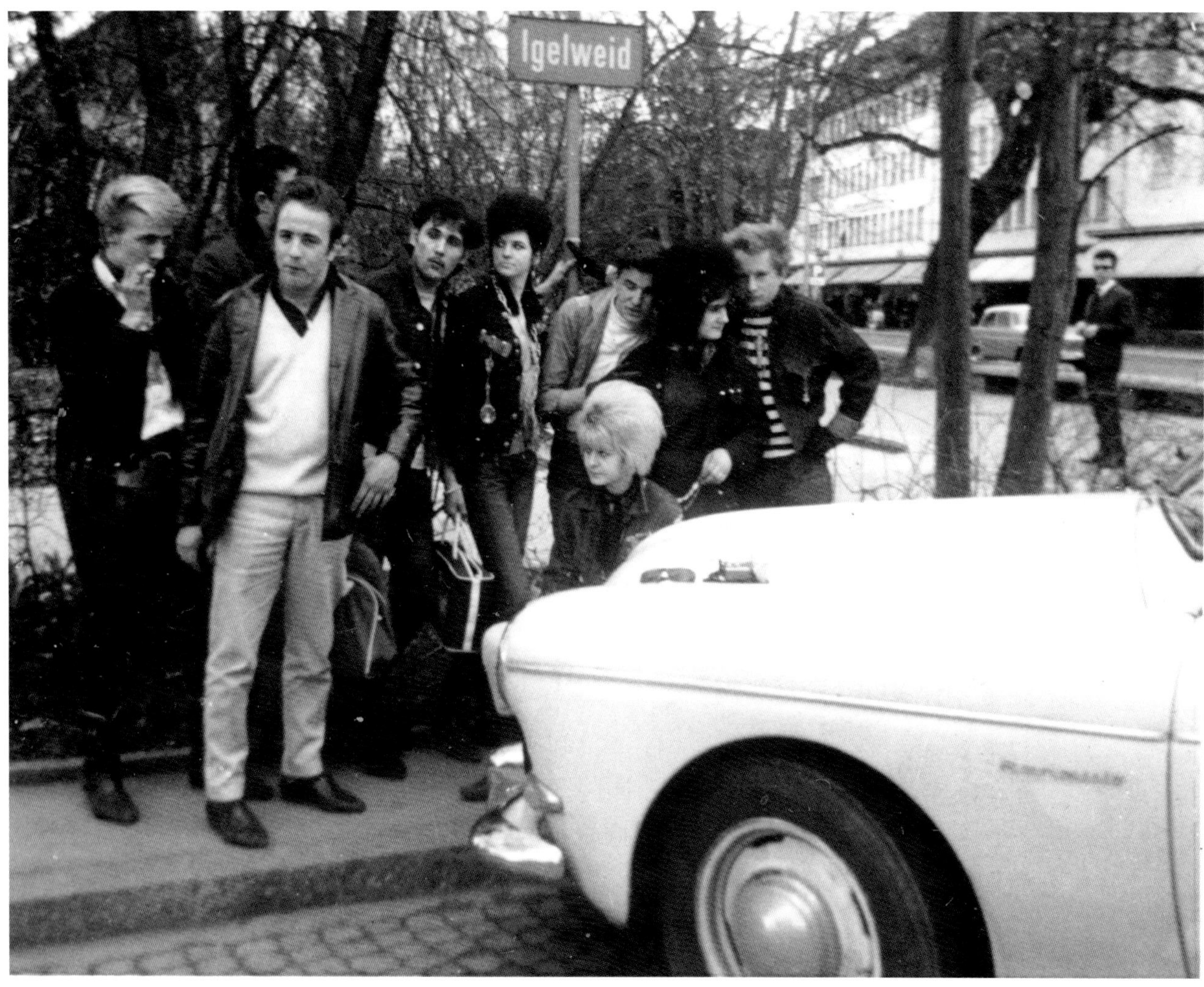

From left: Kid, Robert Molls aka Stadt-Elvis, Tello, Jenny, Vreni, Priska and Igel. There used to be four guys named Elvis in the group.

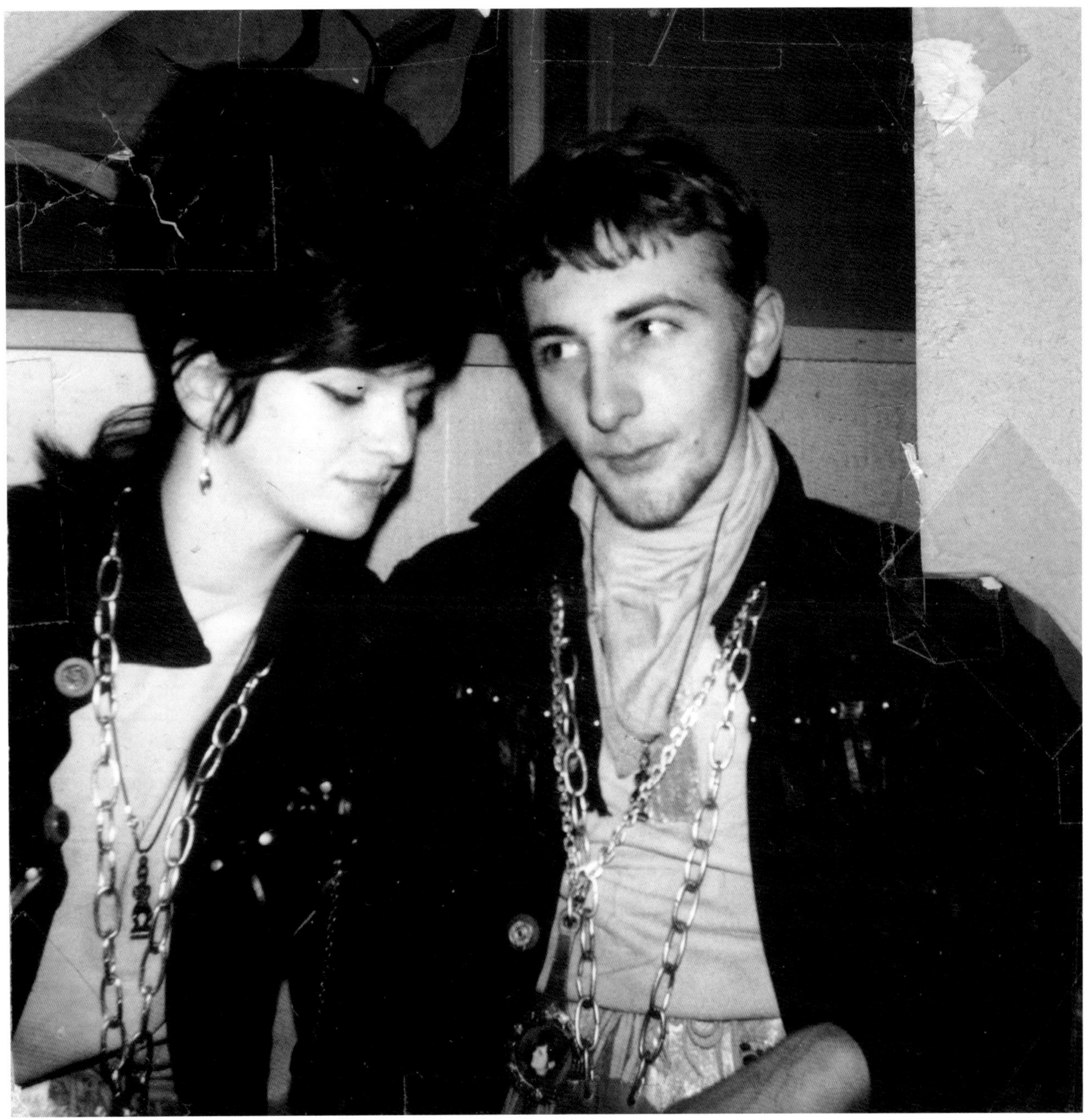

Dream Team: Astrid and Raymond. You didn't see many girls in Basel with chains around their necks at this time.

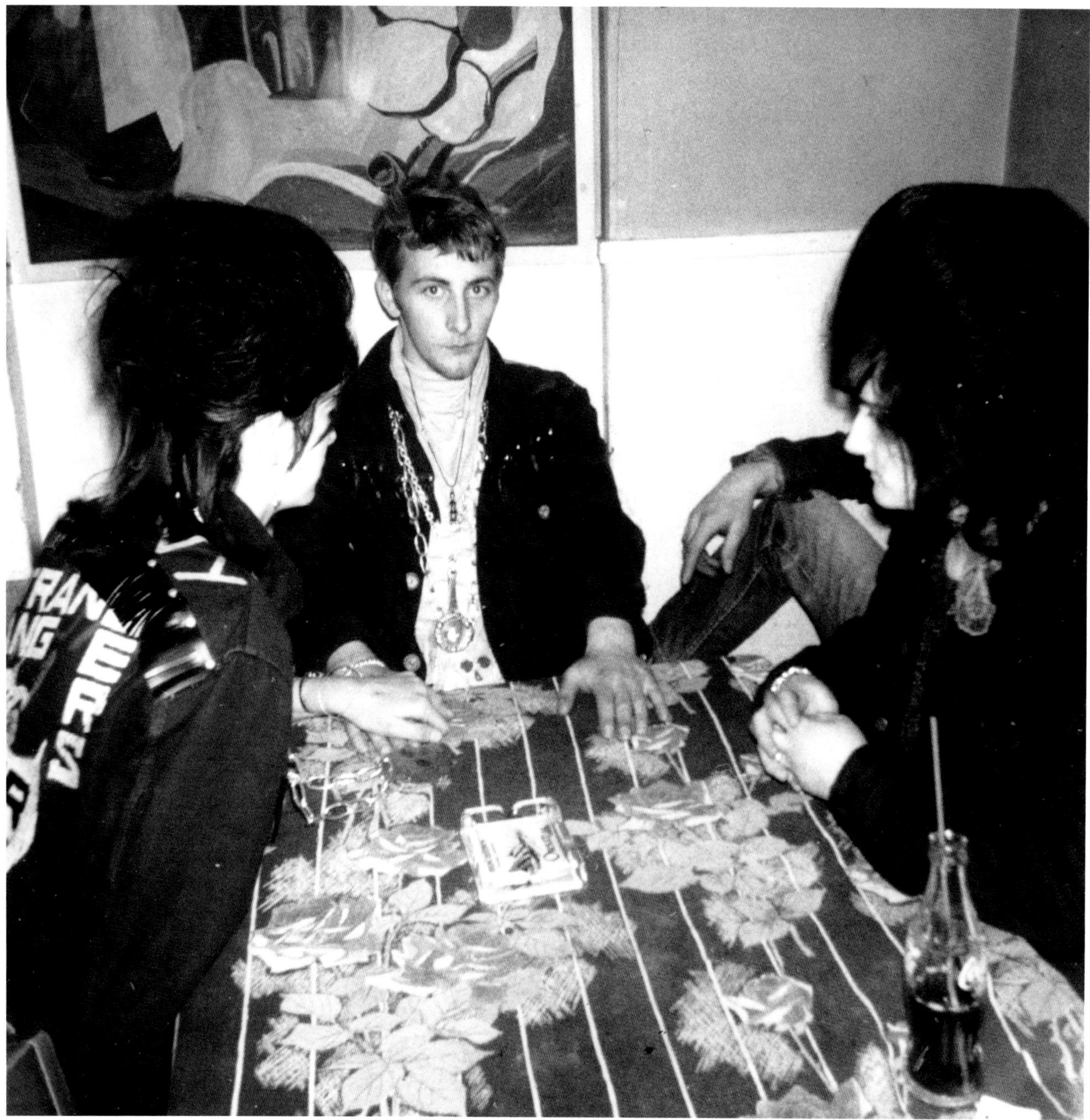

Raymond with Jenny and Rumy—all from the Strangers Gang Vampir Basel.

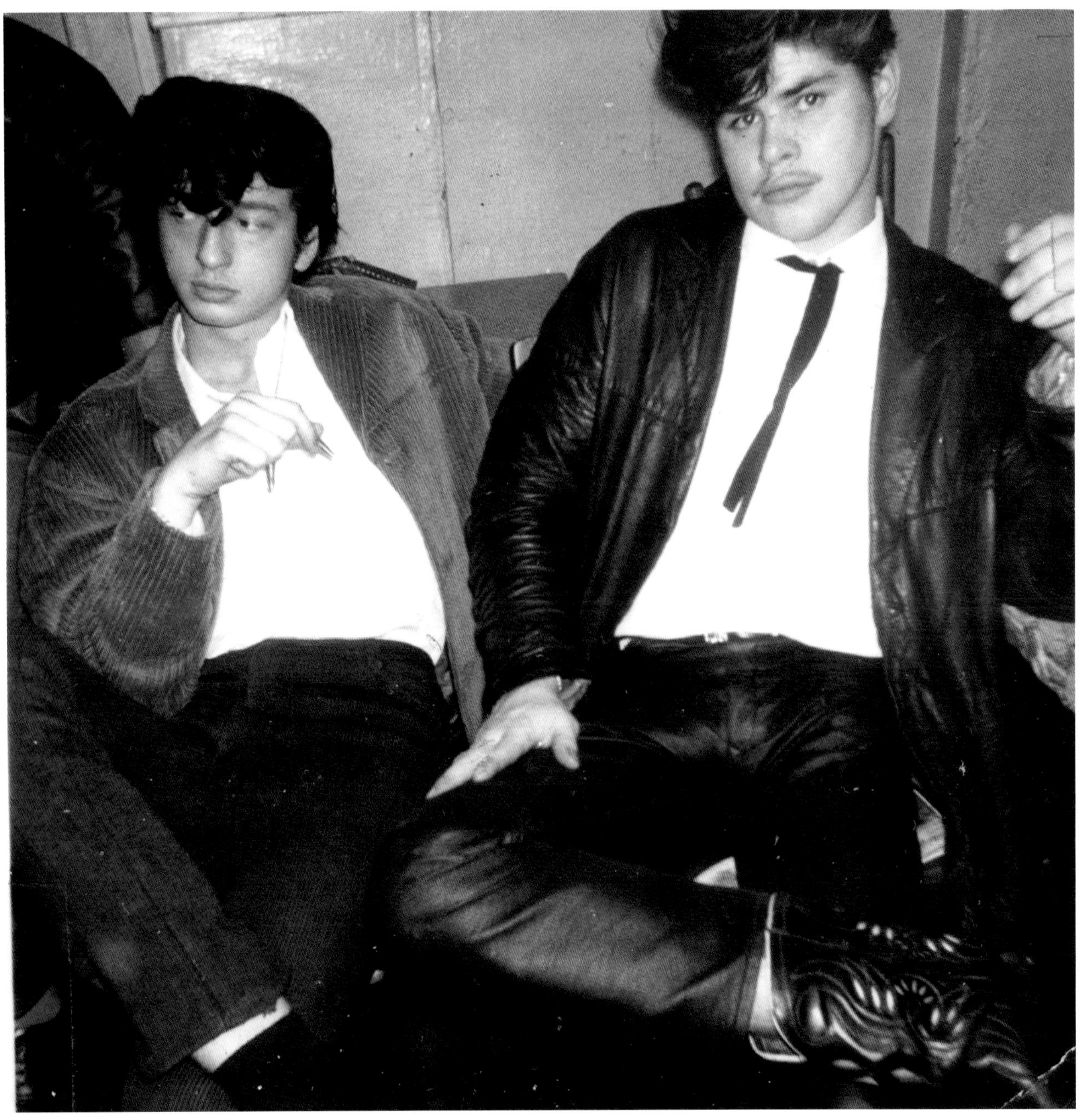

Johnny and Zack-Zack.

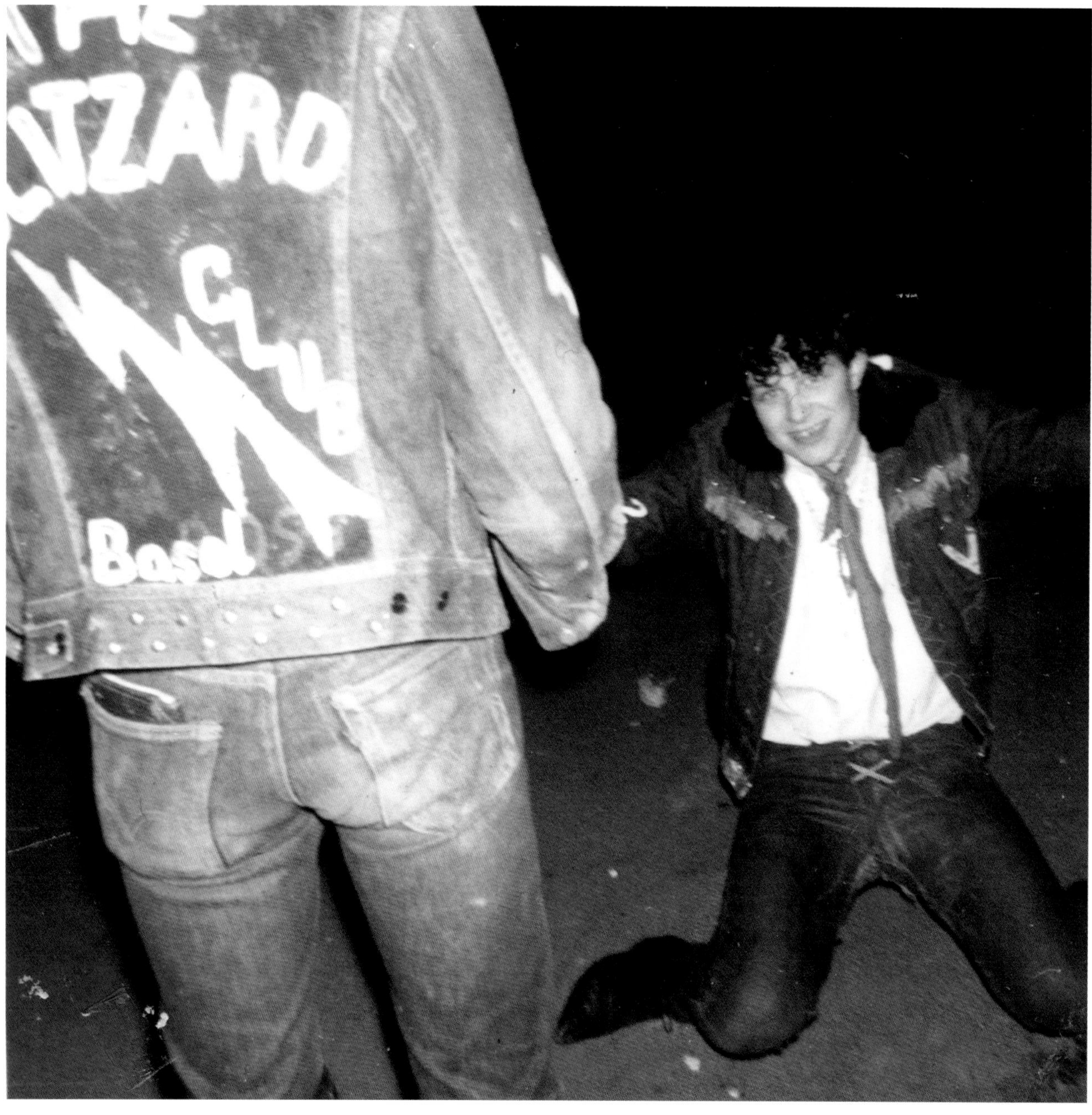

Marcel Zimmerli (Jacky)—here in a Rock'n'Roll pose—was the boss of The Blizzards. Please notice the name on the back of the Blizzards jacket: "Blizzard" was originally in German ("Blitzard" Club Basel).

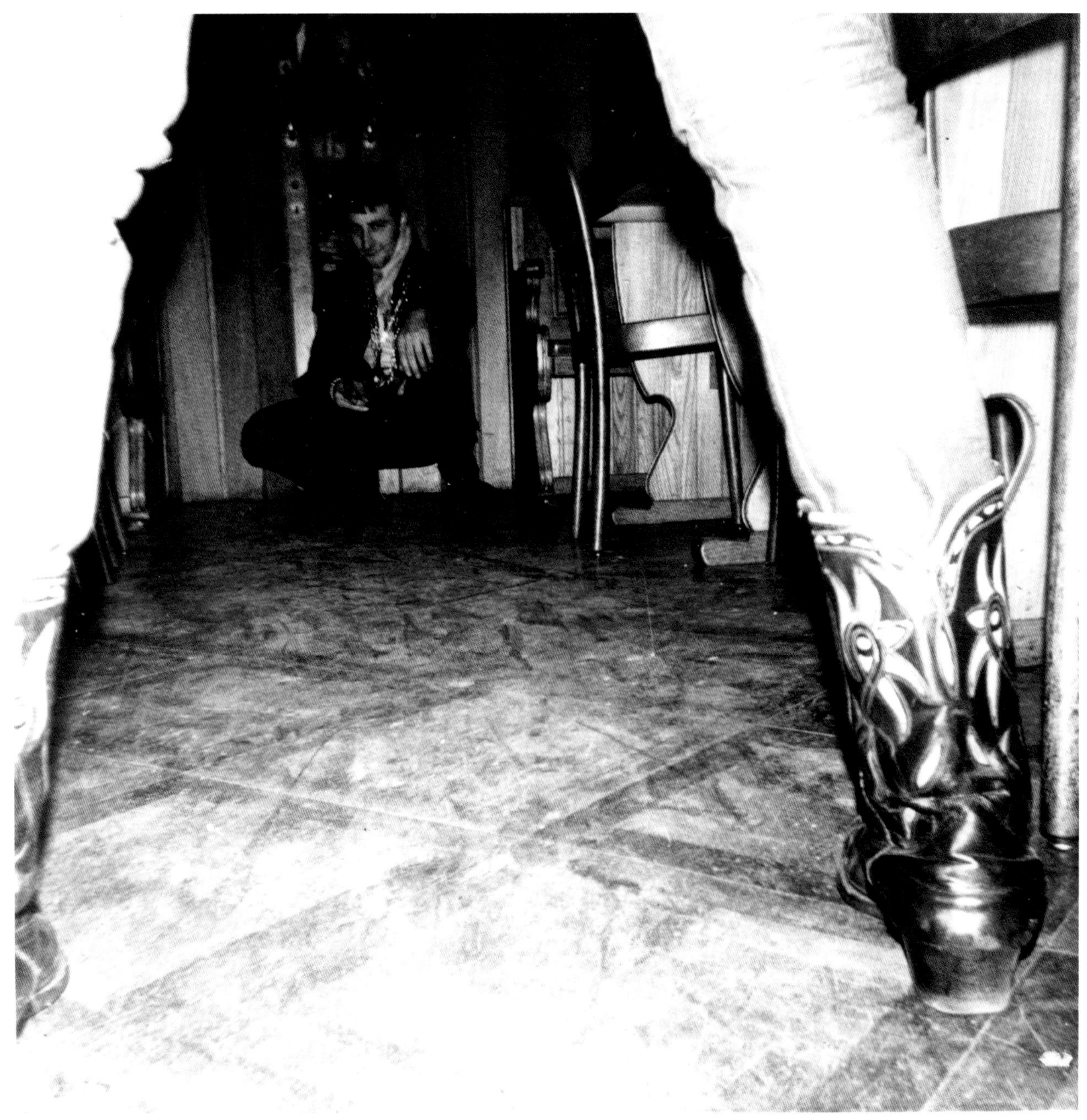

Vampir boss Raymond Christen in action. Cowboy boots were trademark gangwear. Raymond died in 2010.

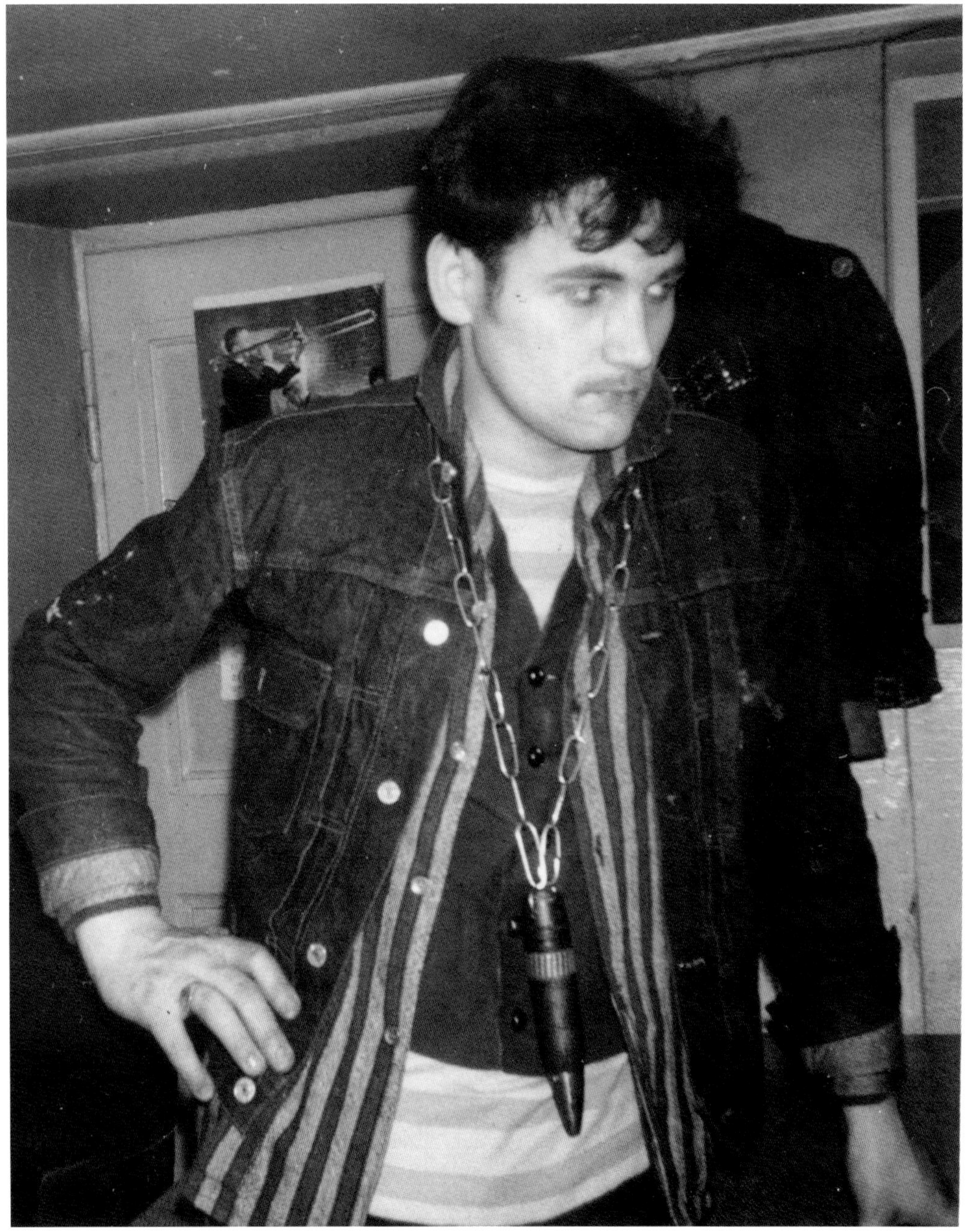

Tello, wearing some heavy ammunition on a chain around his neck.

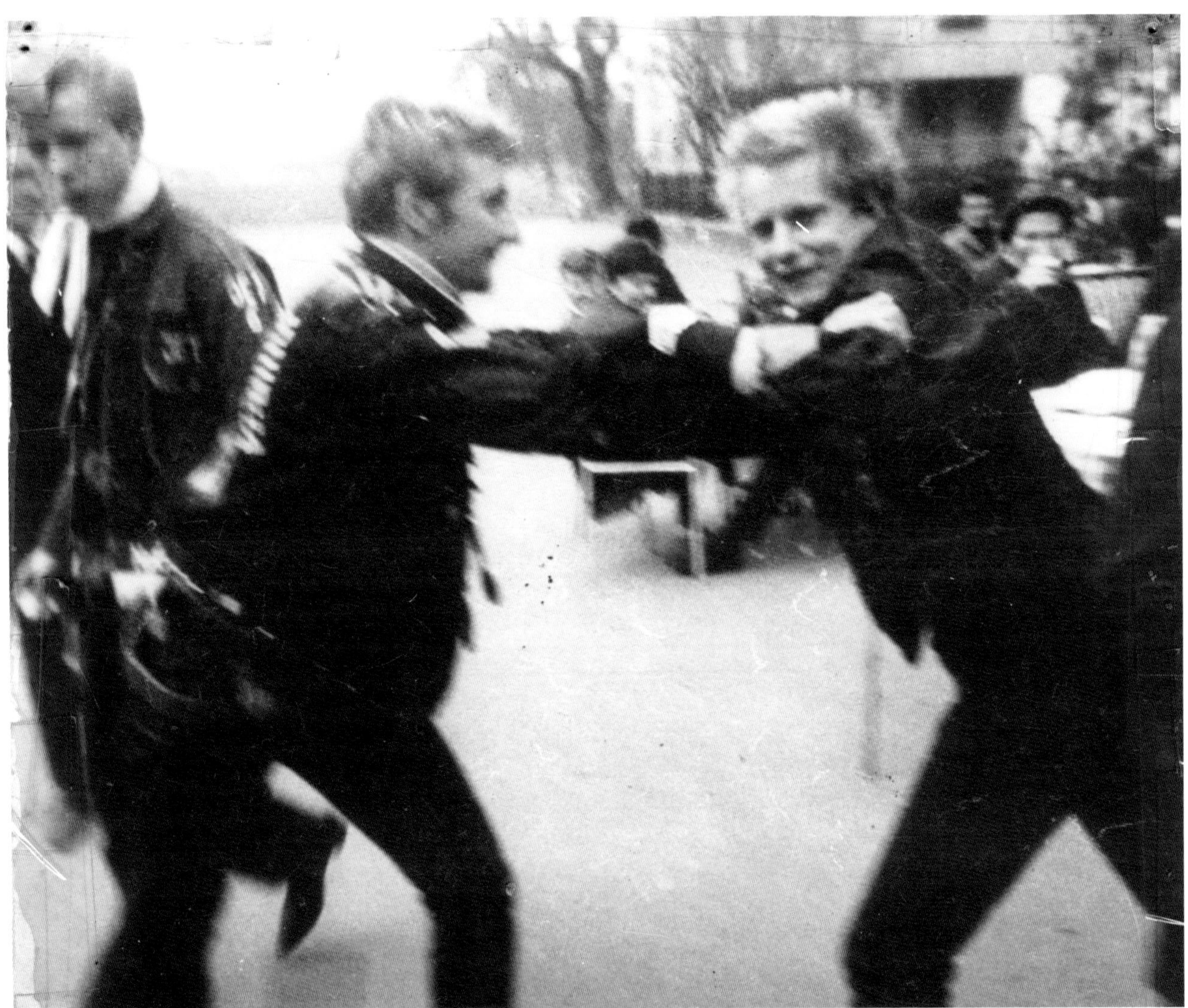

Who has the stronger arms? Wrestling time with Raymond and Igel.

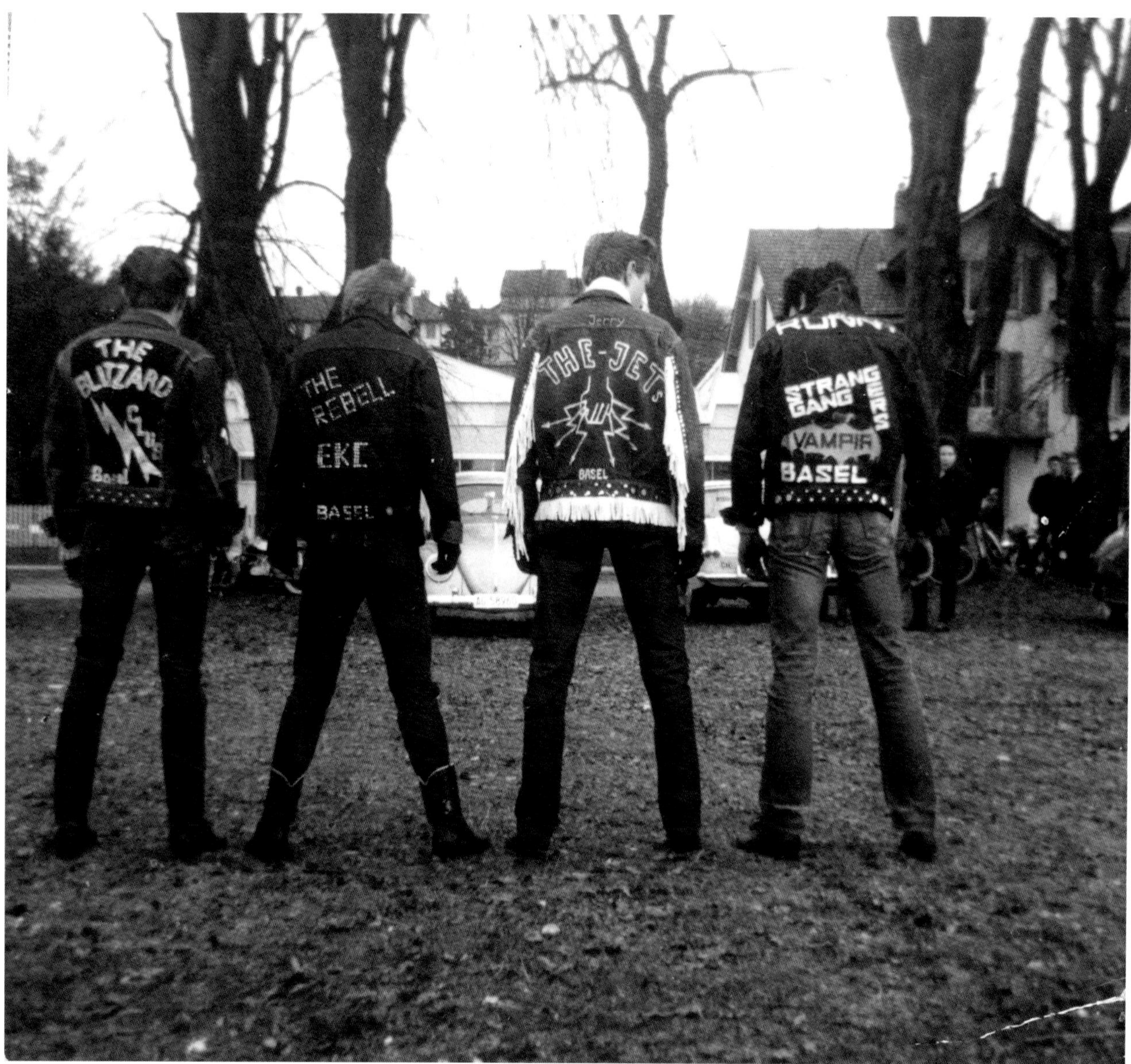

A Blizzard, Igel, Jerry from The Jets, and Ronny from the Vampir, Basel.

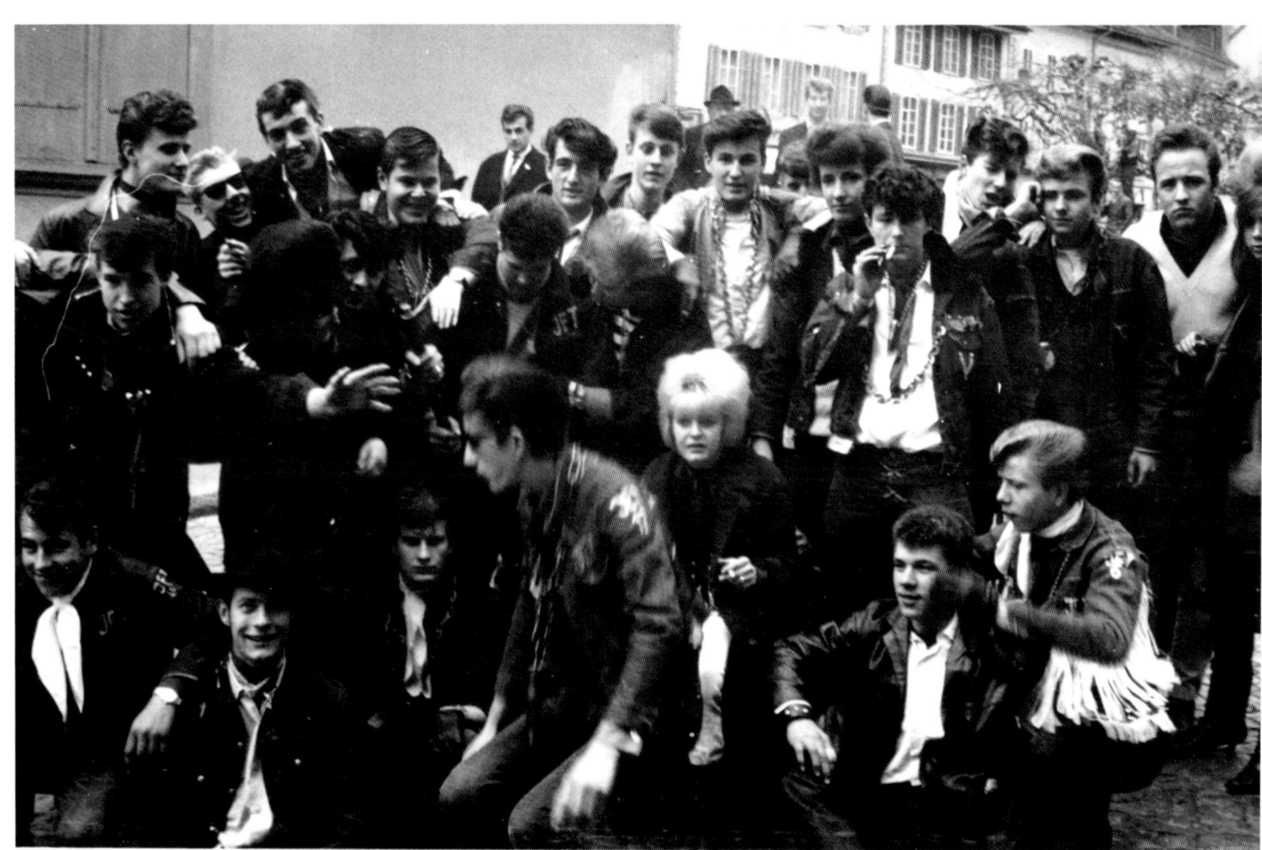

Gang meeting in Aarau.

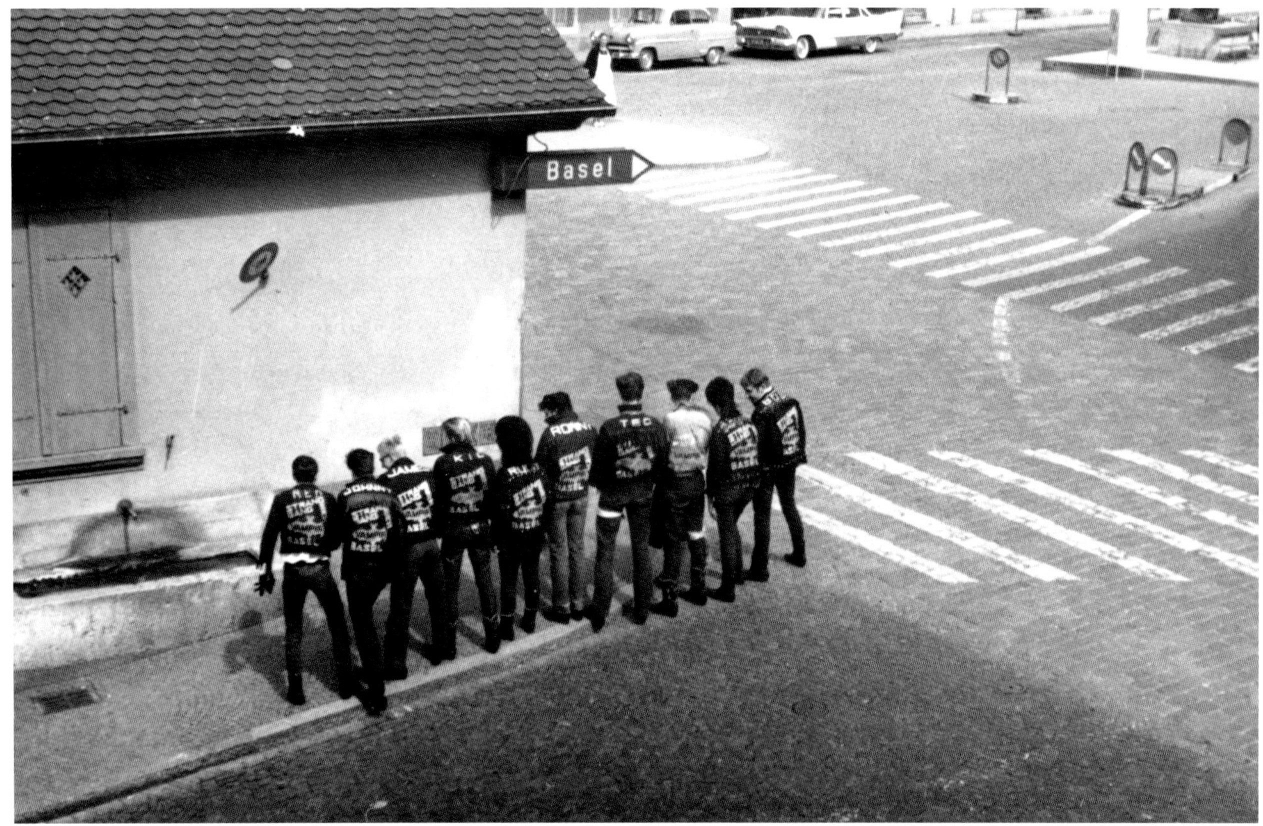

Vampir, Basel from left to right: Red, Johnny, James, Kid, Rumy, Ronny, Ted, unknown guy, Jenny, and their boss Raymond.

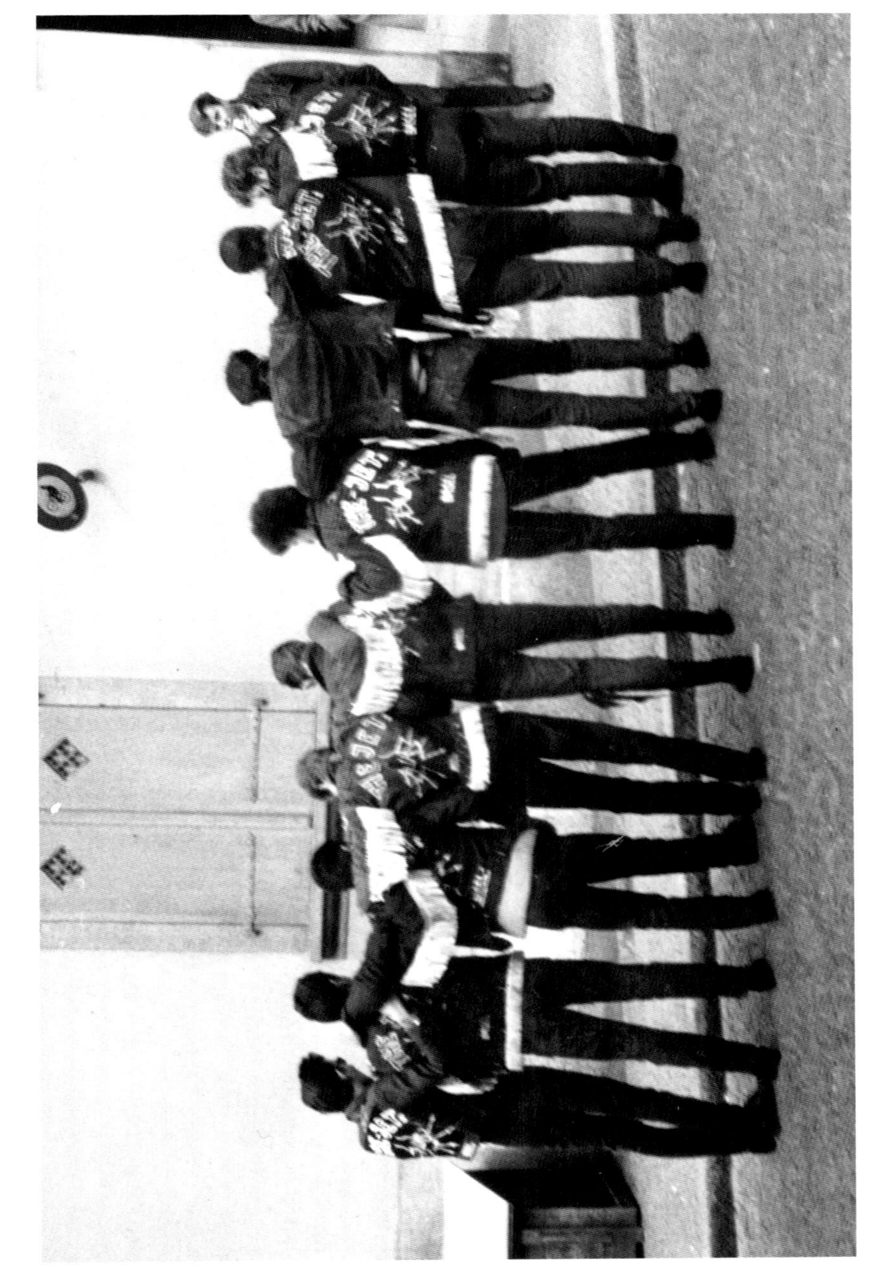

15/trip to bern
april 28, 1963

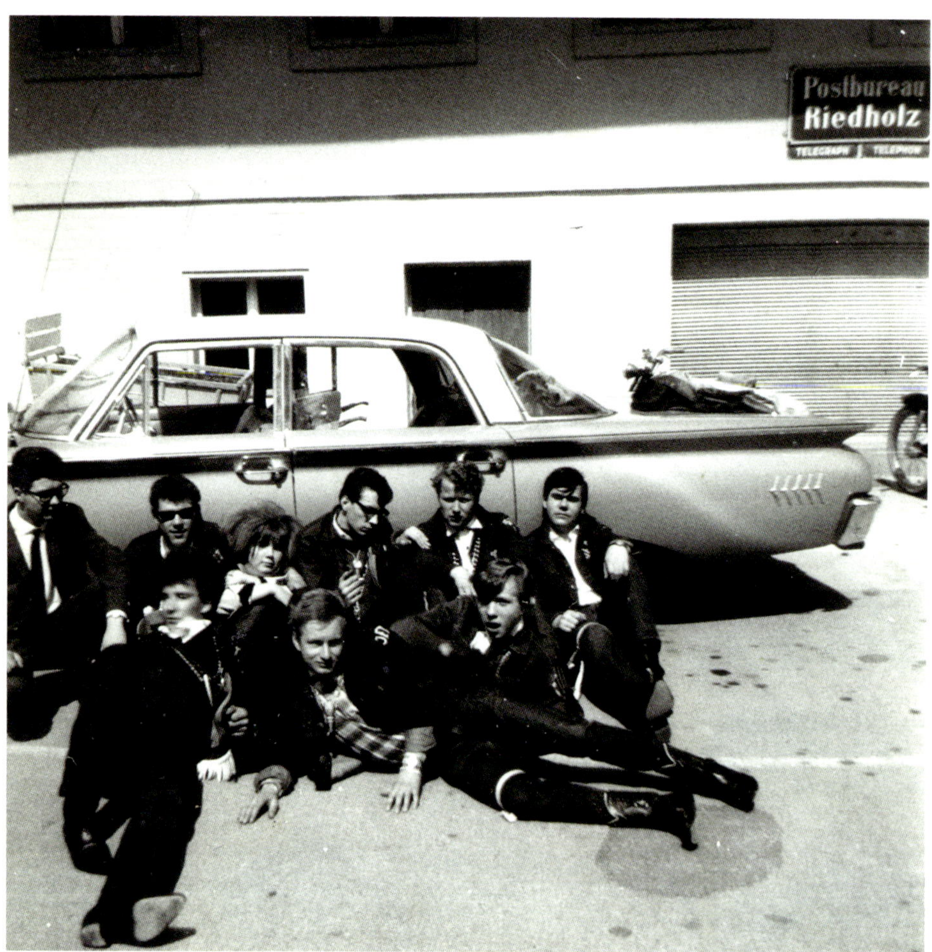

Ten Jets / One auto.

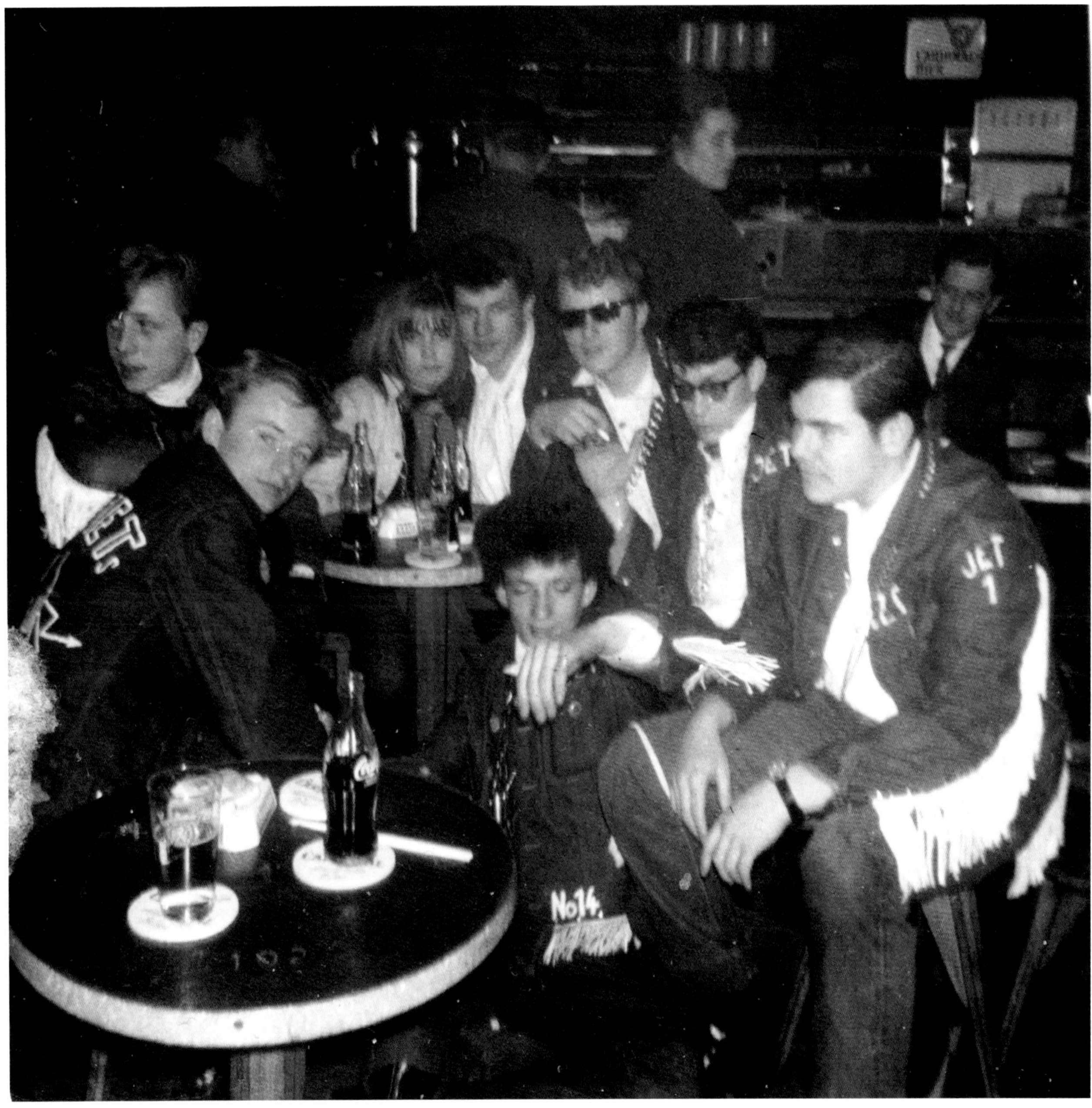

Igel (front left) and Boss Doc (far right) with the number “Jet 1” on his arm. Every gang member had his own number.

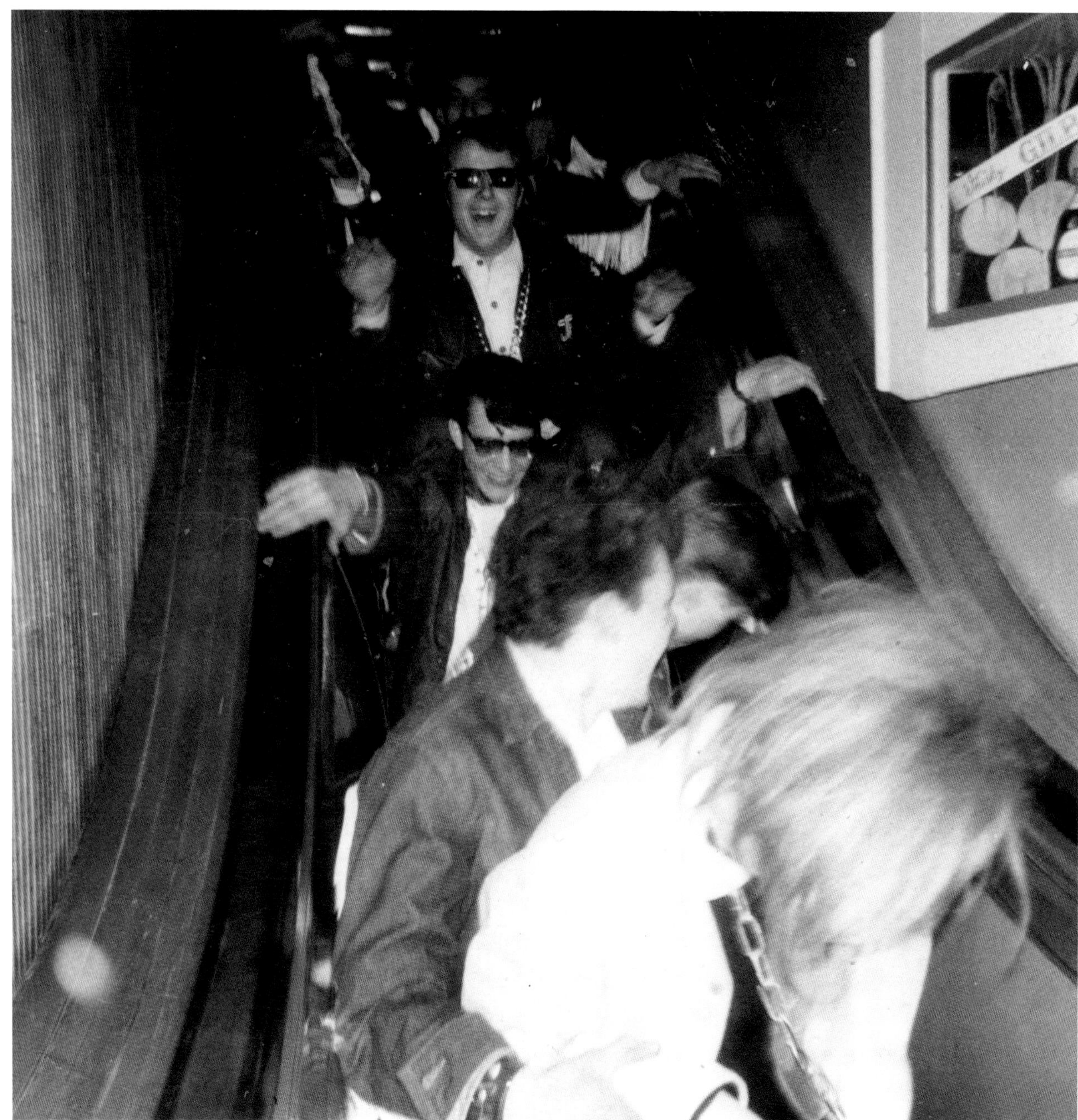

The Halbstarke goofing off on an escalator.

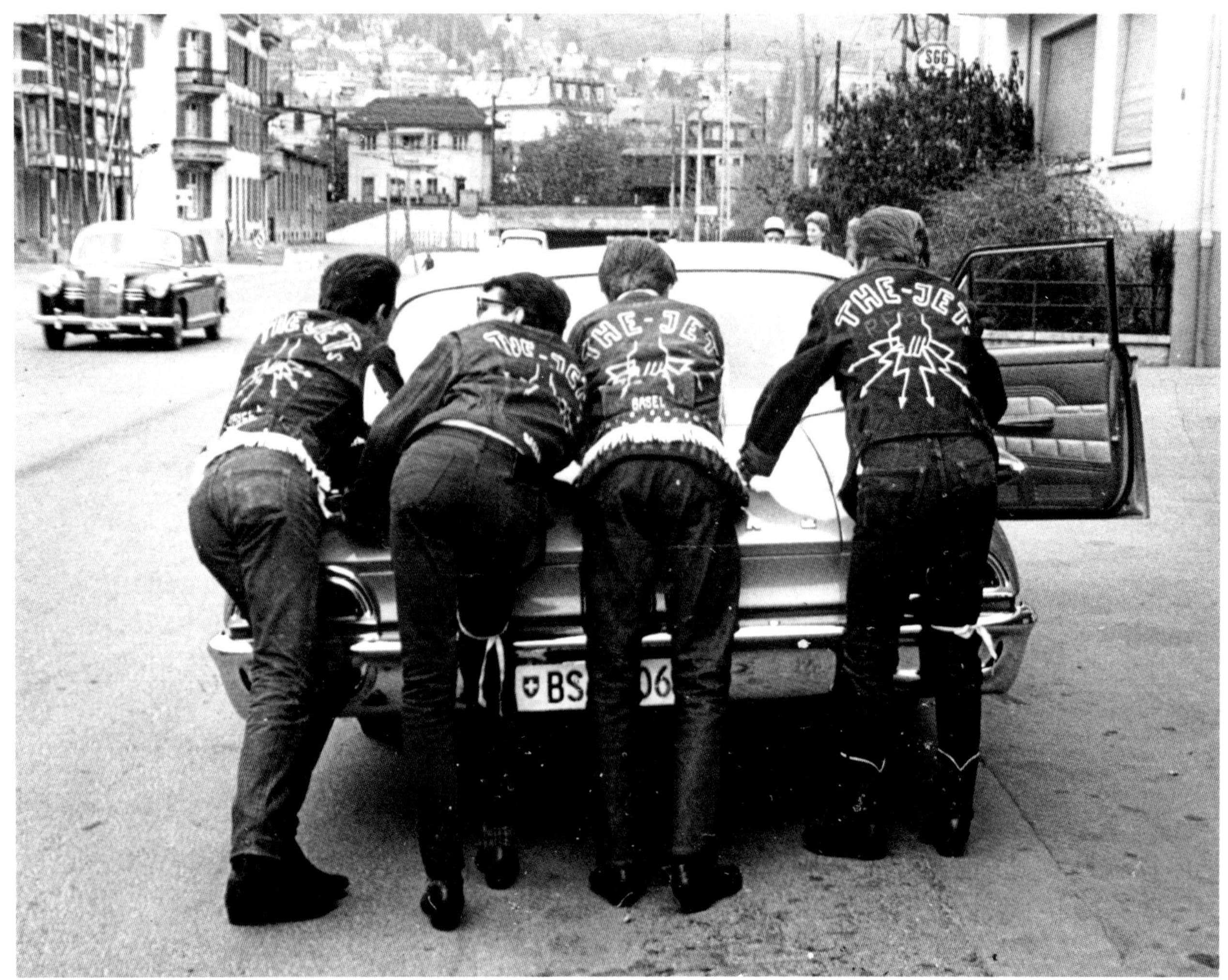

Igel earned his gang jacket. He was now a full-on member.

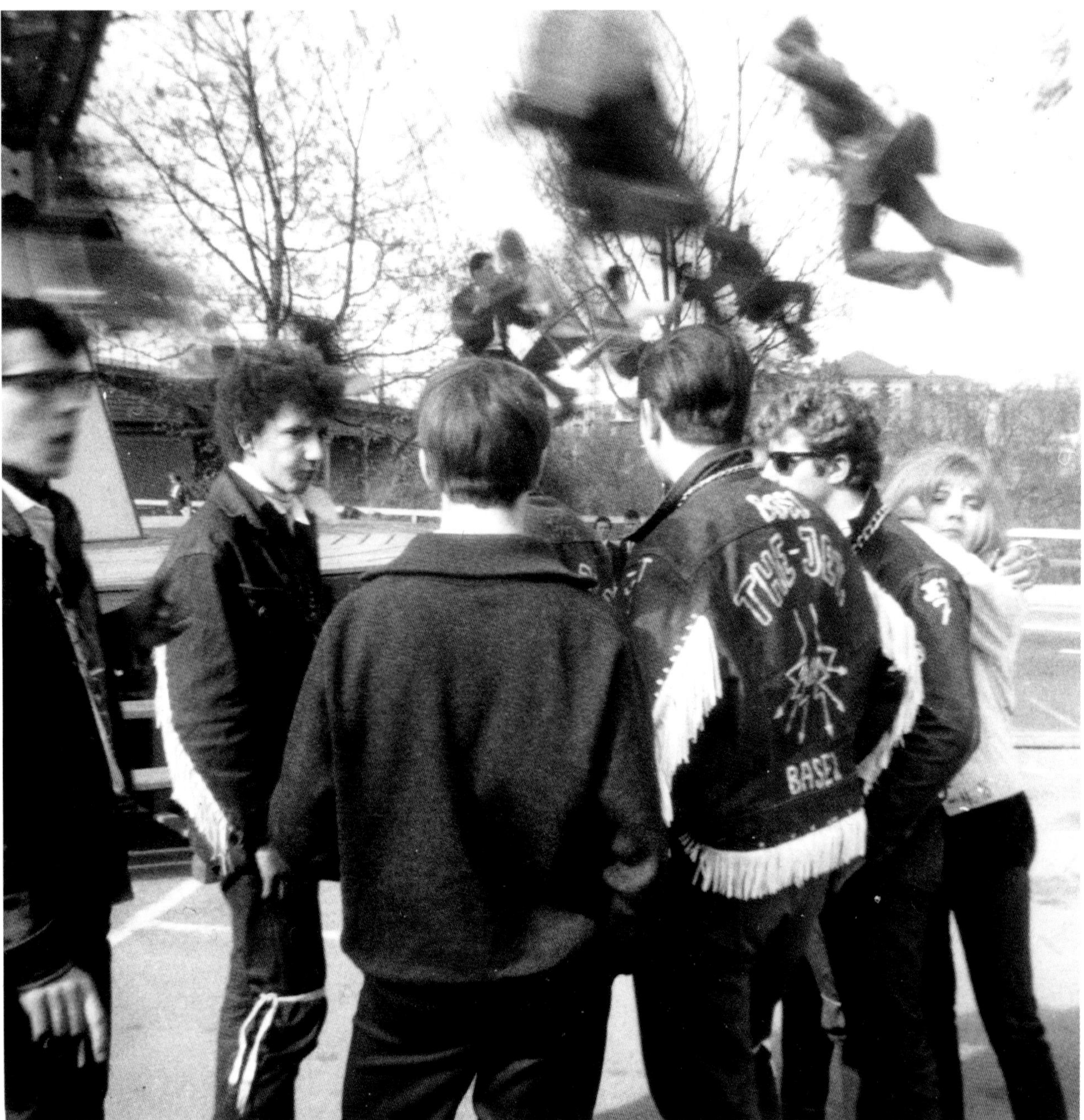

At the fairgrounds.

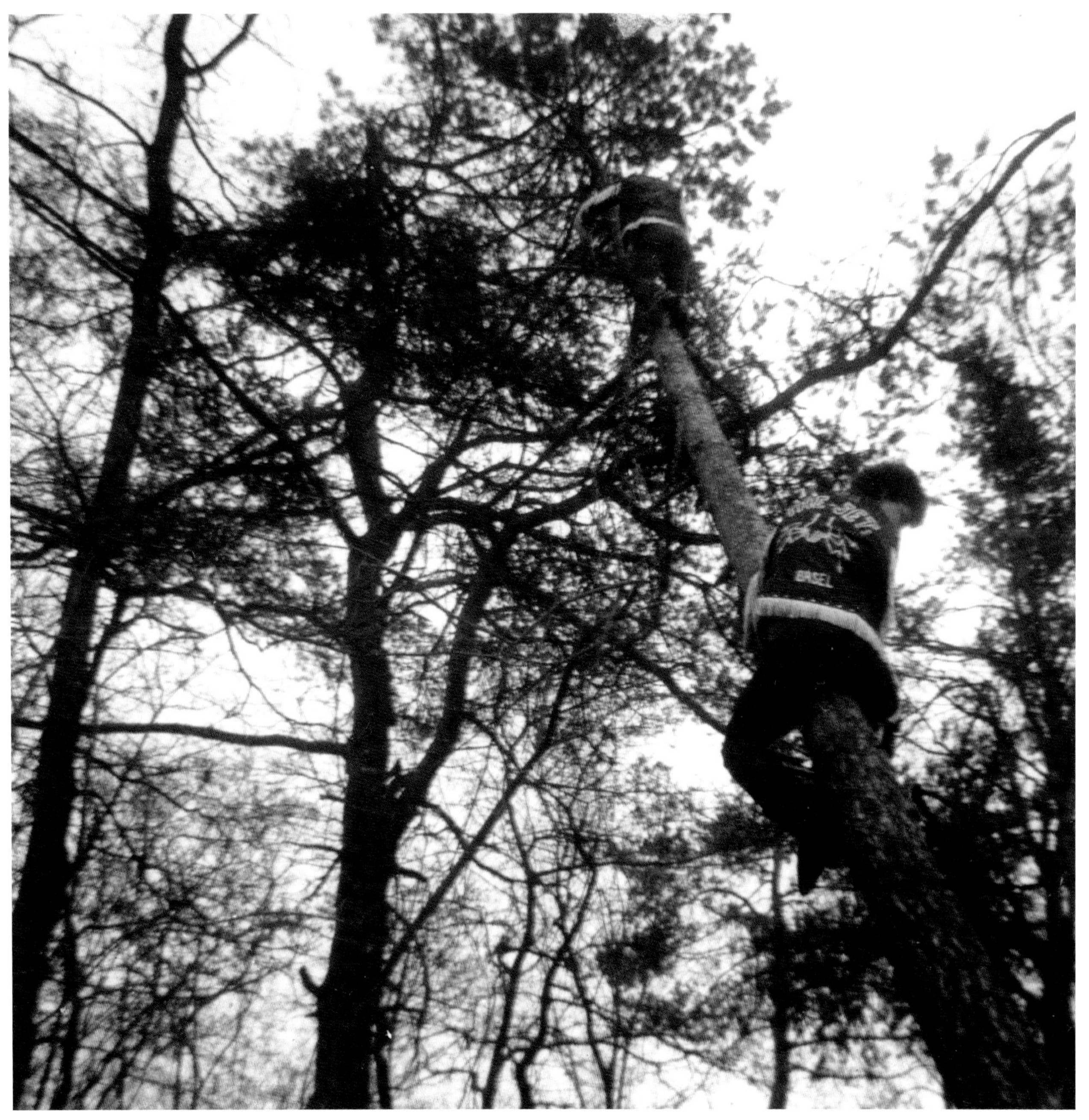

Jenny and Lexi on a dare.

16/zürich
may 5, 1963

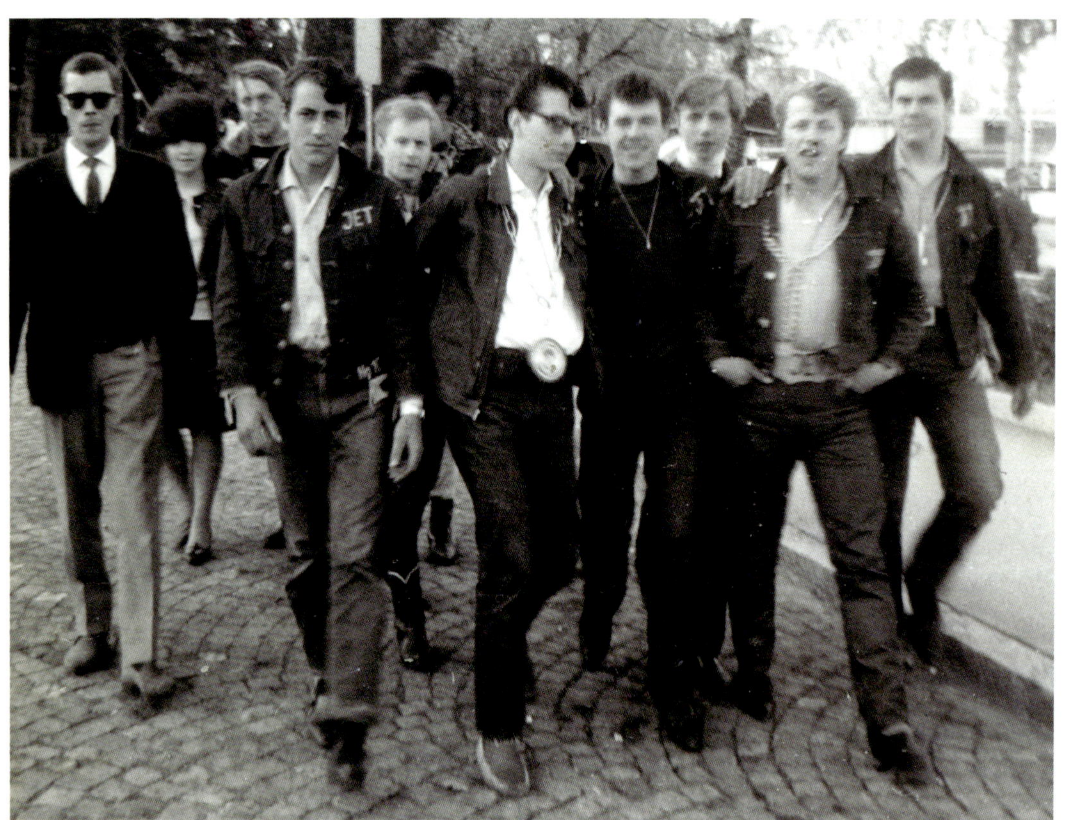

The Jets au grand complet.

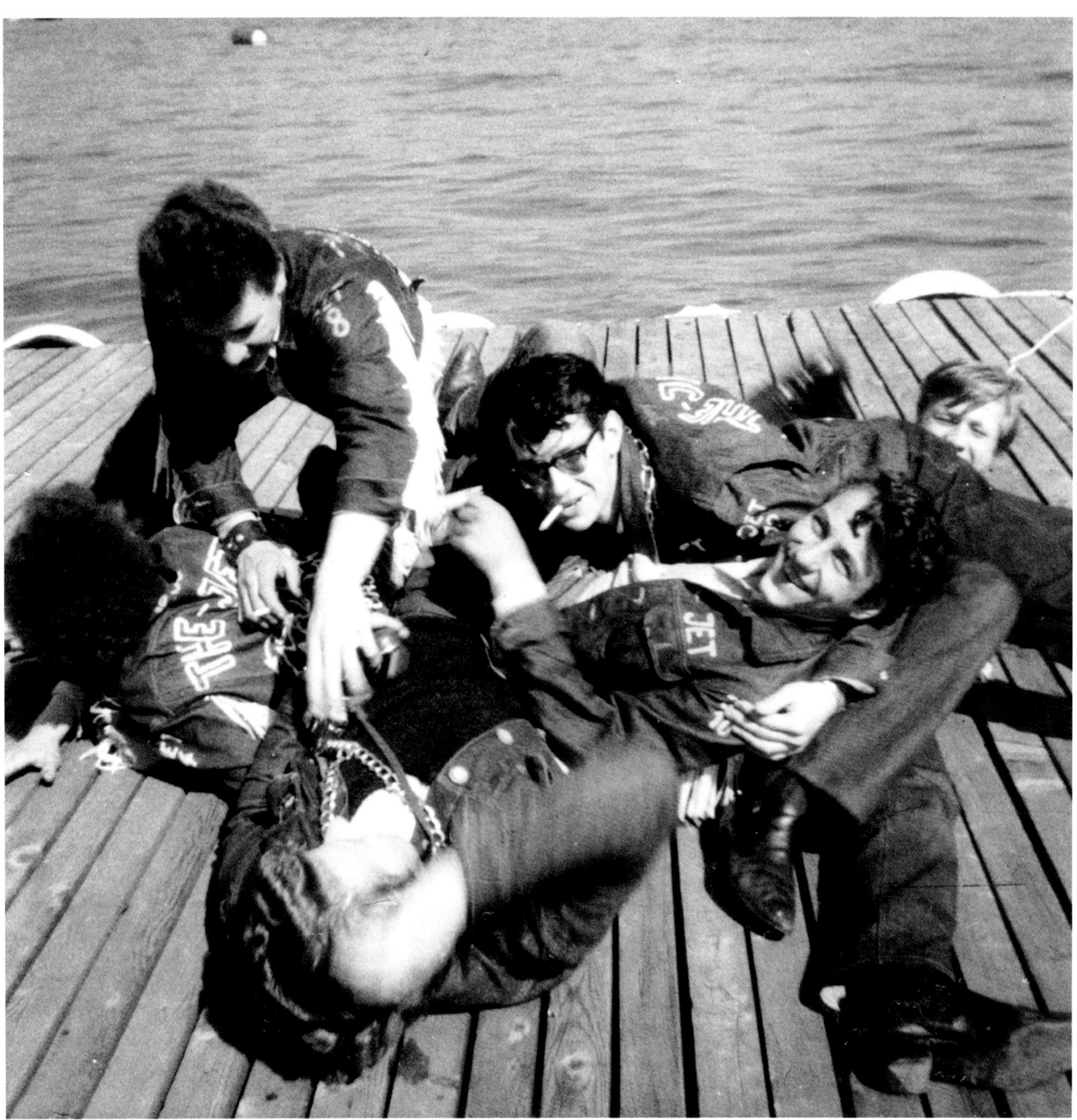

Brawling.

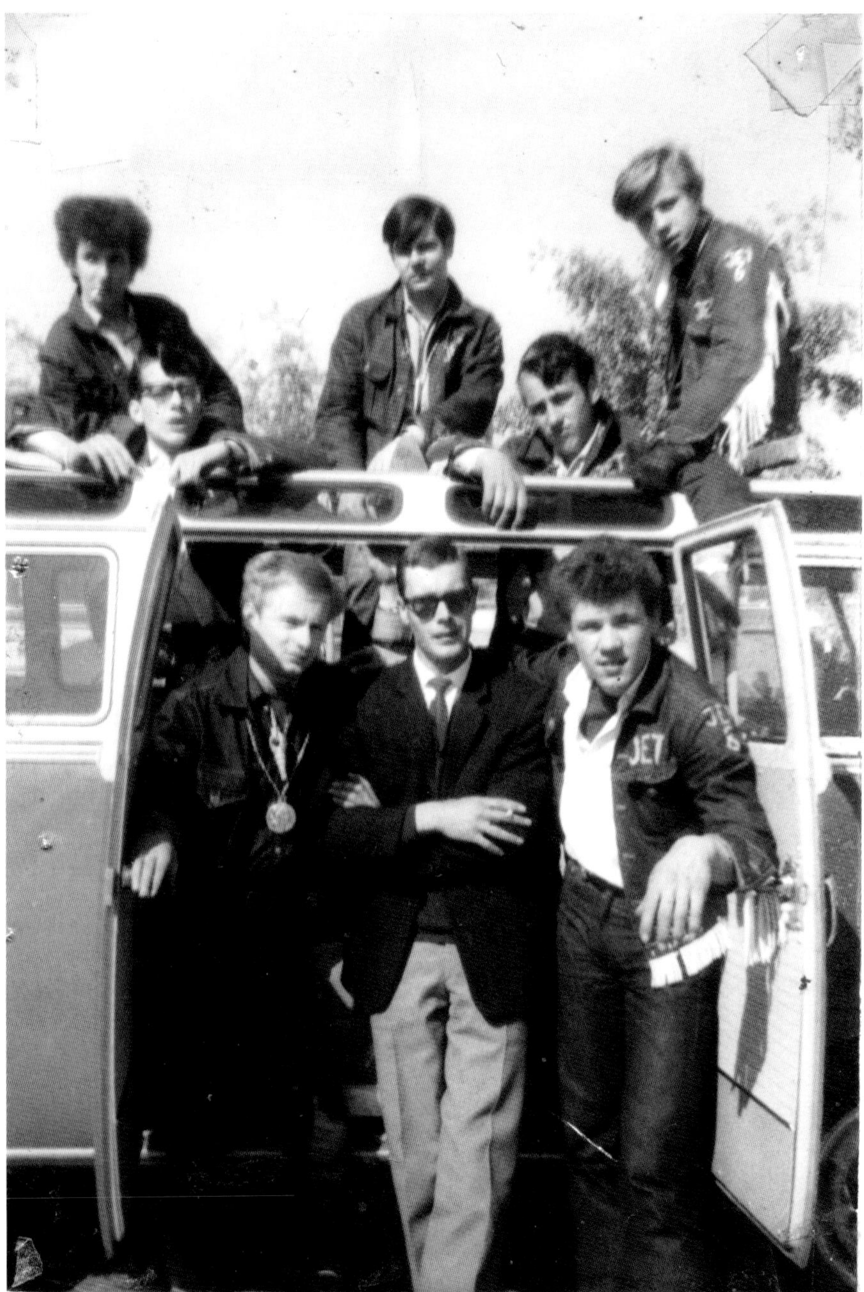

On tour.

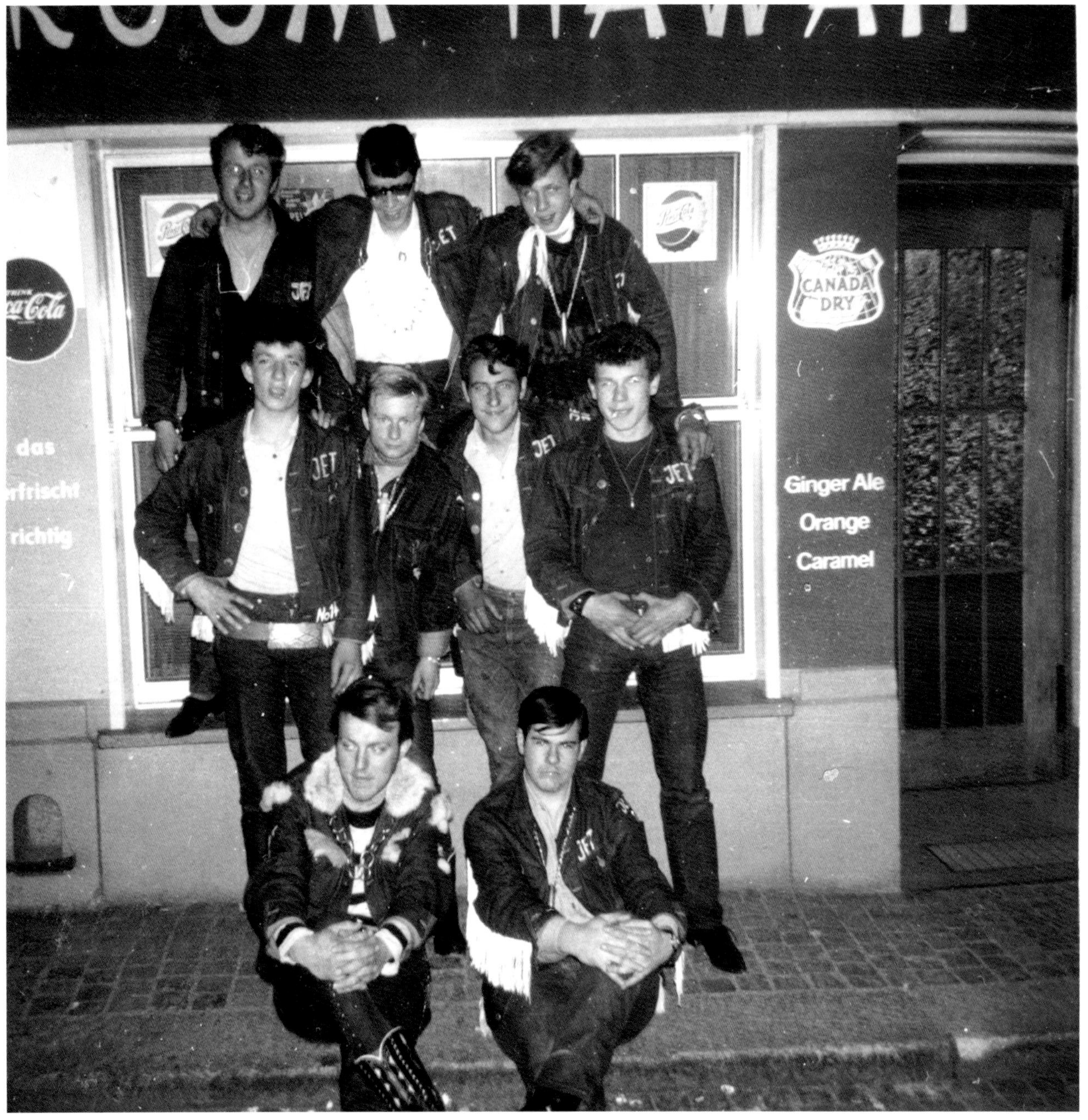

Romeo (boss of the Revenger Gang, Zurich), and Doc with other members of The Jets at Tea Room Hawaii at Rindermarkt.

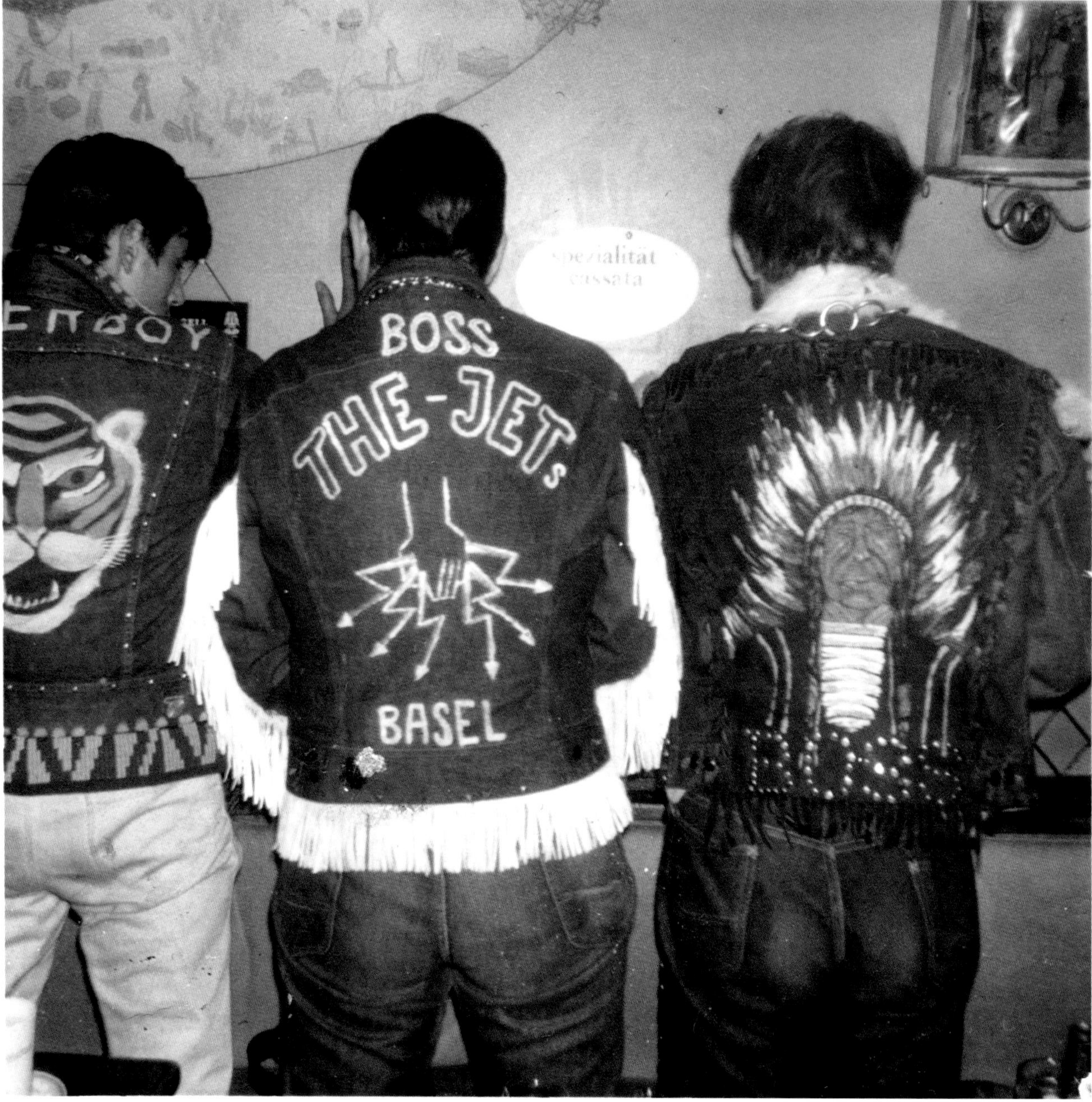

Tiger boy (on right) with two well-known bosses, Paul Marggraff a/k/a Doc (center) and Romeo (boss of the Revenger Gang, Zurich). Romeo was a feared gang member, known for going head to head with the authorities.

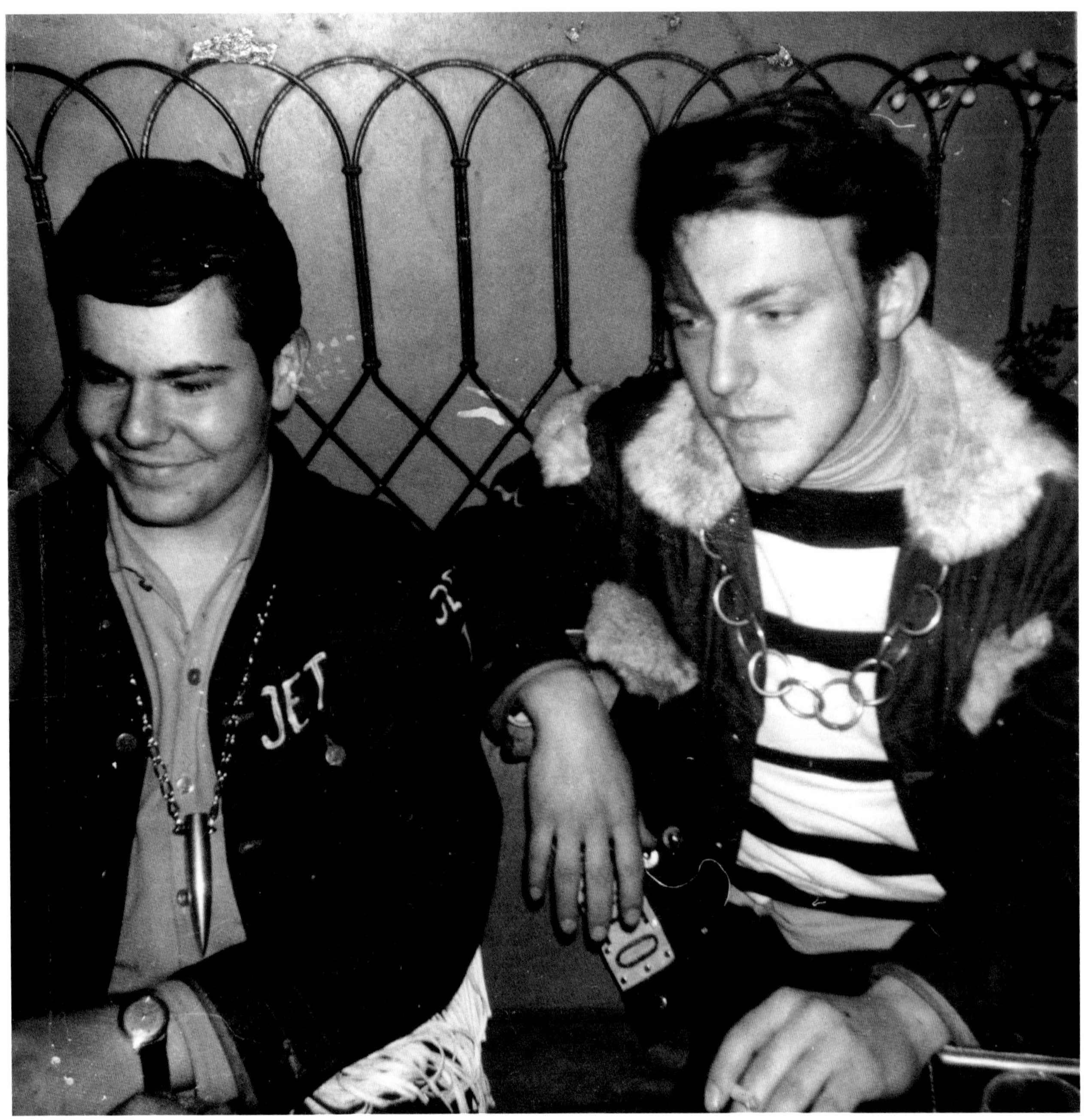

Doc and Romeo.

17/arlesheim, near the castle birseck
may 11–12, 1963

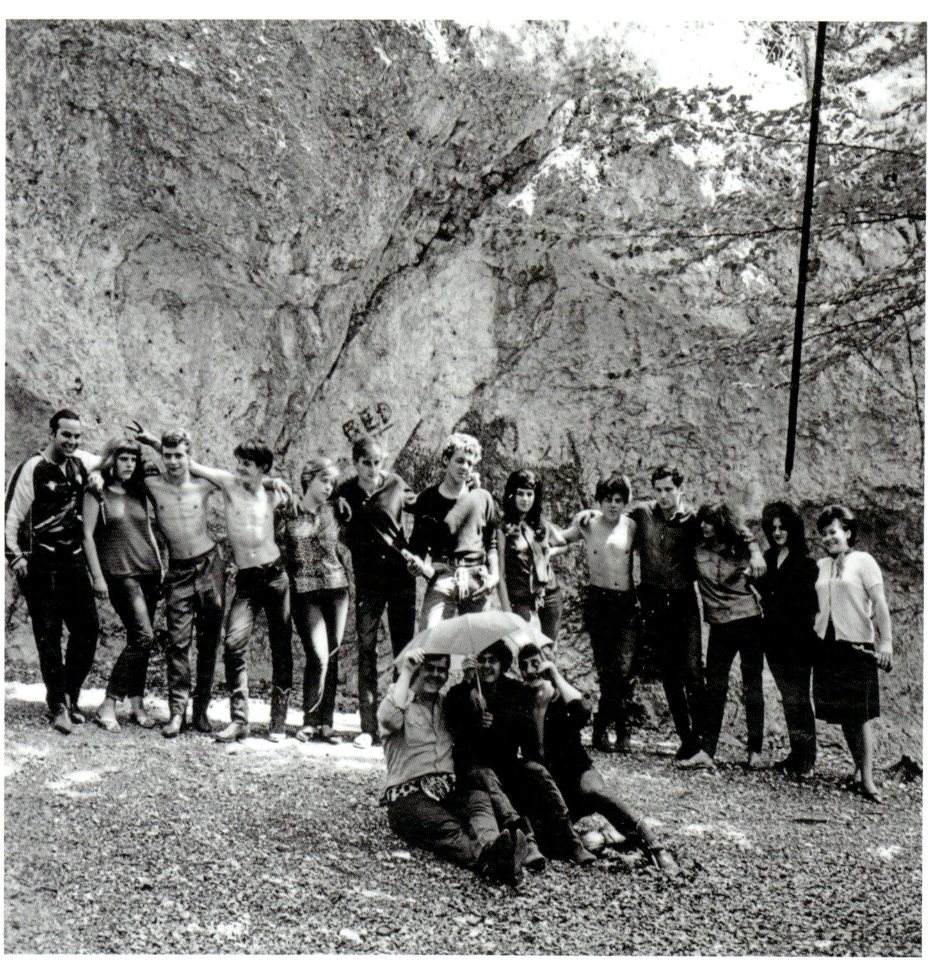

Various Basel gangs posing near the Castle Birseck.

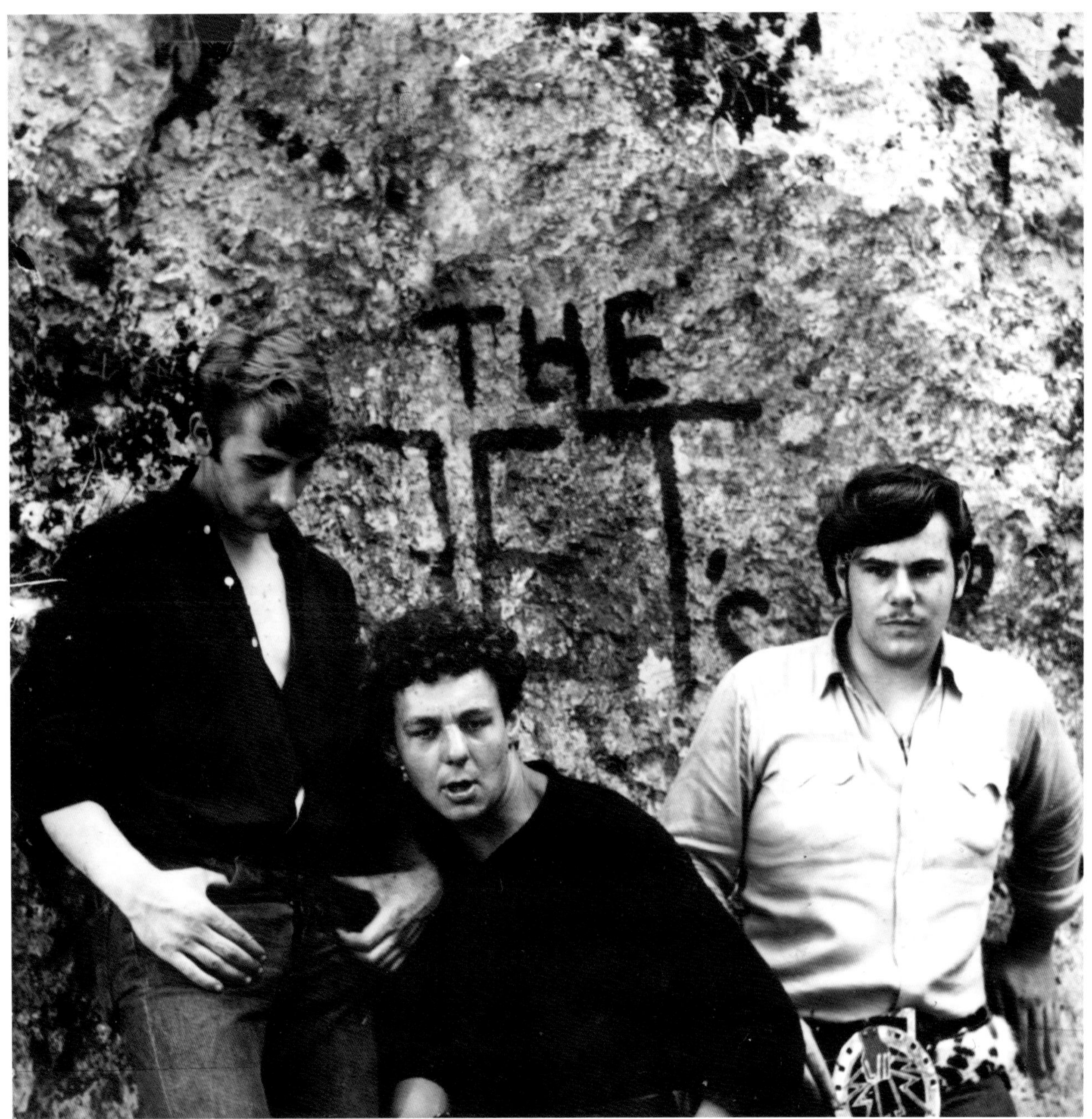

Raymond Christen, Martin Schippert (Tino) and Paul Marggraff (Doc).

18/st. petersinsel, lake biel
big yearly swiss gang meeting
june 2–3, 1963

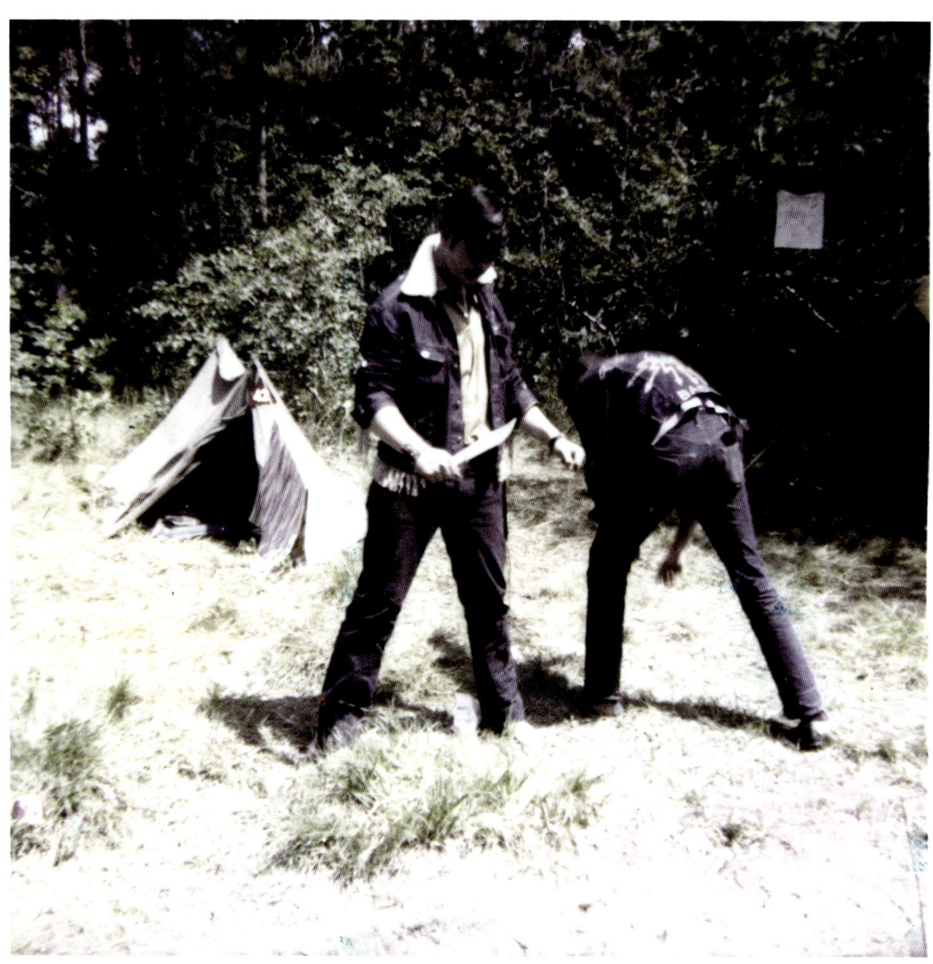

St. Petersinsel 1963. Knife fight in the woods.

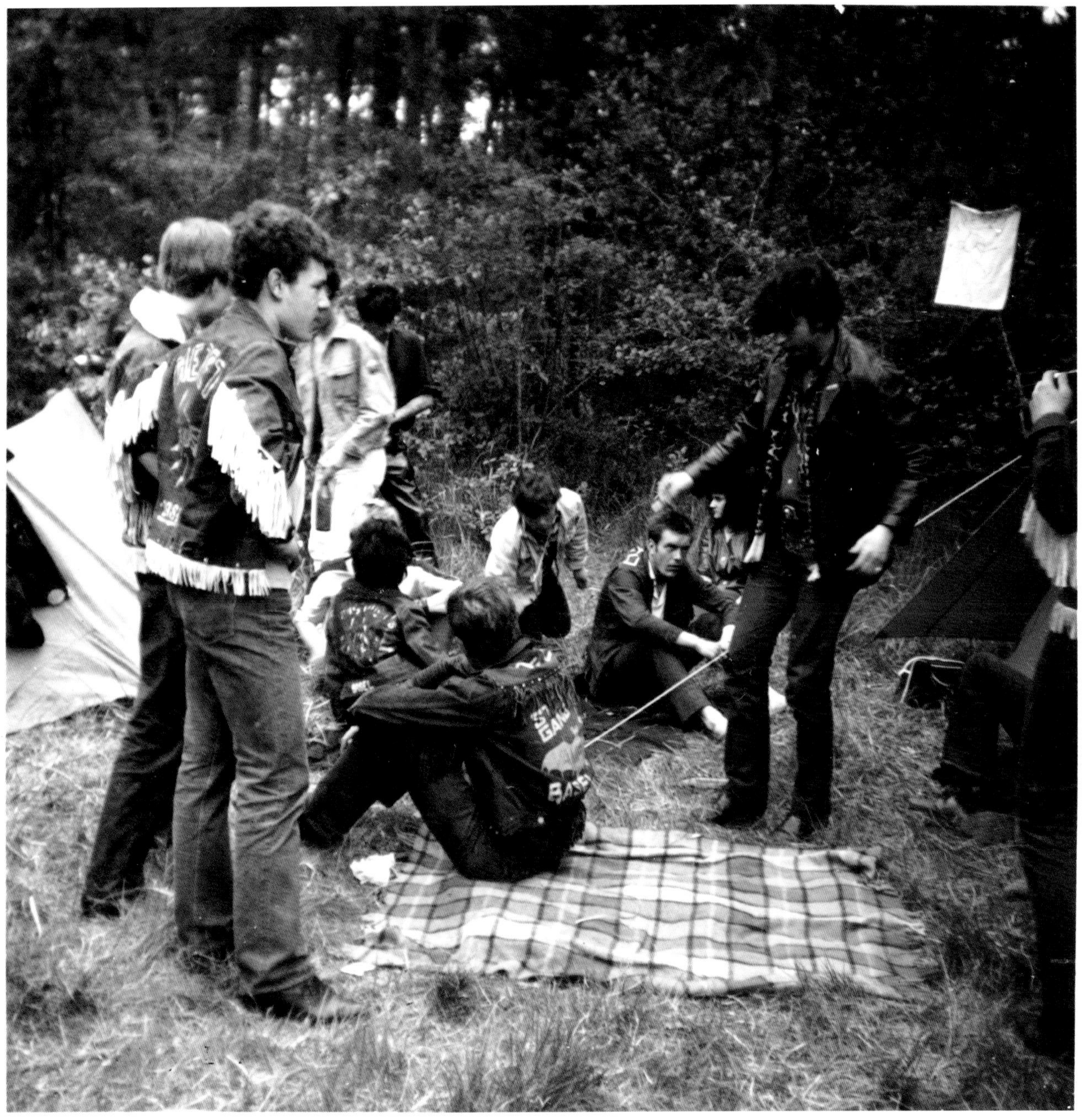

Erwin Metzger (Sunny) from The Jets, Arrigo Prestini (Johnny) from The Strangers Gang Vampir Basel.

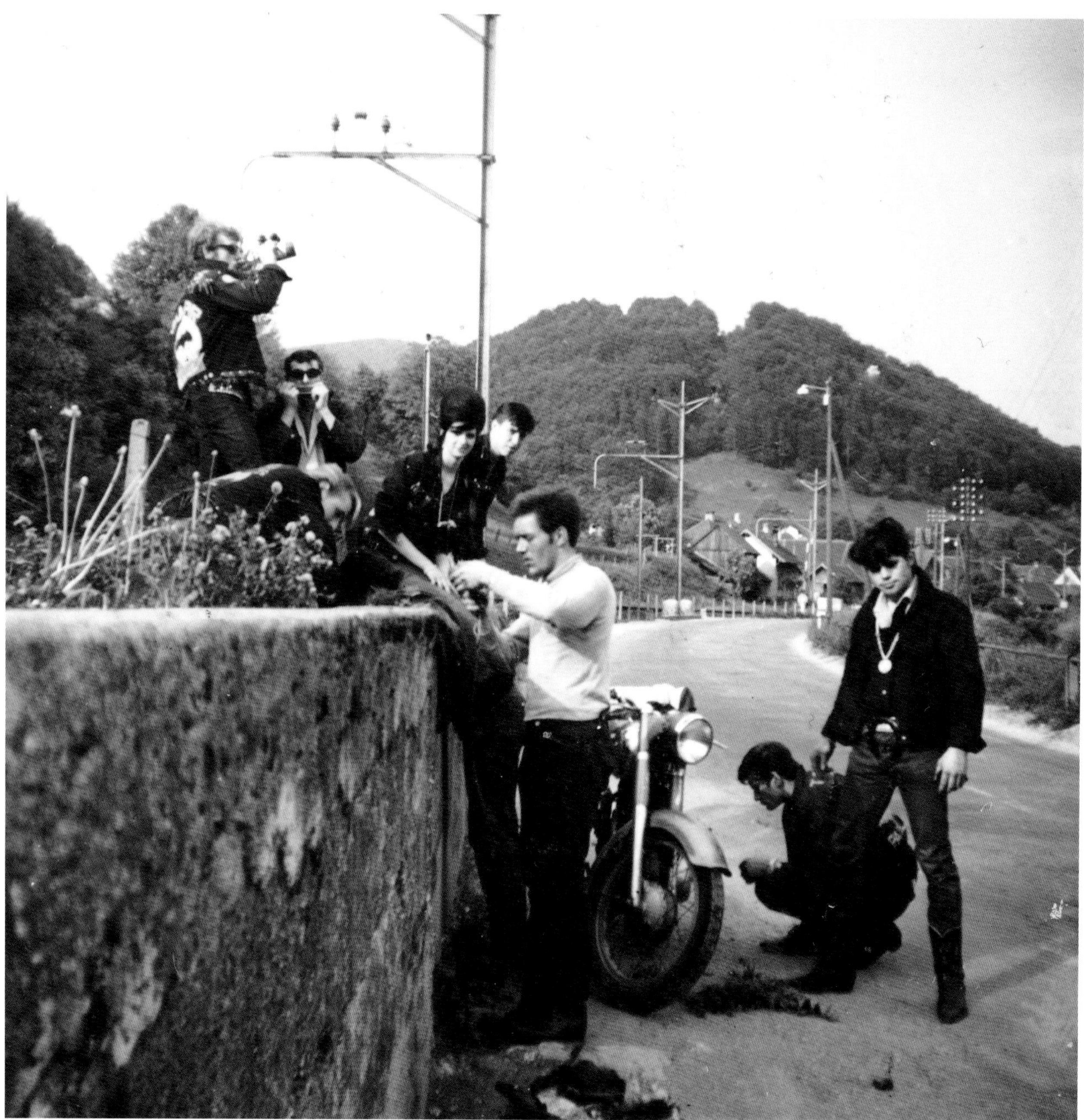

Raymond, Red, Jenny, Cliff, Tschaiko, Ted, and Zack-Zack.

19 / aarau,
july 13–14, 1963

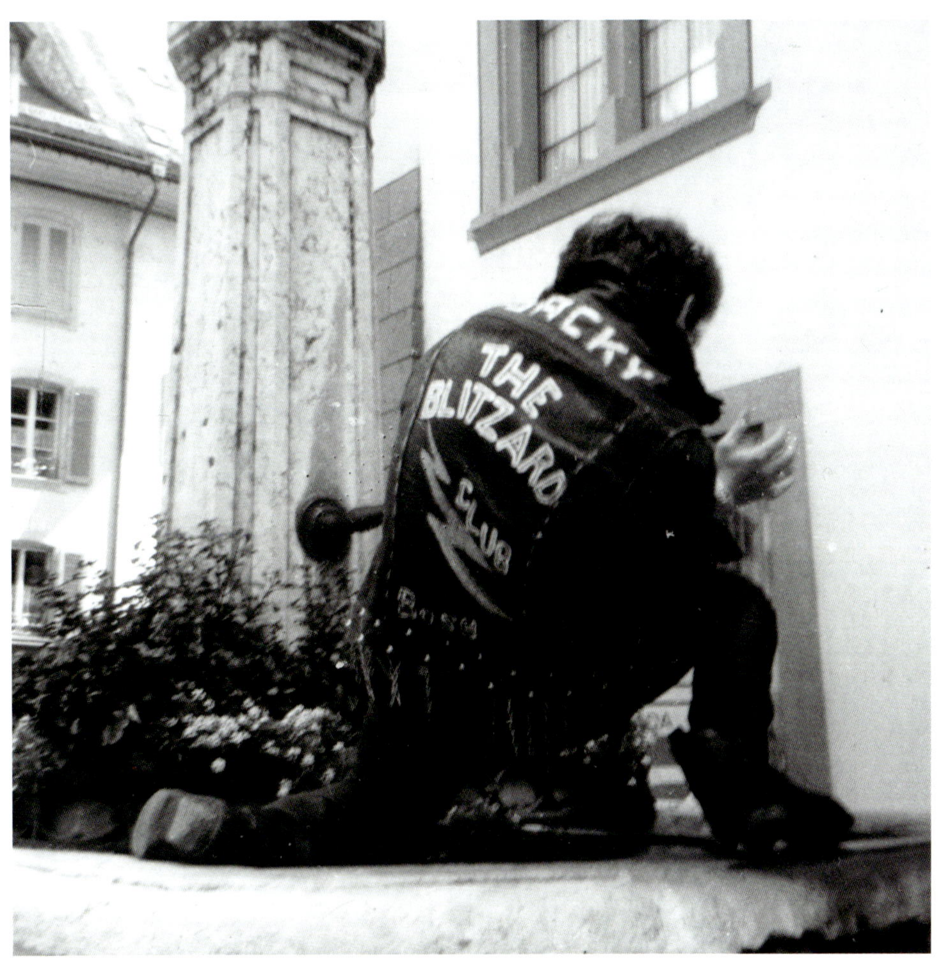

Blizzard Jacky.

20 / knabenschiessen, zürich
september 7–8, 1963

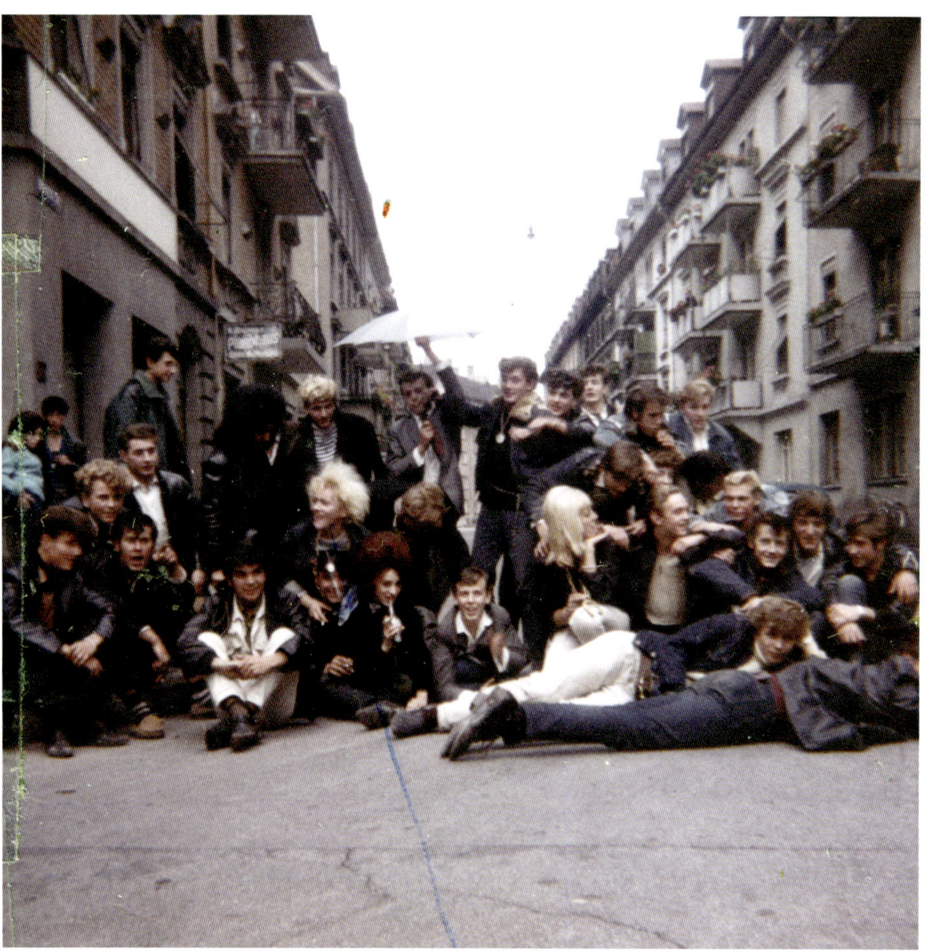

Zurich street gang meeting.

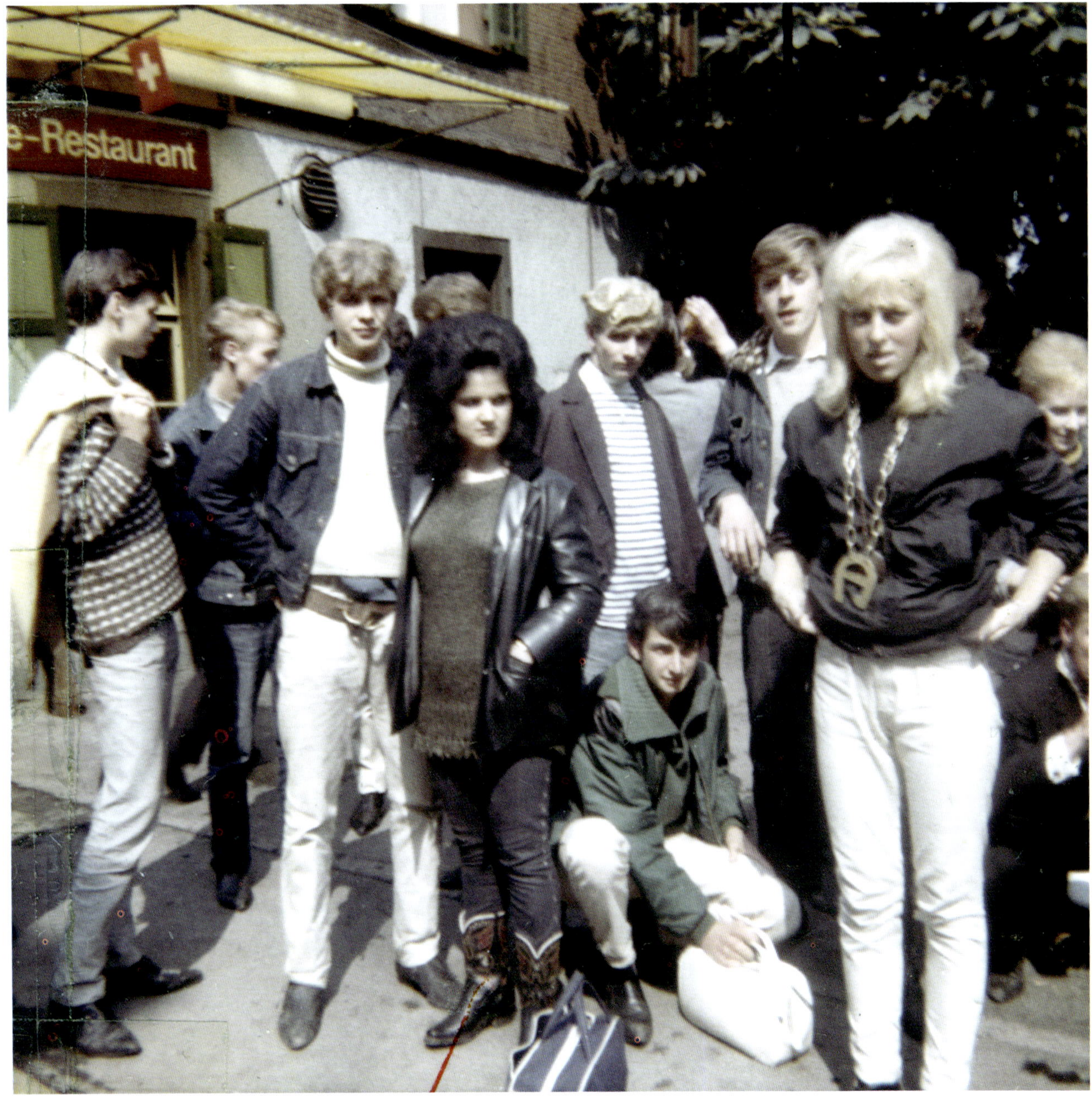

The Halbstarke in front of Restaurant Rauberhohle ("den of thieves"). Jamaica from Hollard at right, Urs Antener, at center, the brother of Dynamites and The Sauterelles lead guitarist Rolf Antener.

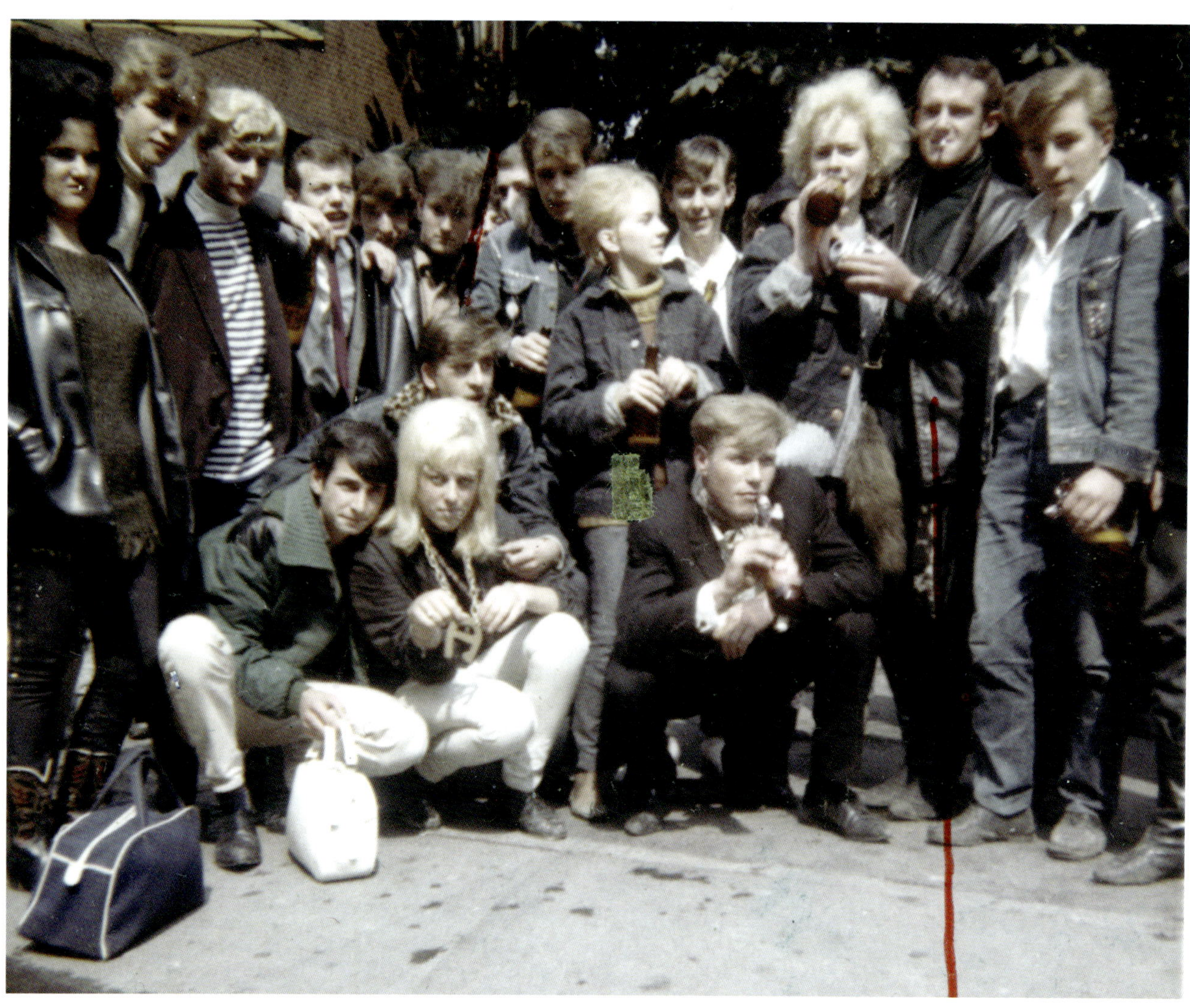

Jamaica and friends. Ex-gang boss Cliff ZH (Cliff from Zurich) is second from right.

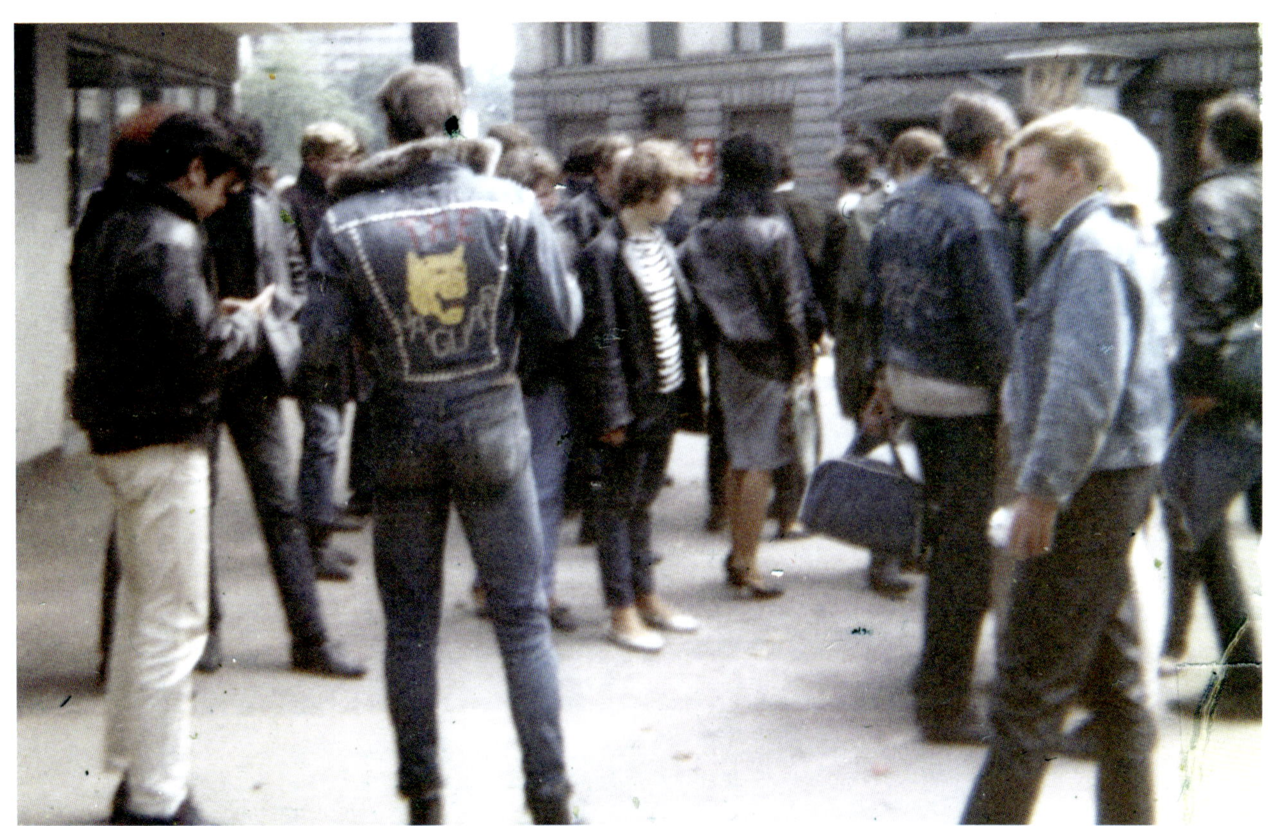

The Jaguars from Zug.

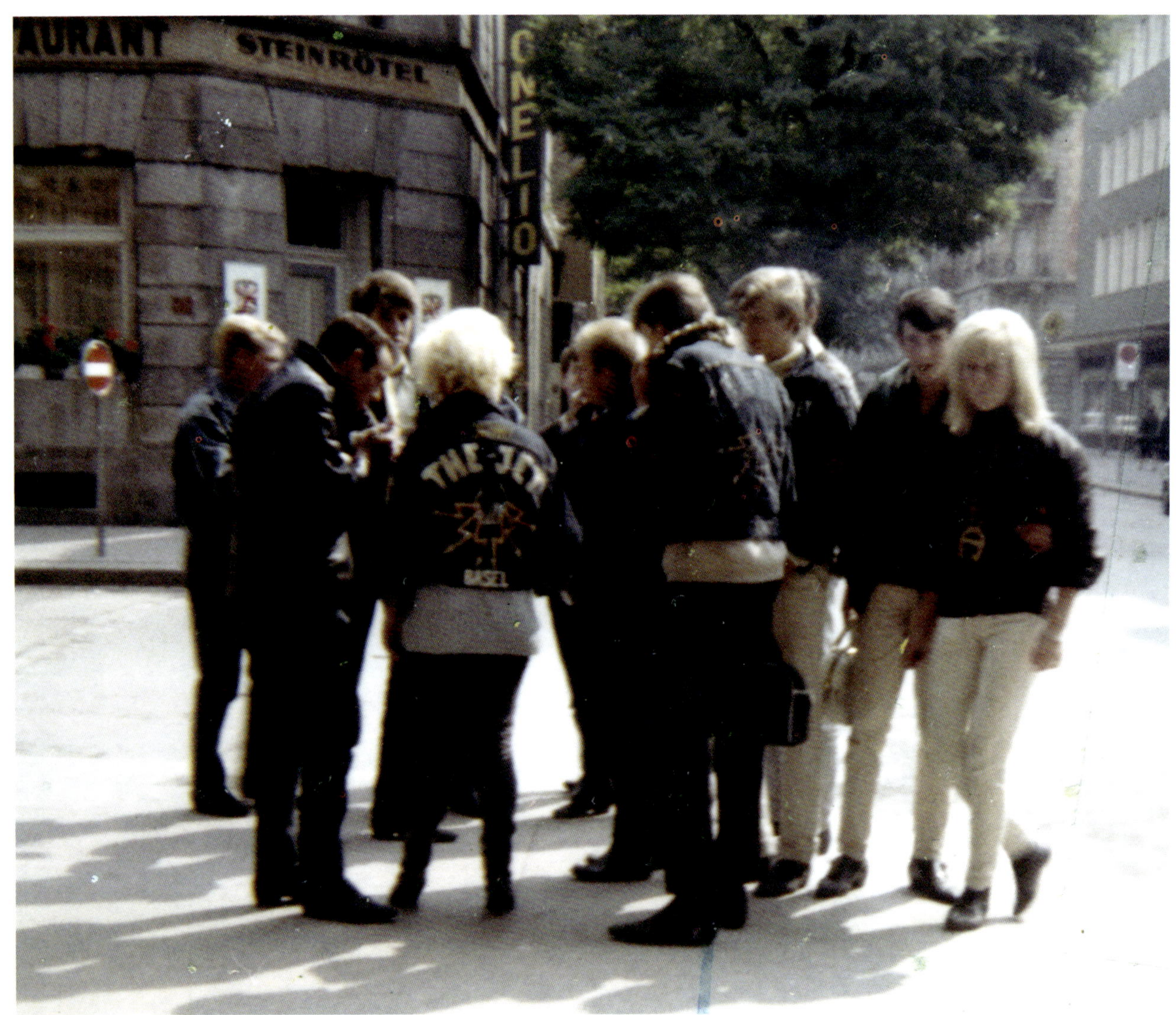

Blondes Jenny (from The Jets) and Jamaica, with Cliff ZH (left), Igel (center) and Urs Antener.

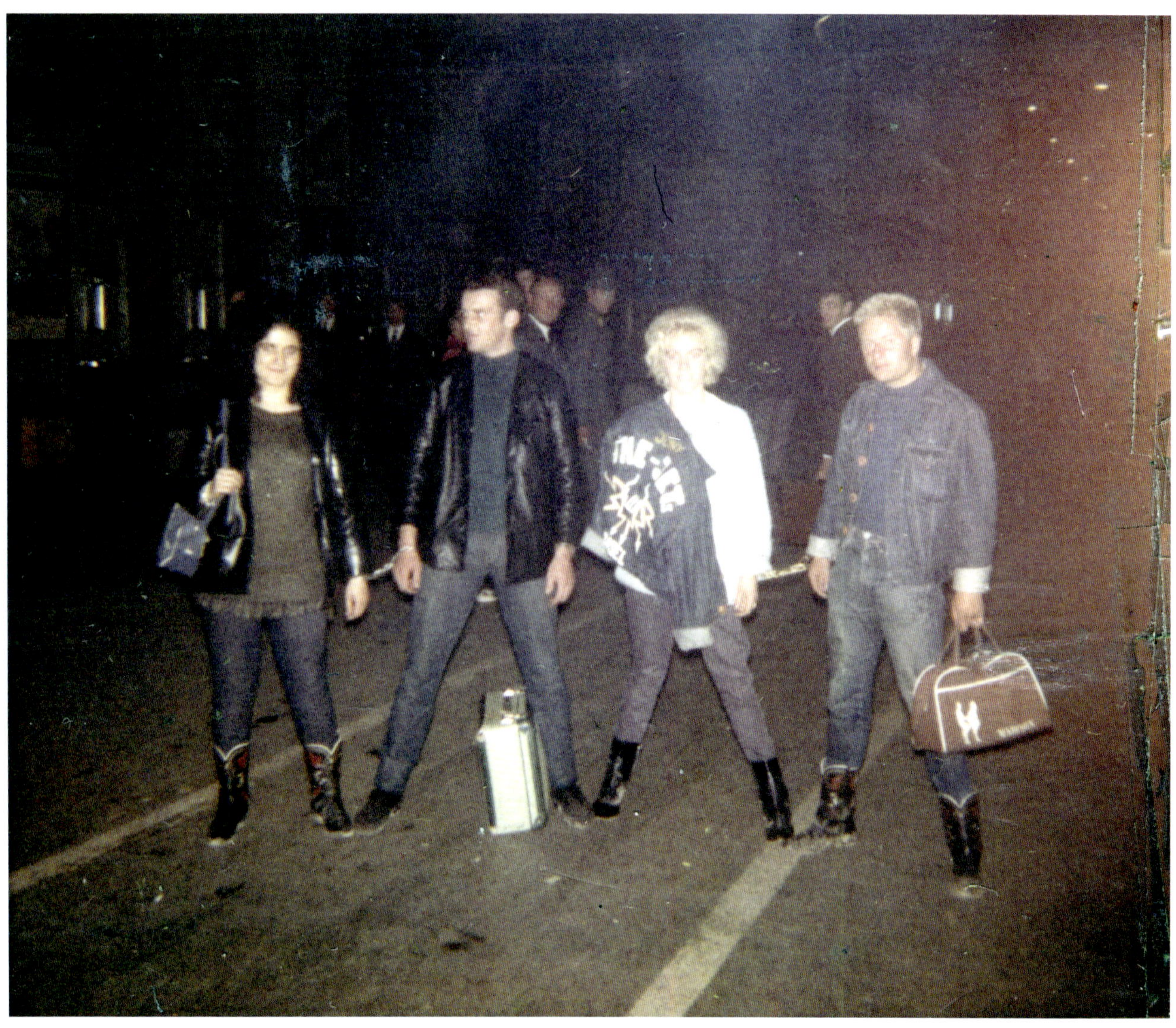

Jenny poses proudly with her Jets jacket. She was one of the girls who were fully integrated into the gang. From left to right: Rumy, Cliff ZH, Jamaica and Igel.

21 / schachen, aarau
september 28–29, 1963

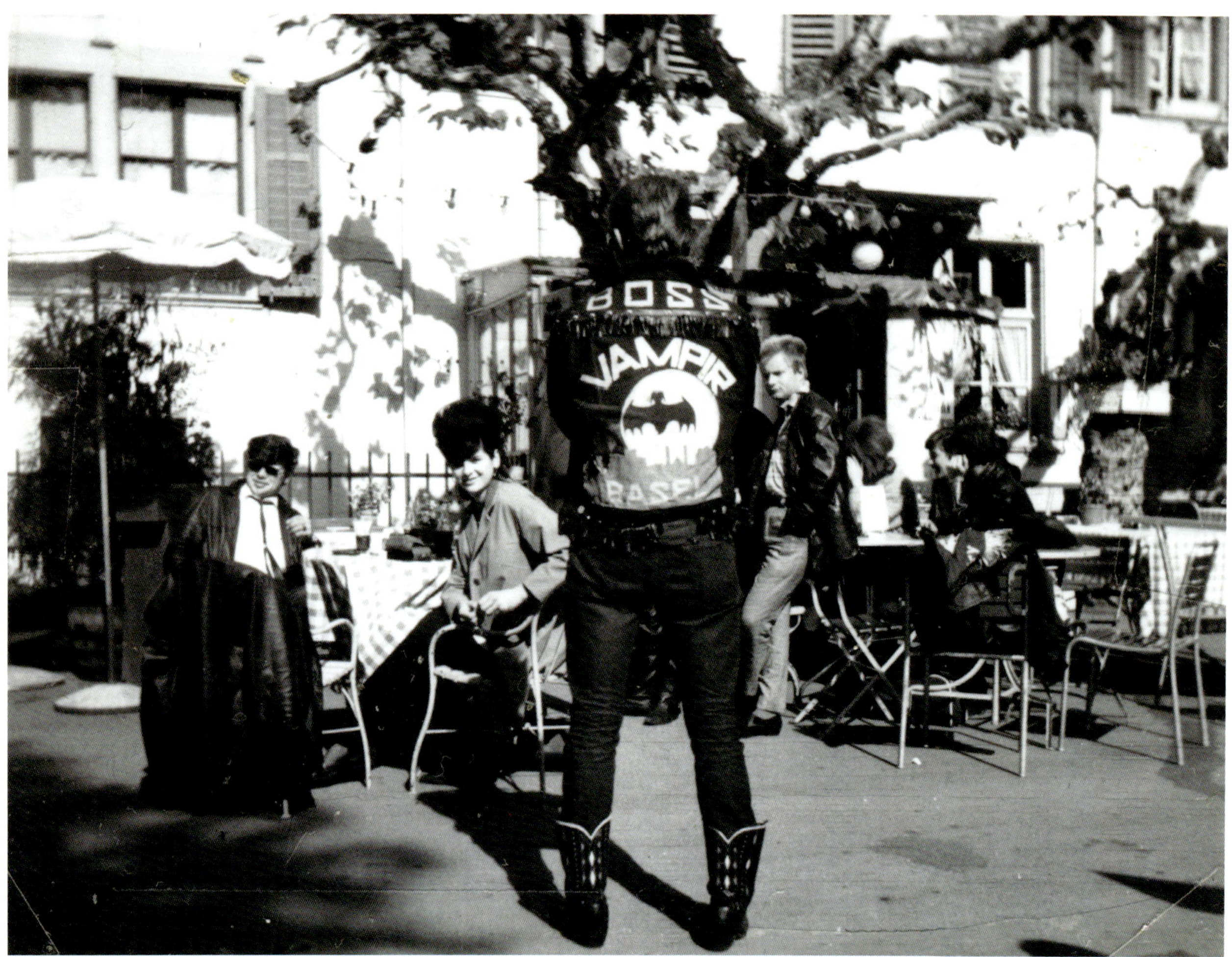

From left to right: Zack-Zack, Jenny, Boss Raymond, and Igel.

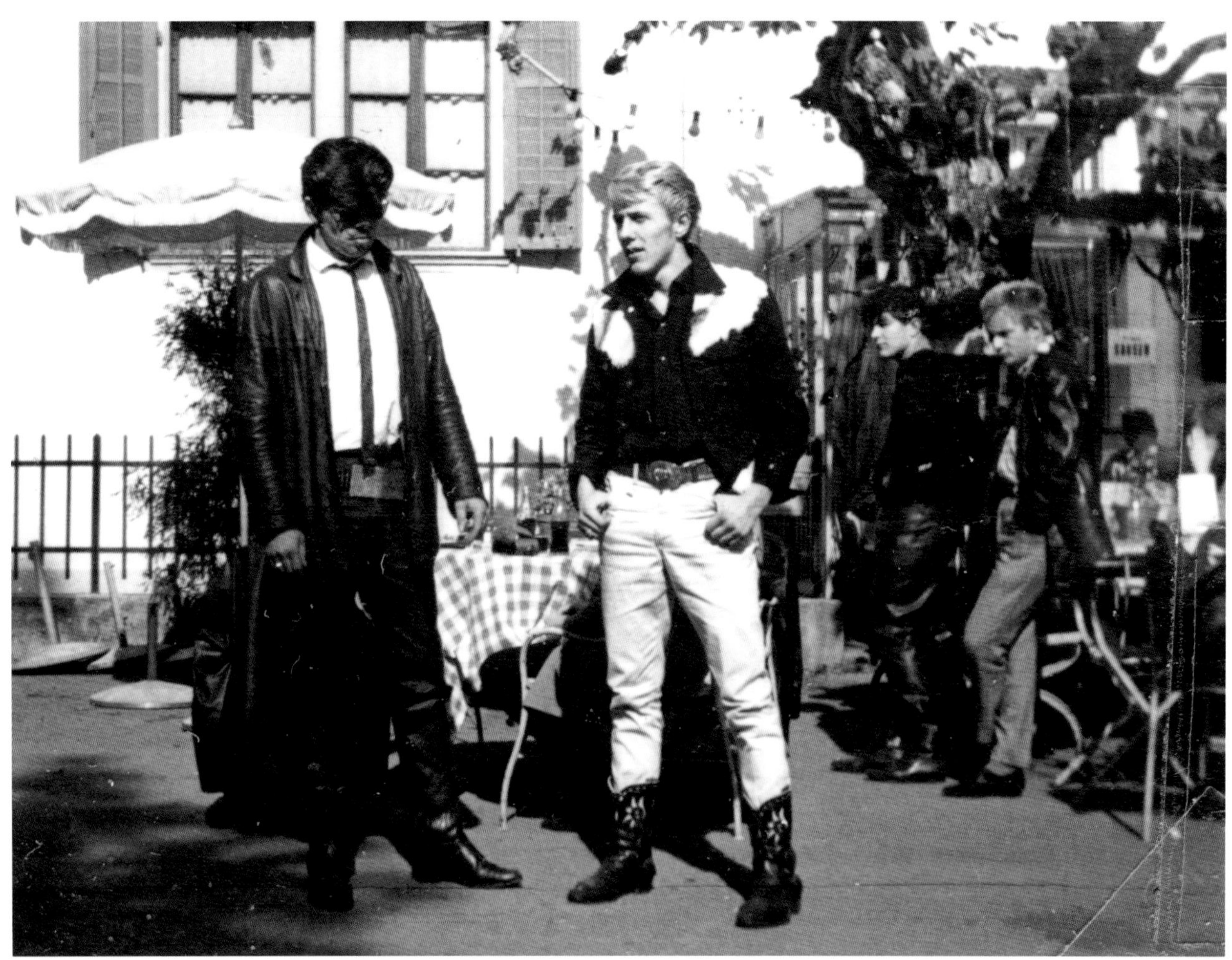

Zack-Zack and Kid.

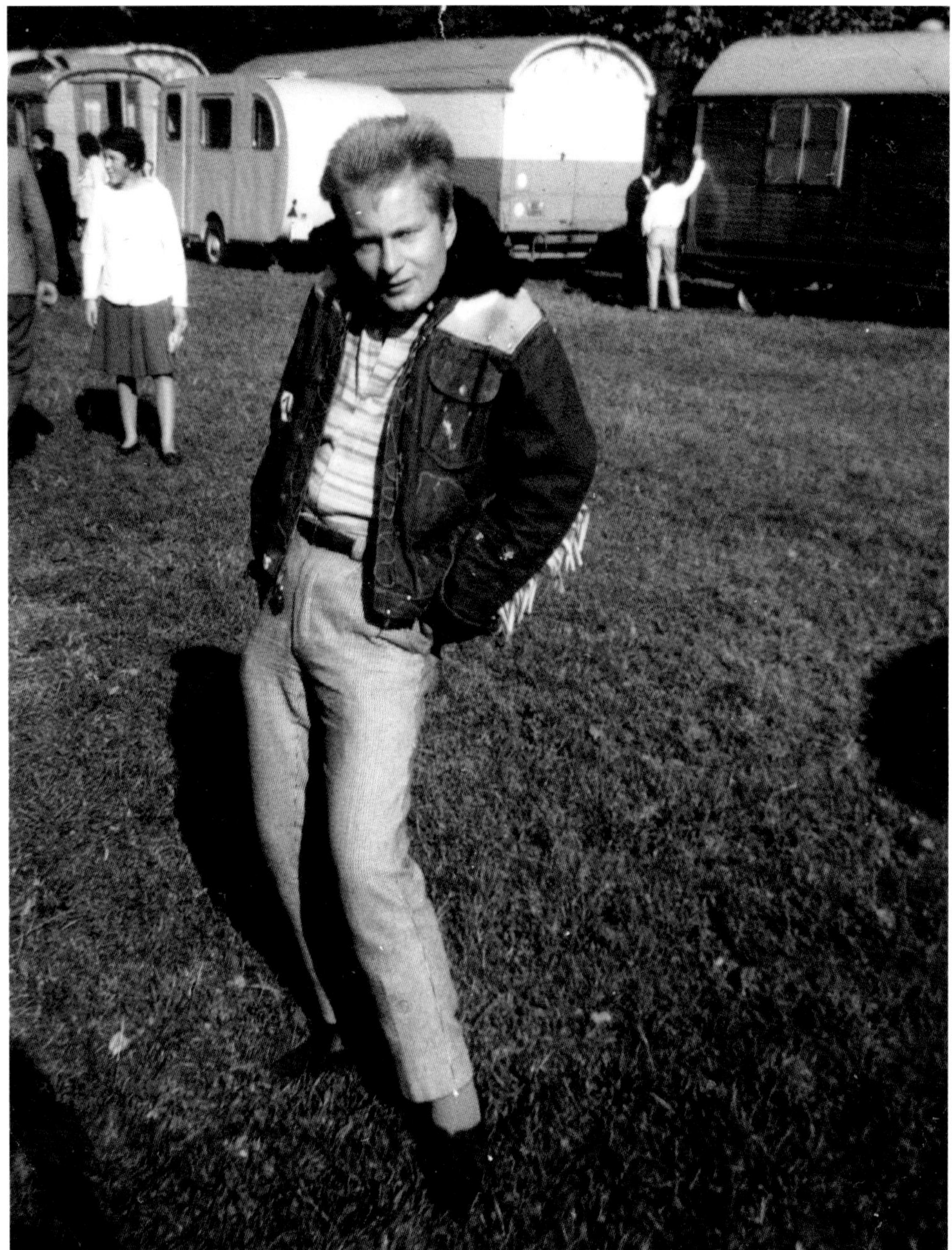

Igel.

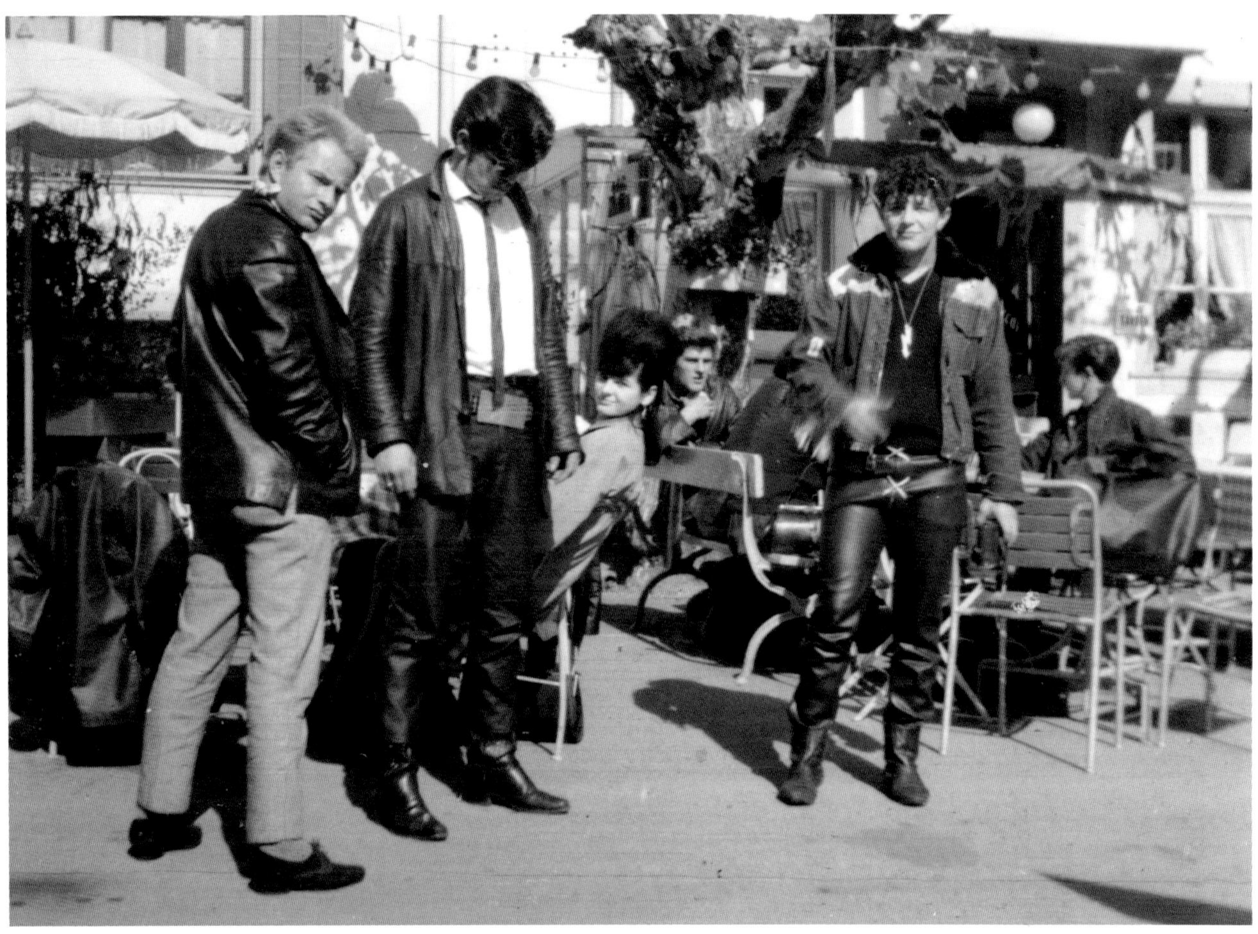

Igel, Zack-Zack and Jenny with Jacky, the boss from The Blizzards (with. lightning bolt around his neck).

22 / herbstmesse, basel
october 27–november 10, 1963

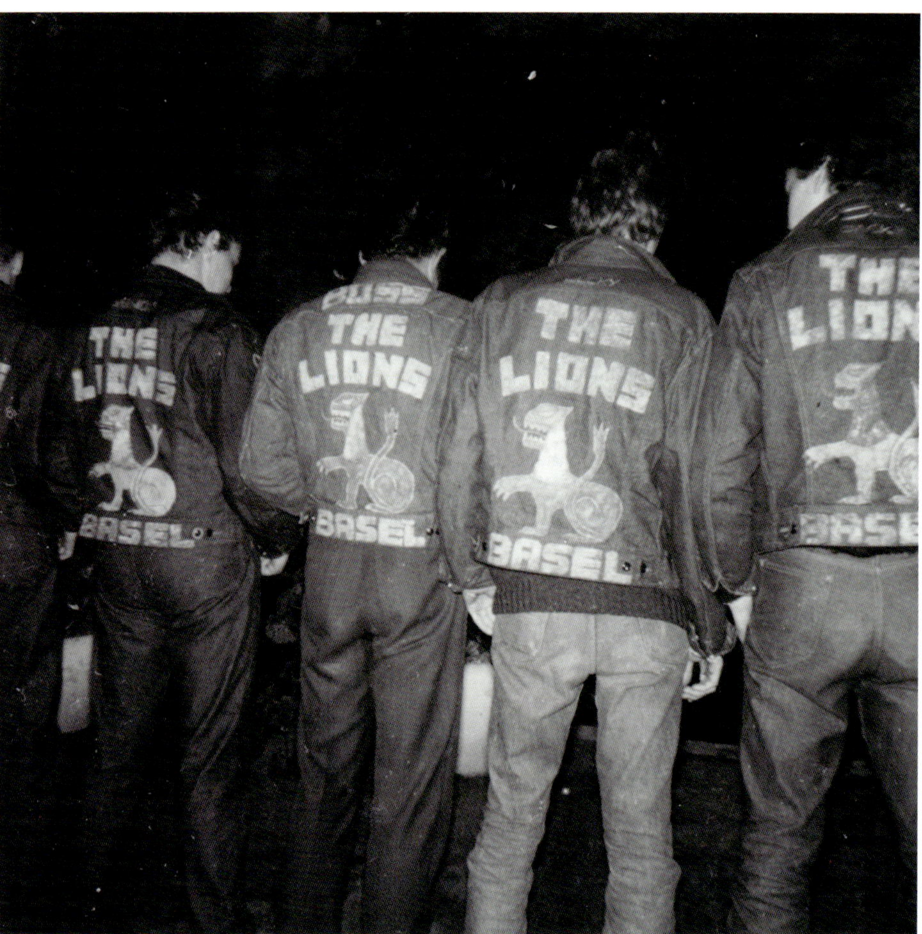

The Lions on Rosentalanlage near Mustermesse, Basel. The jackets were made by Sonny from Zurich who used to live in Basel.

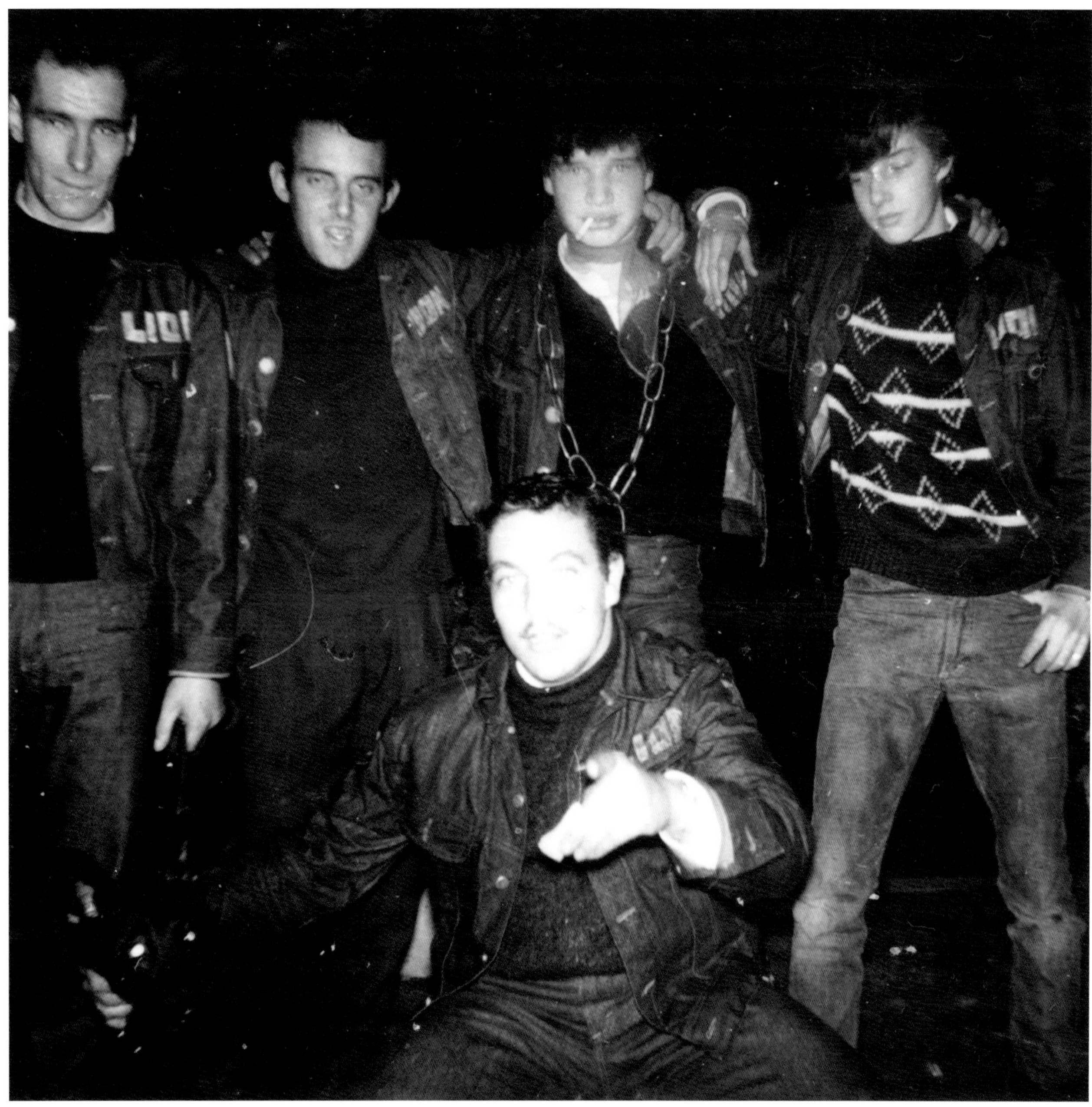

Basel gang The Lions on the road: all three bosses from The Lions—Zorro (second boss), Cliff ZH (The Lions' first boss), Conny Thudium, Jack. Front: Sumo,(third and last boss from the lions).

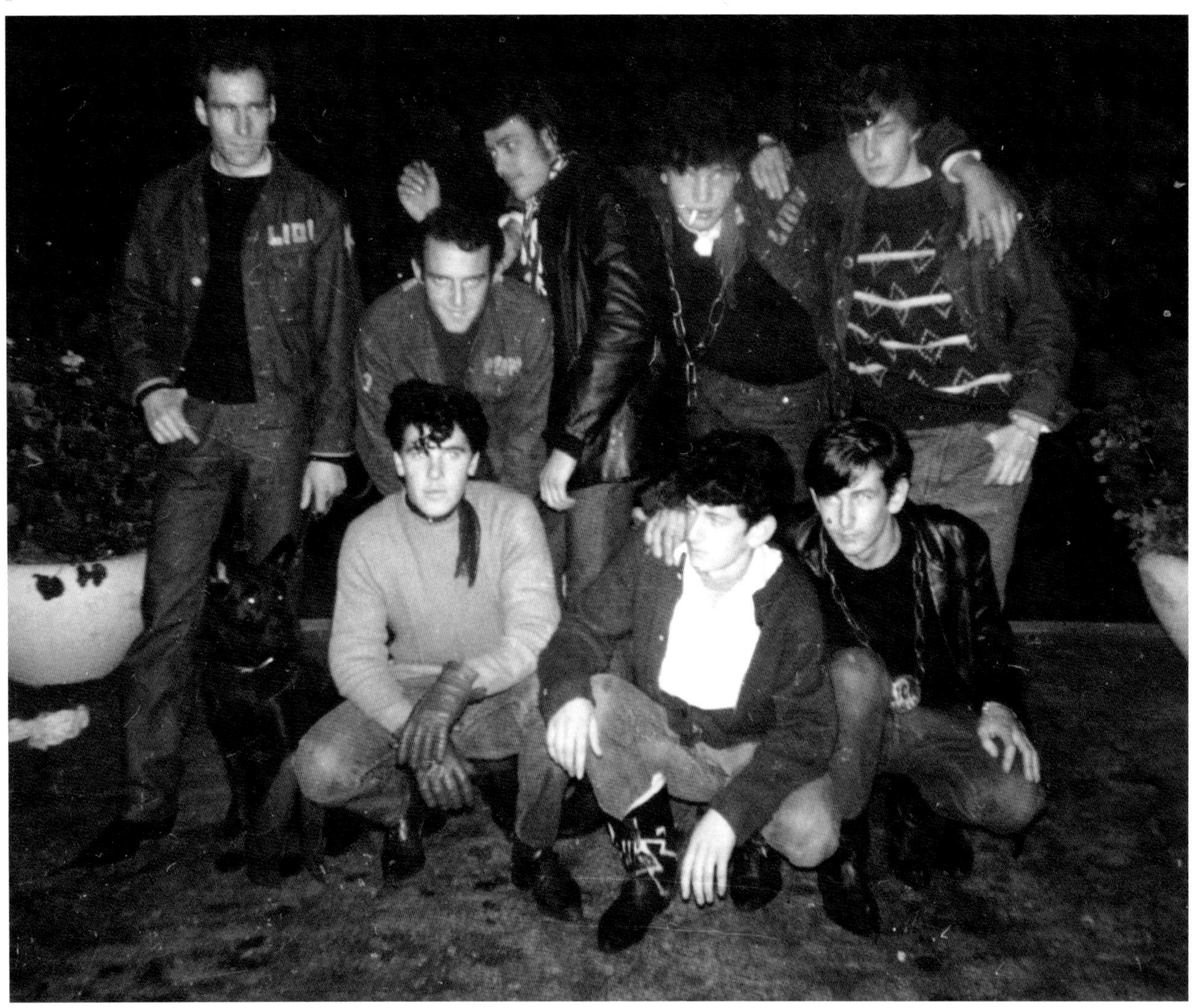

In formation.

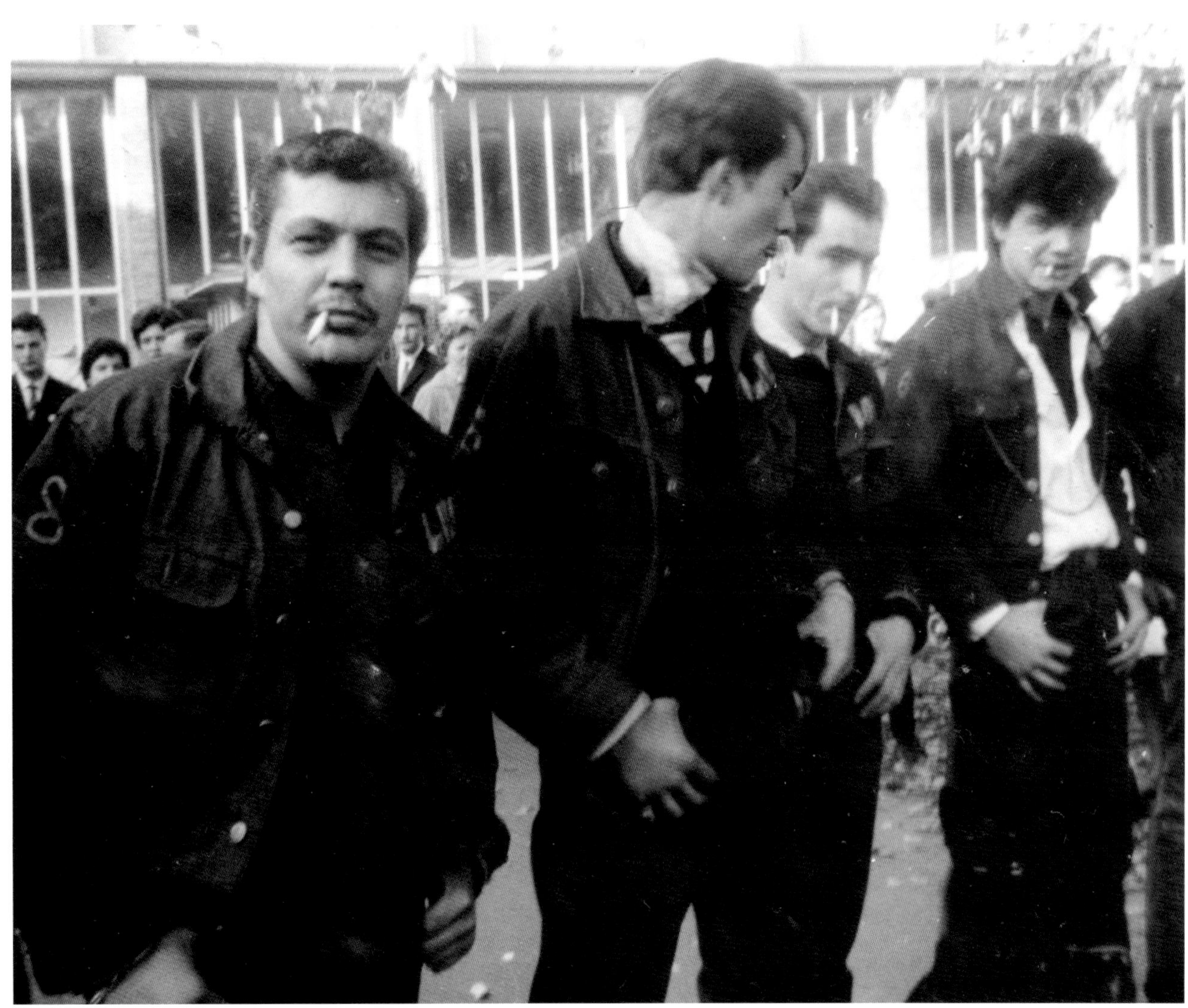

Blue denim Lions in Basel.

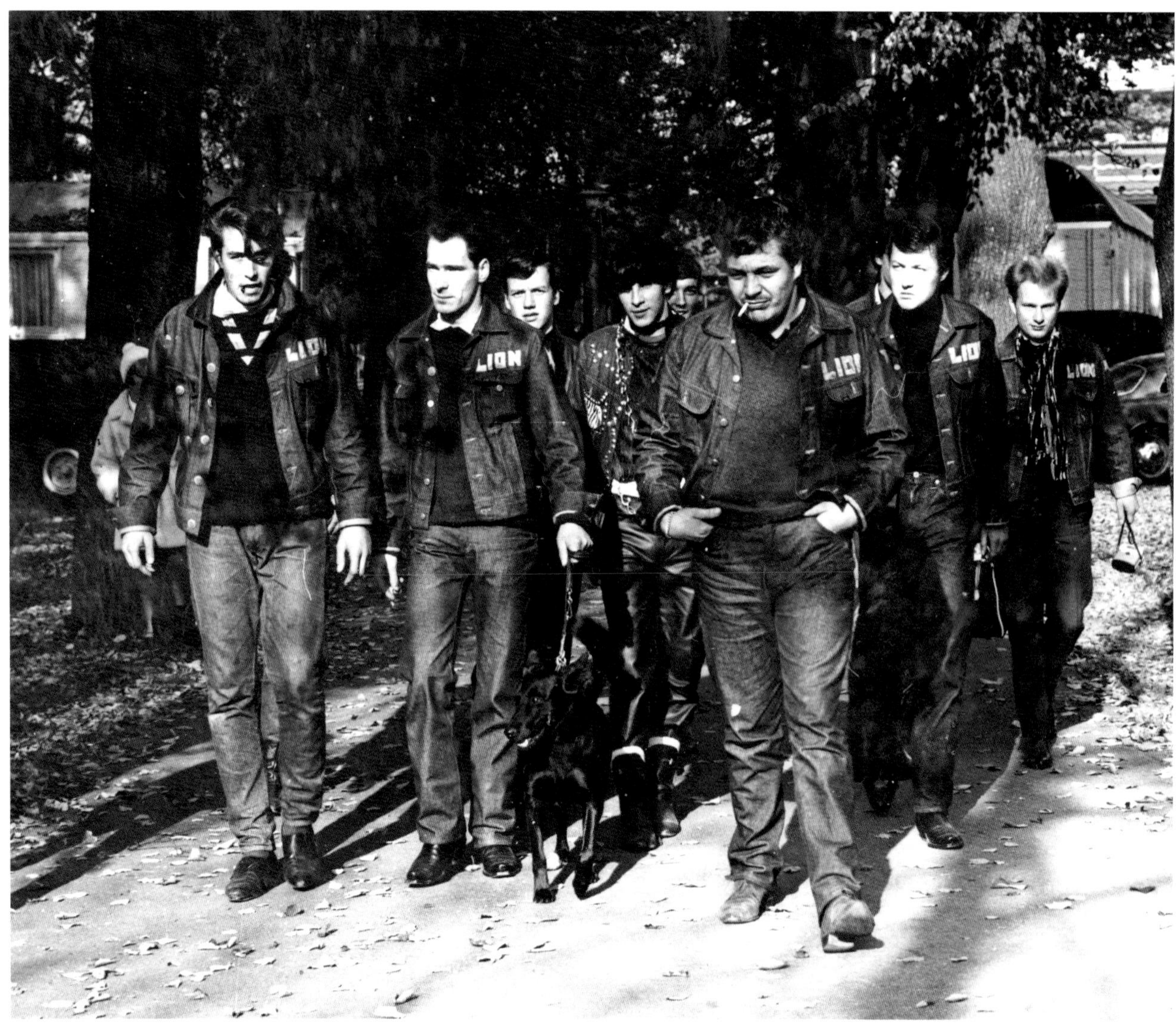

The gang comes to town. Zorro with his dog; Sumo with his cigarette.

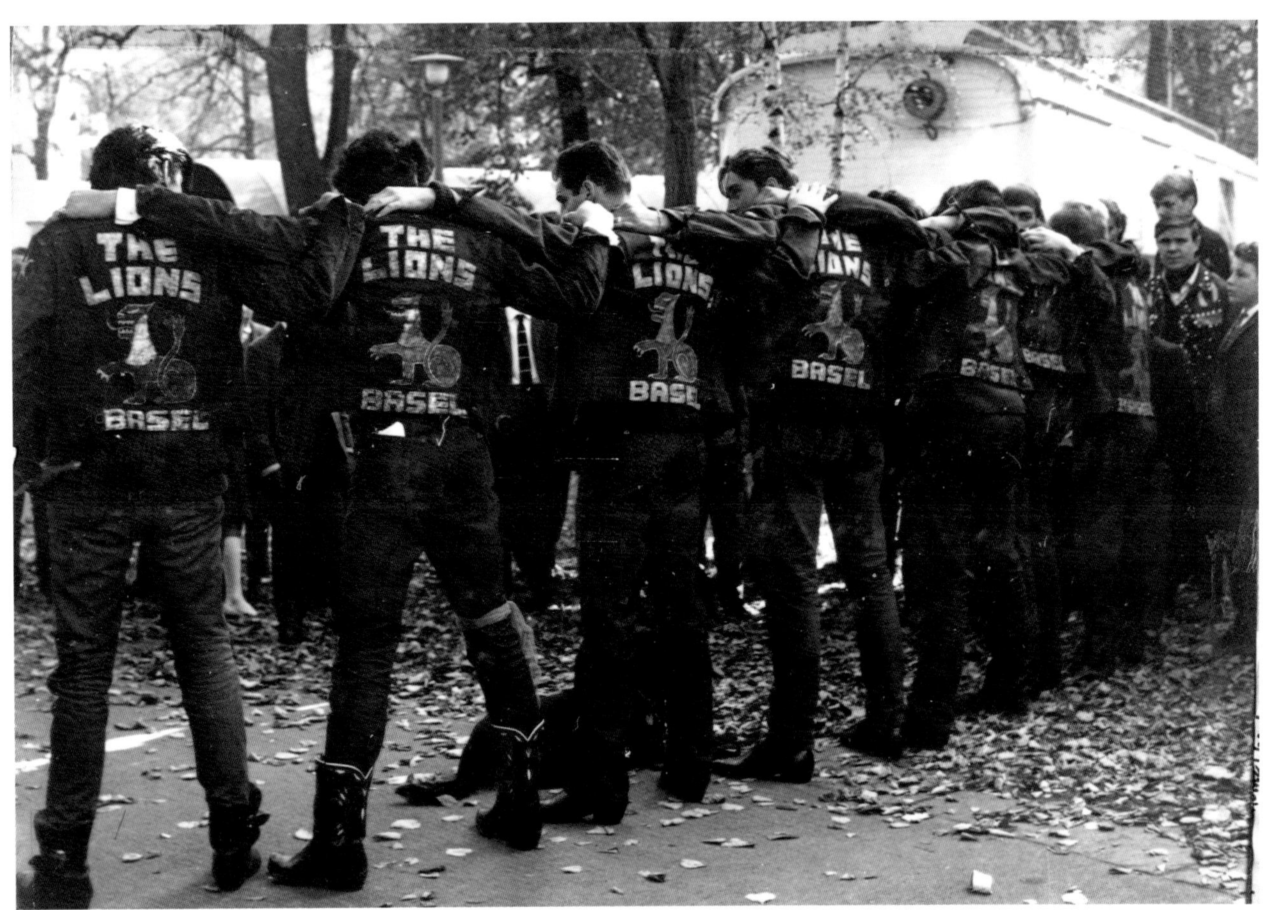

Brute force.

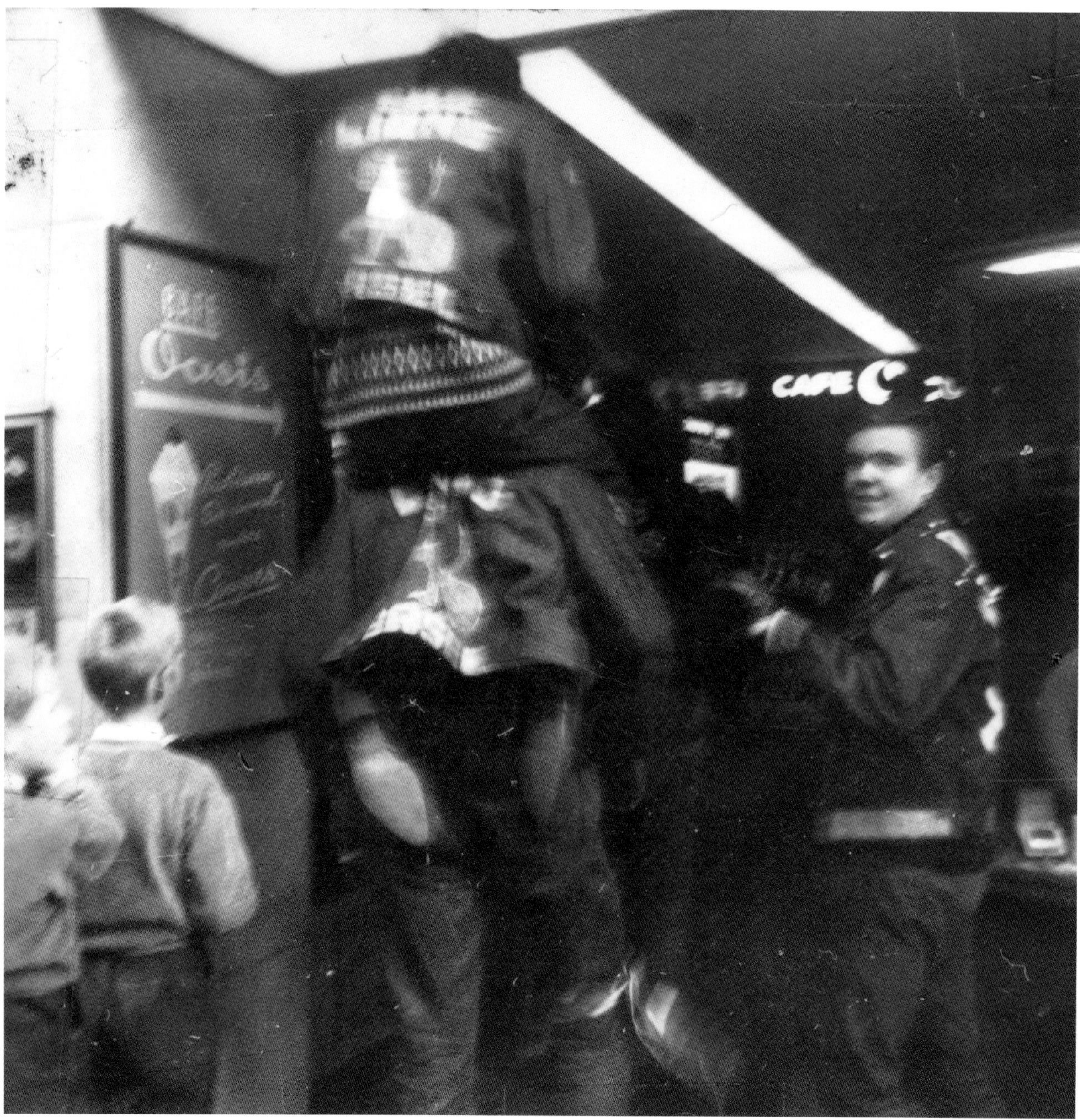

Cafe Oasis, Greifengasse, Basel.

23 / express-bar, rheingasse, basel

november 1963

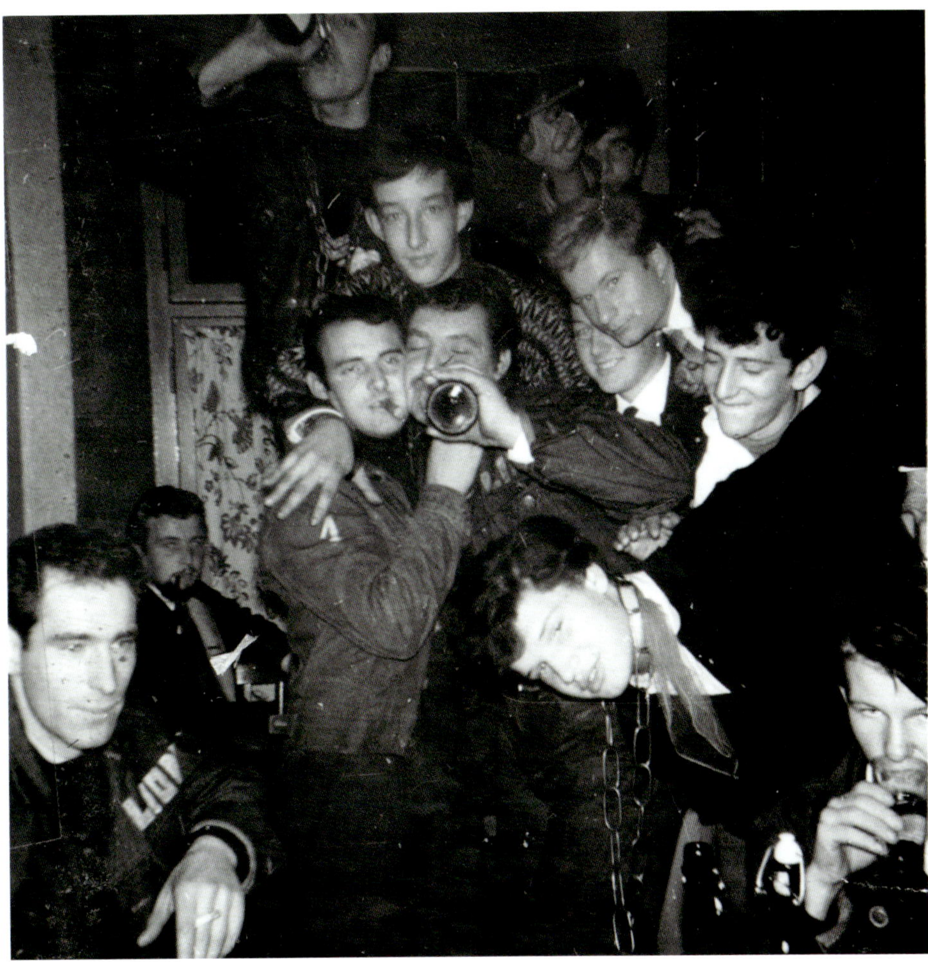

Express Bar was the big hotspot for Halbstarke. Zorro (far left), Cliff ZH (number 1 on his arm) with Sumo (drinking), Romeo from Zurich (top), Sonny (smiling), Igel and Conny Thudium with his big chain.

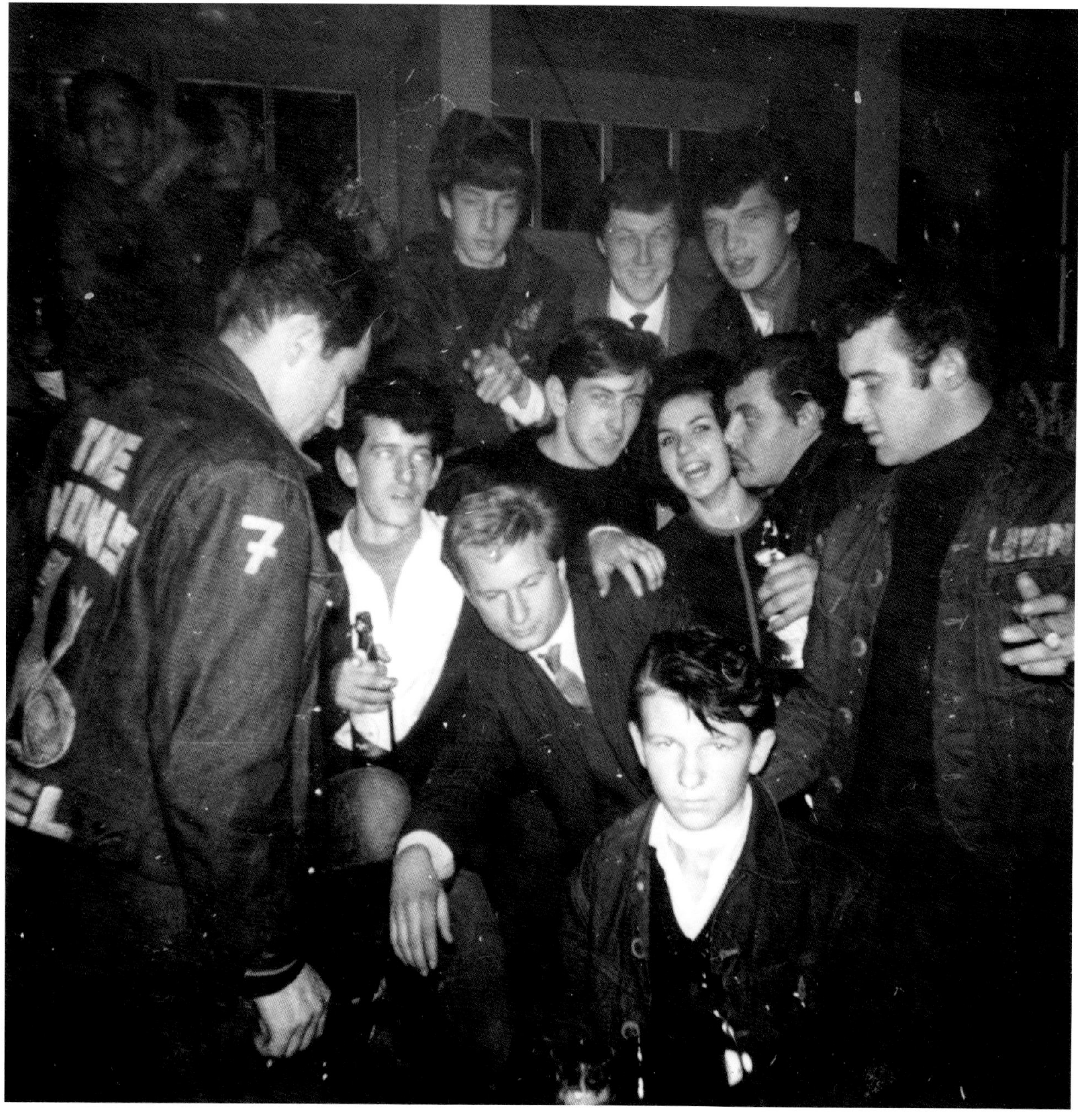

Barmaid Brigitta and Sumo, surrounded by various Halbstarke from Basel.

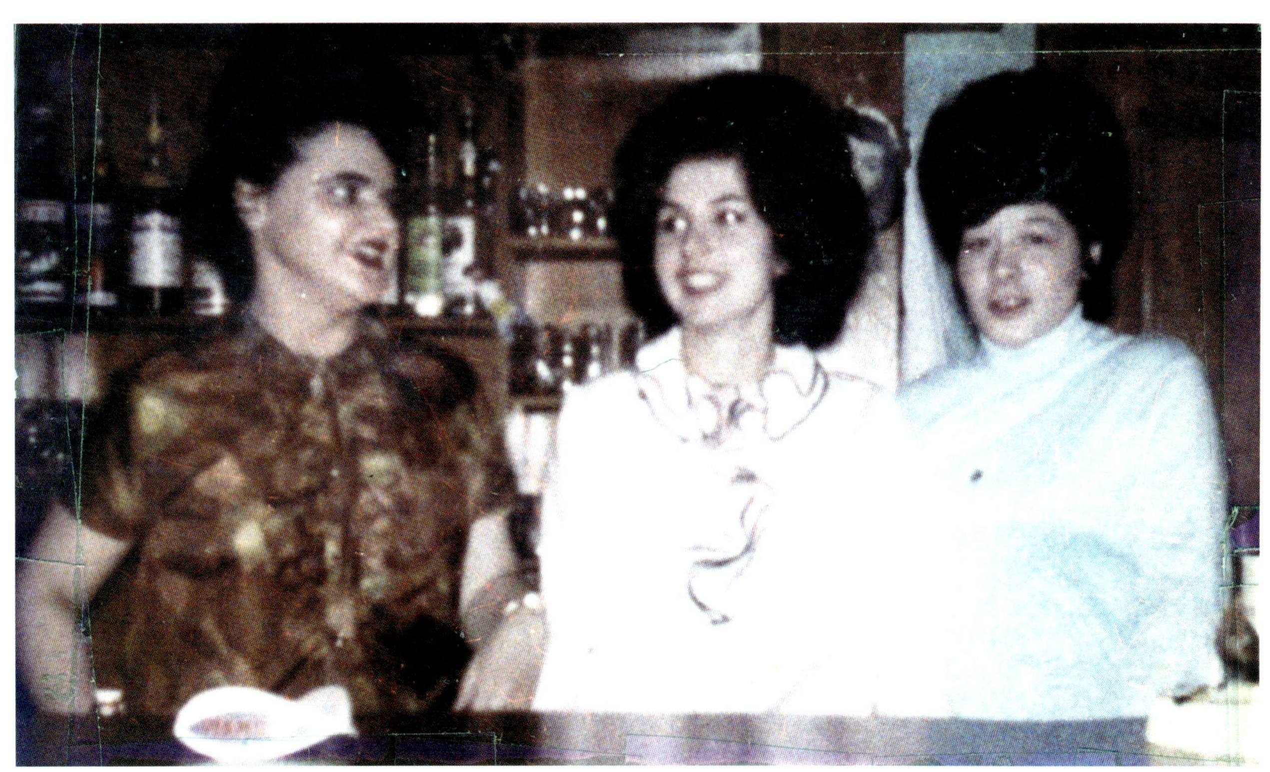

Express Bar barmaid Brigitta with guests Vreni Sonderegger (left) and Vreni Stebler from Riehen (right).

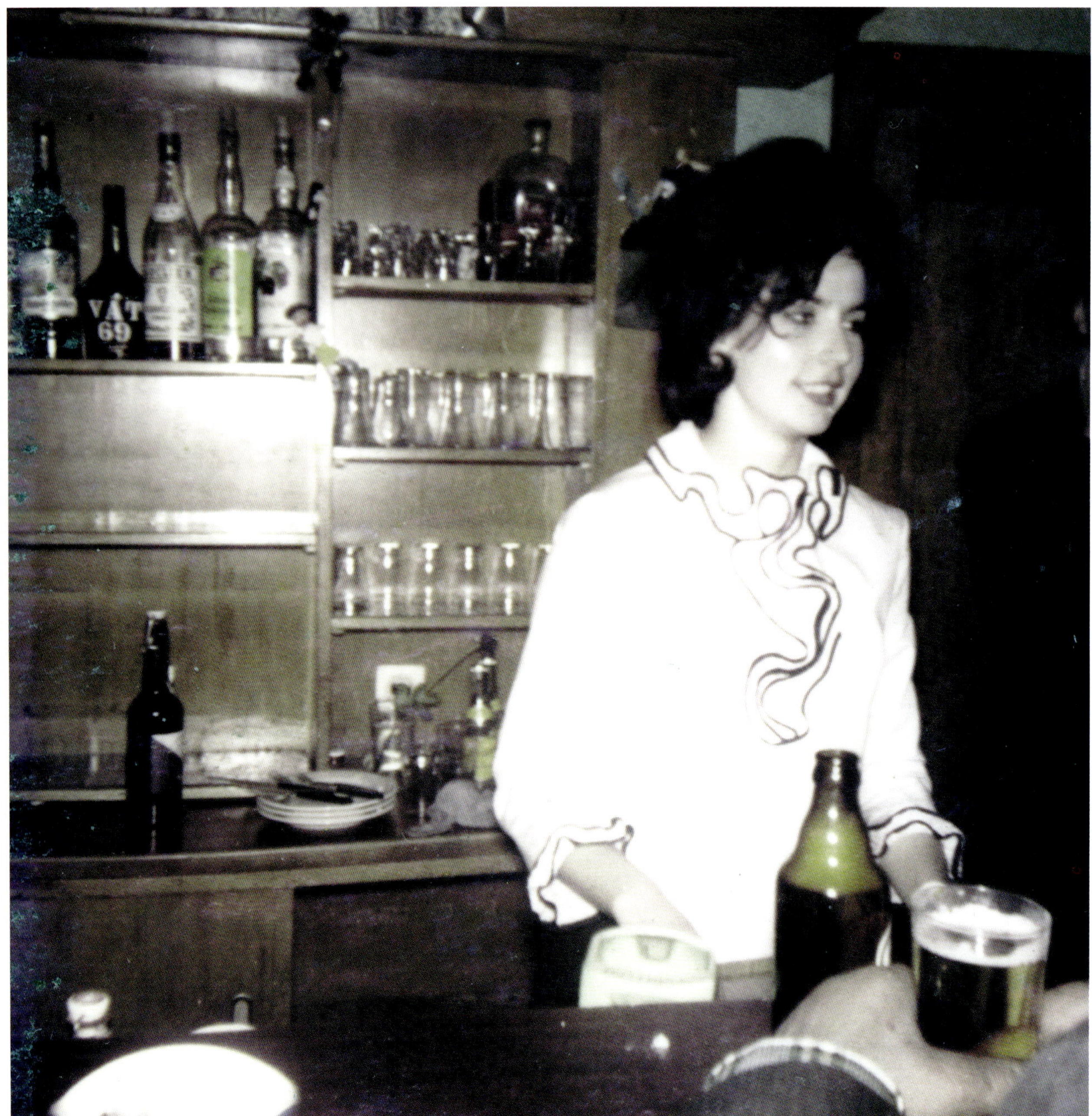

At the bar with charming Brigitta.

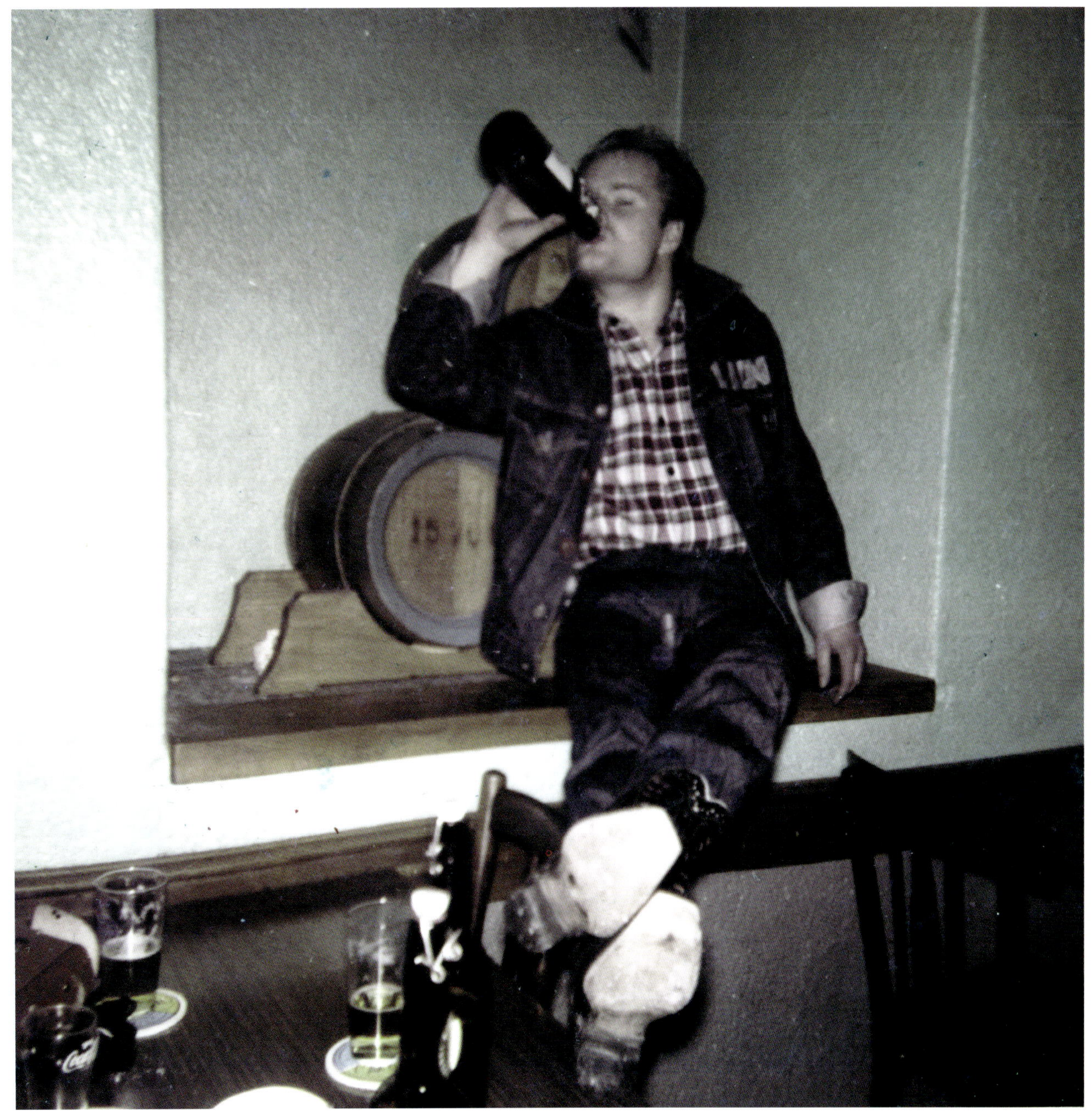

After a long, long, night, Igel takes one last guzzle.

24 / uetliberg, zürich
december 1963

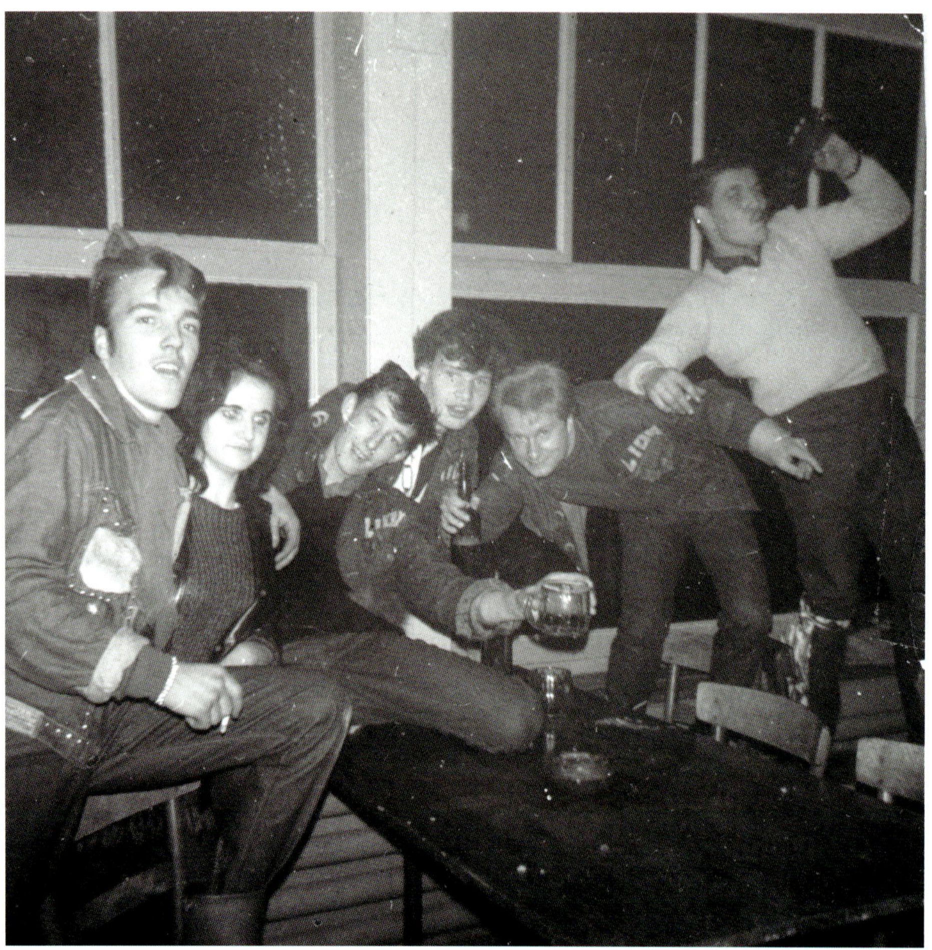

Uetliberg, Zurich: Rumy with Priska, unknown Lion, with Conny Thudium, Igel, and Hans Breitenstein aka Sumo.

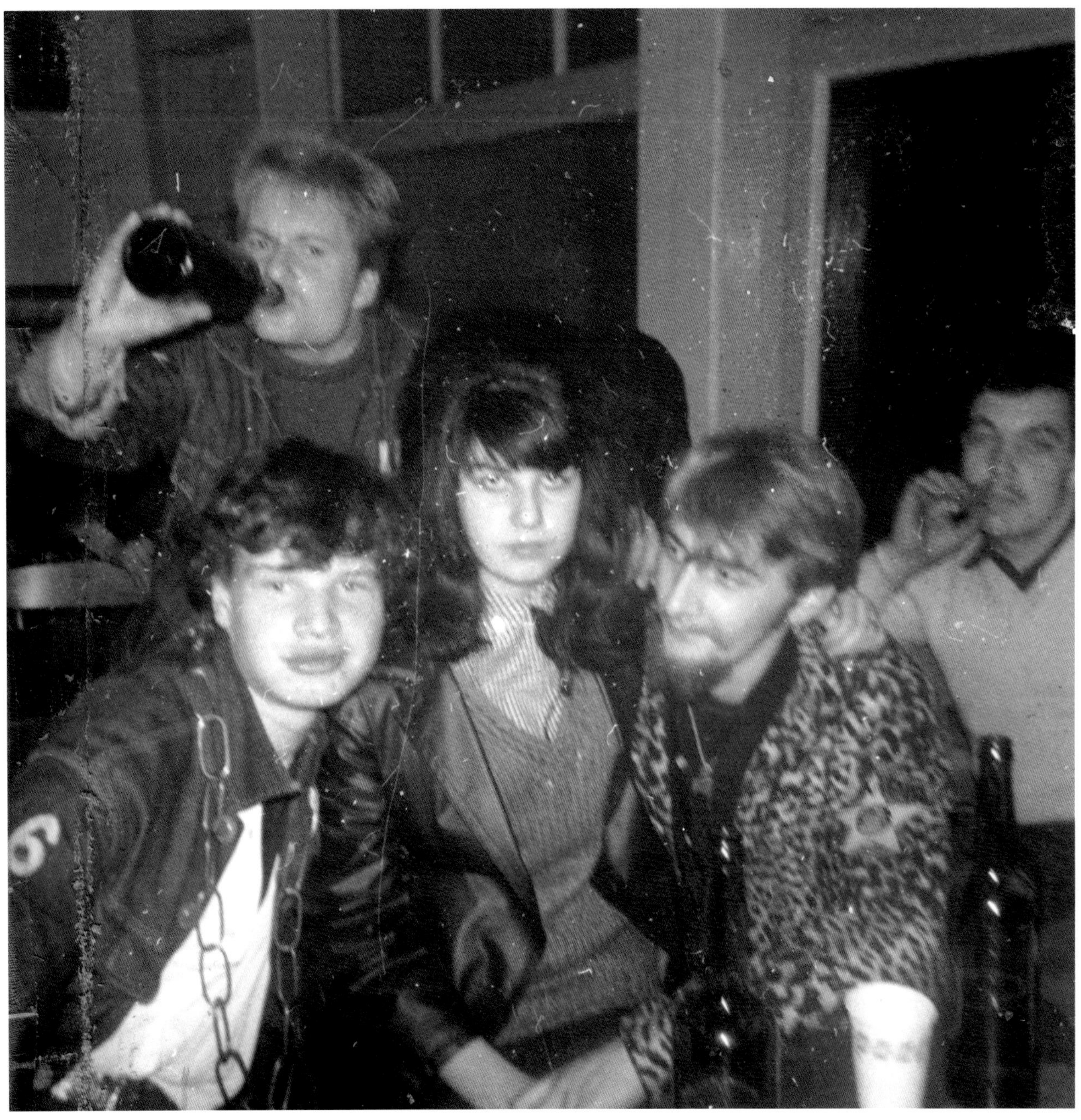

Silvia Nebel with gang boys Conny Thudium, Igel, Raymond, and Sumo.

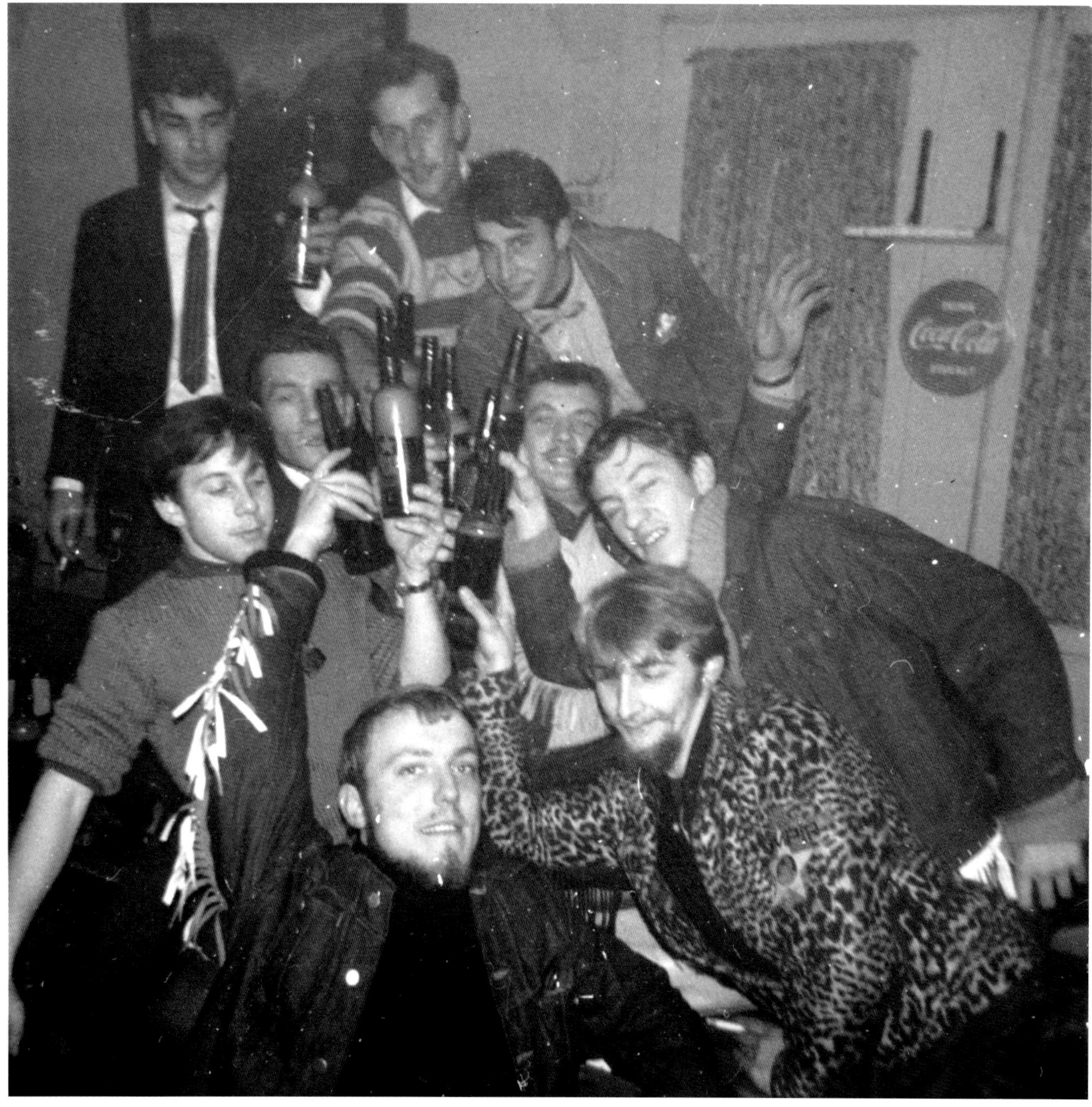

Proscht! Pictured upfront is Romeo (boss of the Revenger Gang, Zurich), along with Ray Christen (boss of the Vampir Basel) wearing a leopard jacket.

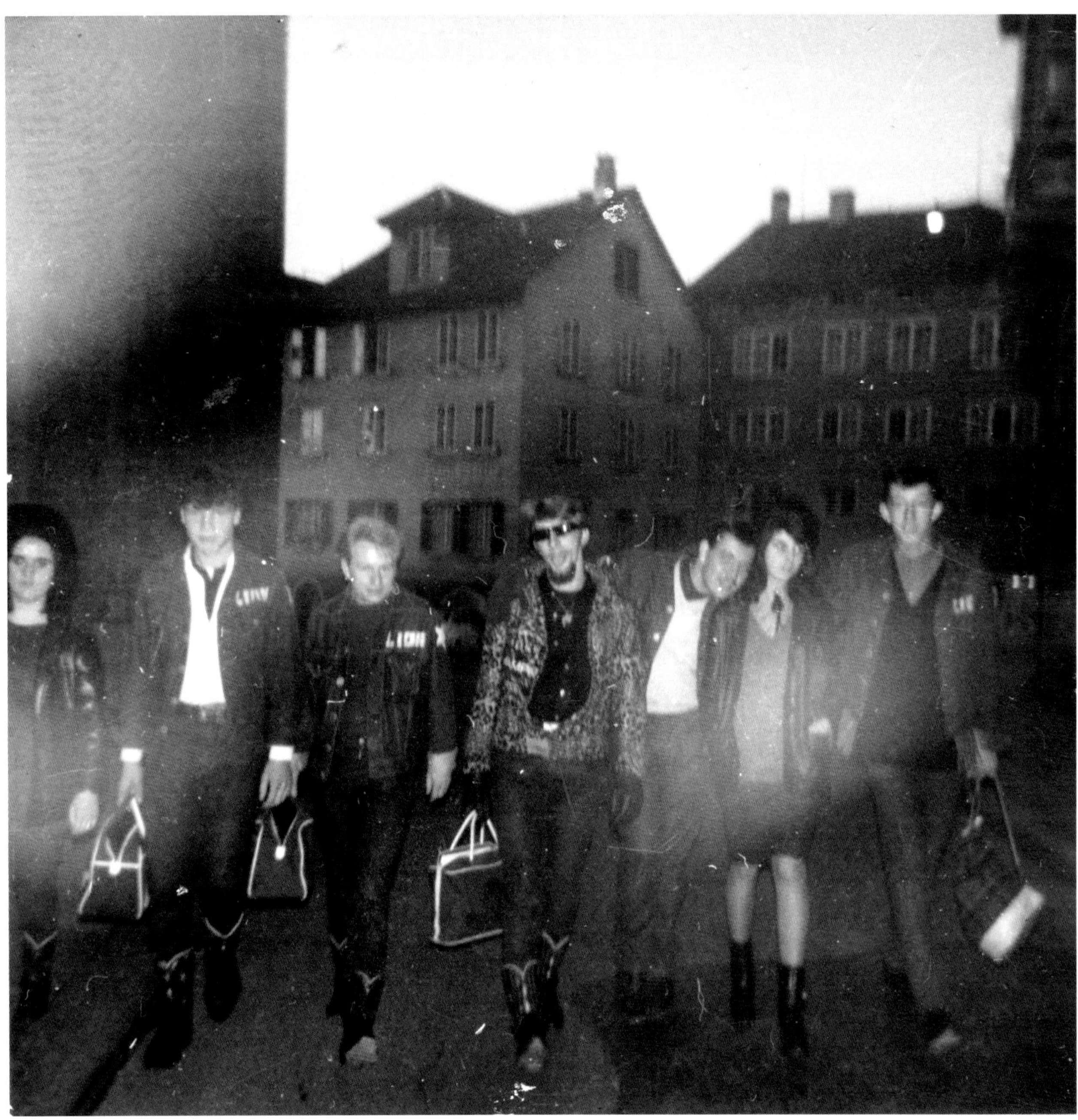

Igel and the Lions head for the next bar.

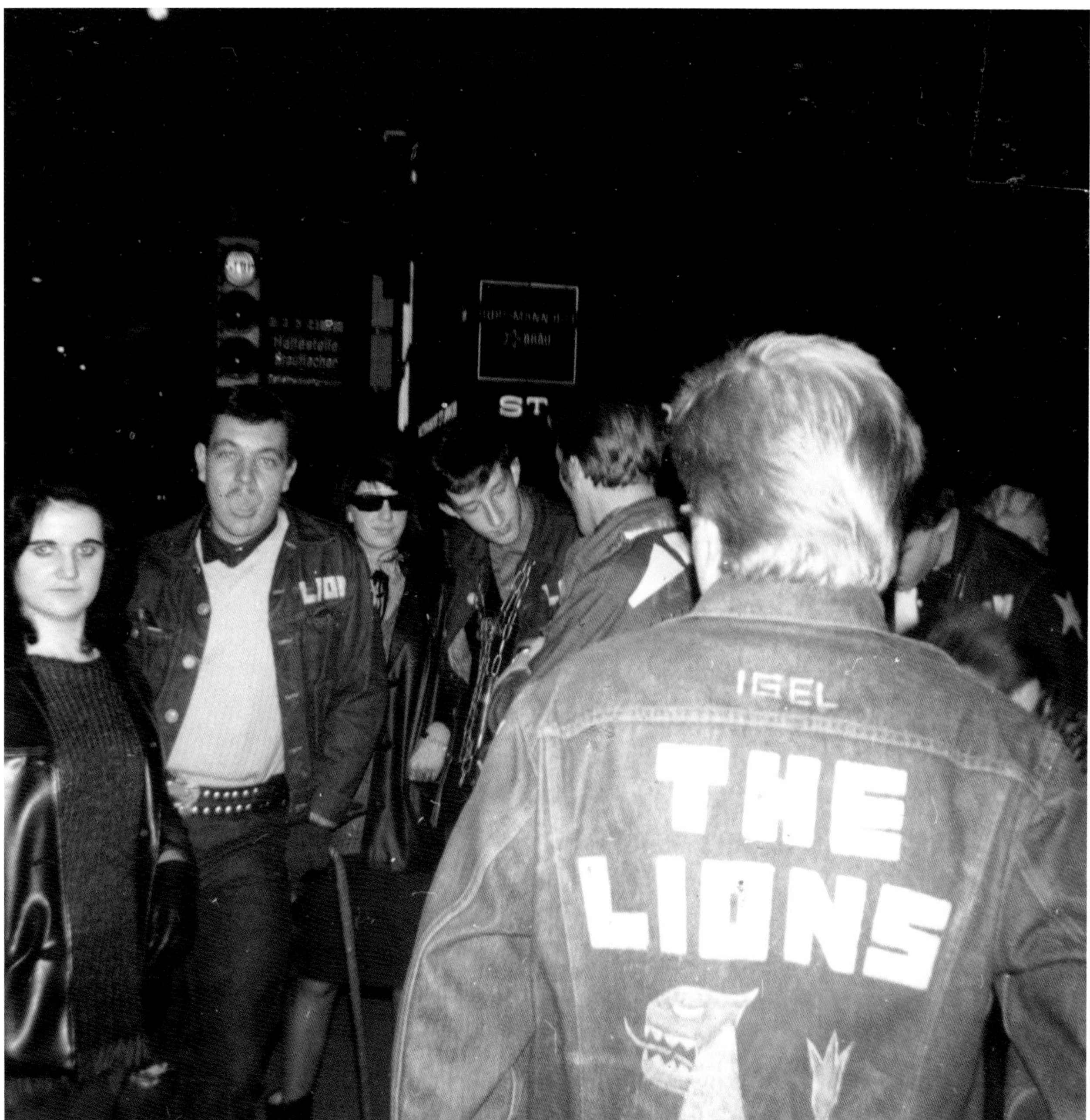

Igel with his new Lions jacket.

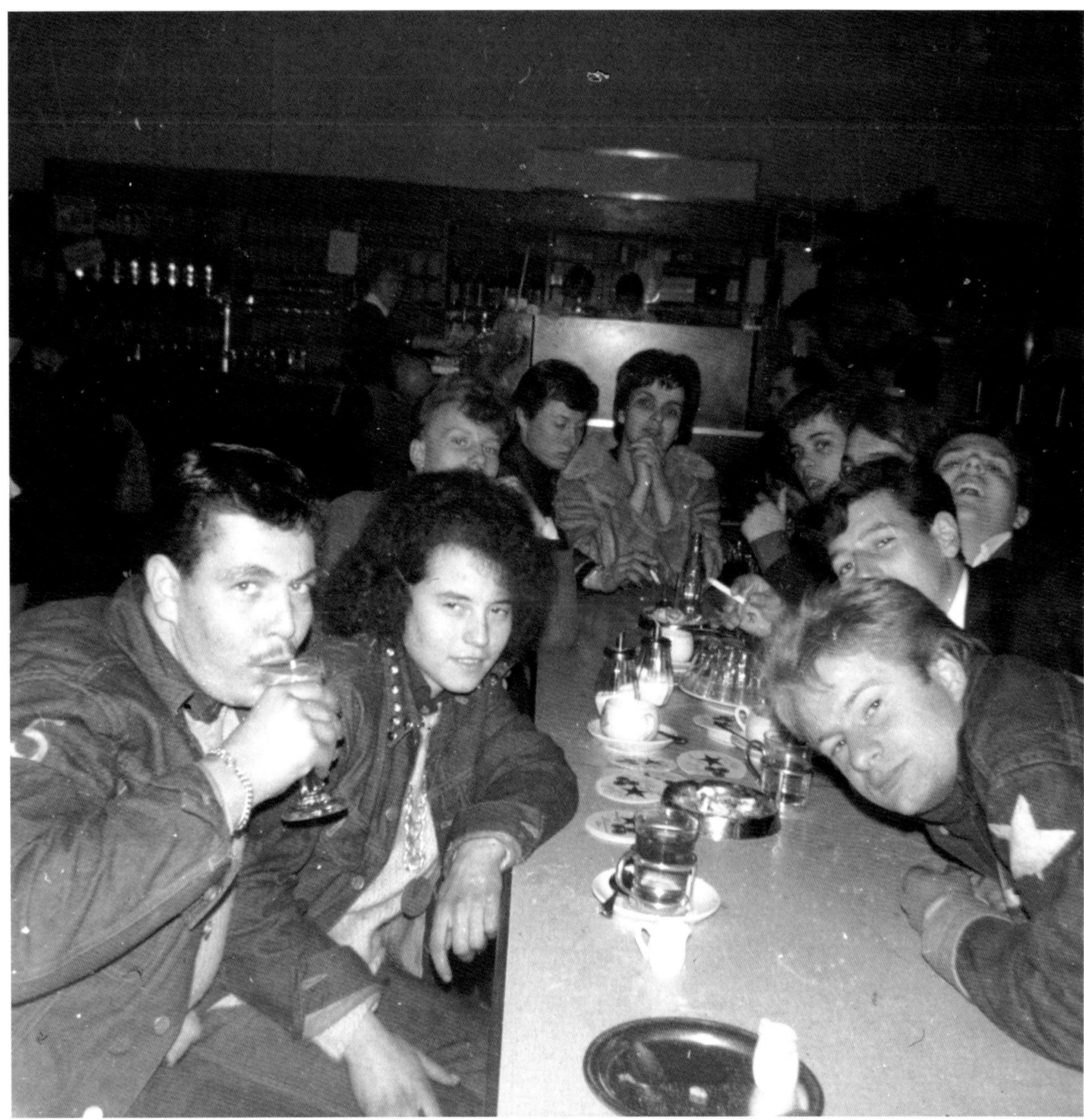

Sumo and Igel having one last drink in the crowded Bahnhofbuffet at the central train station, Zurich.

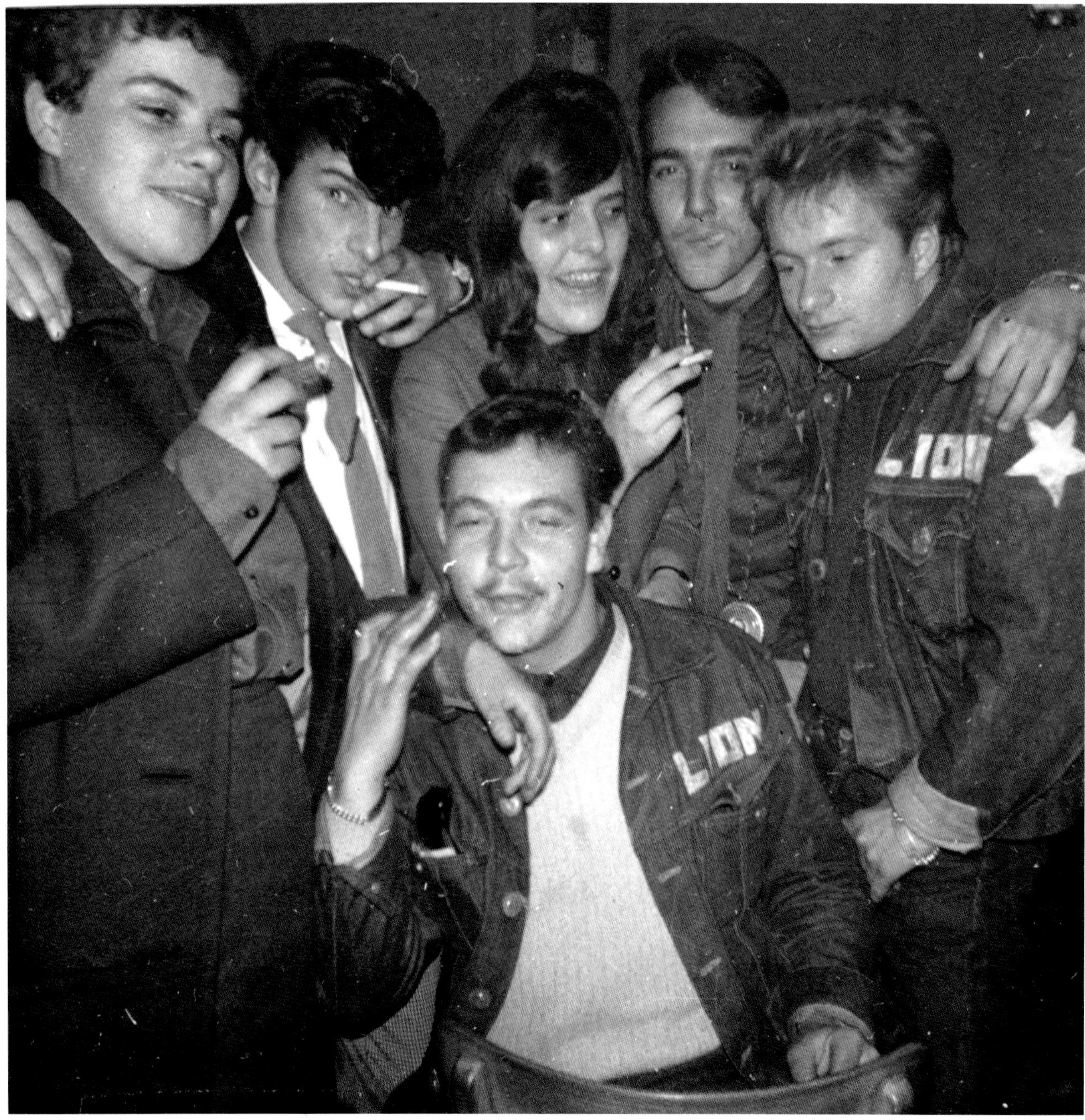

Lions with friends in Basel. All photos featuring Igel were taken using Igel's camera.

1964

25 / new years eve in lucerne
december 31, 1963 – january 1, 1964

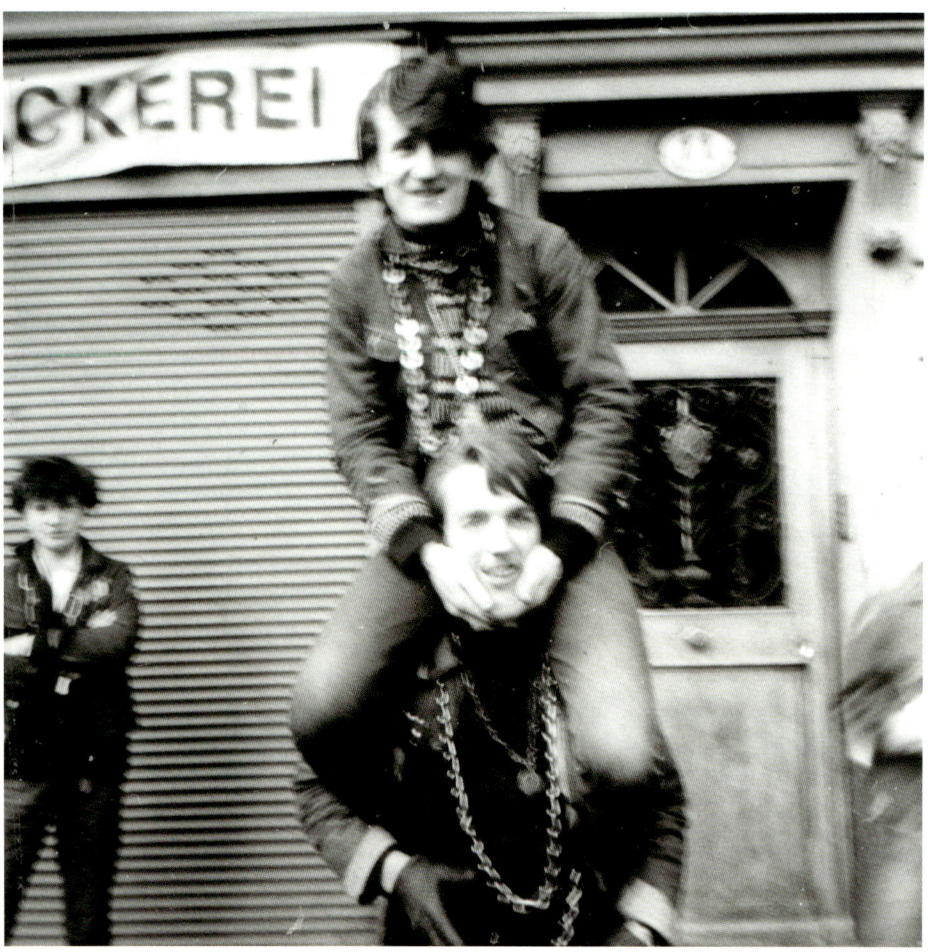

During their roadtrips to Lucerne and Zurich, the Halbstarke had good fun. Conny from The Lions (left), and Schlangepfiff on the shoulders of an unknown gang boy. The name Schlangepfiff in English means "whistle of a snake."

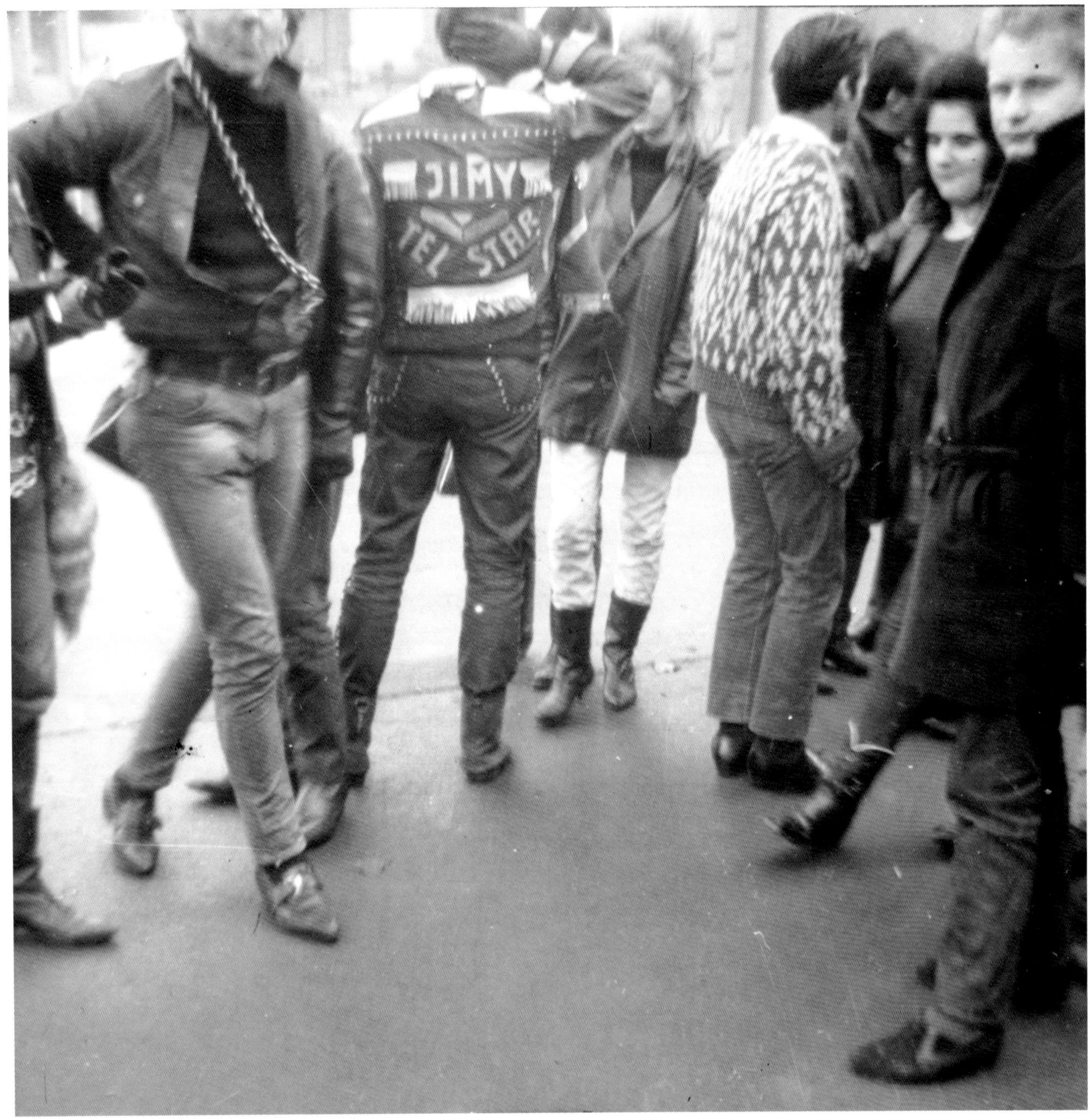

Jimy from the Tel Star gang joins the Basel bunch. At right we have Rumy and Igel.

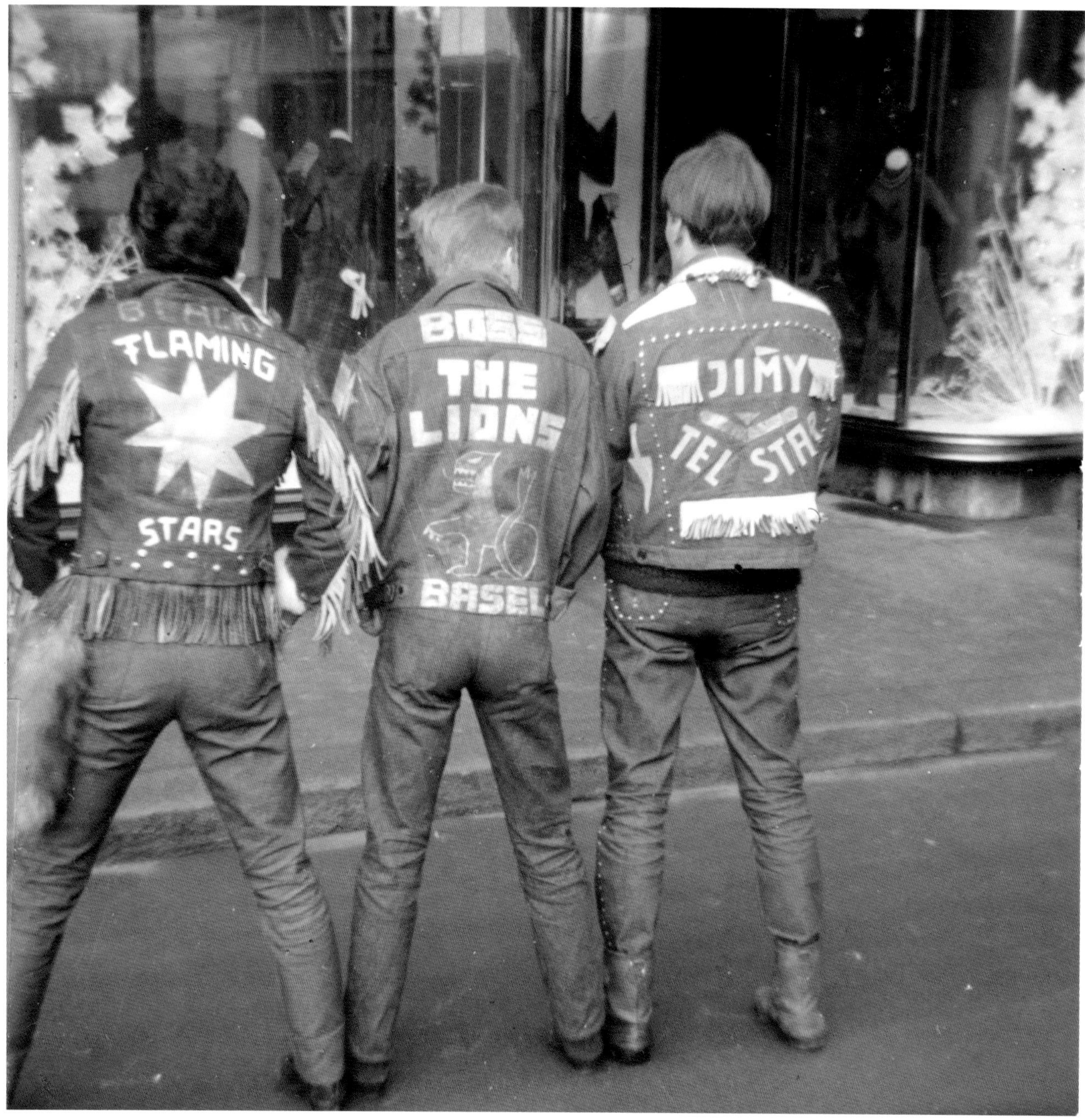

Blacky from The Flaming Stars, Igel wearing the jacket of his ancient Lions boss, and Tel Star Jimy.

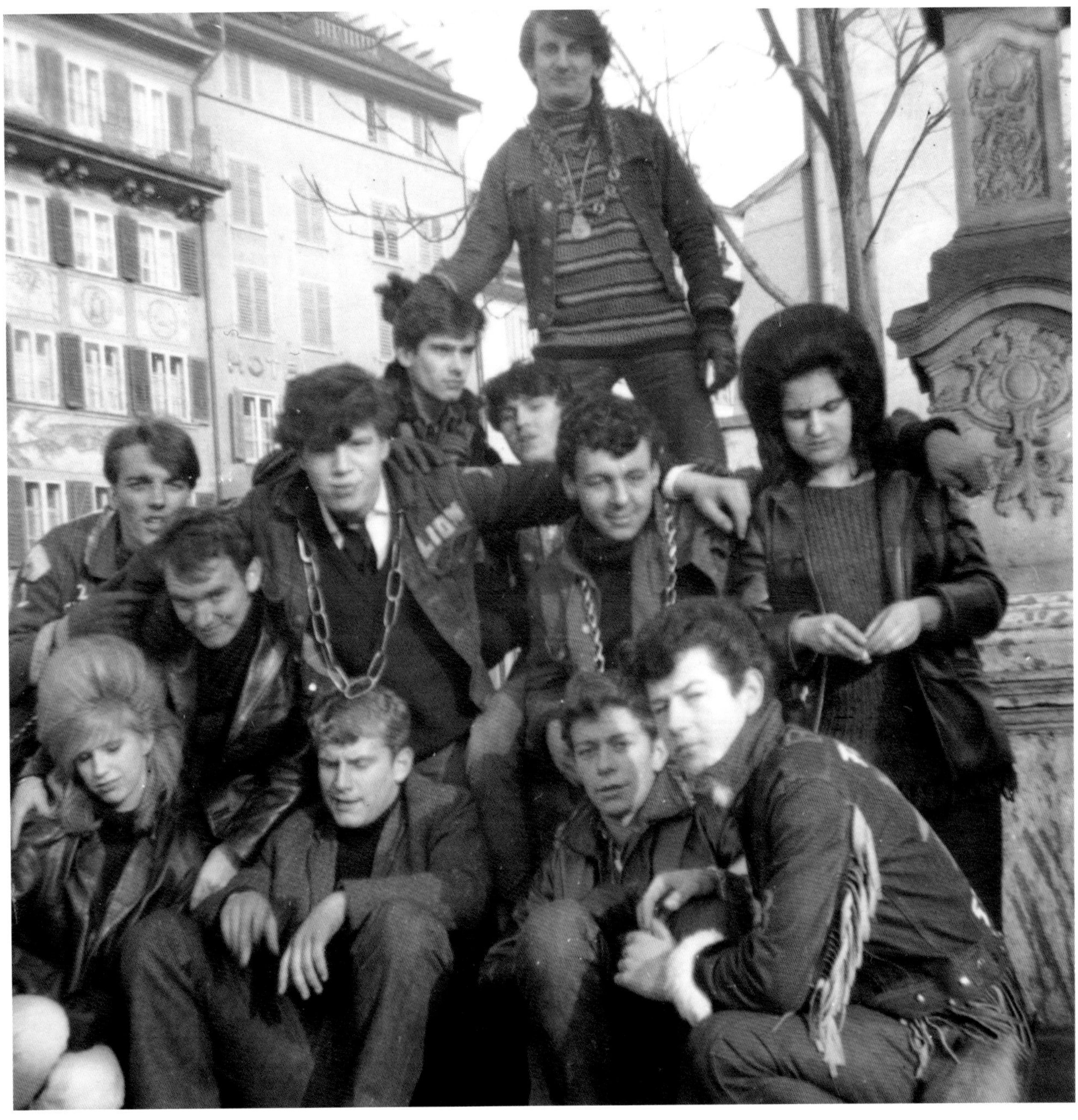

Halbstarke together. Second row: Martin Schippert aka Tino, who later founded the Swiss Charter of Hells Angels.

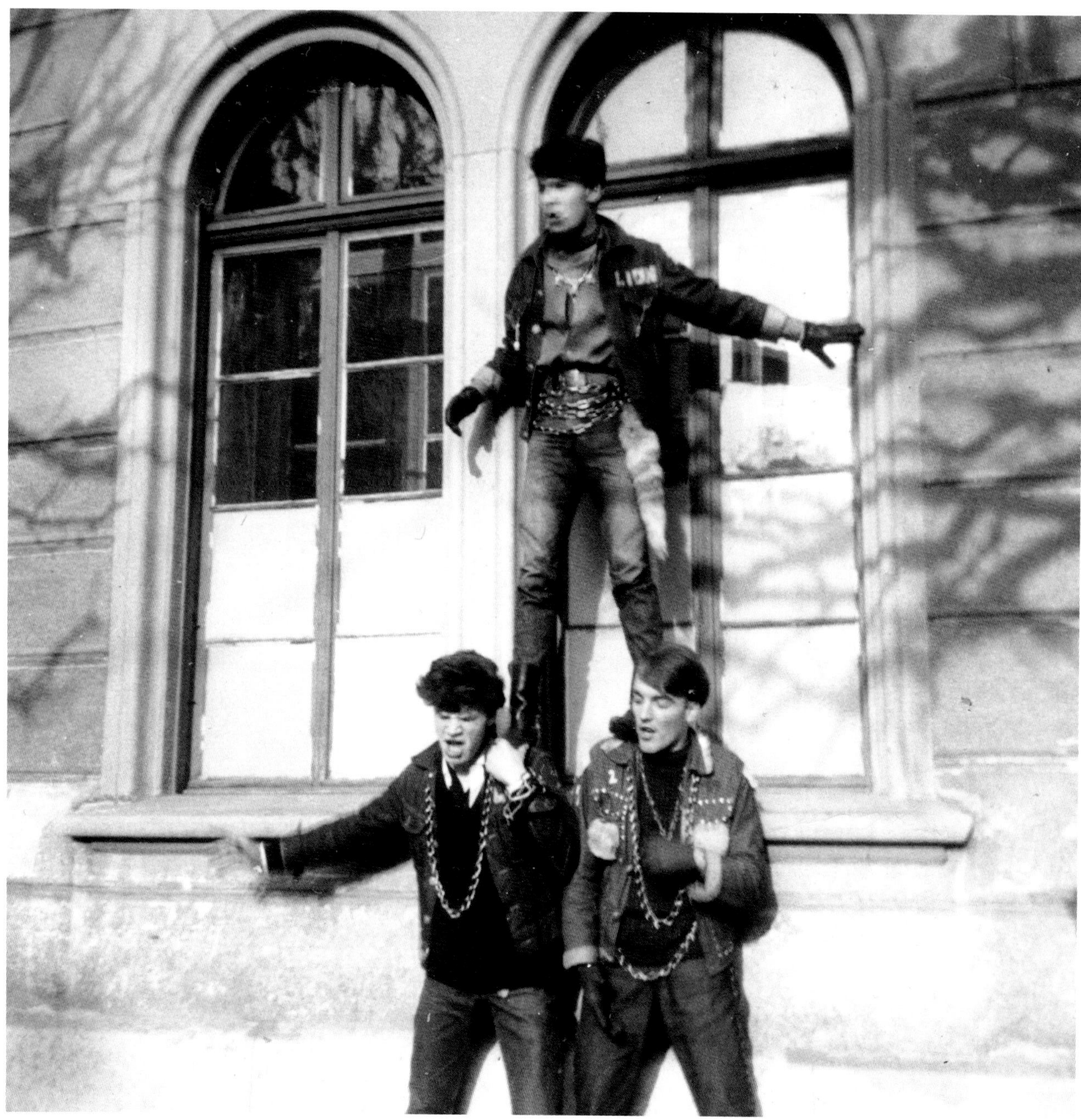

Dracula (top), Conny Thudium (left) and a gang member from Aarau.

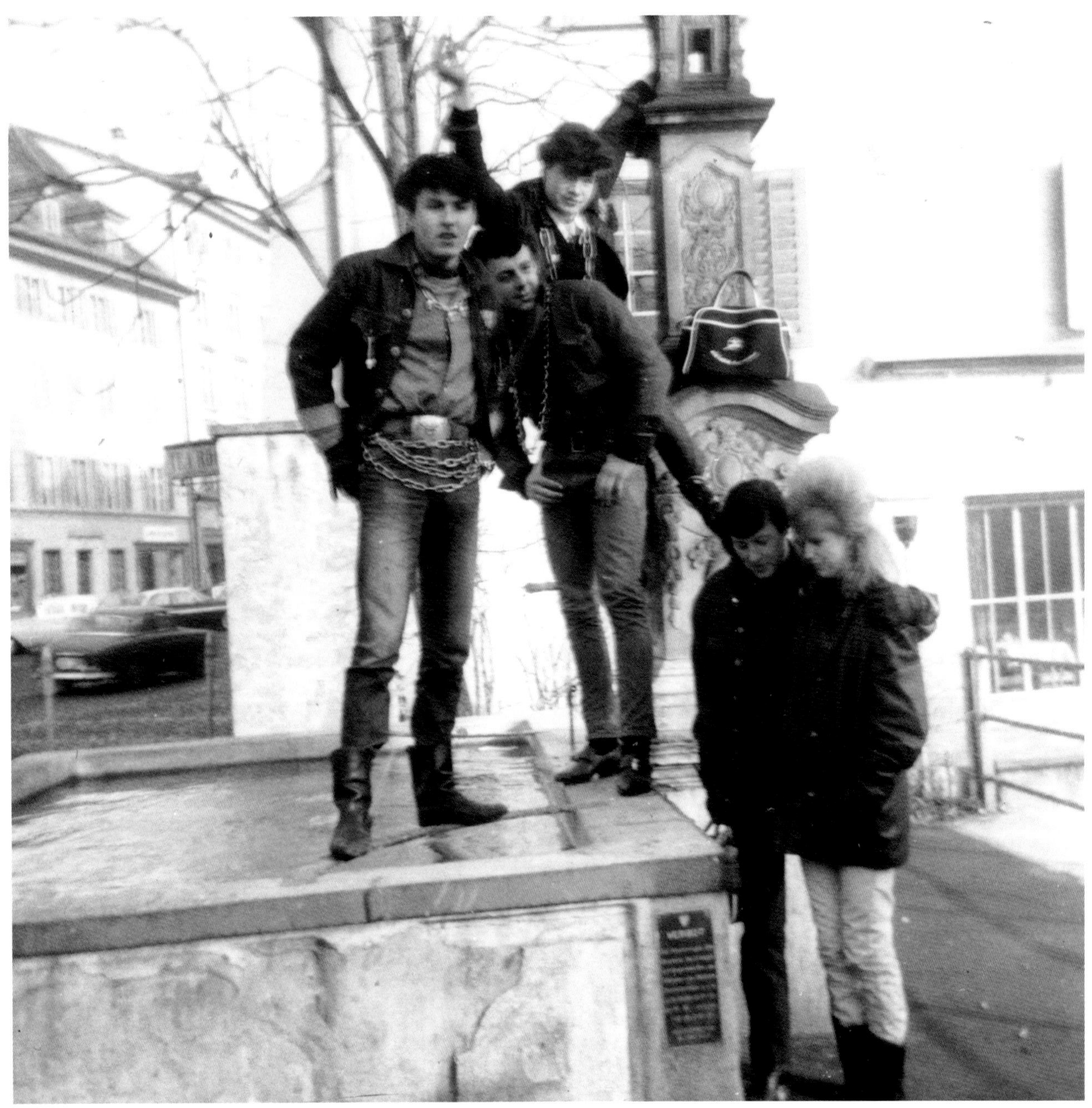

Center: future Swiss Hells Angels founder Tino (with chain around his neck). At right, Dracula, with four chains around his chest and waist. Right: Sonny and Vreni. Top: Conny Thudium.

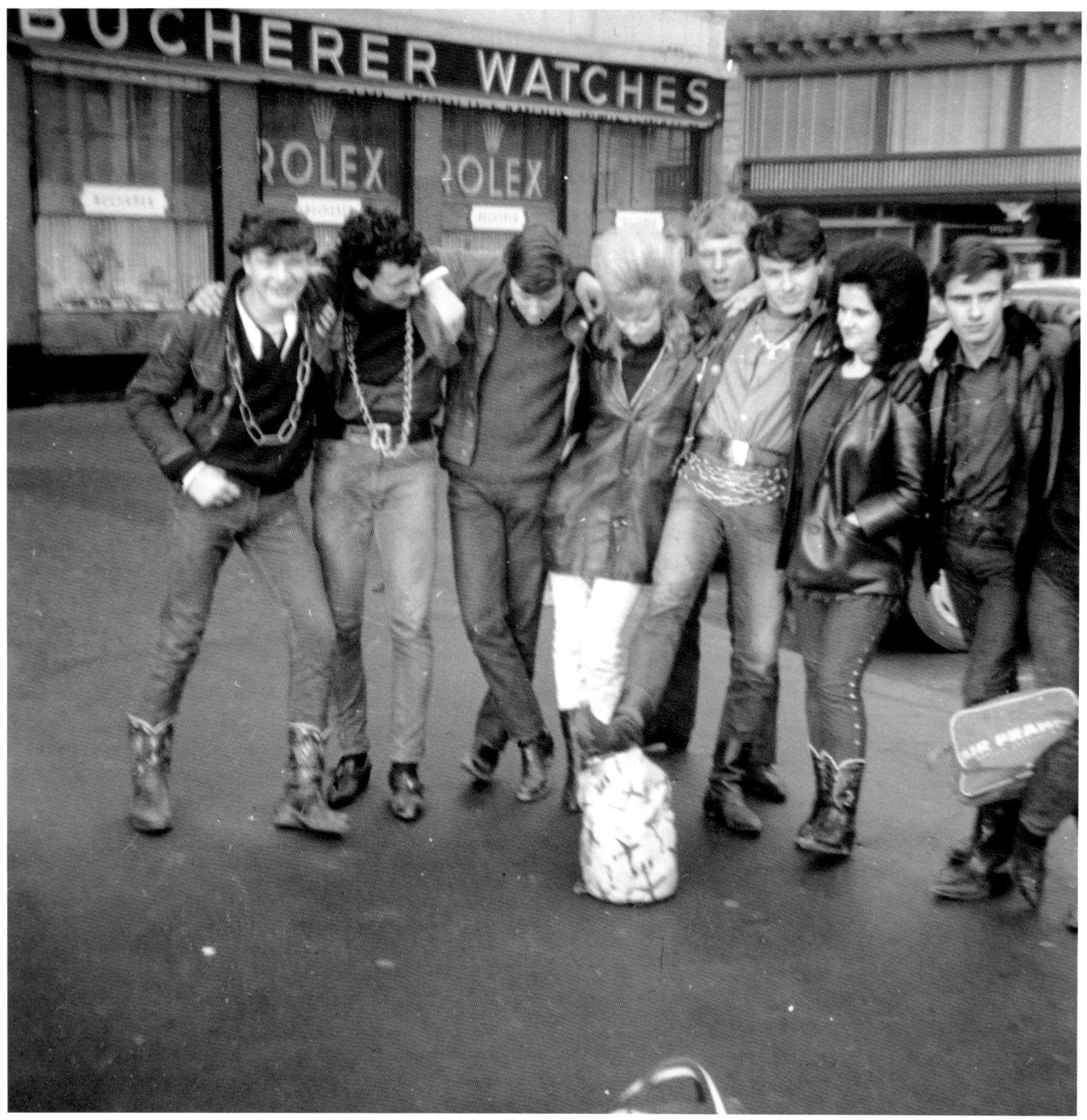

From left: Conny, Tino, Sonny, Vreni, Marti, Kelly, Dracula and Rumy with an unknown hangaround.

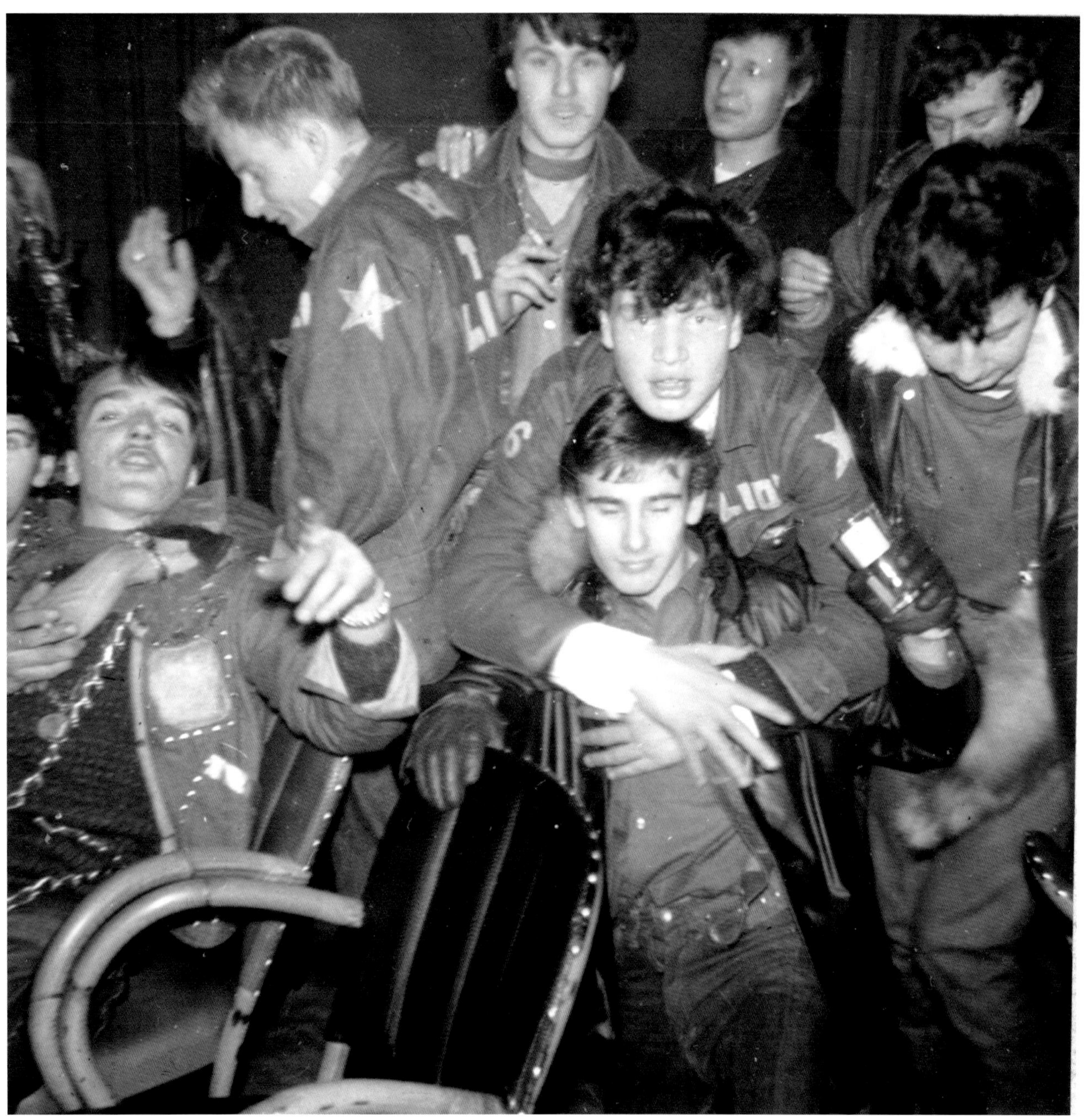

Hully Gully with the usual suspects.

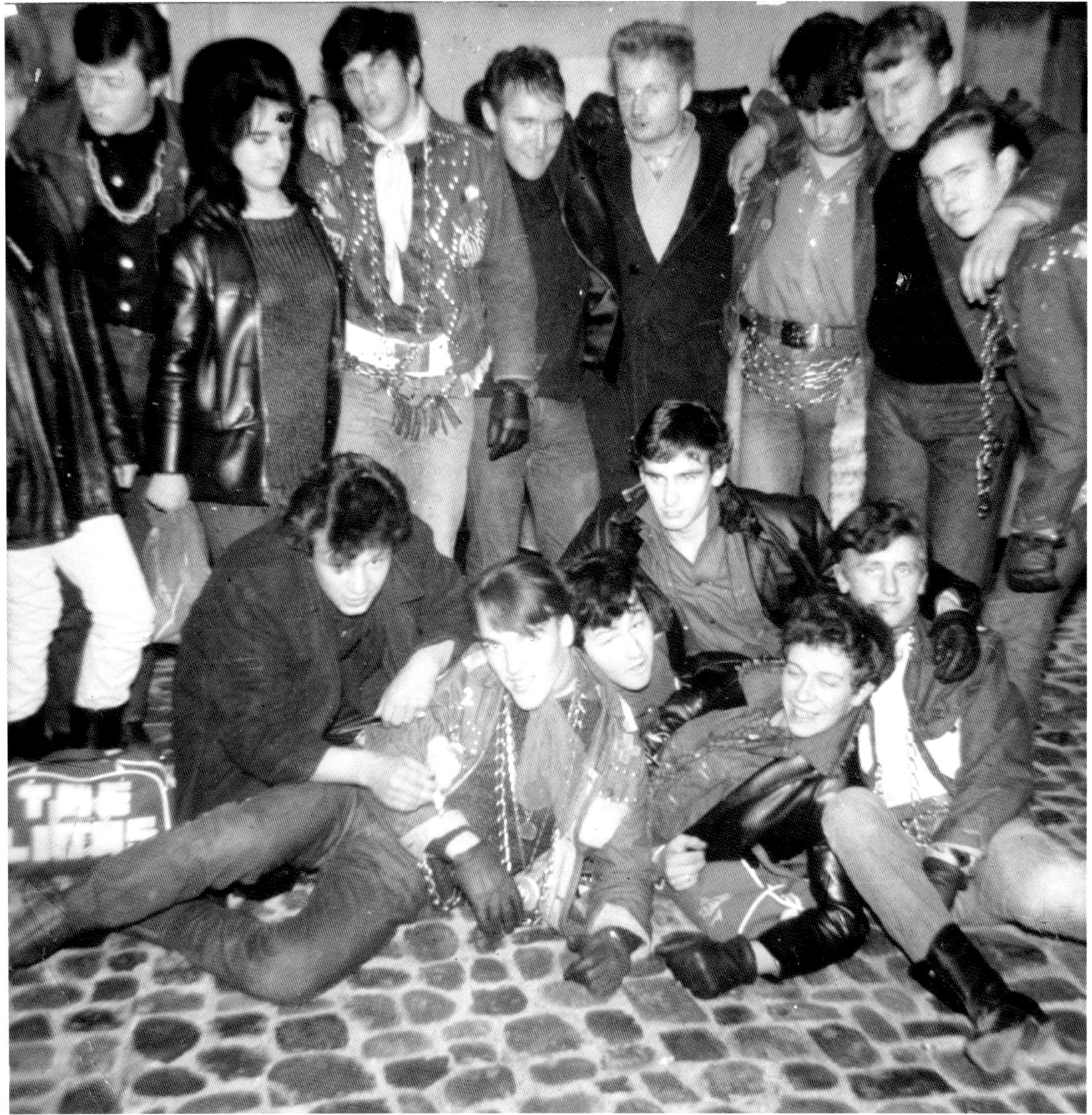

Rumy, Johnsy, Igel and crew.

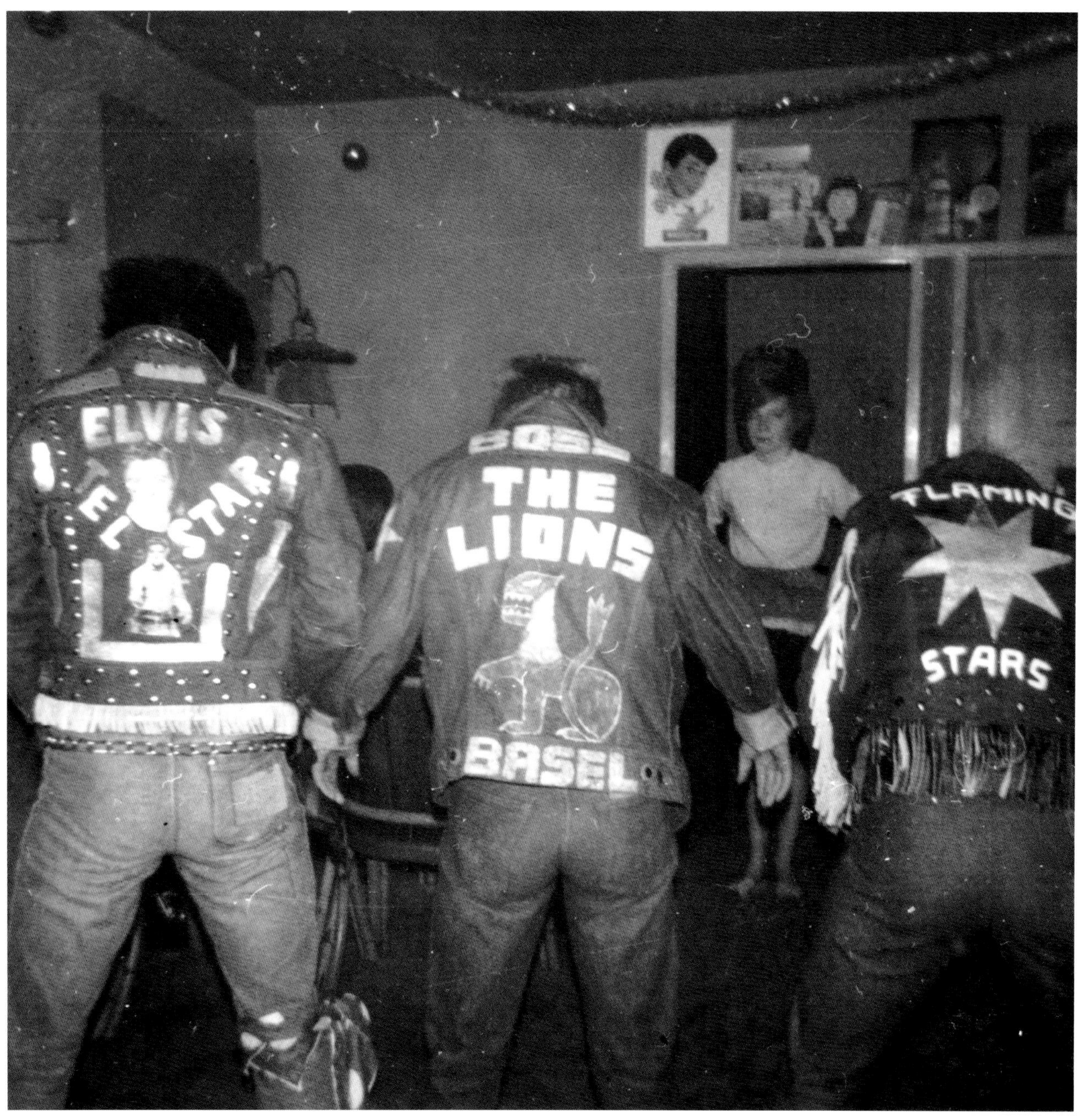

The triumvirate: Elvis (Tel Star), Igel (Lions) and an unnamed gang member of The Flaming Stars.

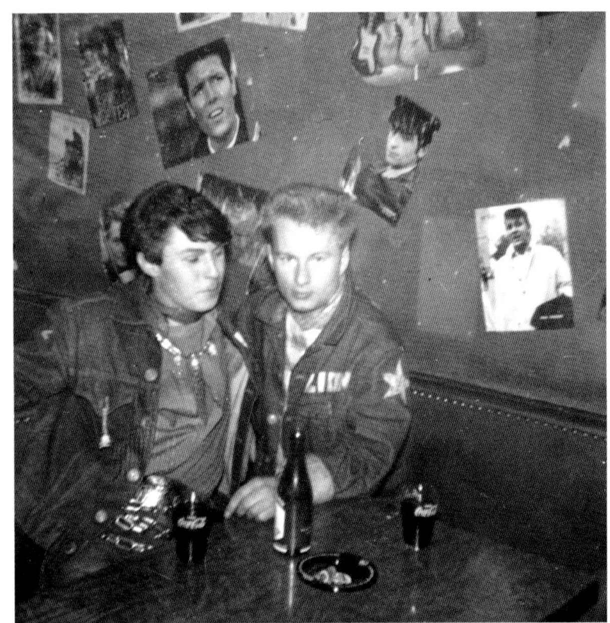

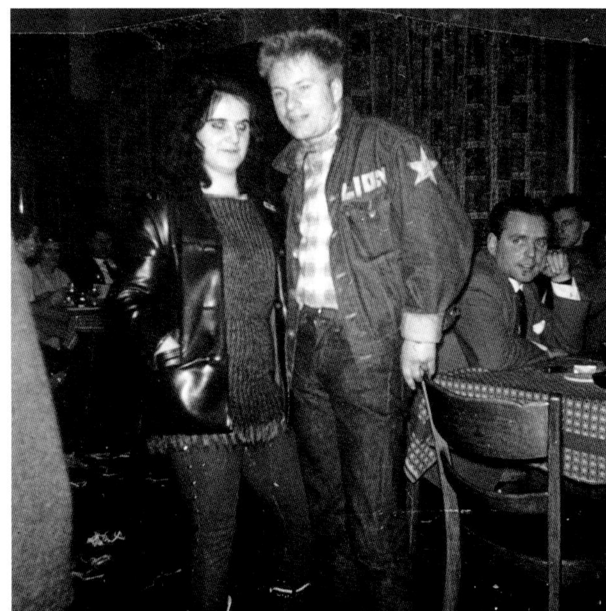

Left: Cafe Nebelspalter, Lucerne. Dracula and Igel. Right: Priska with Igel at a restaurant in Lucerne.

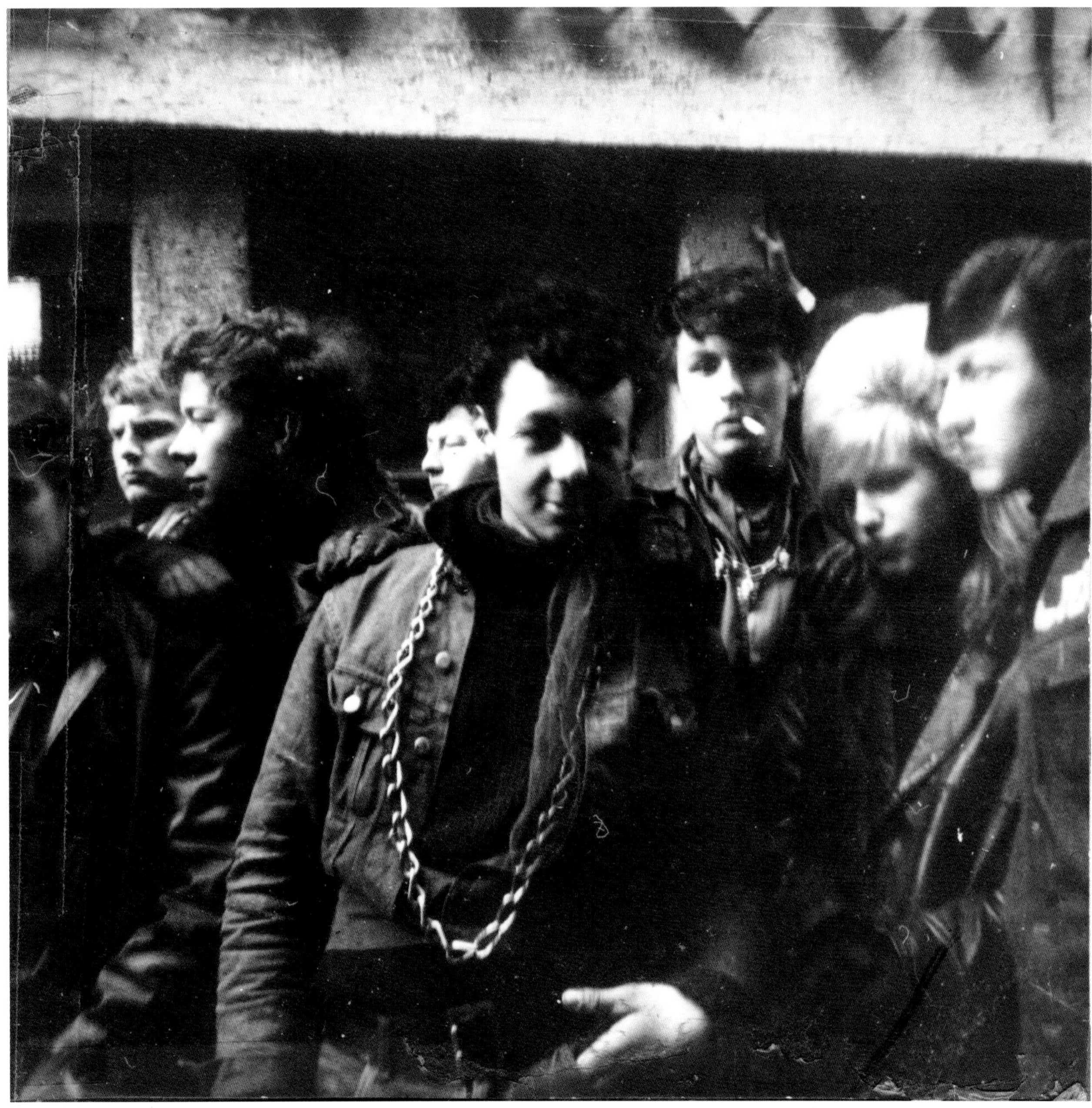

Historic photo outside the Restaurant Nebelspalter taken by Igel. Center: Martin Schippert aka Tino who later founded the Swiss chapter of Hells Angels. Right: Dracula, Vreni and Sonny.

26 / basler fasnacht (carnival in basel)
february 1964

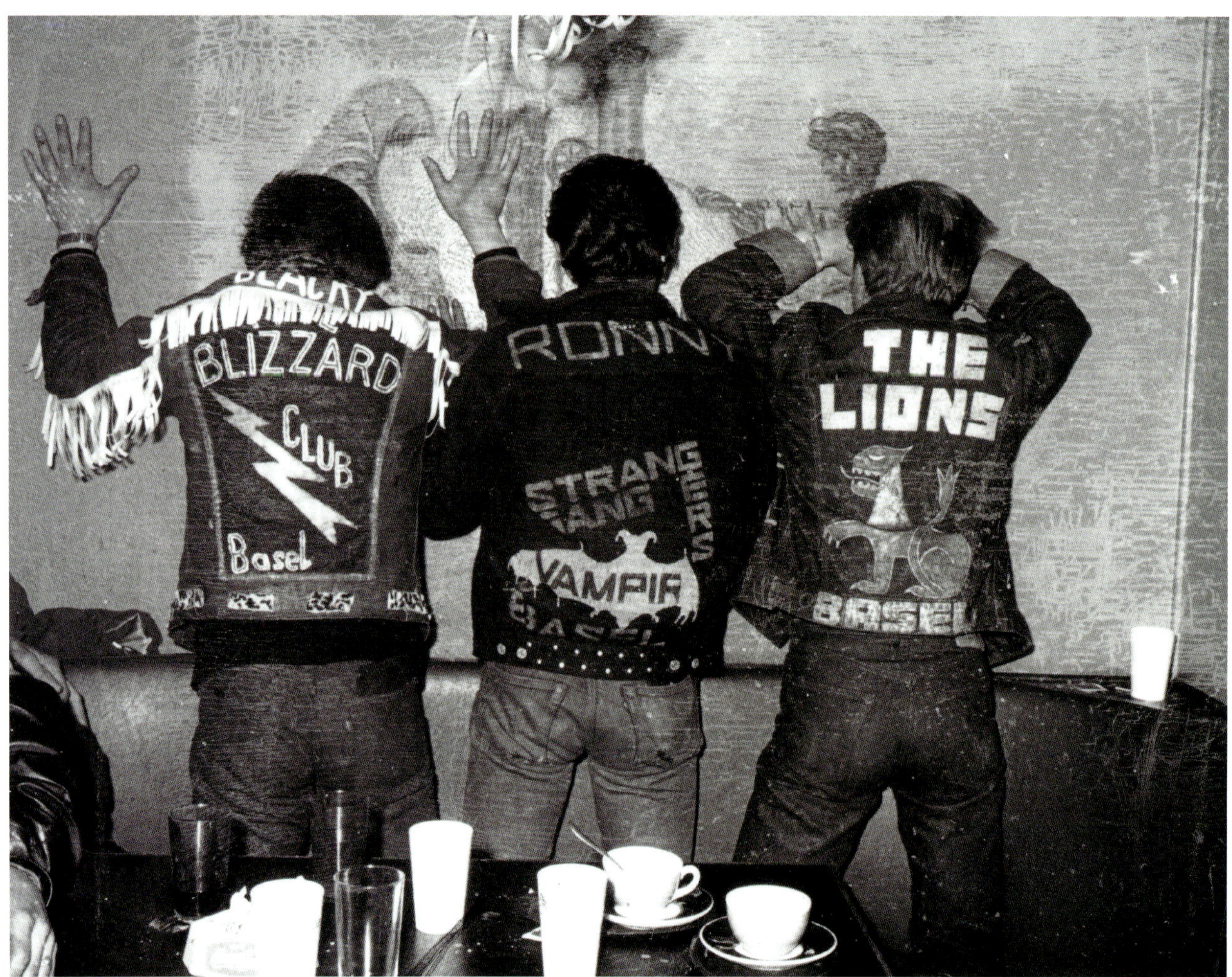

Up against the wall at Cafe Oasis, Greifengasse, Basel.

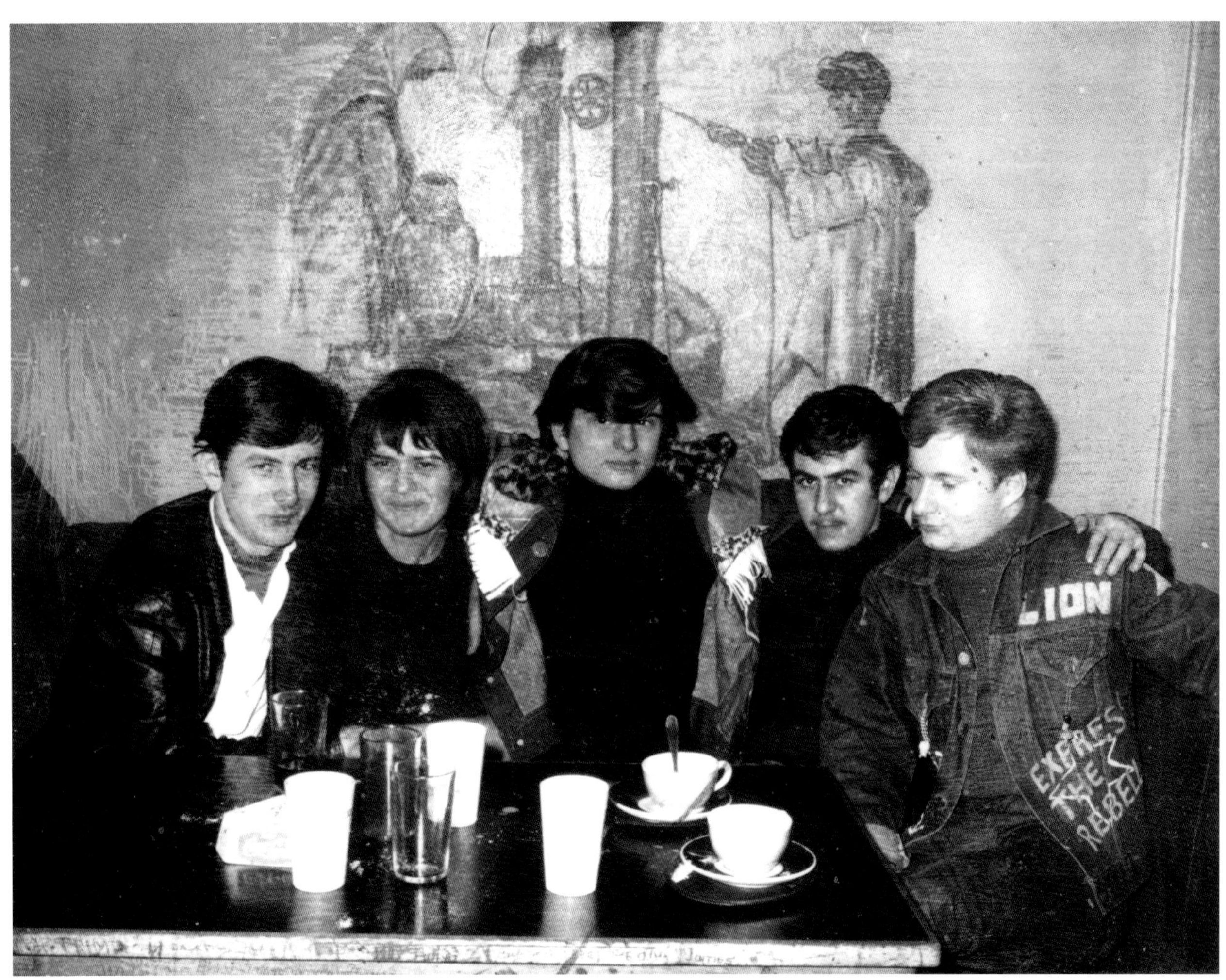

At Cafe Oasis: unknown couple with Blacky (middle), Whisky and Igel.

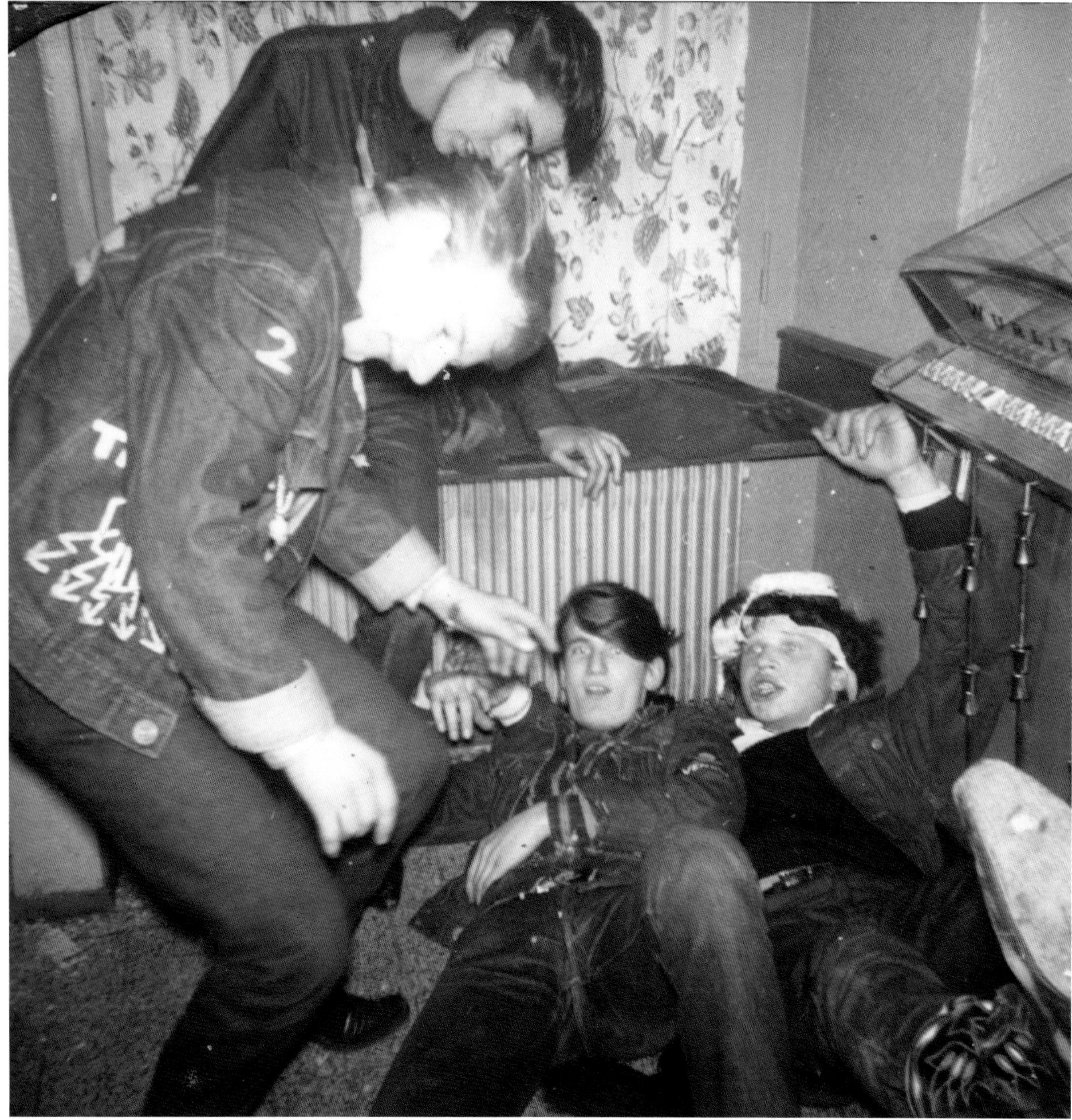

Wild scene in front of the jukebox at Express Bar, Basel - with Schlangepfiff and Conny on the floor. Igel at this point was second in command for The Lions.

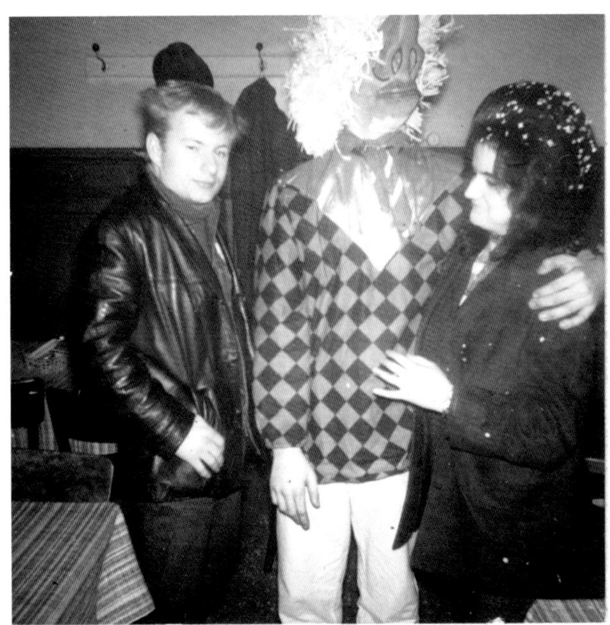
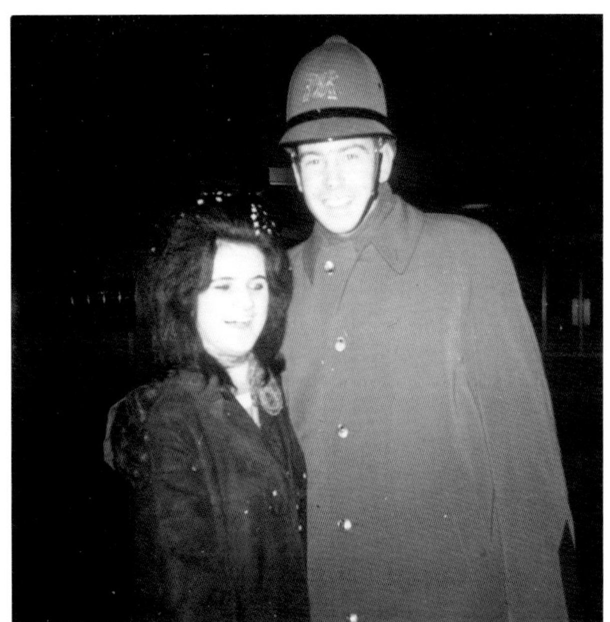

Left: Igel and Priska meet a Waggis with a big nose. Right: Priska has a good laugh with a policeman.

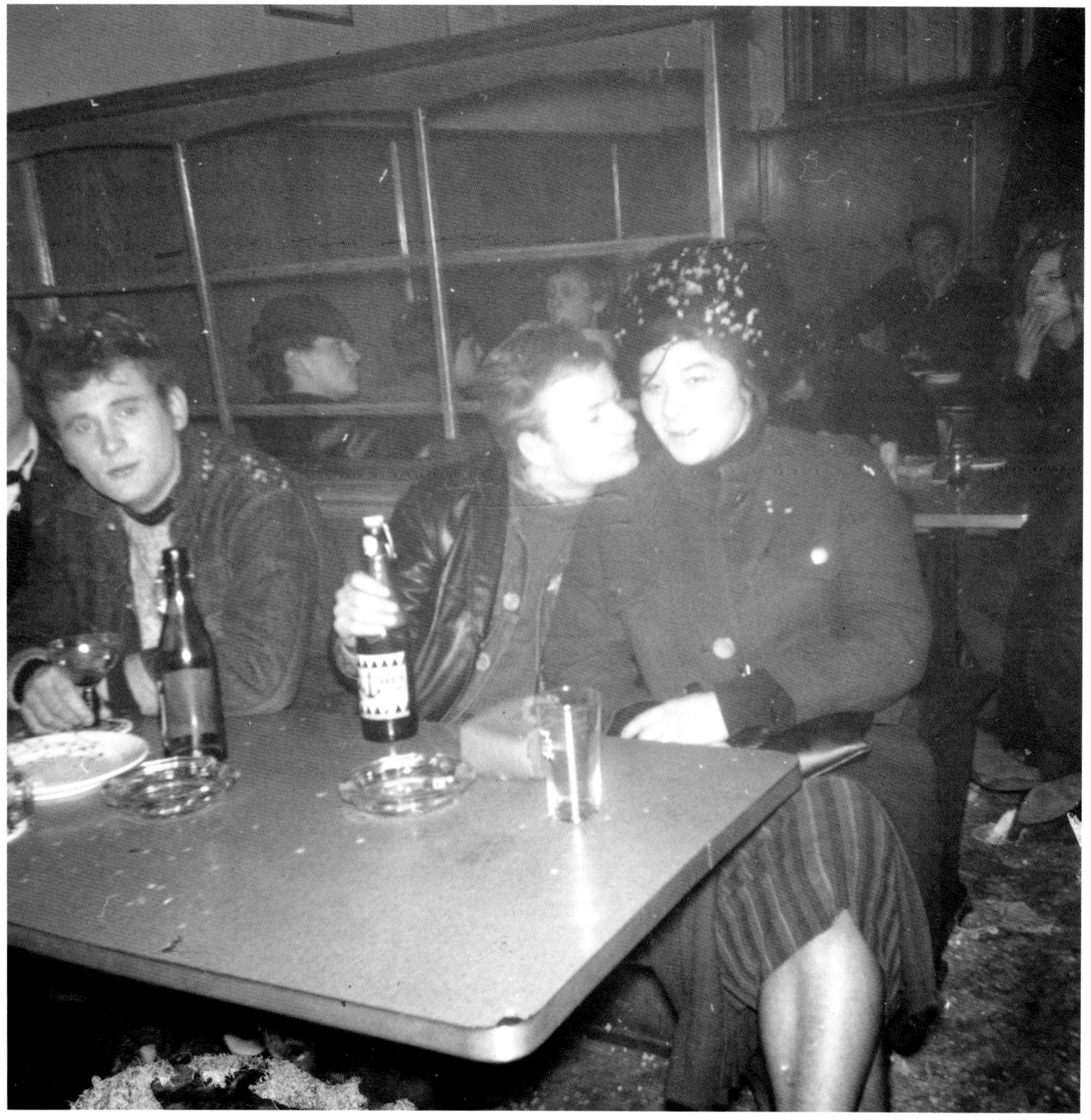

Basel: Tello, Igel, and Vreni Stebler at Restaurant Sonne, Rheingasse 25.

27 / express-bar, basel
march 1964

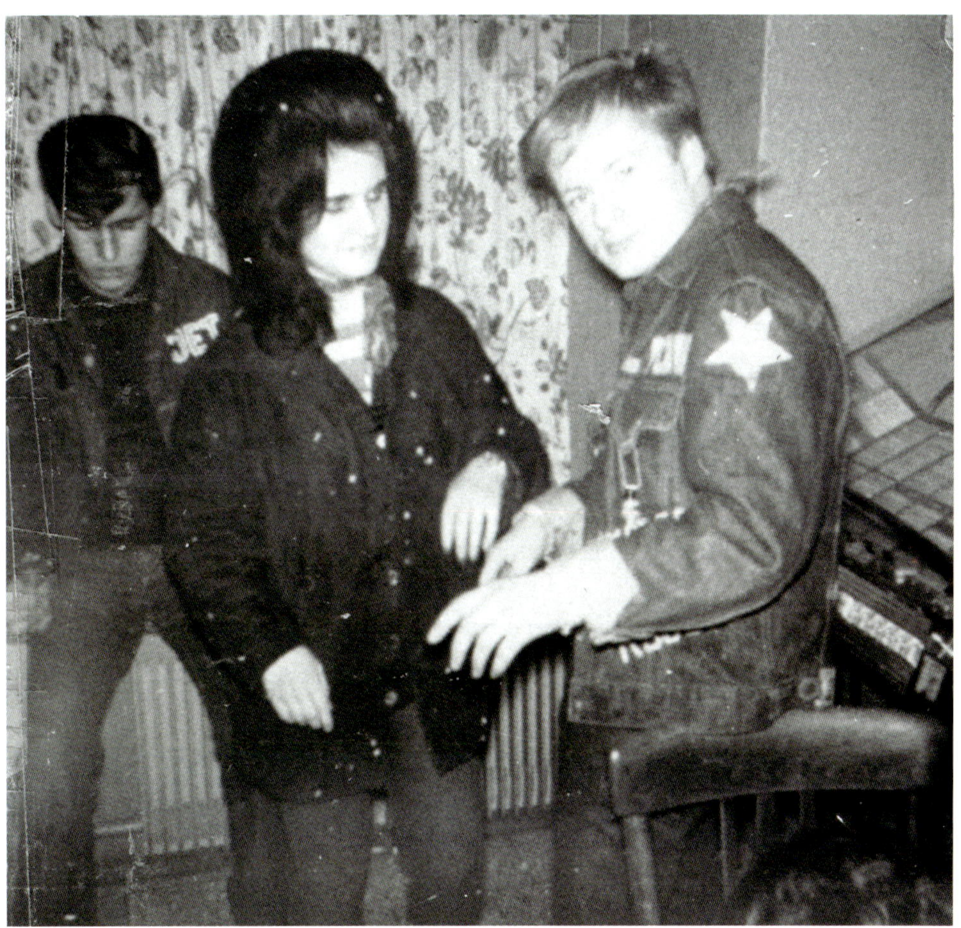

Priska (Rumy) and Igel hit the dance floor.

28 / schachen, aarau

march 29, 1964

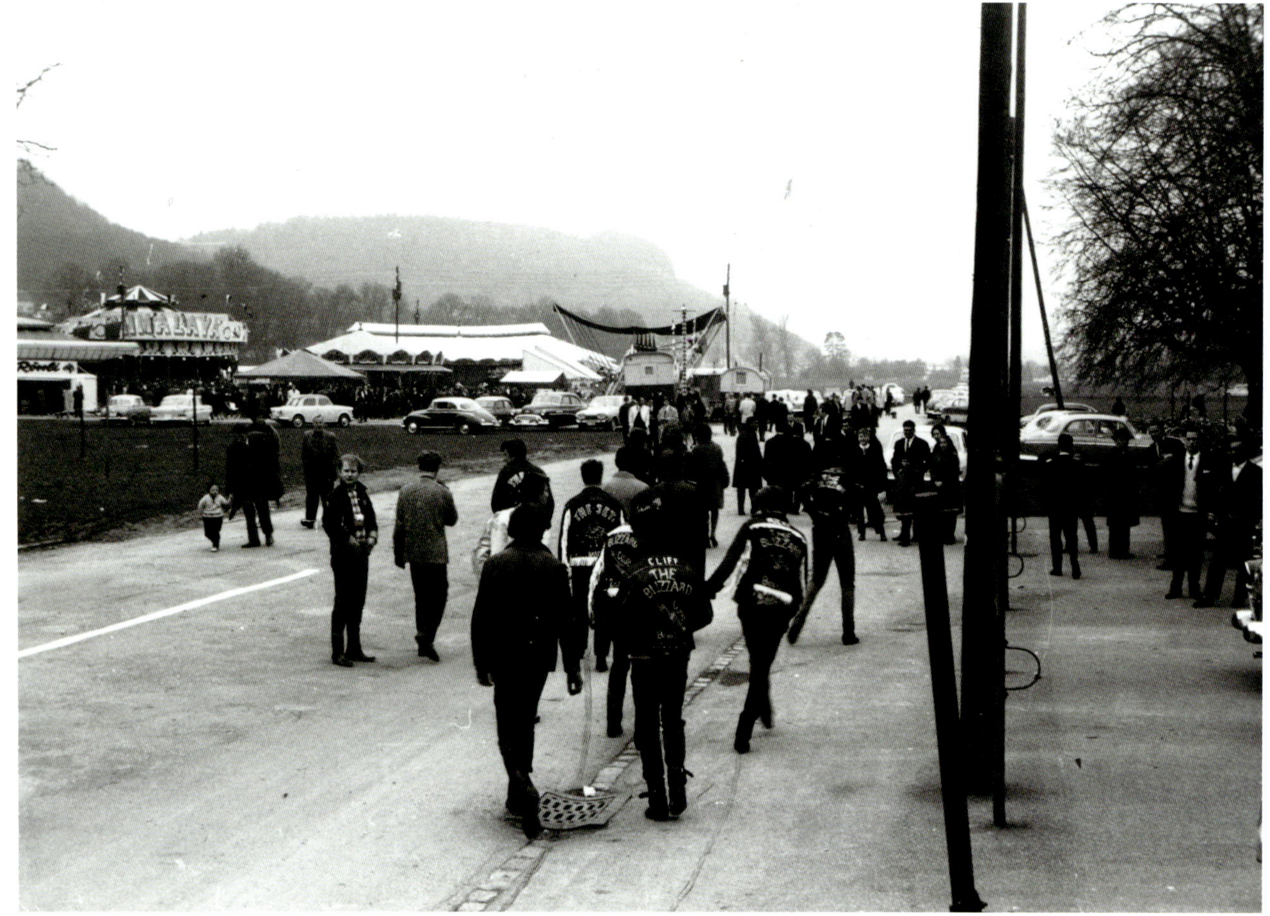

Schachen in Aarau was a magnetic field for the gangs of Basel and nearby towns.

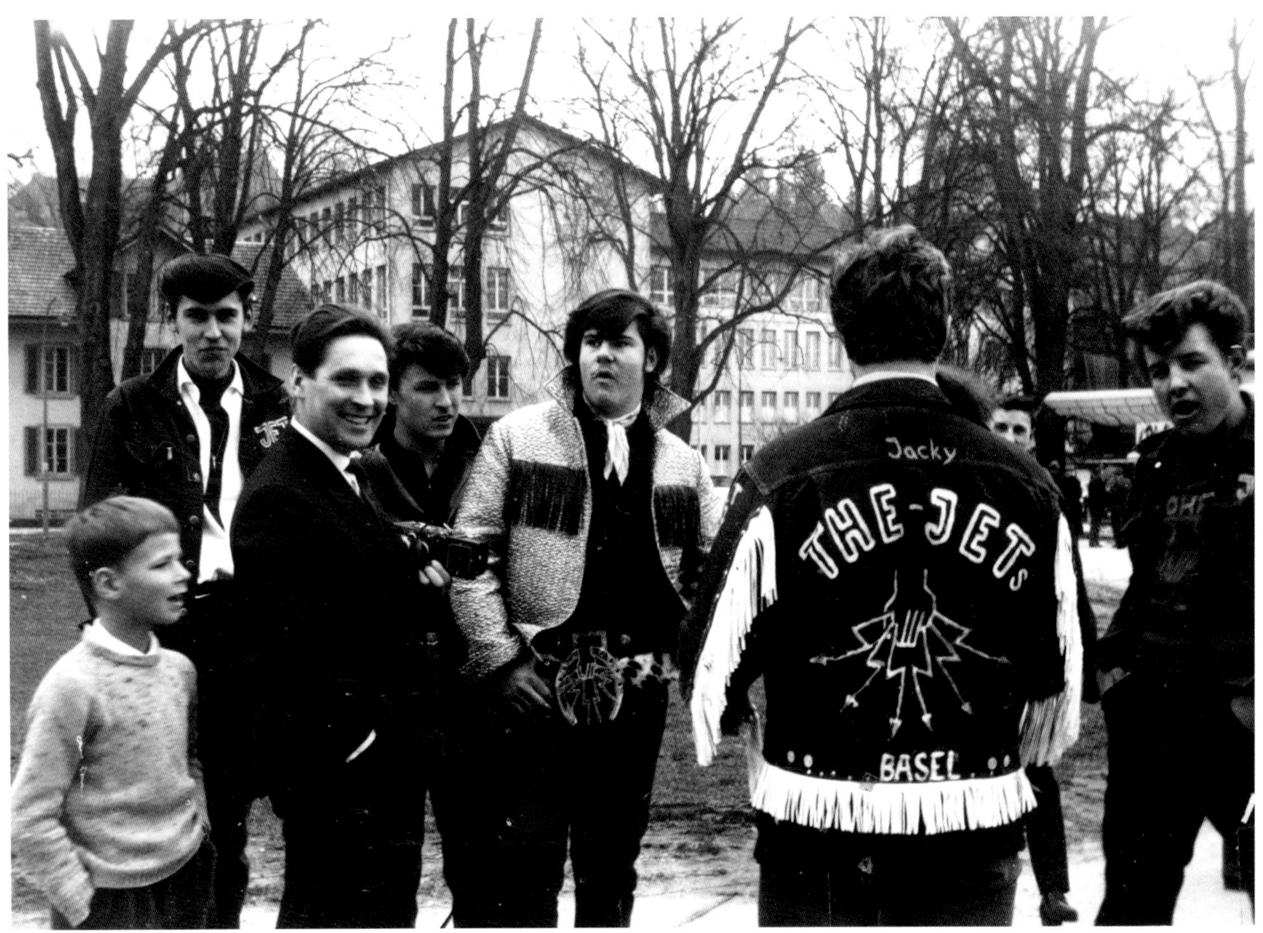

The Jets with boss Paul Marggraff a/k/a Doc (middle, white scarf), vice boss Jacky Jacquiery a/k/a Jacky (forefront, back to camera) and Jimmy from The Lions.

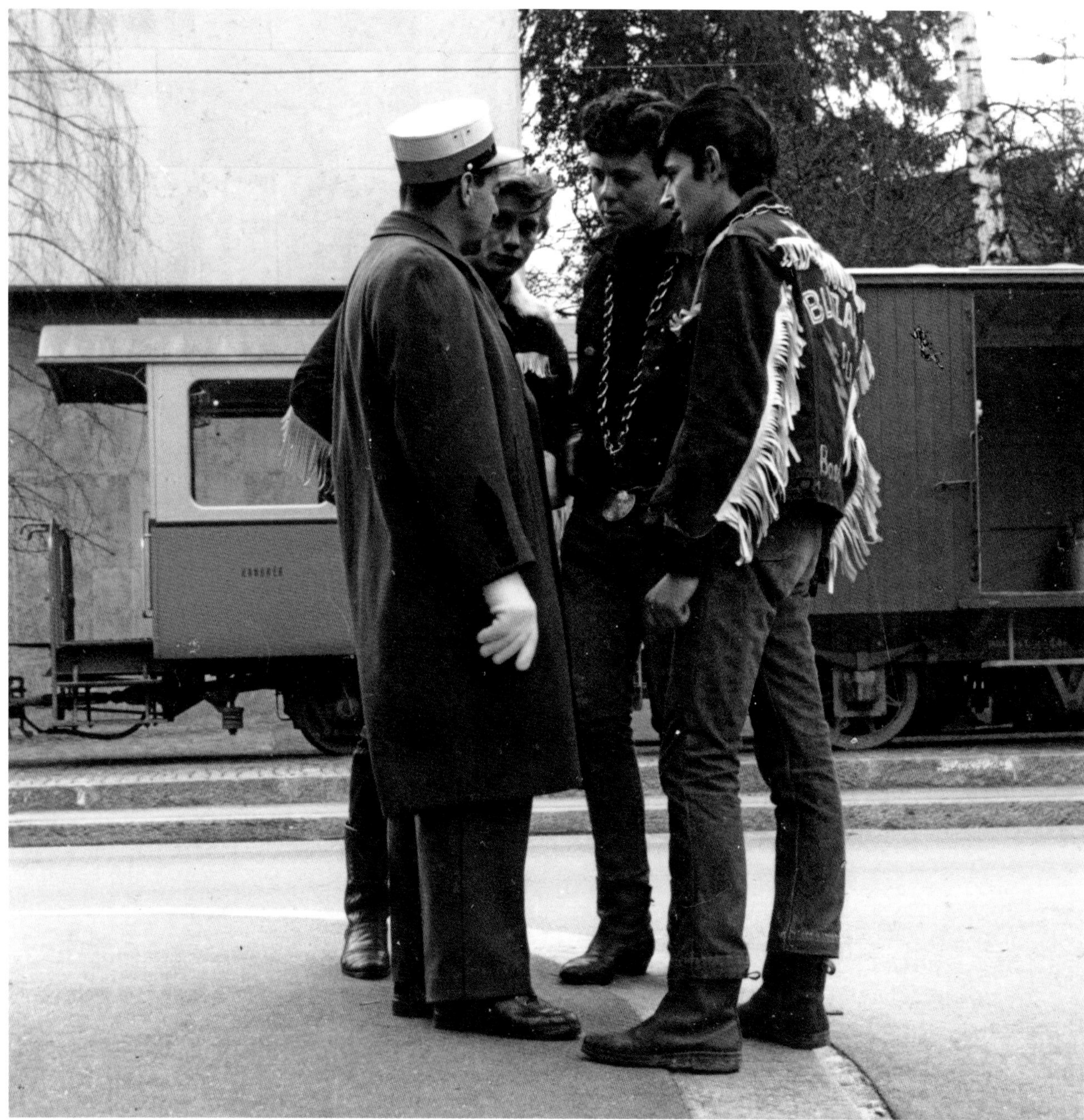

Rail guard has a word with the gang boys.

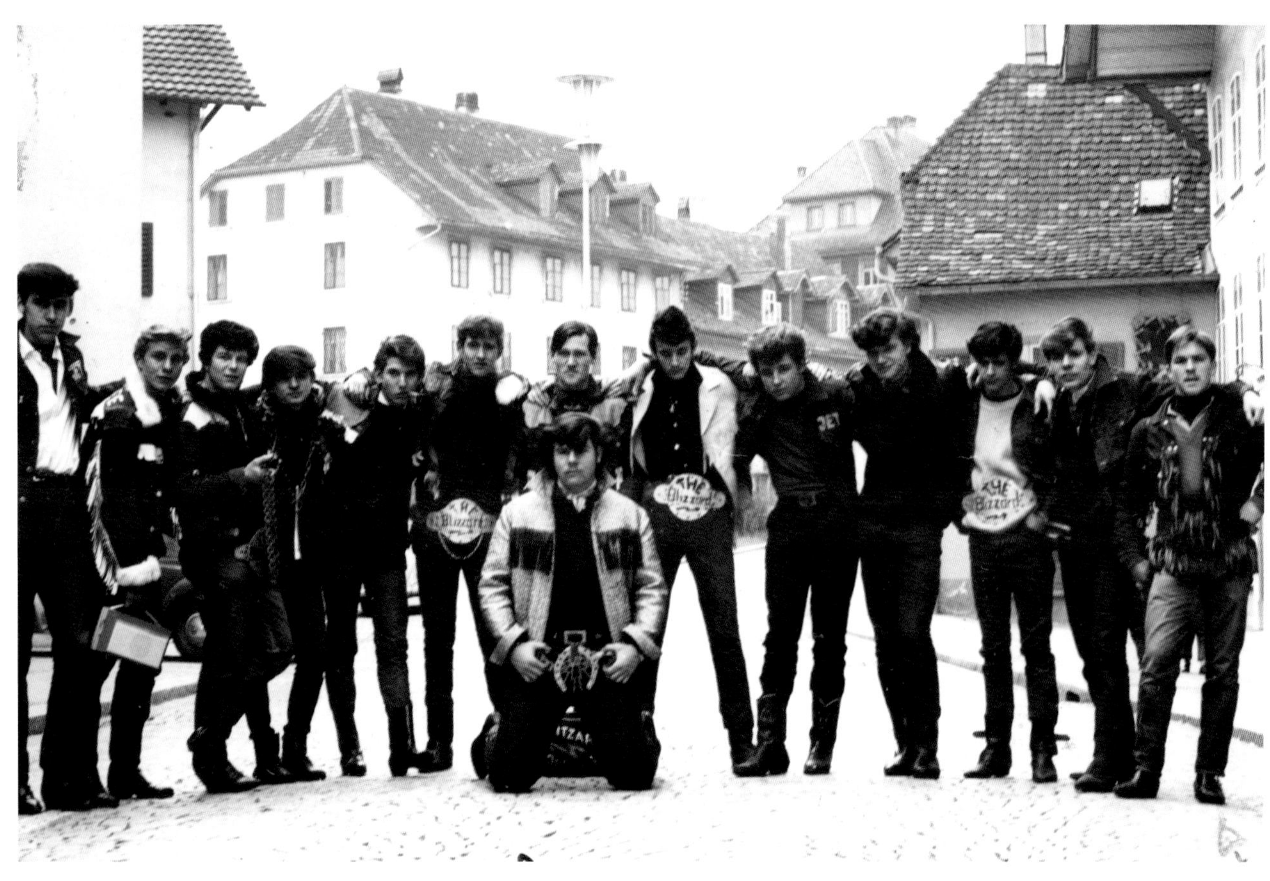

The Jets with headmaster Paul Marggraff called Doc in his white fringed jacket.

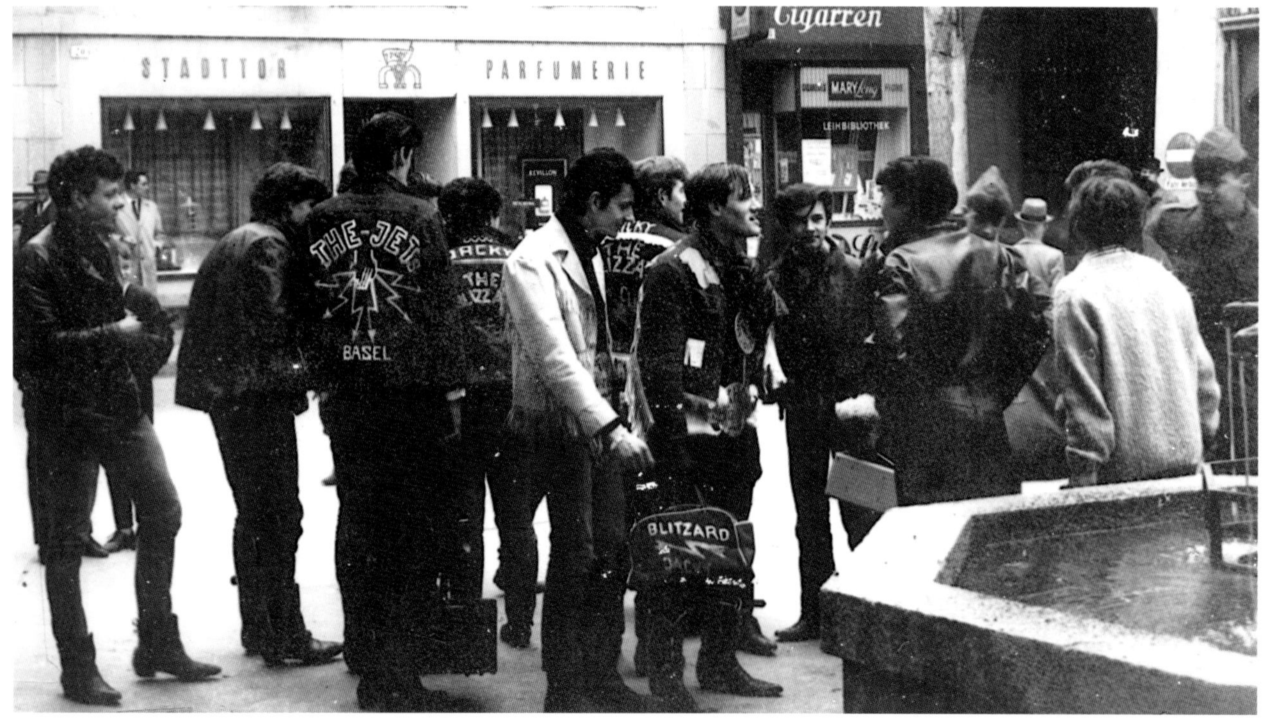

Aarau. Far left: Martin Schippert aka Tino; fourth from left: Jacky from The Blizzards, fifth from left: Mischuta. Beside him is Clochard with the big belt buckle.

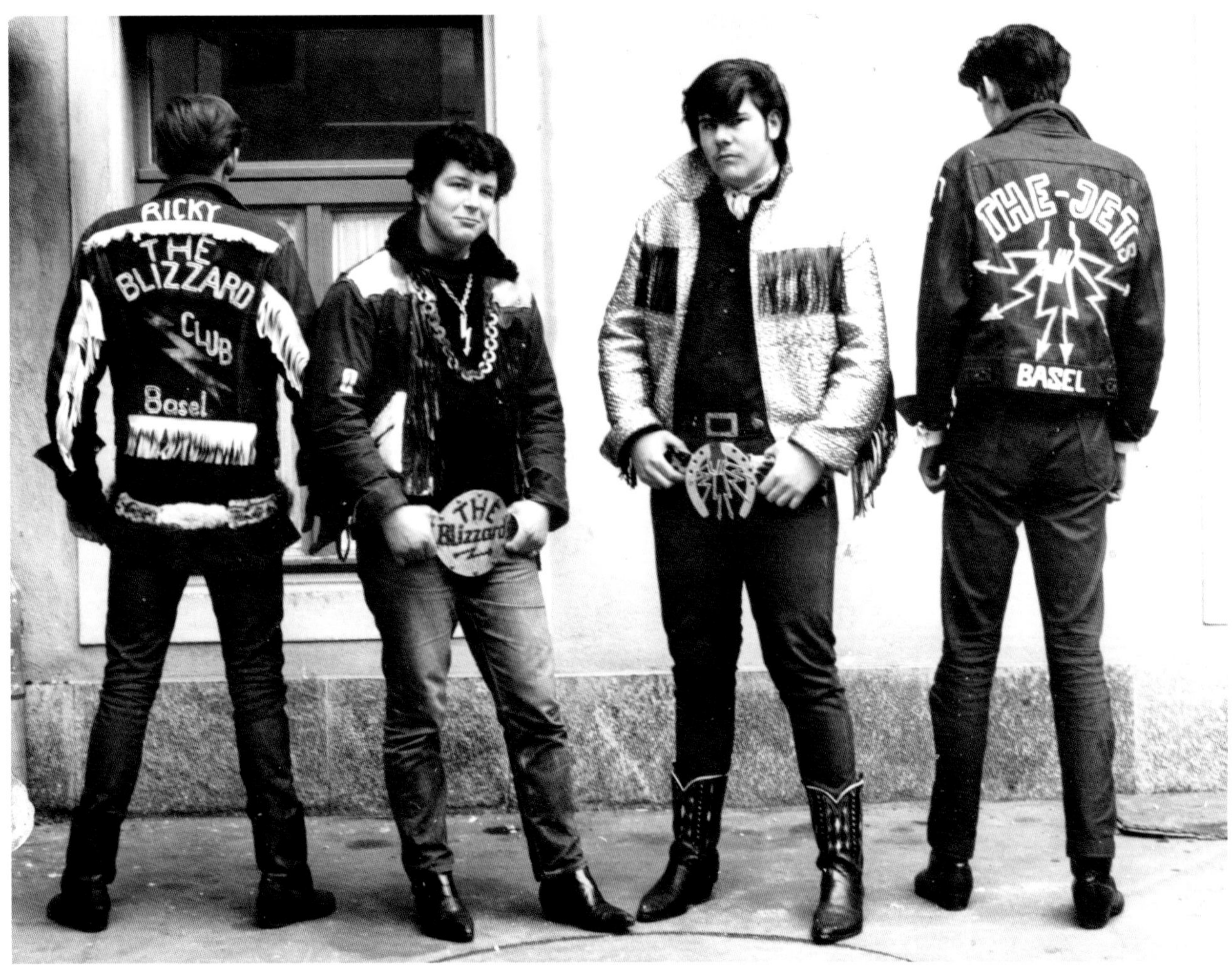

Ricky, Jacky, Doc and a tall guy from The Jets. Doc wears a massive horseshoe on his belt, and Jacky has a handmade metal Blizzard shield on his belt.

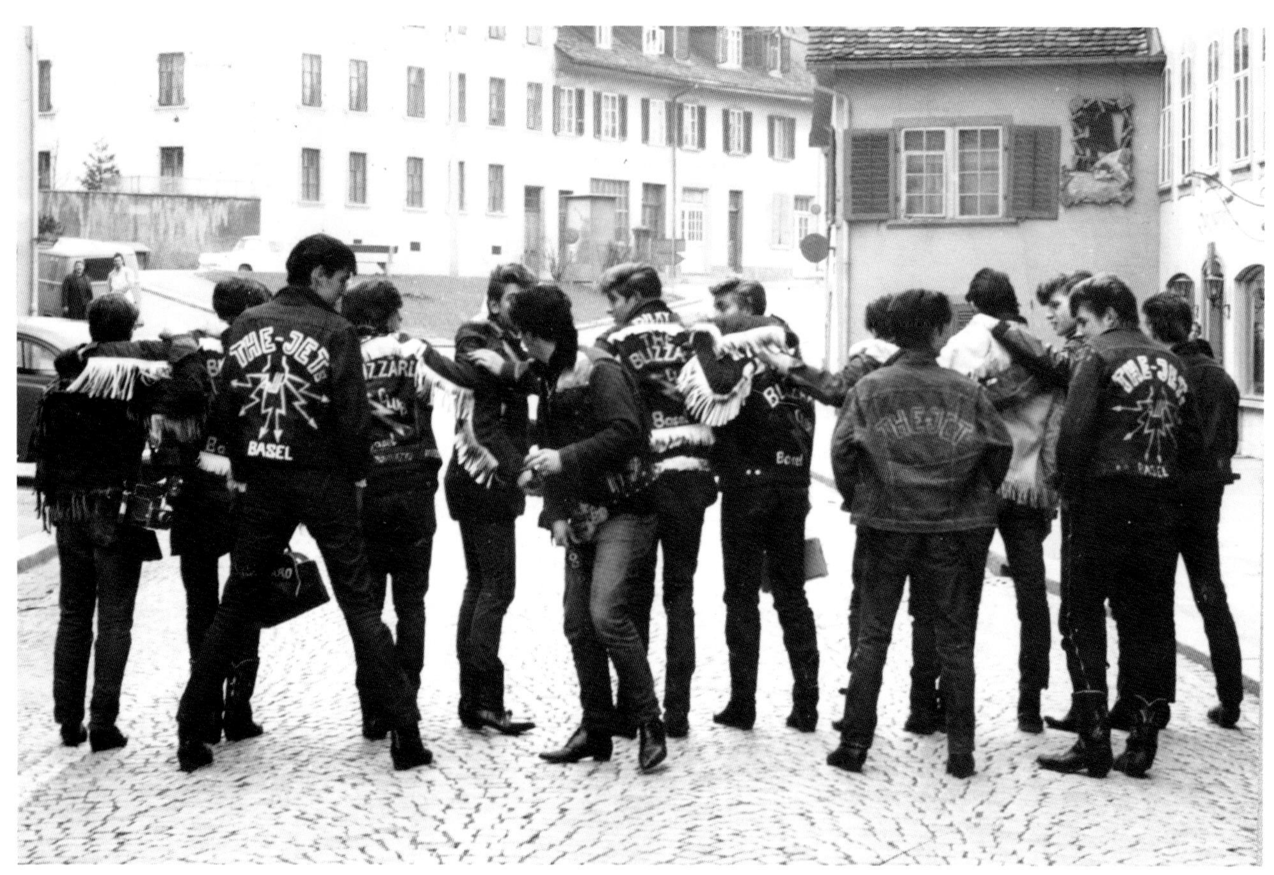

Jets vs. Blizzards.

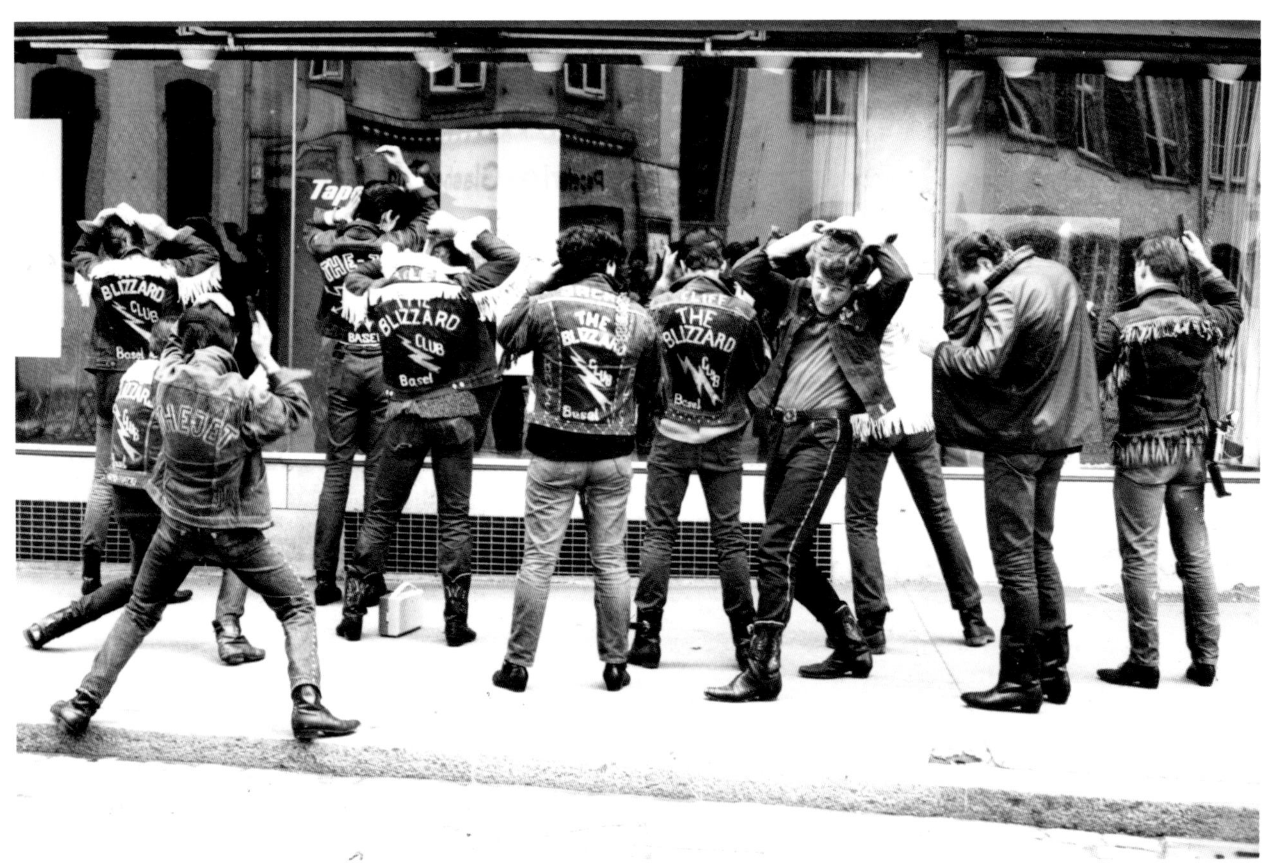

Greasers style their manes in a shop window.

29 / st. petersinsel, lake biel big yearly swiss gang meeting may 16–17, 1964

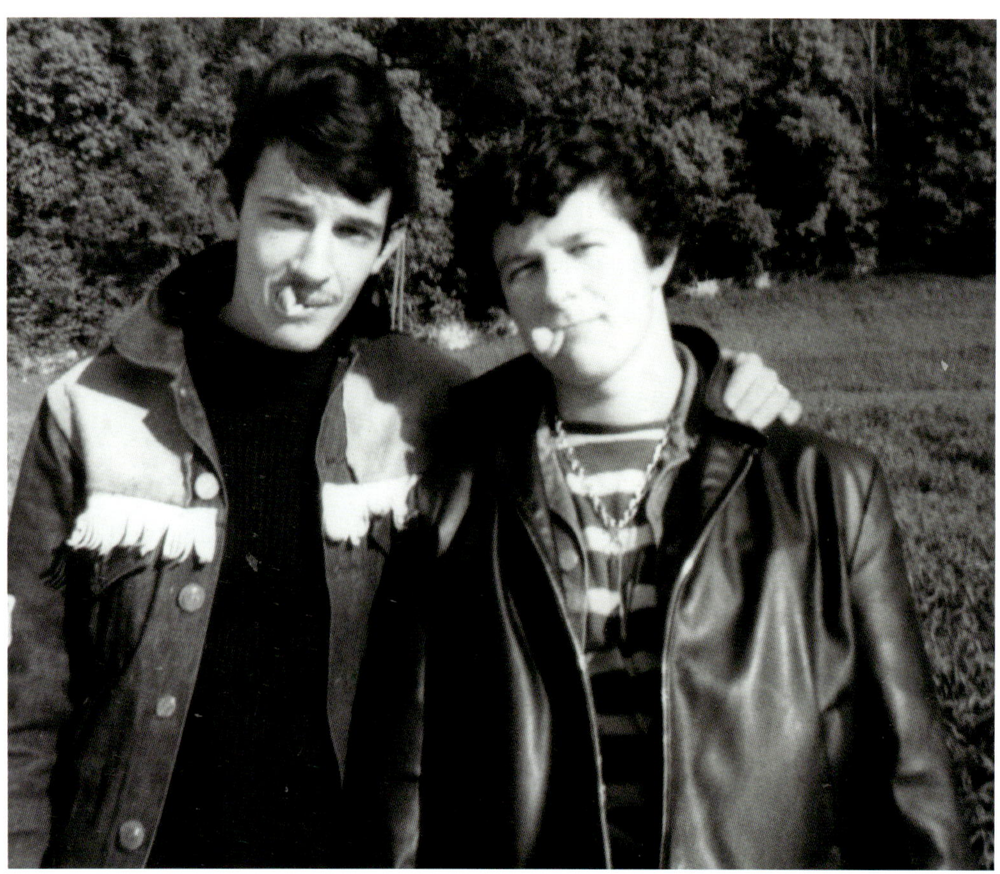

Mischuta and Jacky.

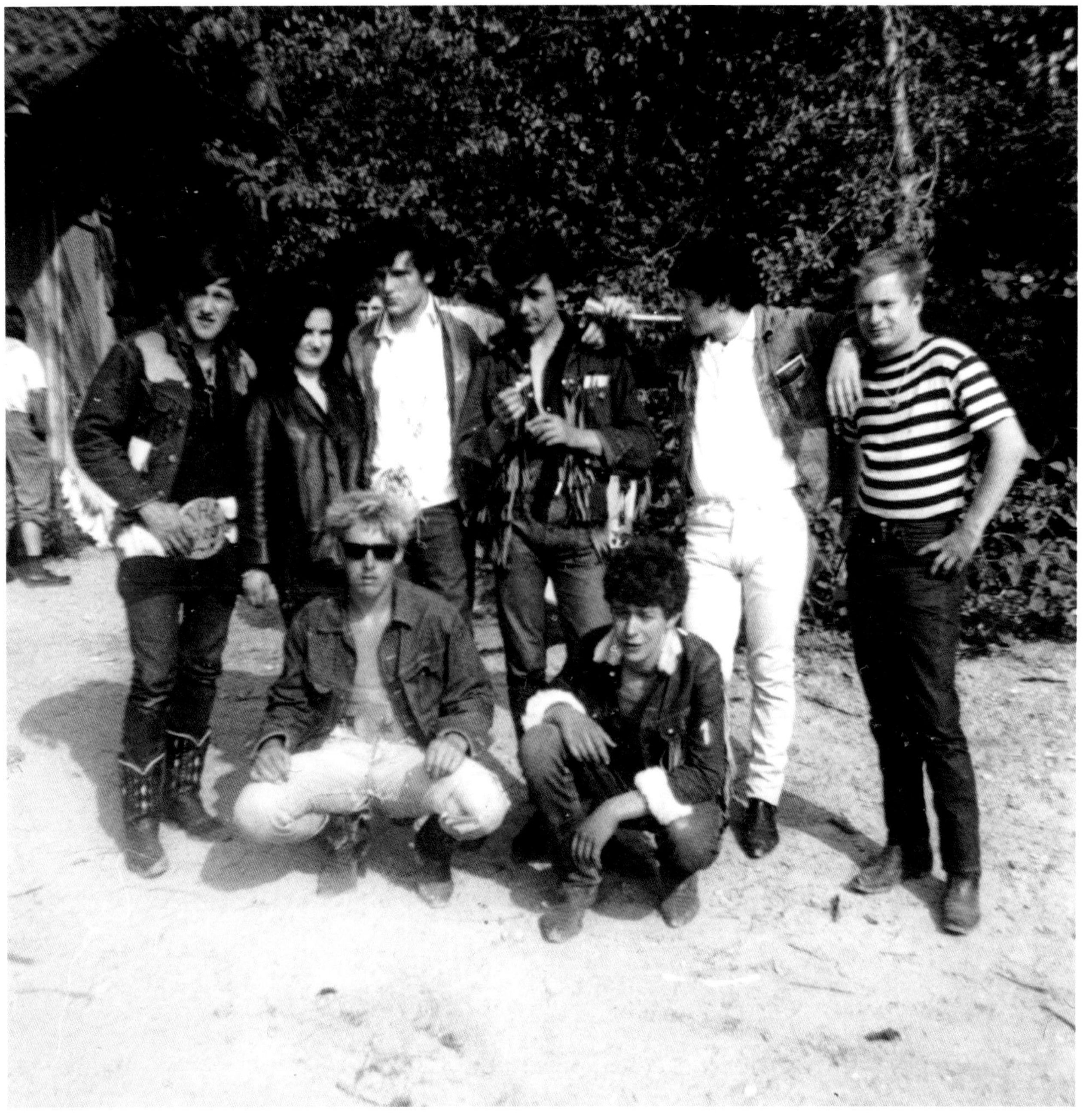

Clochard from The Blizzards, Rumy, two unknown gang cats, Jacky, and Igel. Front row: James and friend.

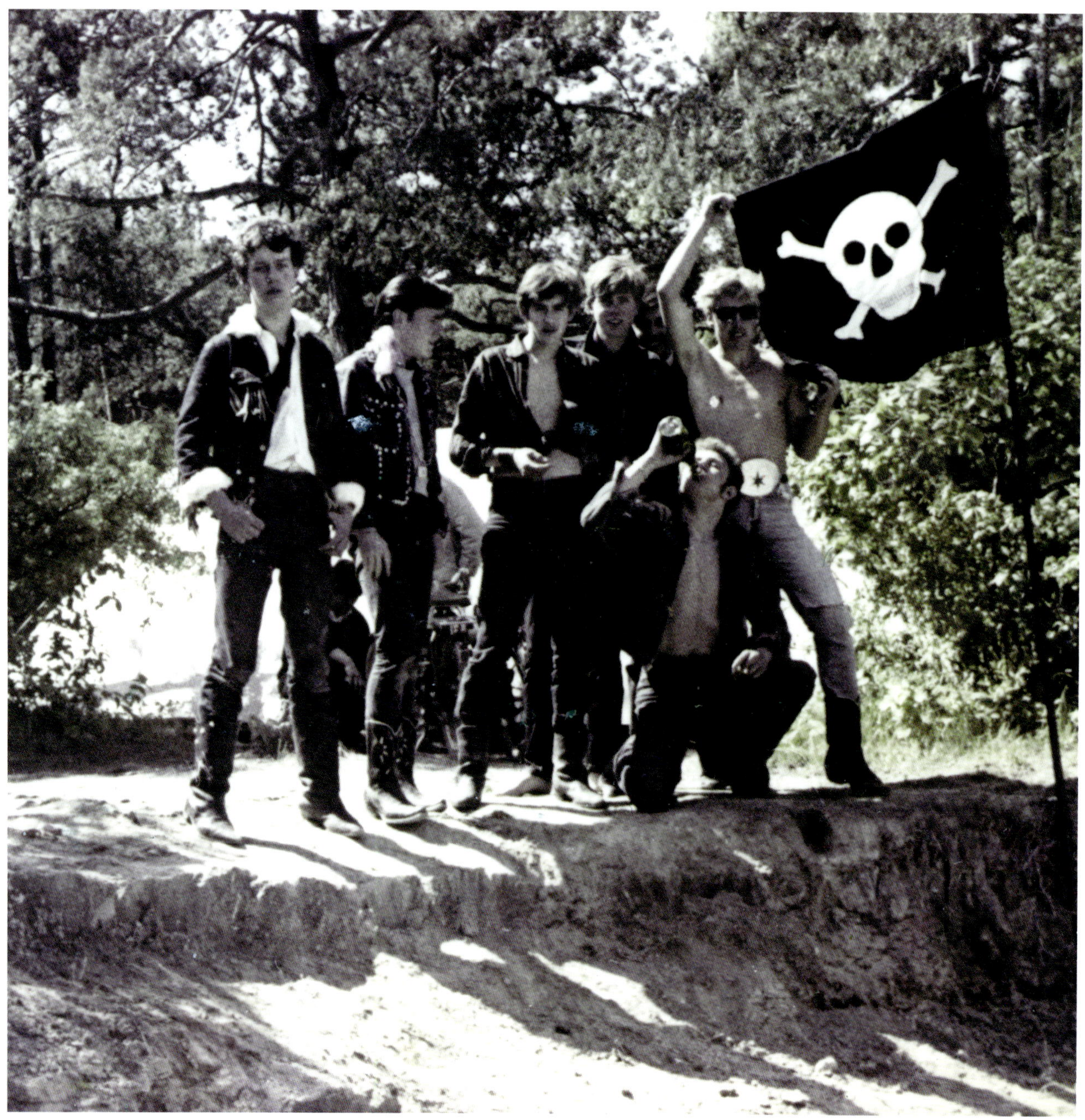

At St. Petersinsel.

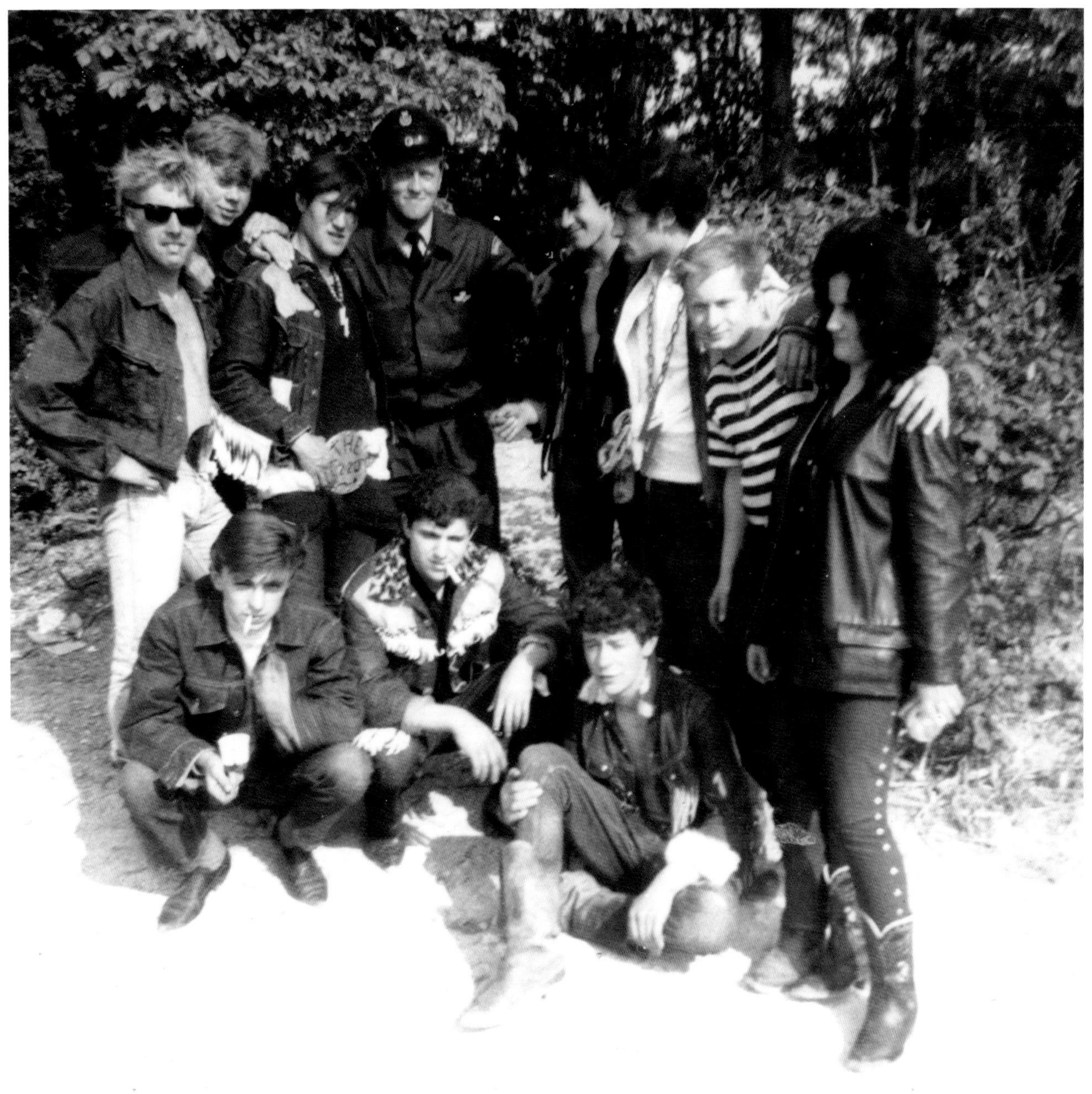

Igel handed his camera to a fellow gangster to pose with Rumy and friends in the woods. A friendly cop crashes the photo.

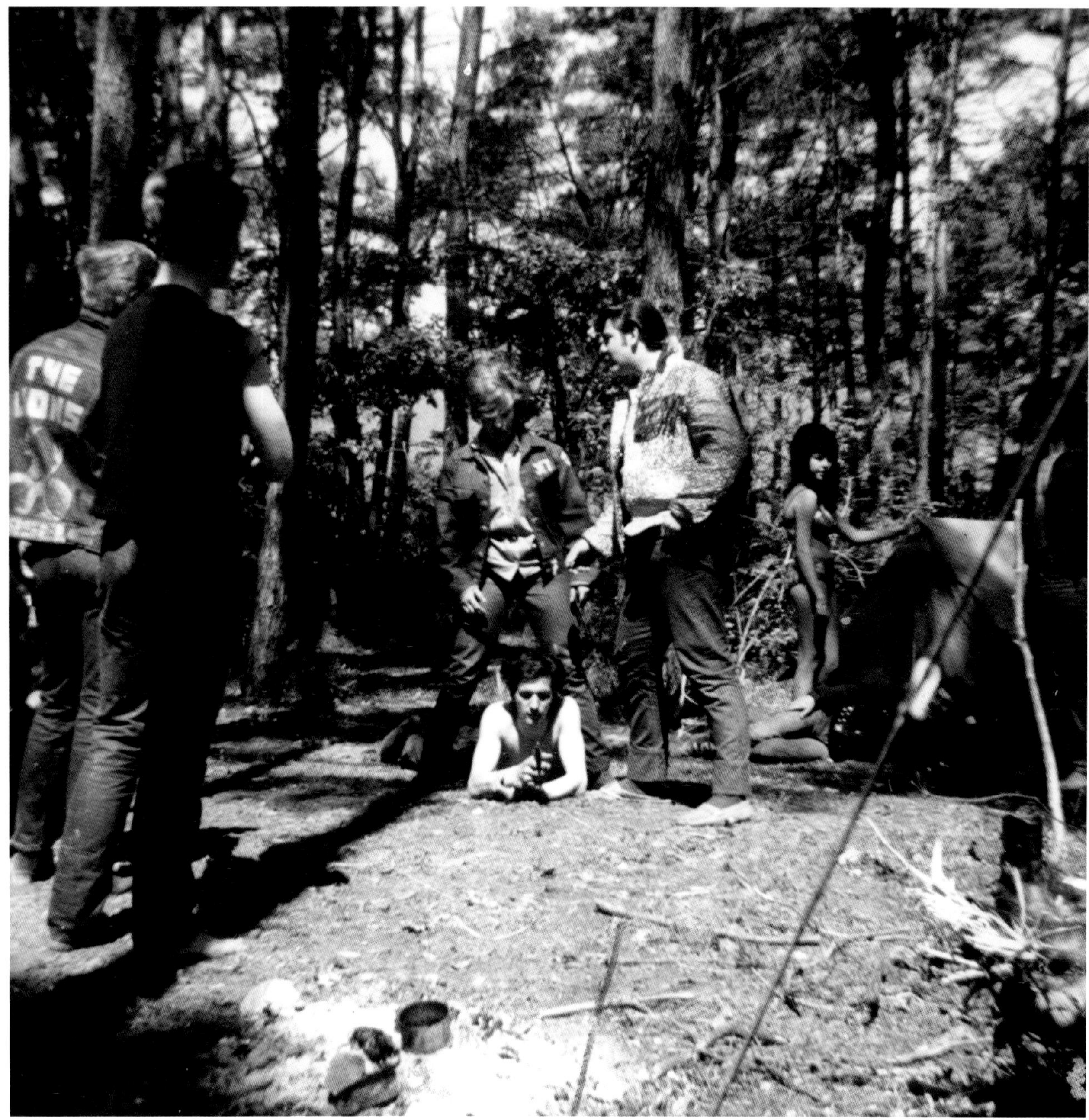

Camp gangland.

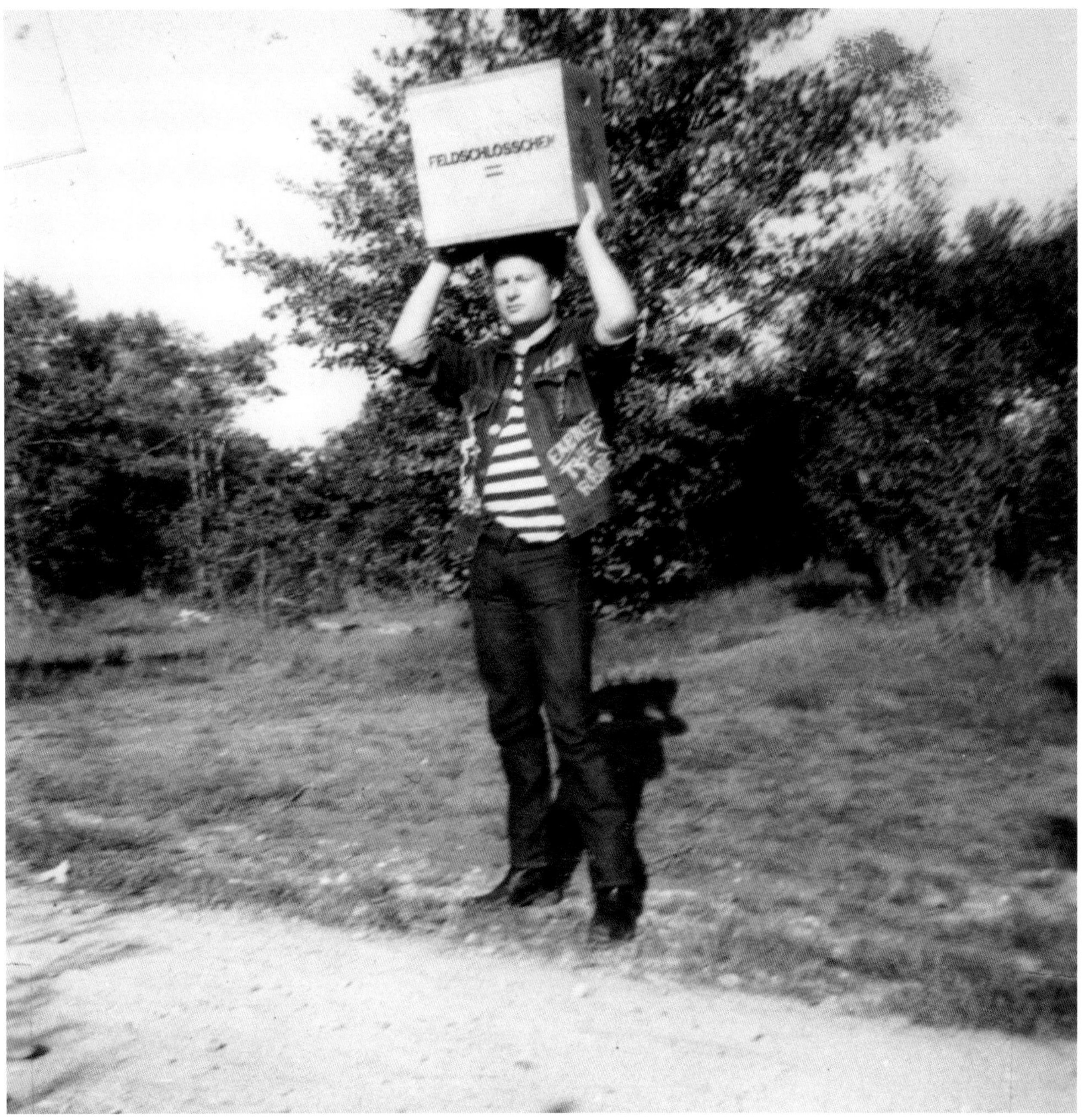

Igel producing one of countless crates of beer.

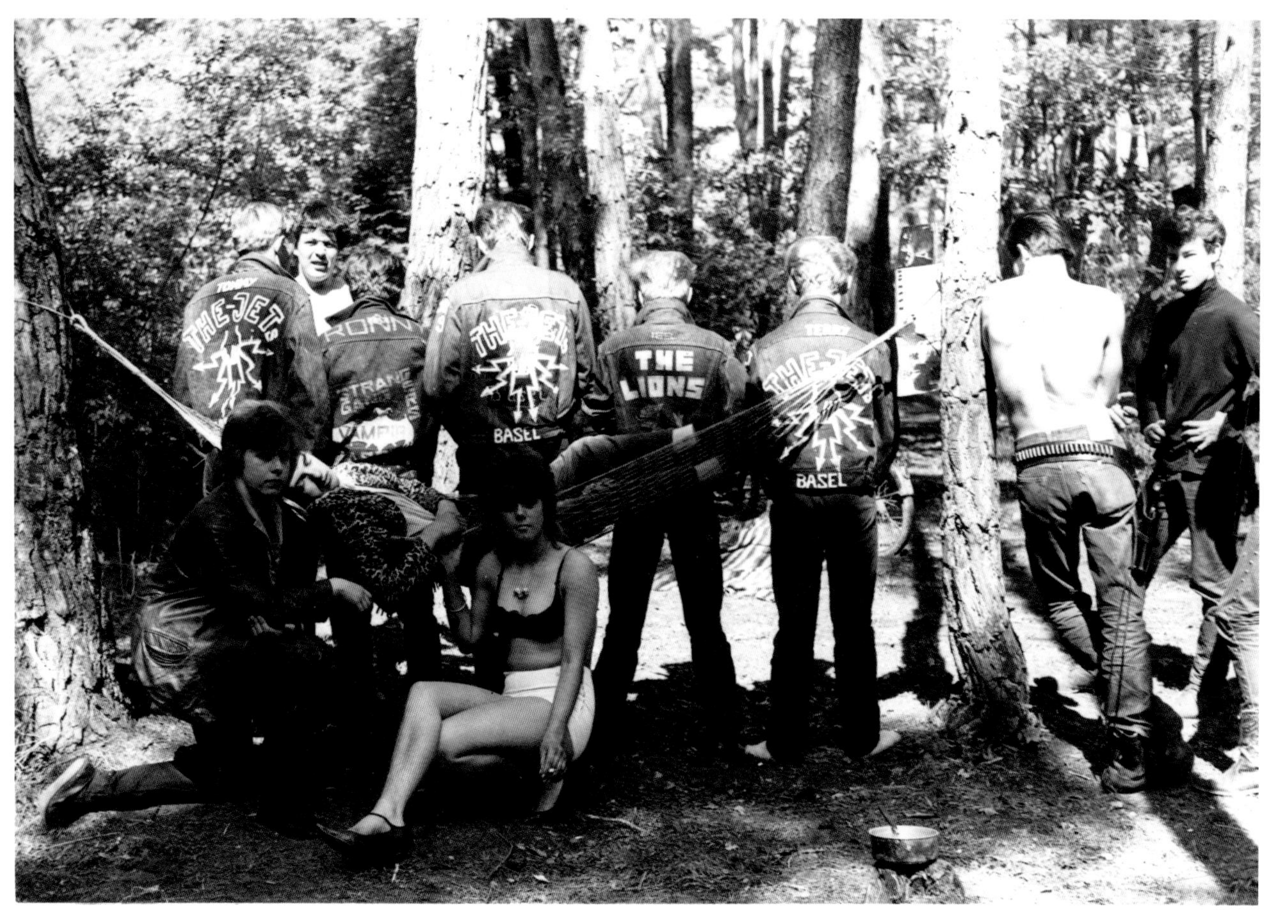

Evelyne Antener (sister of The Dynamites lead guitarist Rolf Antener), with Heidi Widmer and the usual suspects.

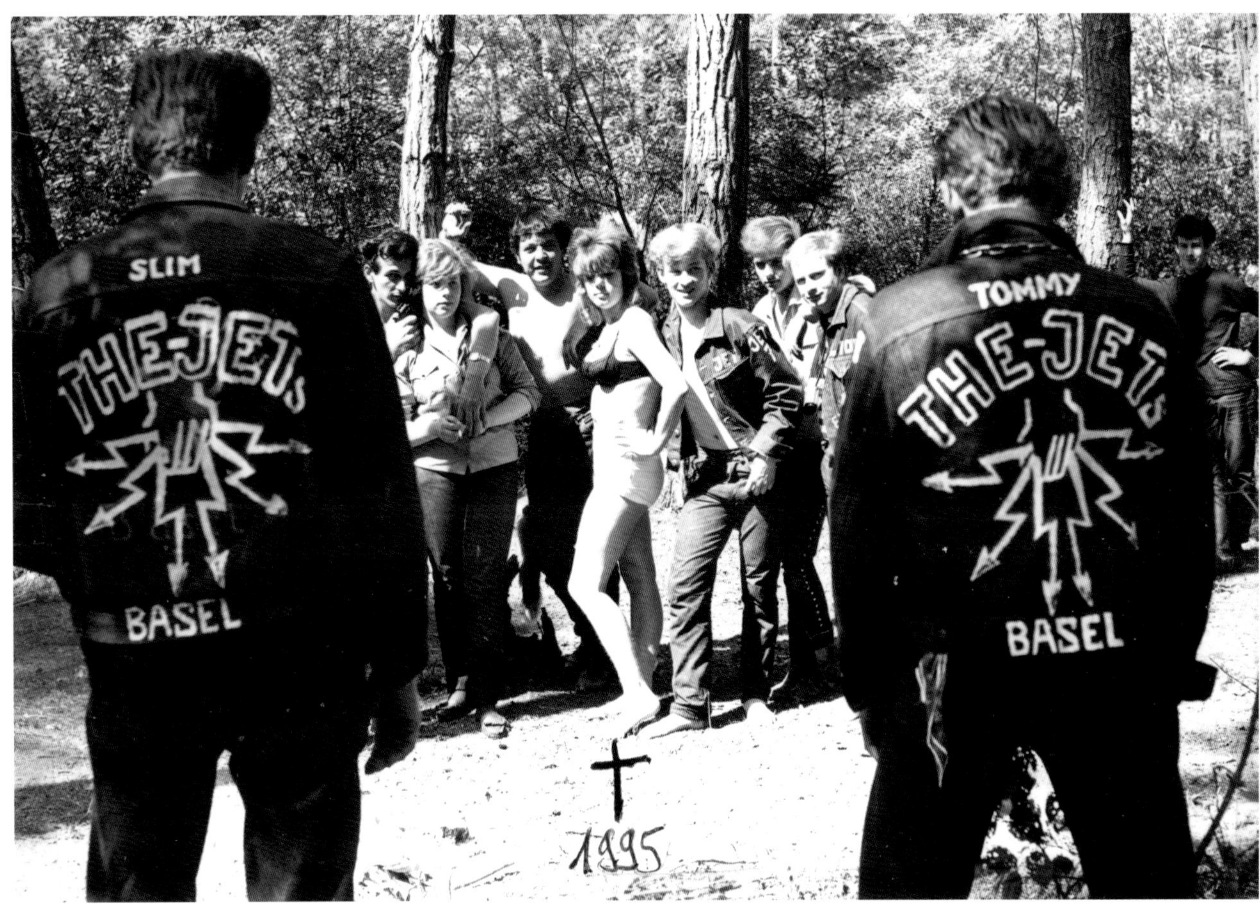

Slim and Tommy from The Jets control the scene. Cross and year, inscribed by Igel, marks Heidi's death in 1995.

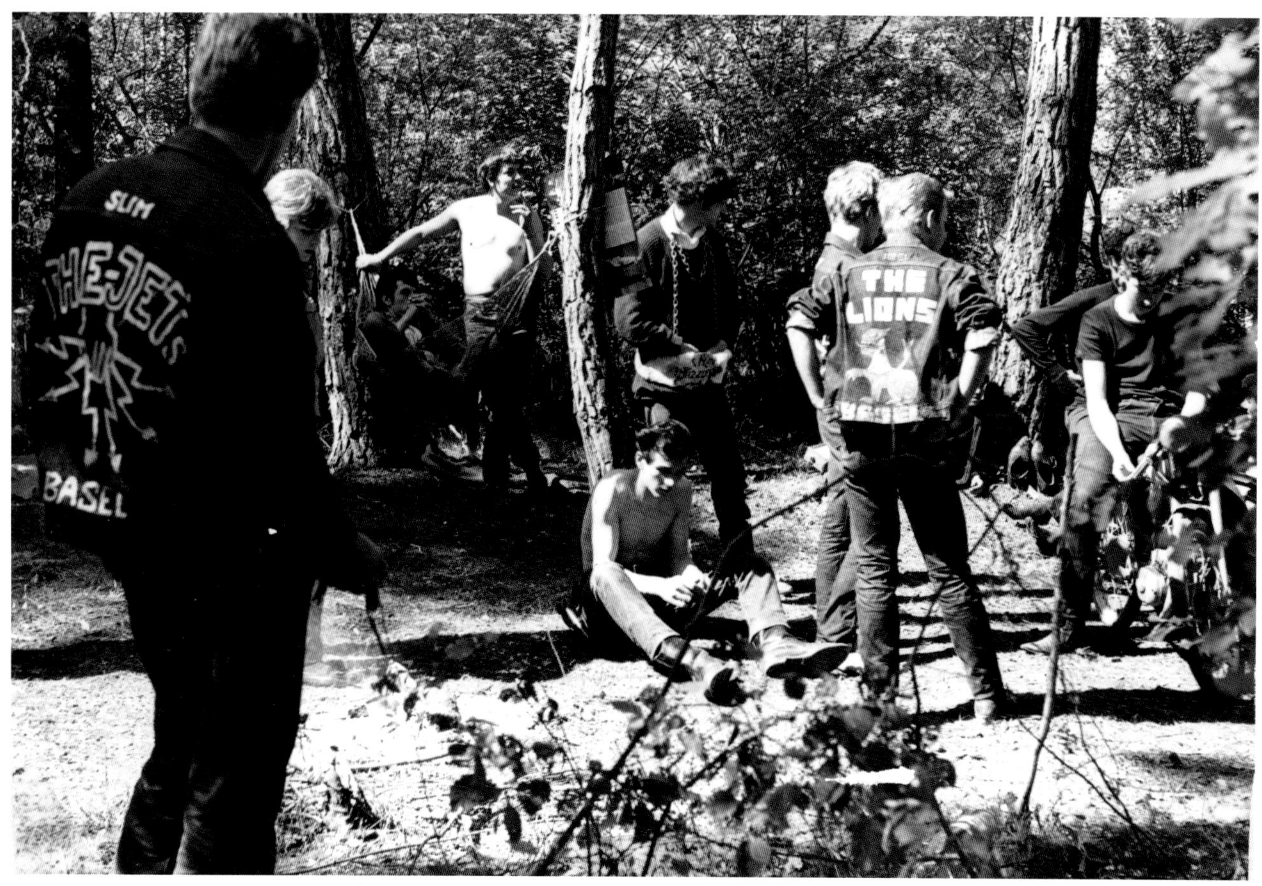

Slim, Sumo, Terry and Igel with Pecos (seated).

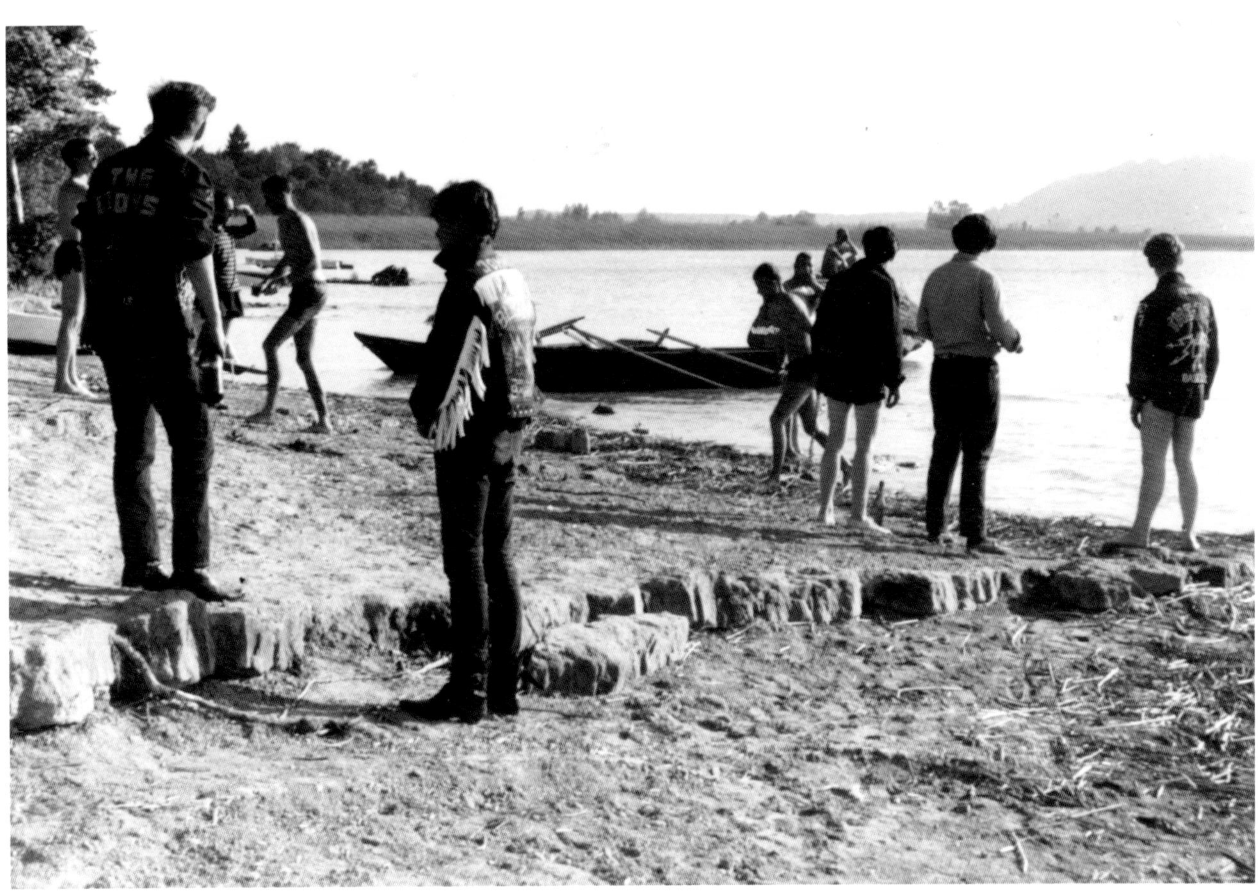

Igel (left) gets another beer on the beach.

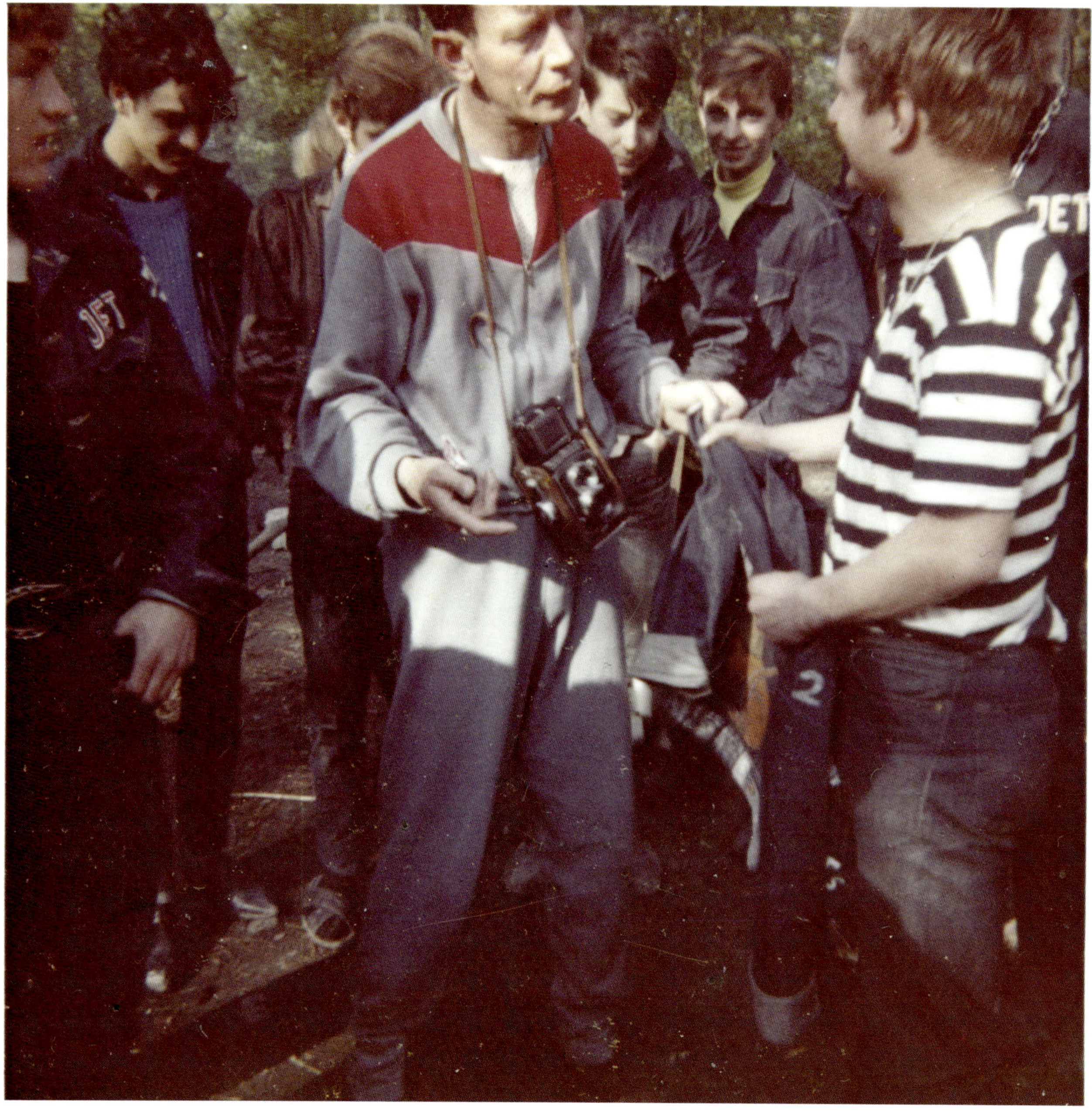

Karlheinz Weinberger, photographer from Zurich, pleaded with Igel not to burn his jacket, offering him fifty Swiss Francs for it. Igel took a match to his uniform.

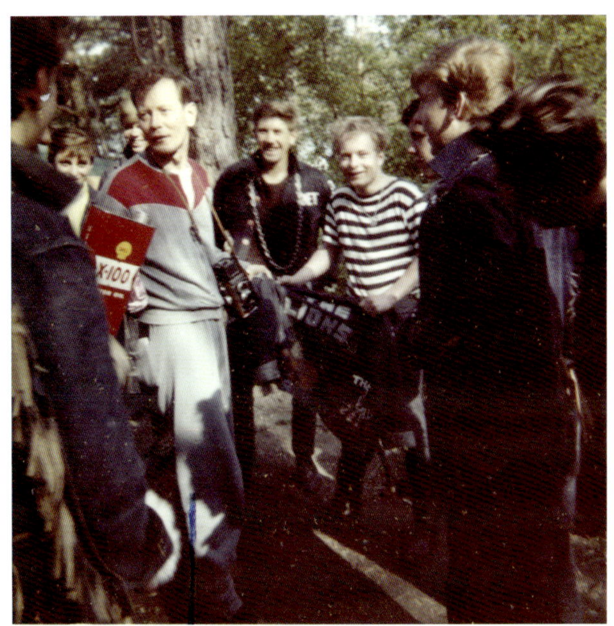

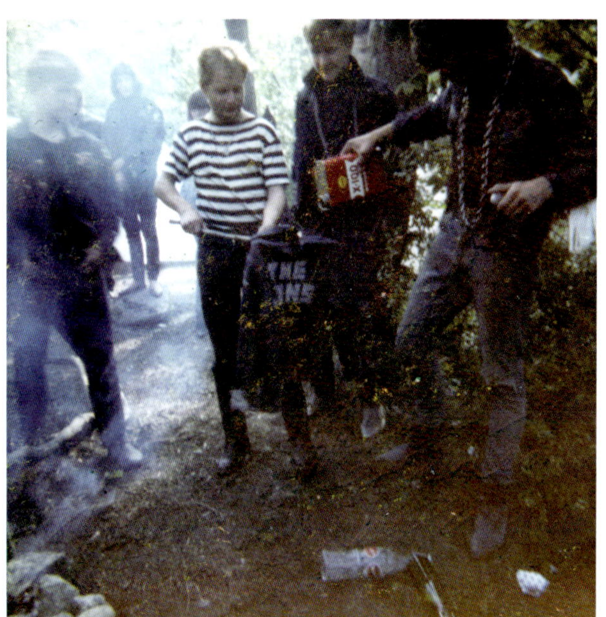

Weinberger disapproves of the jacket-burning ritual and leaves the scene.

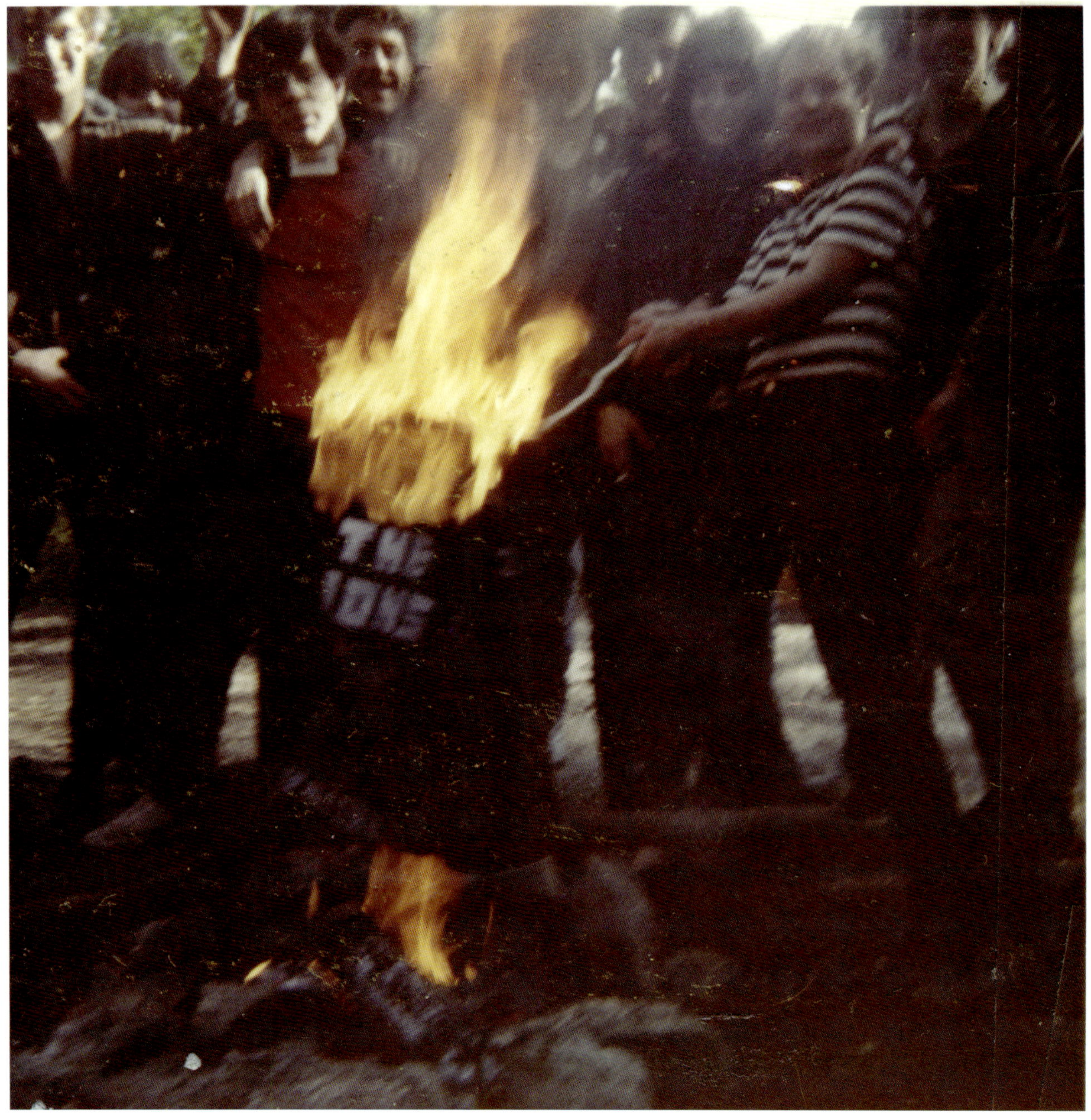

The burning of Igel’s Lions jacket.

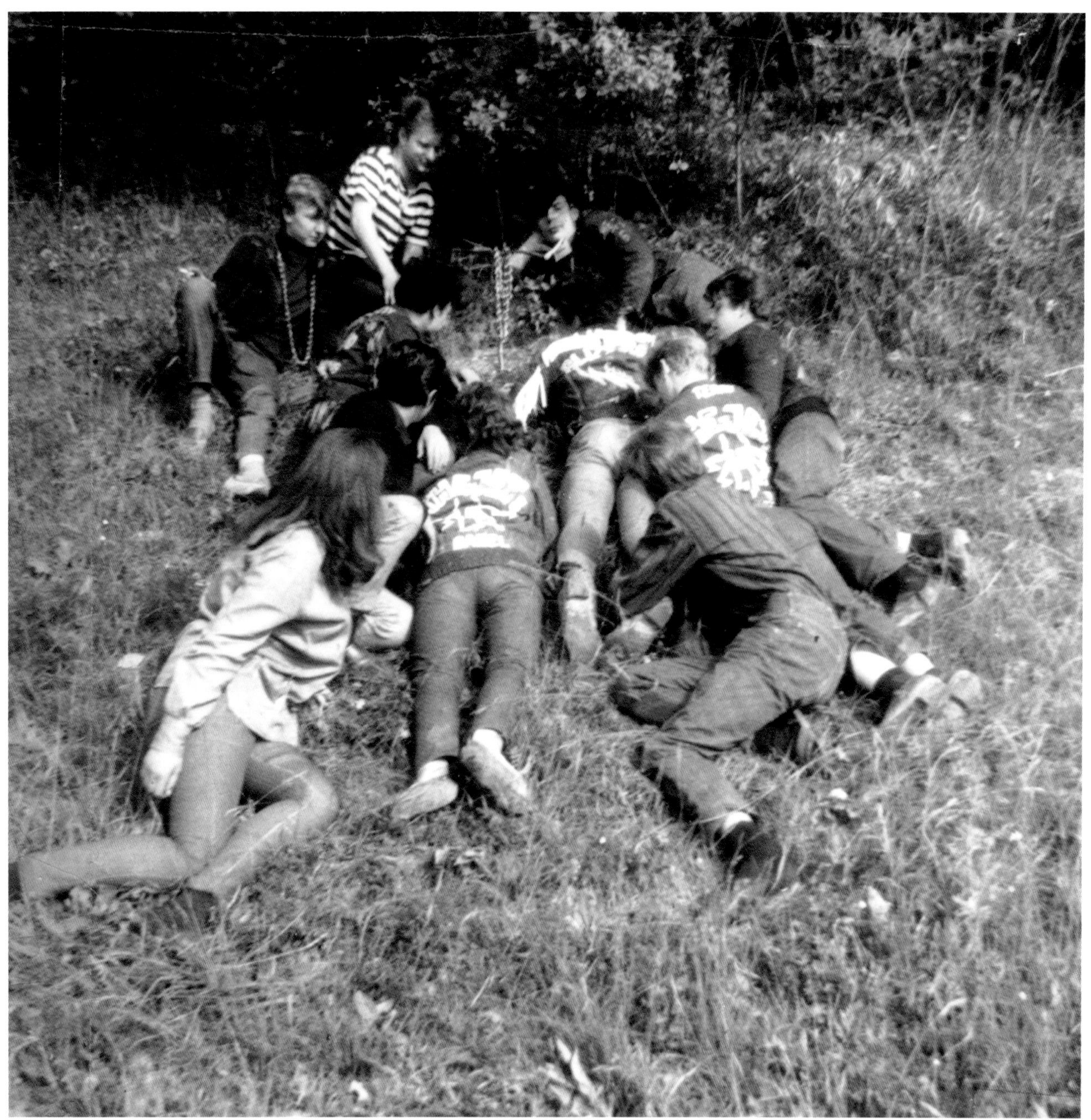

Paying respects.

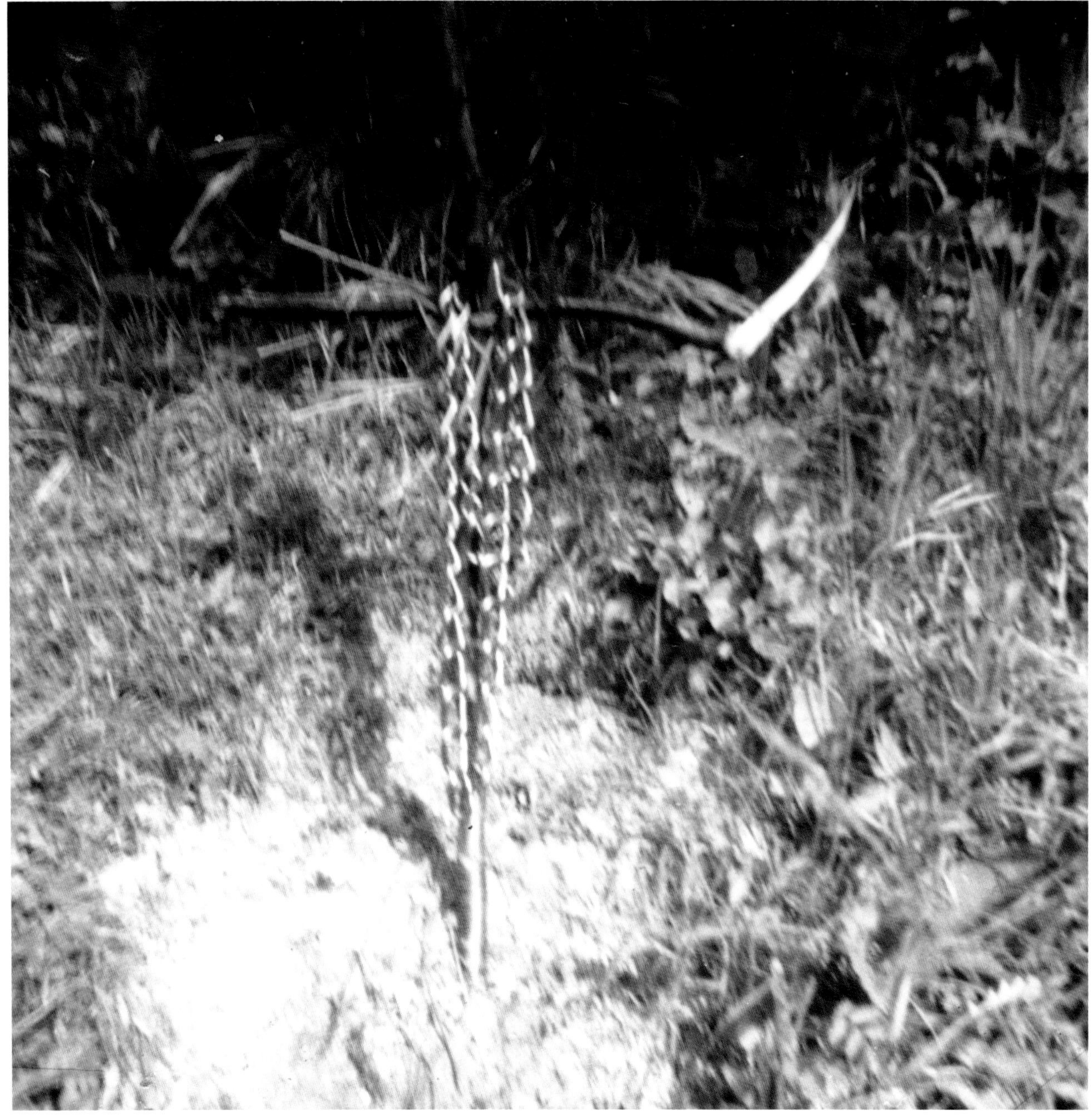

After the burning of his Lions jacket, Igel buried the remains in a small grave. He didn't want any mementos of gang life.

30/unknown first motorcycle gang from basel
1964

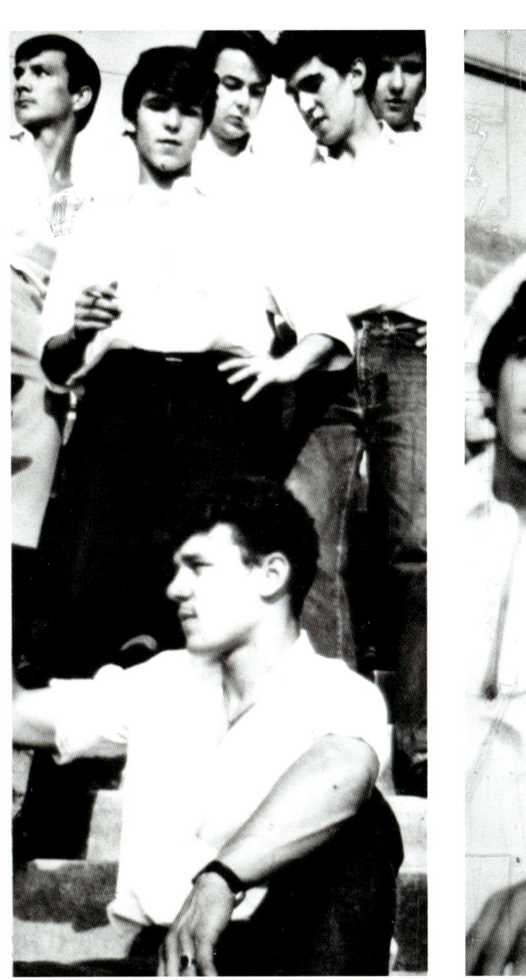

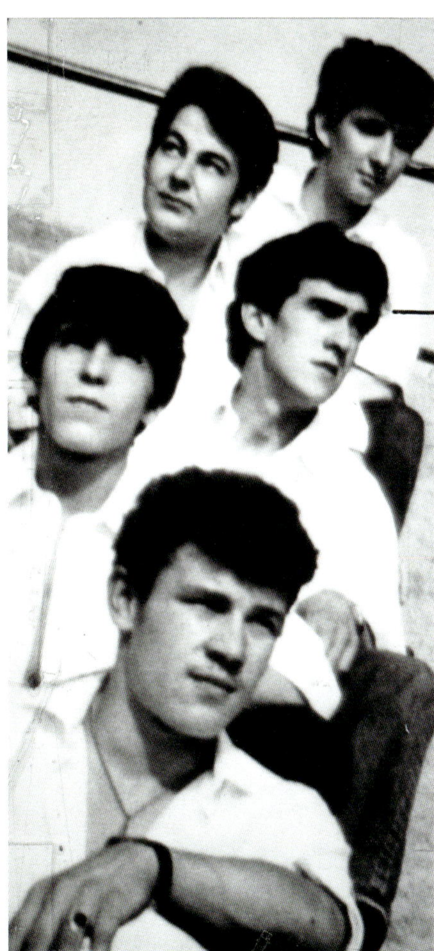

Left: Erwin Metzer was the leader of the first motorcycle gang from Basel in 1964, comprised of six members. The name of their first gang remains unknown. Right: Boss Erwin Metzger with four of his pack.

31 / seenachtsfest, lucerne
june 27–28, 1964

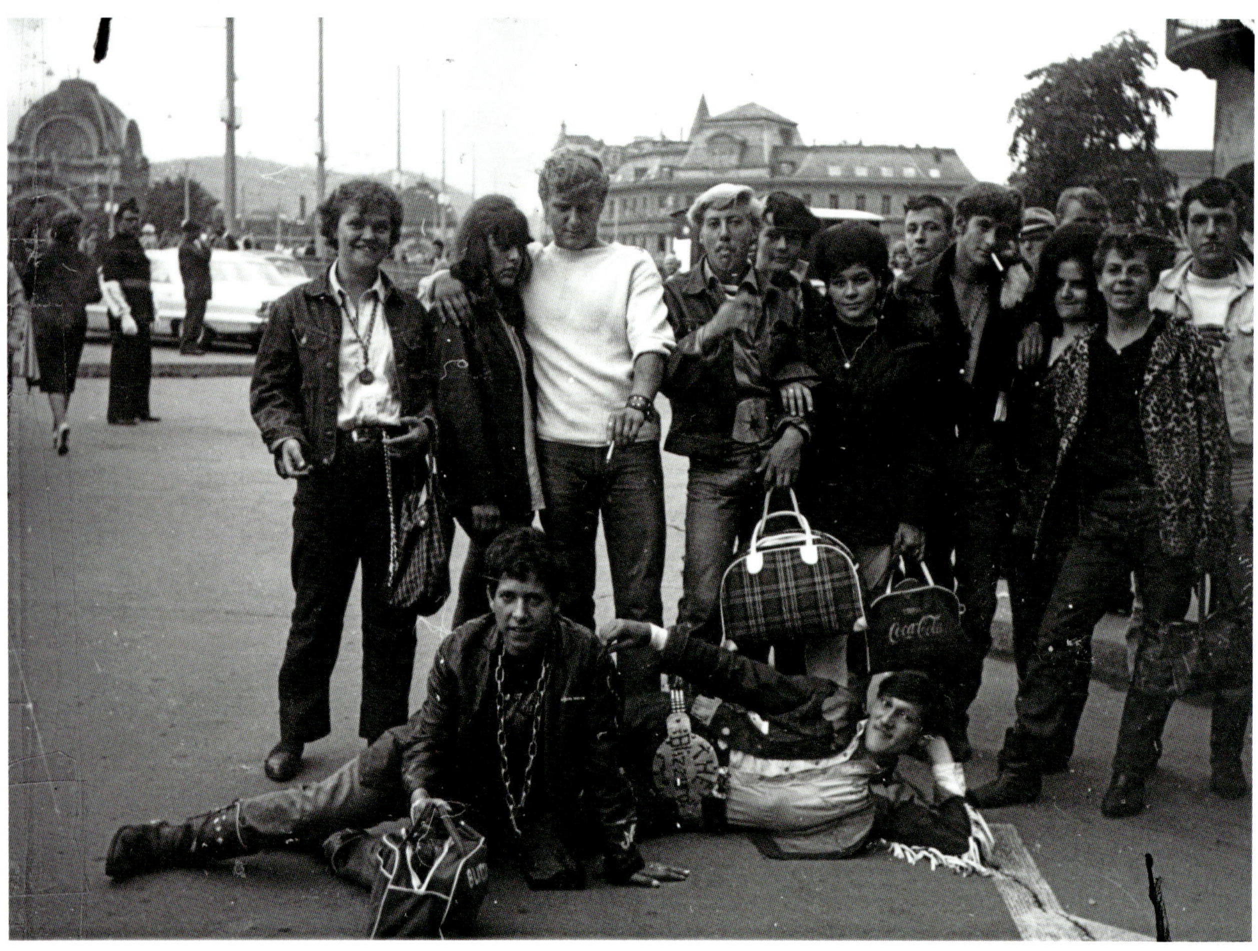

Clochard from The Blizzard Gang Basel (right front), surrounded by his friends upon arrival in Lucerne.

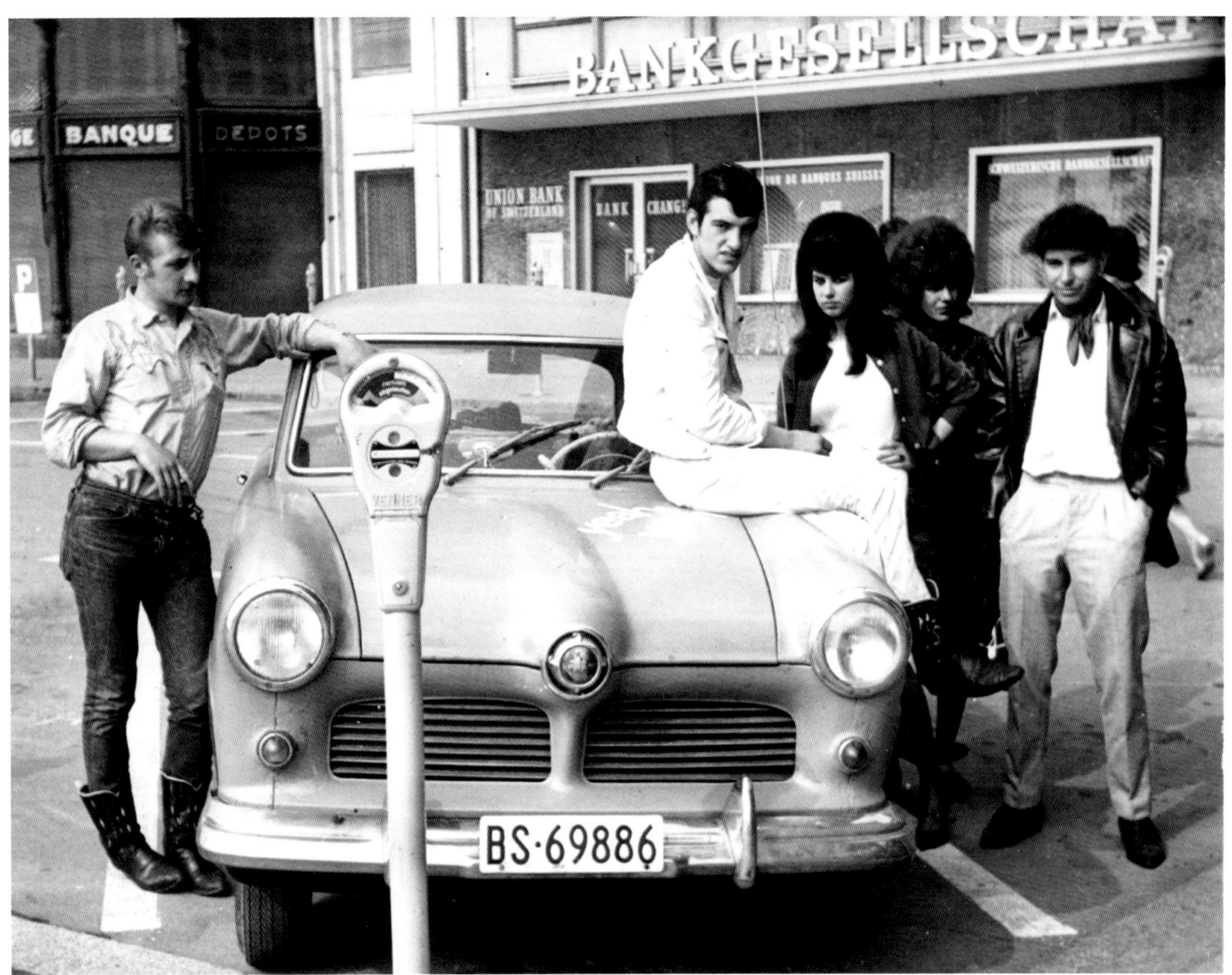

Ray Christen, Red, Sylvia Nebel, and unknown couple.

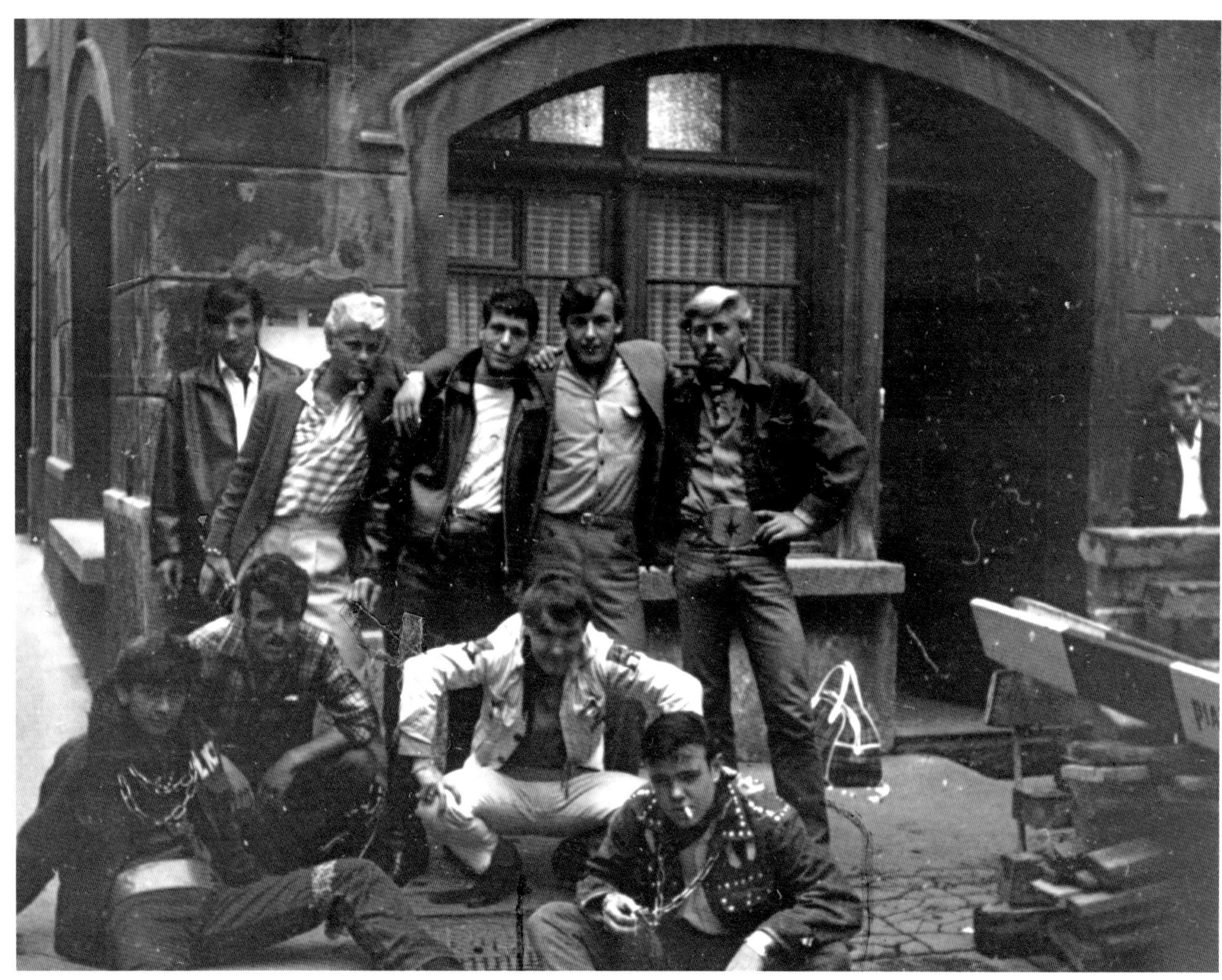

Johnsy (in white) surrounded by various Swiss gang members.

32/the black devil gang, photo session including clochard and tino, basel
september 1964

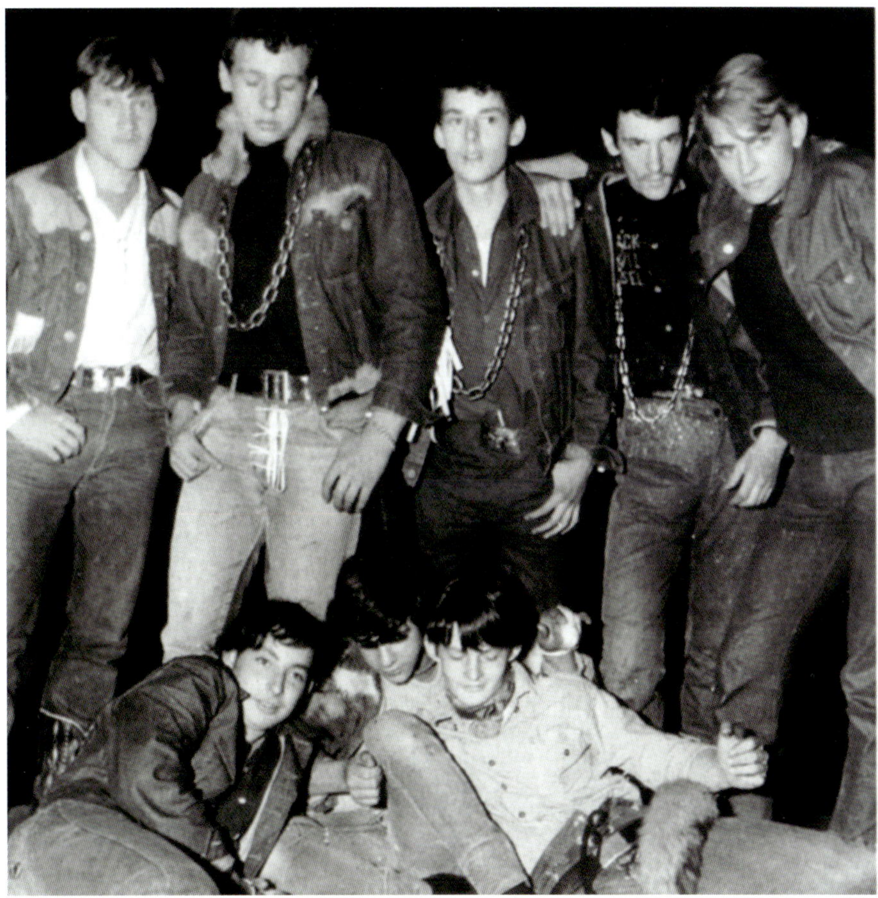

The Black Devil Gang are misidentified in this photo, published by the Swiss press in September, 1964. Clochard and Tino (top left) were actually from the rival Blizzard Gang Basel. The pair were never members of The Black Devil Gang. BD Gang boss Mischuta is fourth from left in top row, in a black shirt that reads "Black Devil Basel." (Photographer unknown)

33/rächer basel, in biel
october or november 1964

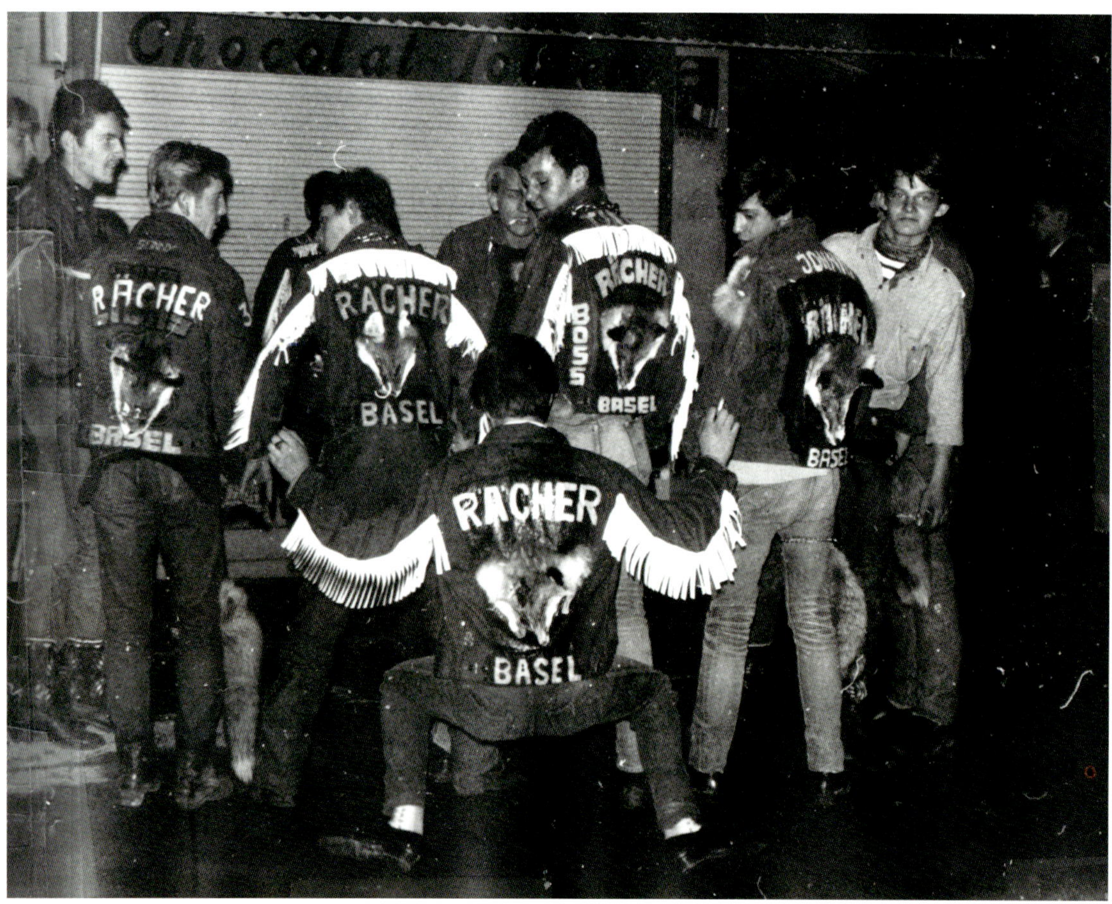

Early photo of Tino's Racher gang, an offshoot of Romeo's Racher gang (The Revenger Gang) from Zurich. Founded by Tino, they are known as the last Halbstarken gang from Basel. Tino is shown wearing the boss jacket. Heads of dead foxes were sewn as emblems onto the backs of their jackets, effectively creating the wildest club jackets in Swiss gang history. Black Devil Basel boss Mischuta is at far left.

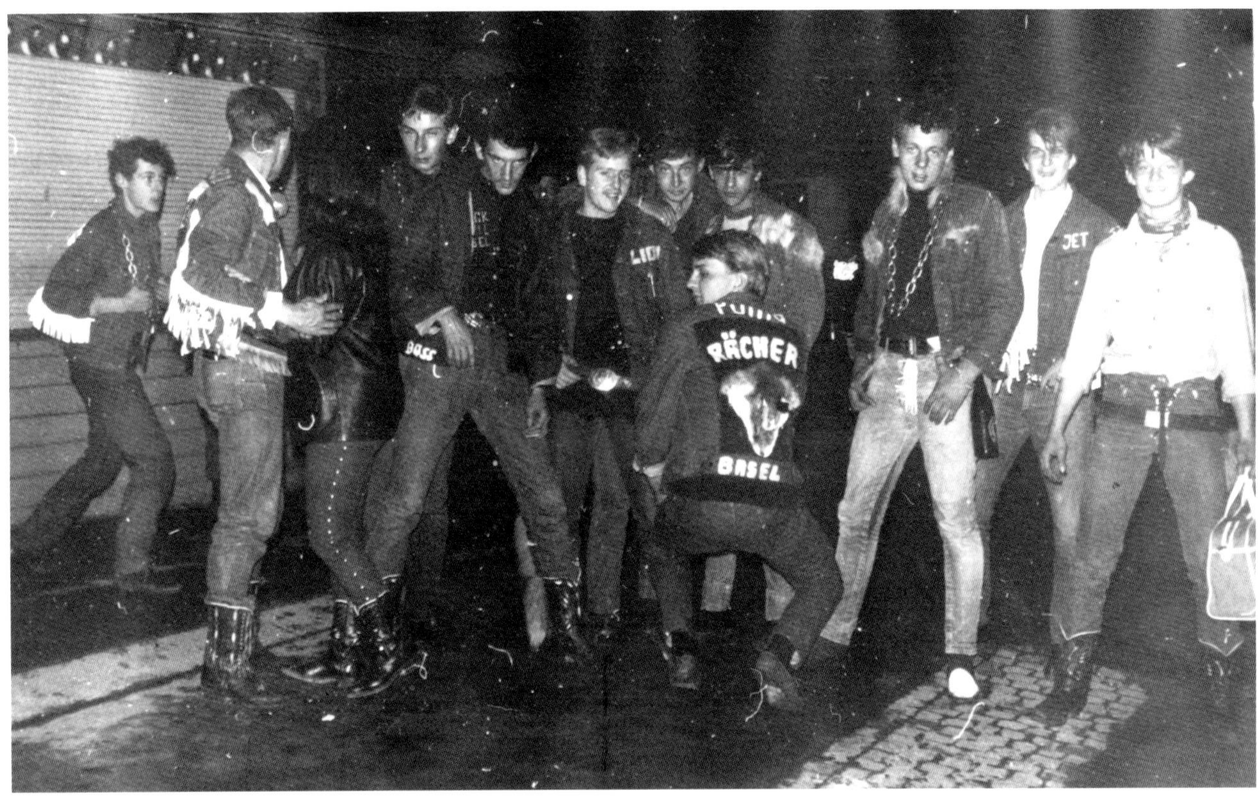

The Racher Basel existed only for a couple of short months with Tino as boss, as he would leave the Racher Basel to join Romeo's The Revenger Gang Zurich (aka Racher Zurich) to become their vice-boss. After Tino's departure, the Racher Basel continued for two years with Jet (originally from the Venom gang) as their leader. Tino is third from right (washed out jeans with crazy zipper). Jet is second from right. Black Devil boss Michuta is fifth guy from left.

34/wine-festival in neuenburg with the jets
october 3–4, 1964

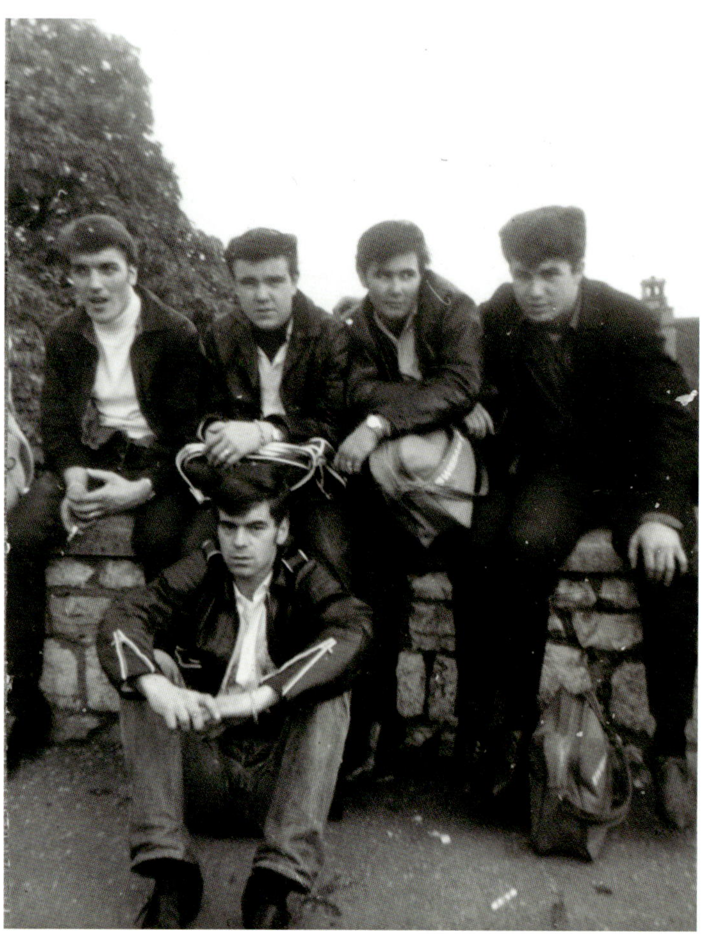

Even though Igel quit being a Blackboard Jungle type of Halbstarken rebel gang member when he burned his Lions jacket at St. Petersinsel on Sunday, May 17, 1964, he stayed friendly with his old pals from the gangs afterwards.

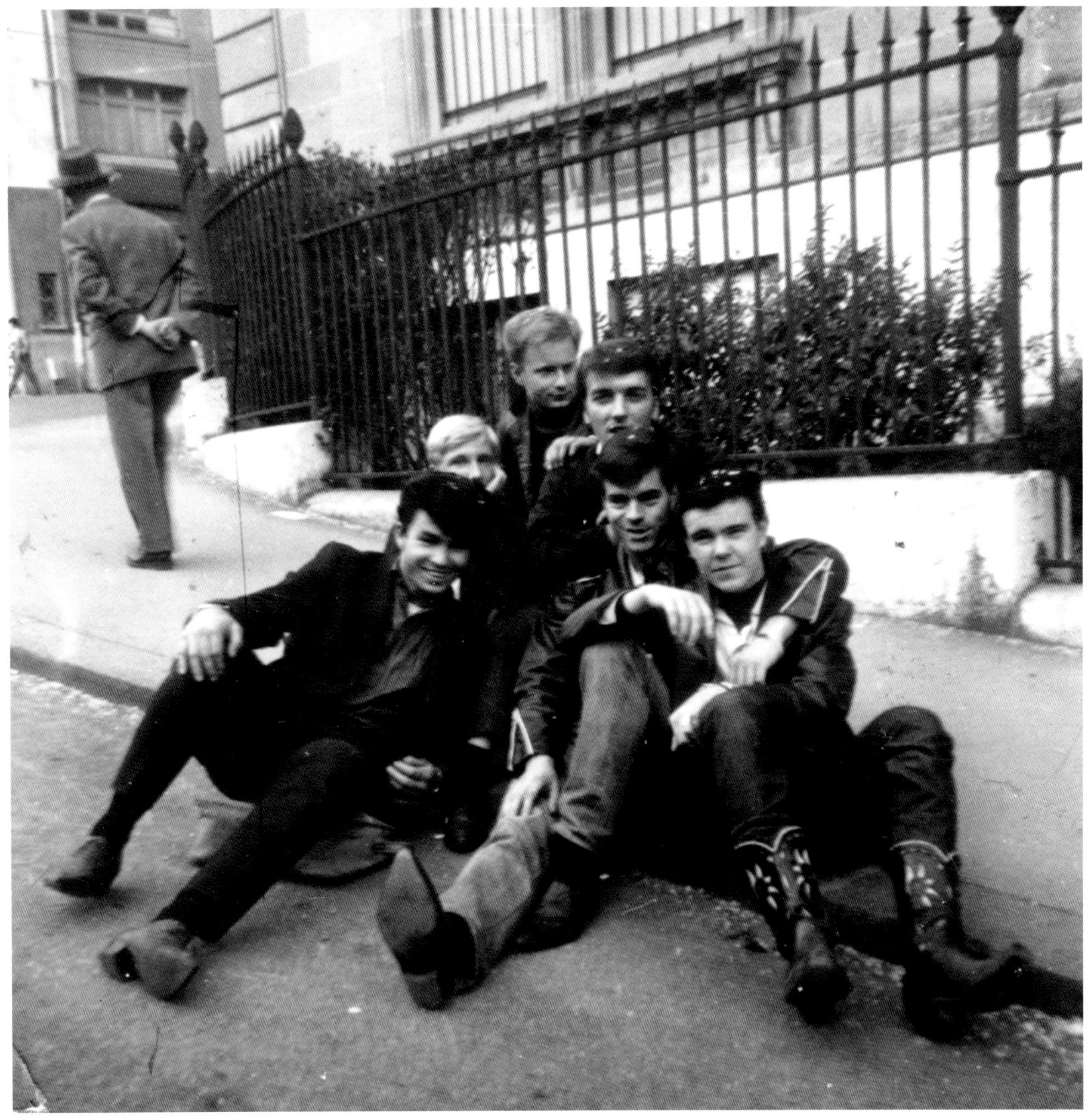

Igel, at back with fellow gang members.

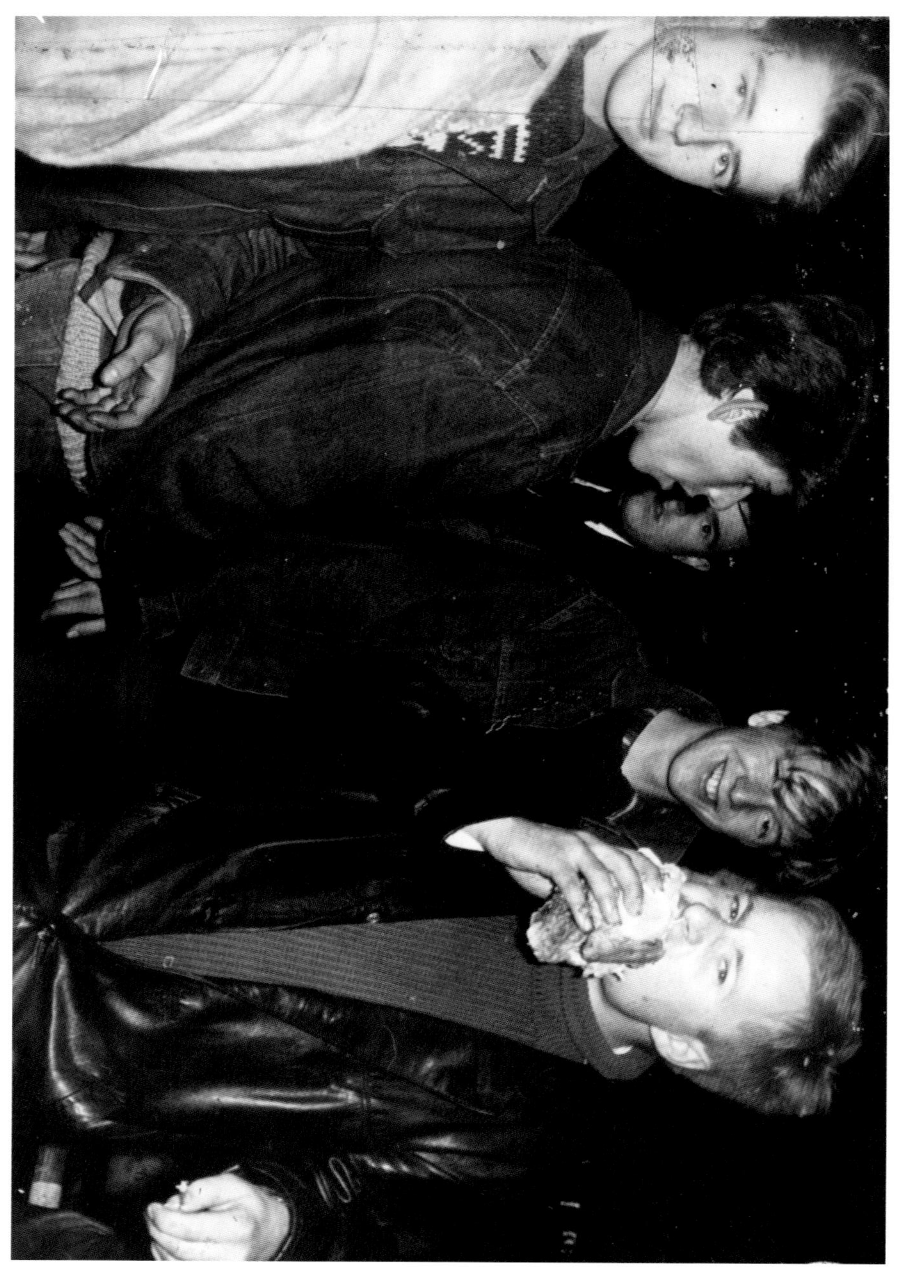

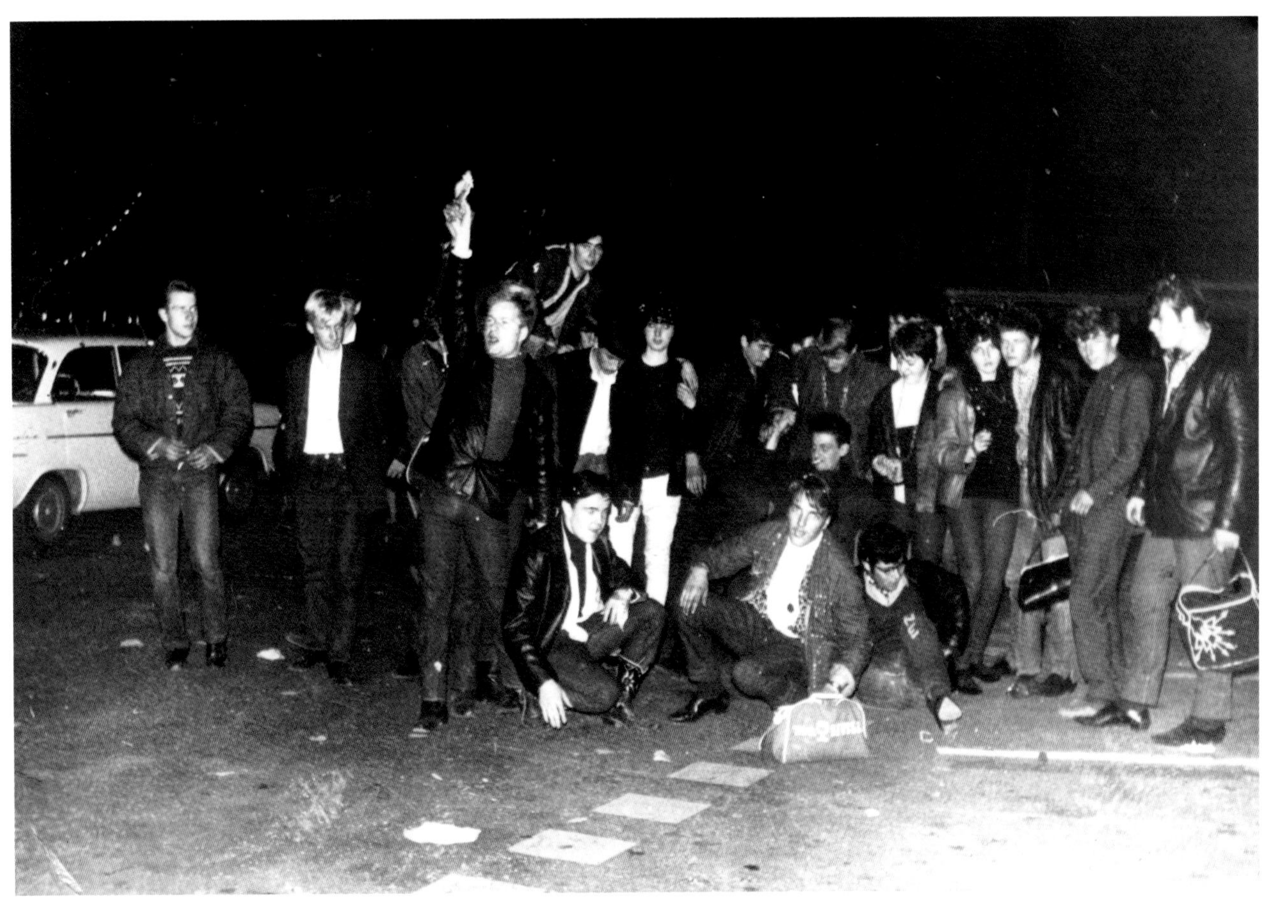

Igel controls his mob by waving a turkey leg at them.

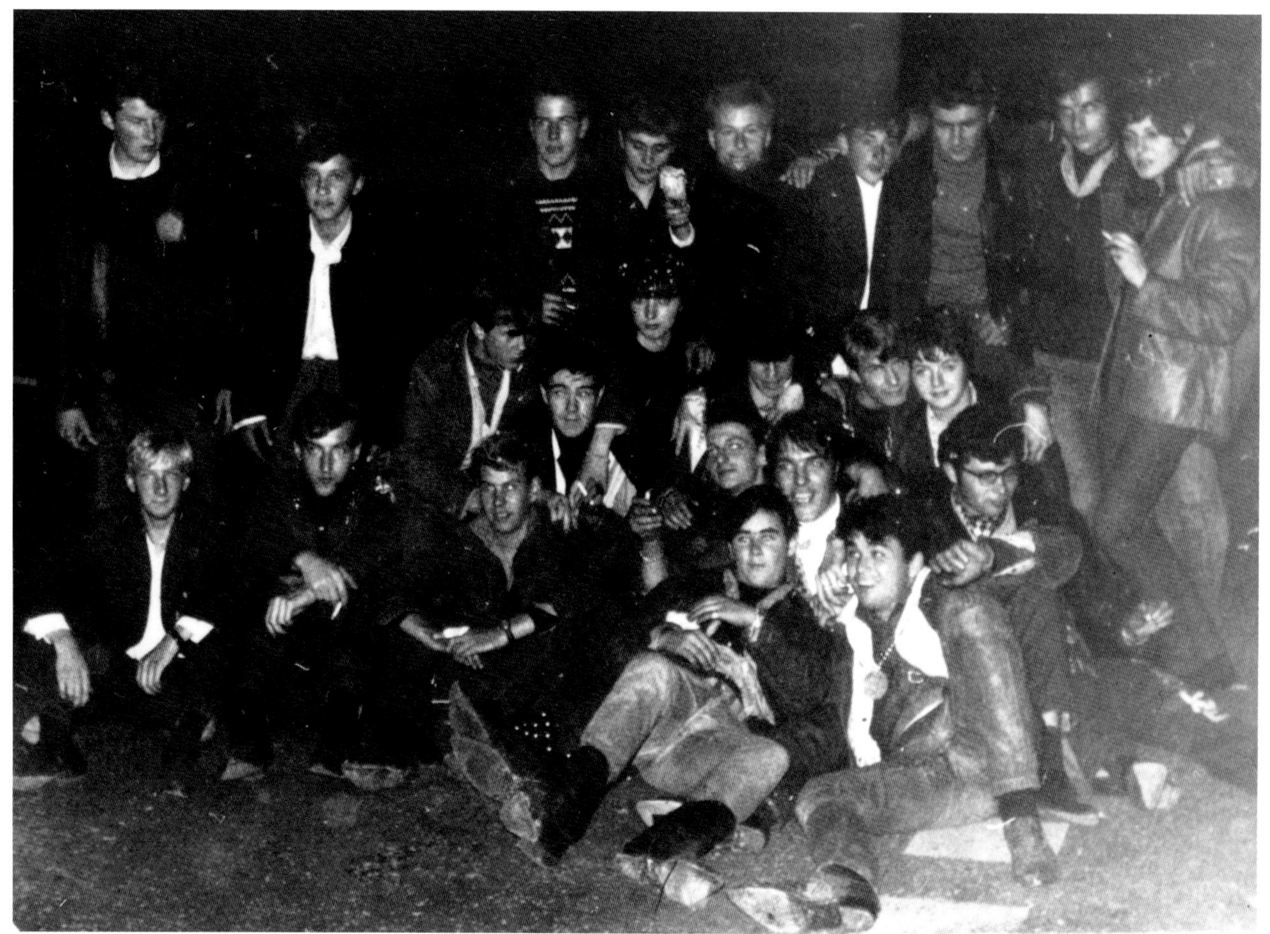

Igel surrounded by various members of different gangs.

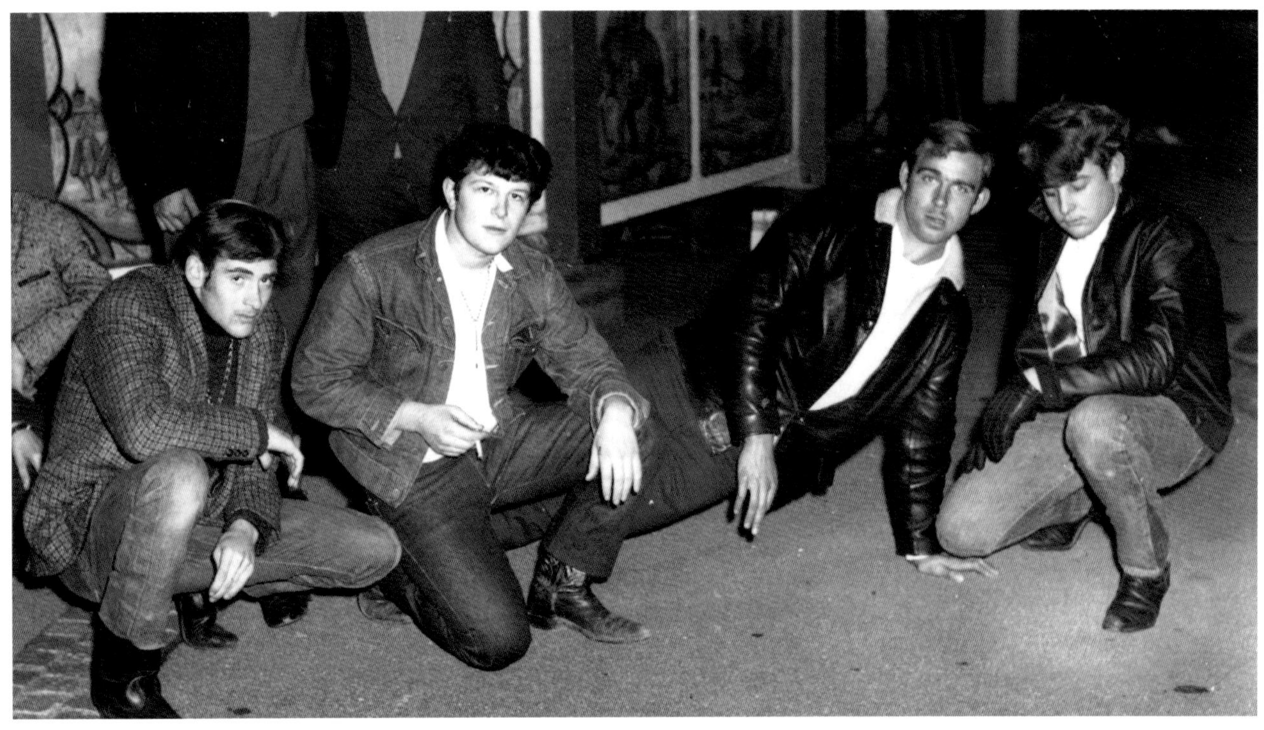

Four members of the Blizzard Club, Basel. Their boss Jackie appears as the second guy from the left. Photo from the collection of Marcel "Jacky" Zimmerli.

35/herbstmesse, basel at mustermesse
october 24–november 8, 1964

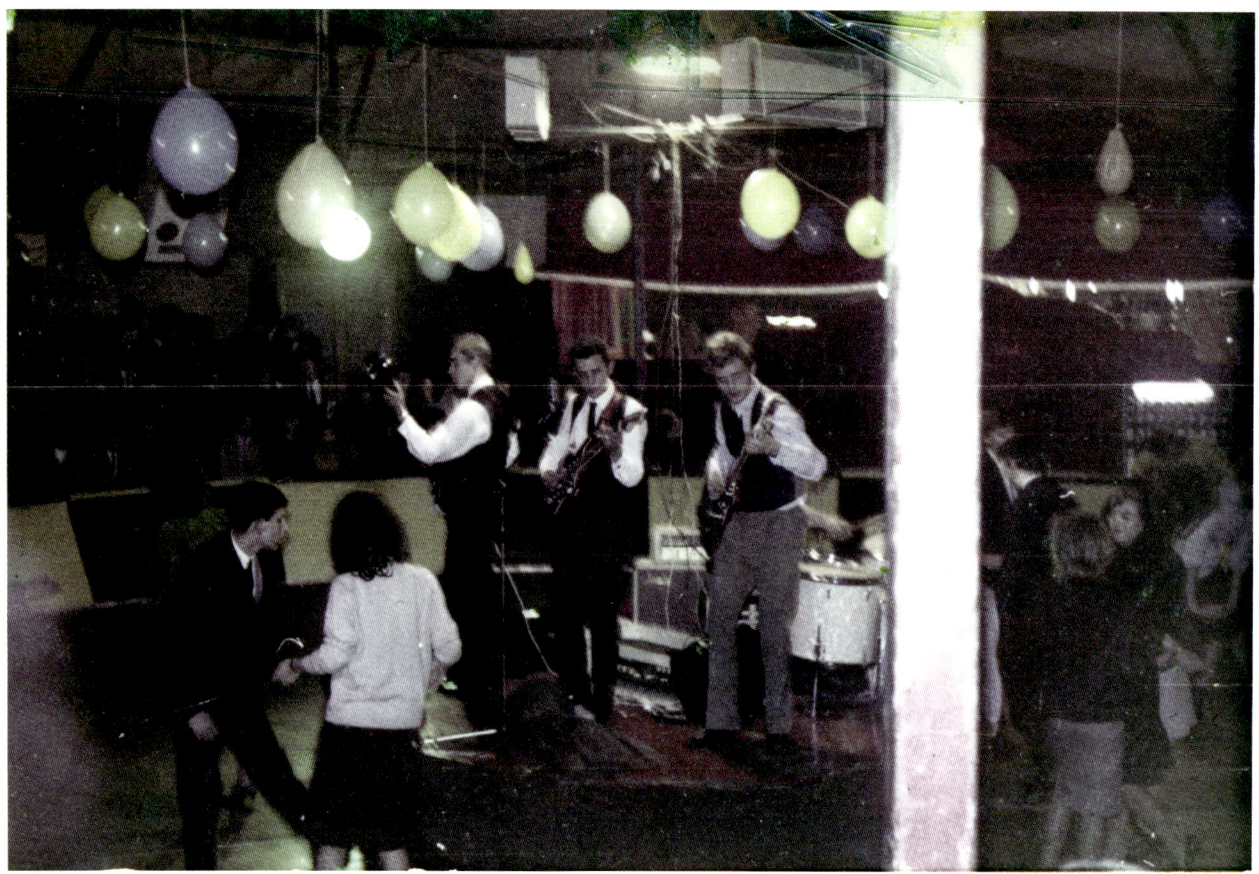

At Basel Herbstmesse, there were many now-extinct fairground attractions. Here we see the interior of the legendary Tanzrad, the dancing wheel, which hosted beat bands from Basel and abroad. Teens would dance in the turning wheel.

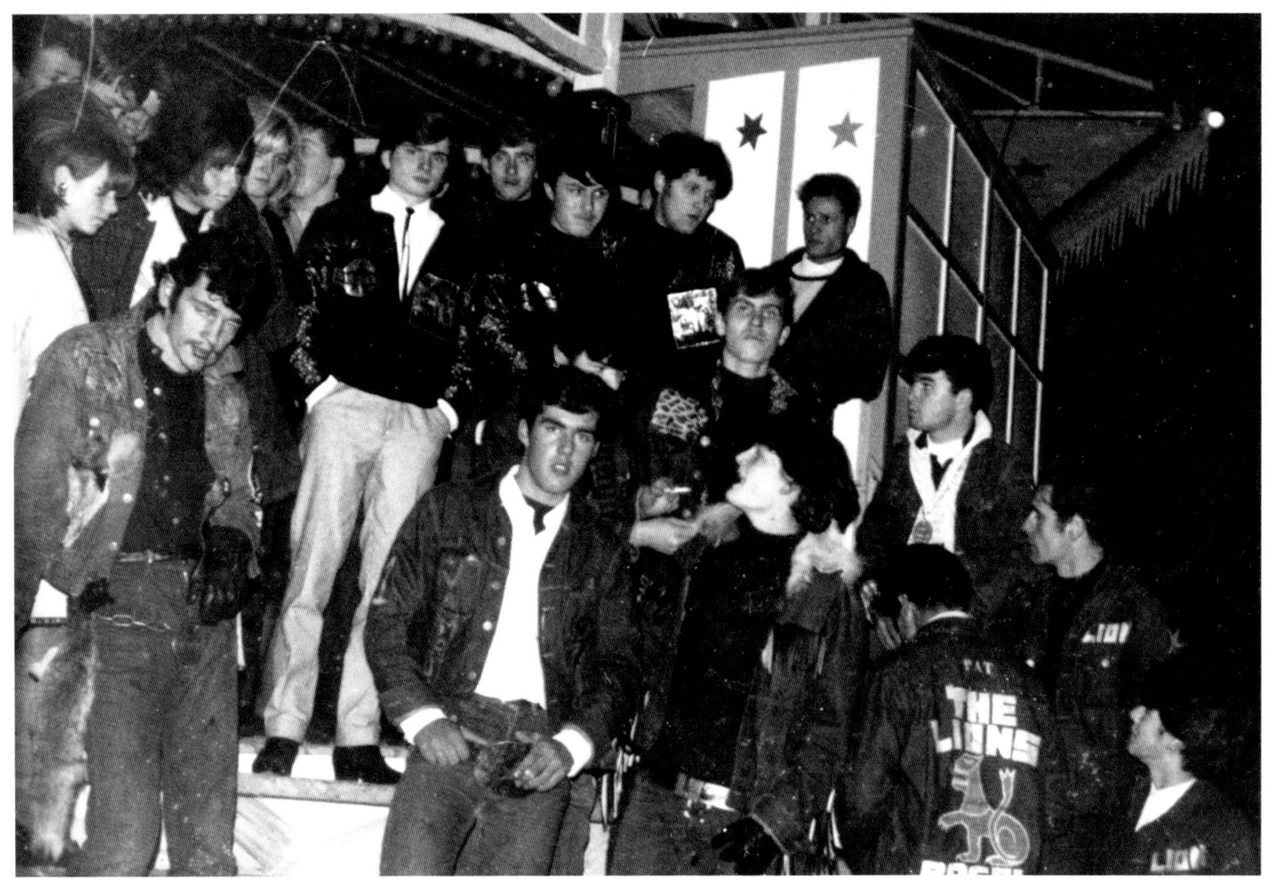

Gang members from Strangers Gang Vampir Basel and from The Lions await their turn at the Cortina Bob. On the left, Mischuta.

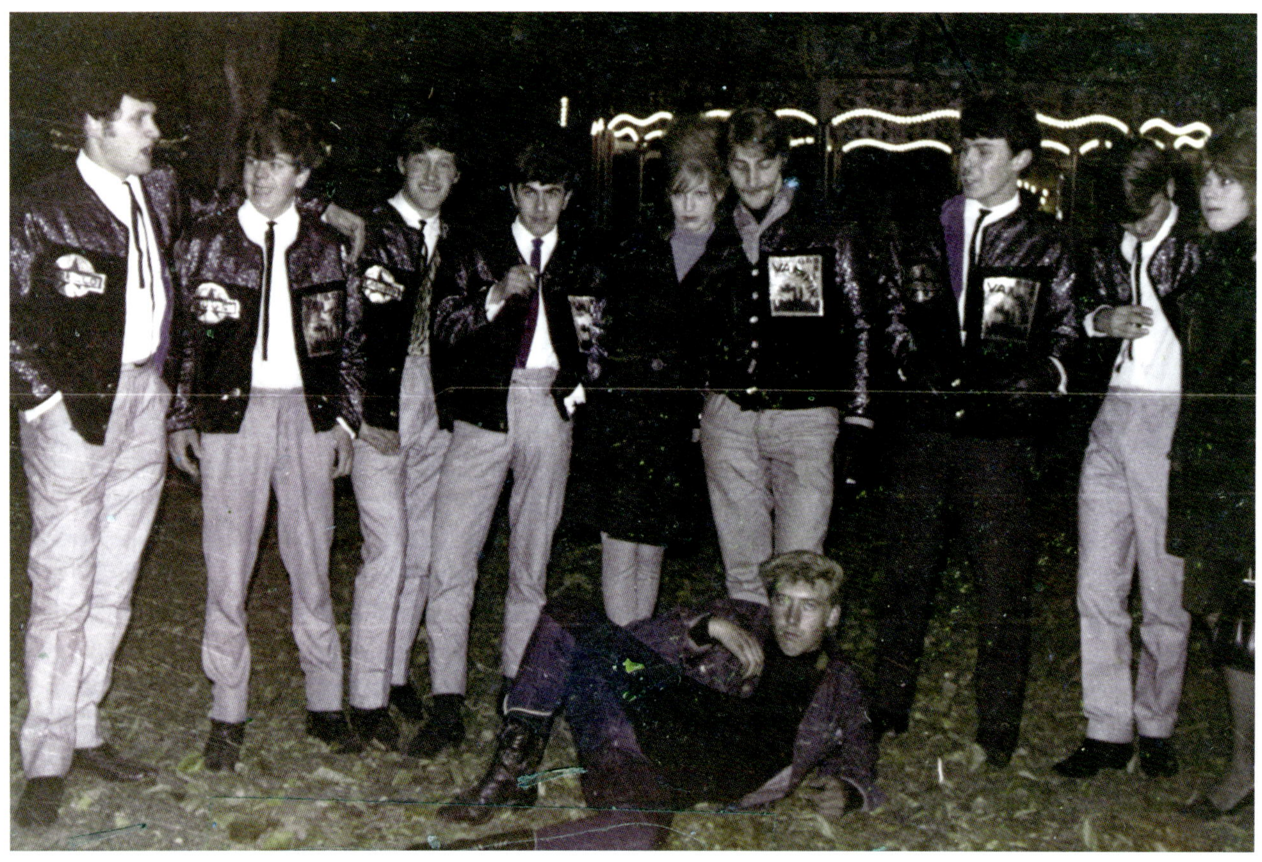

Fashion-conscious Vampir boss Ray "Killer" Christen, together with his girlfriend Vreni, and his crew, is shown sporting brand new Vampir gear. Clochard (third from left) came out of The Blizzard Gang. Muus is second from left; second from right is Dracula.

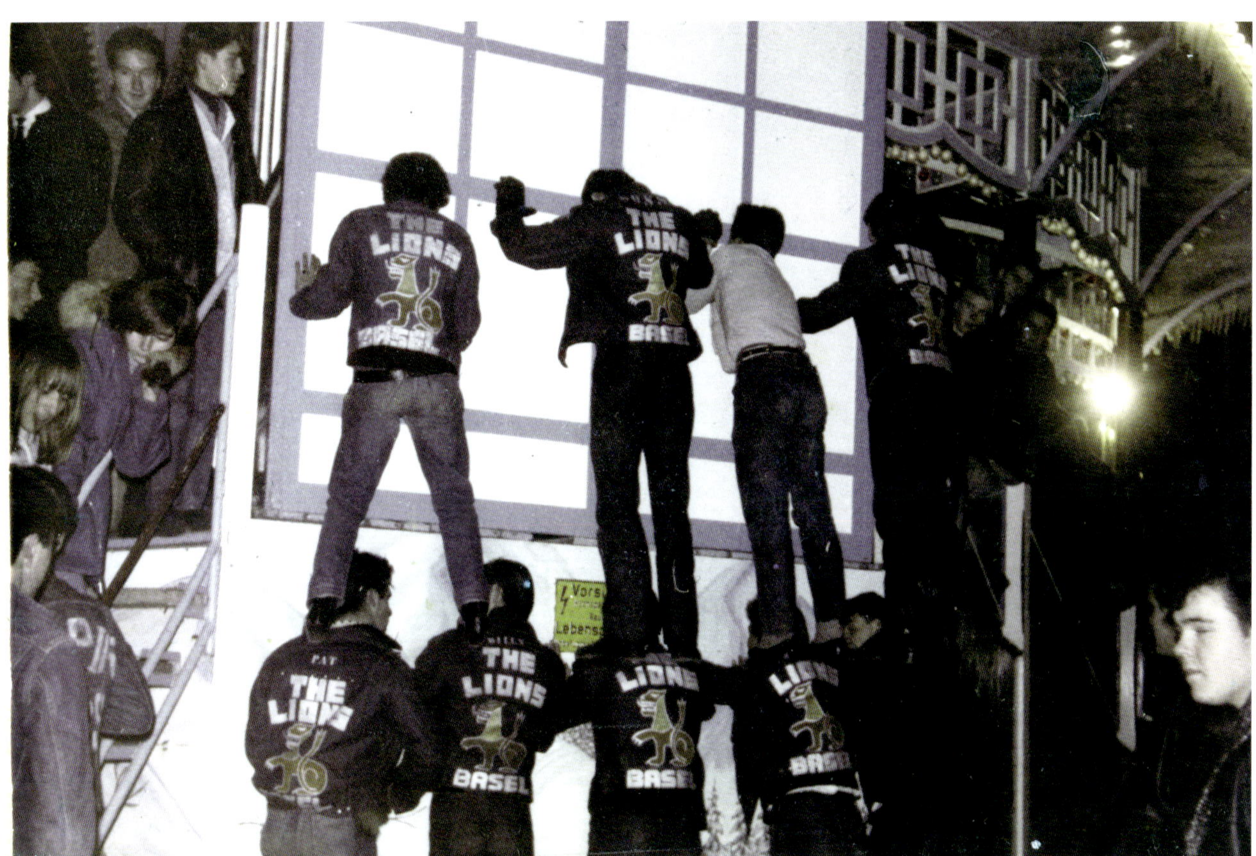

The Lions form a pyramid at the Cortina Bob.

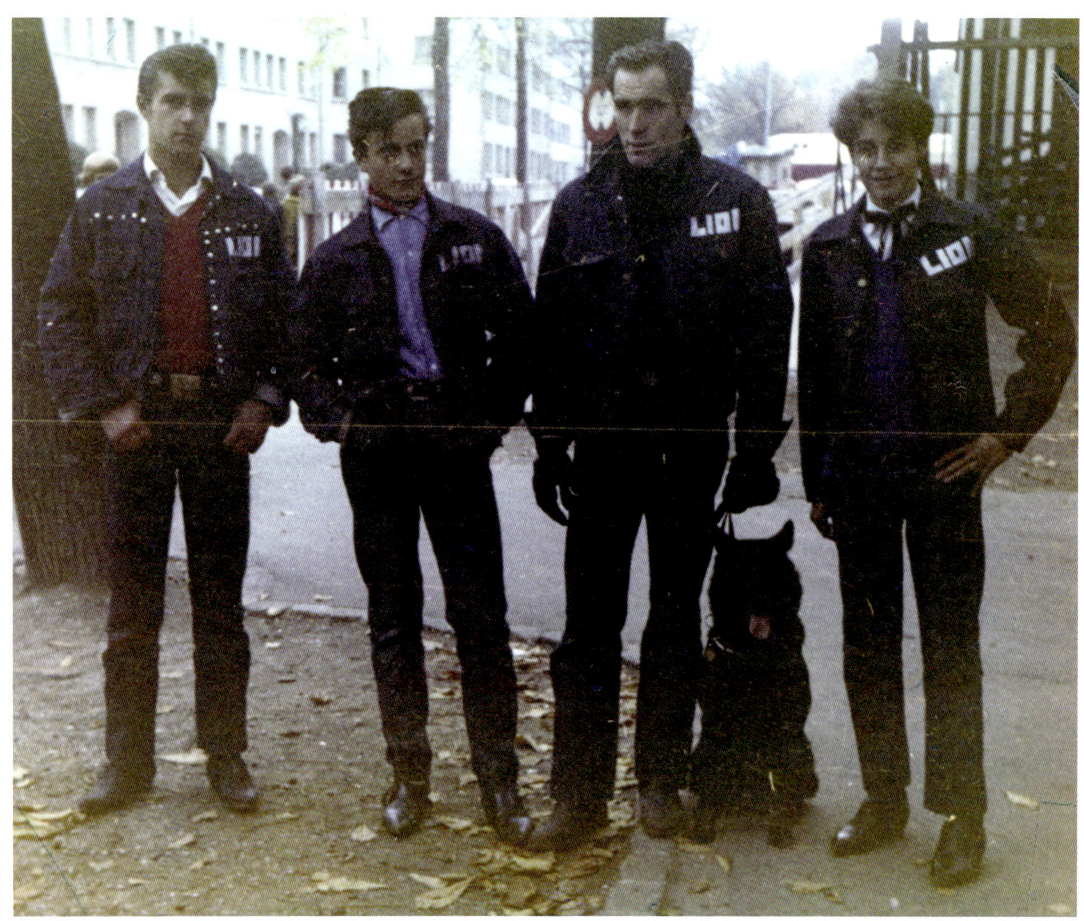

Lions boss Zorro (third from left) with his dog.

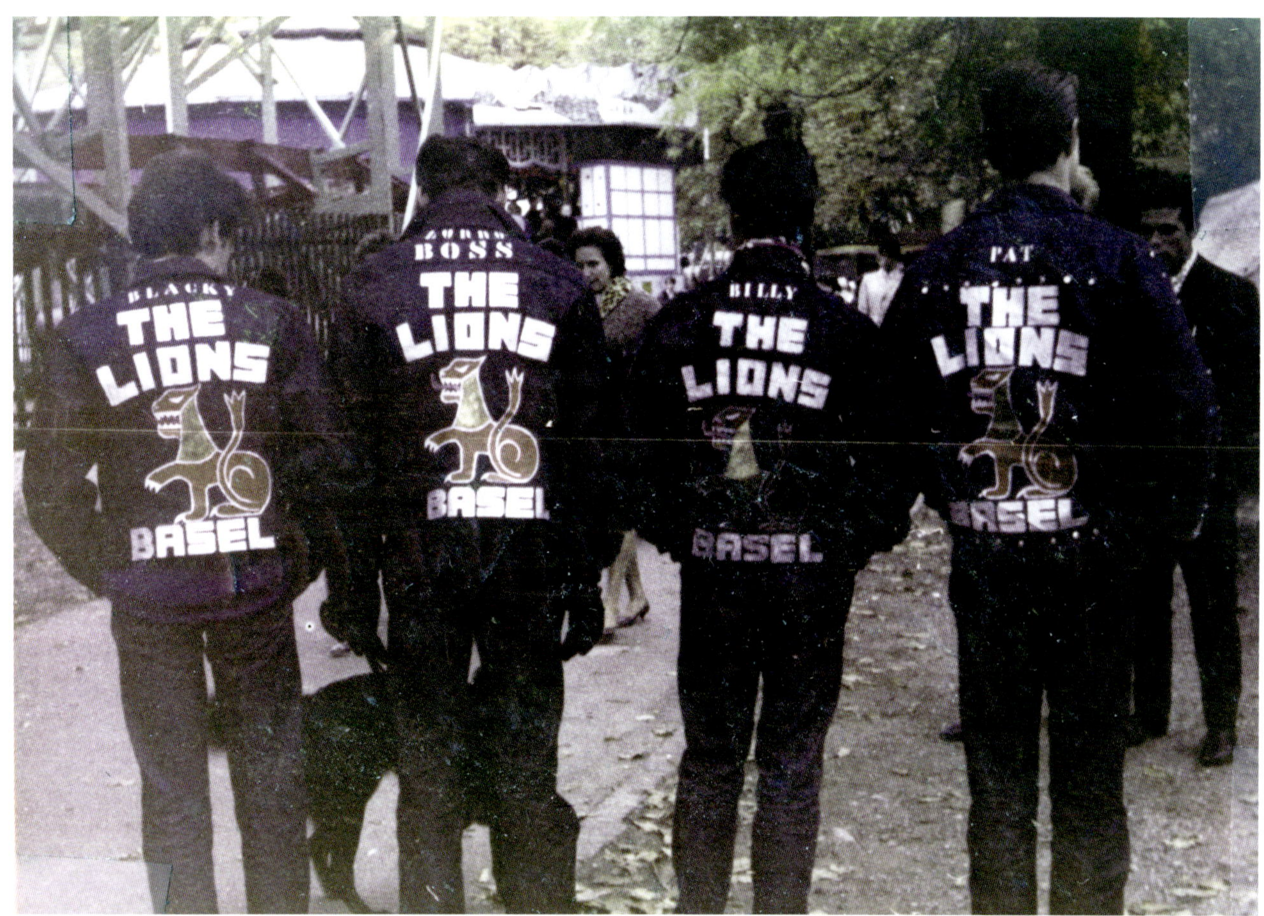

Blacky, Zorro, Billy and Pat from The Lions at the entrance of Rosentalanlage.

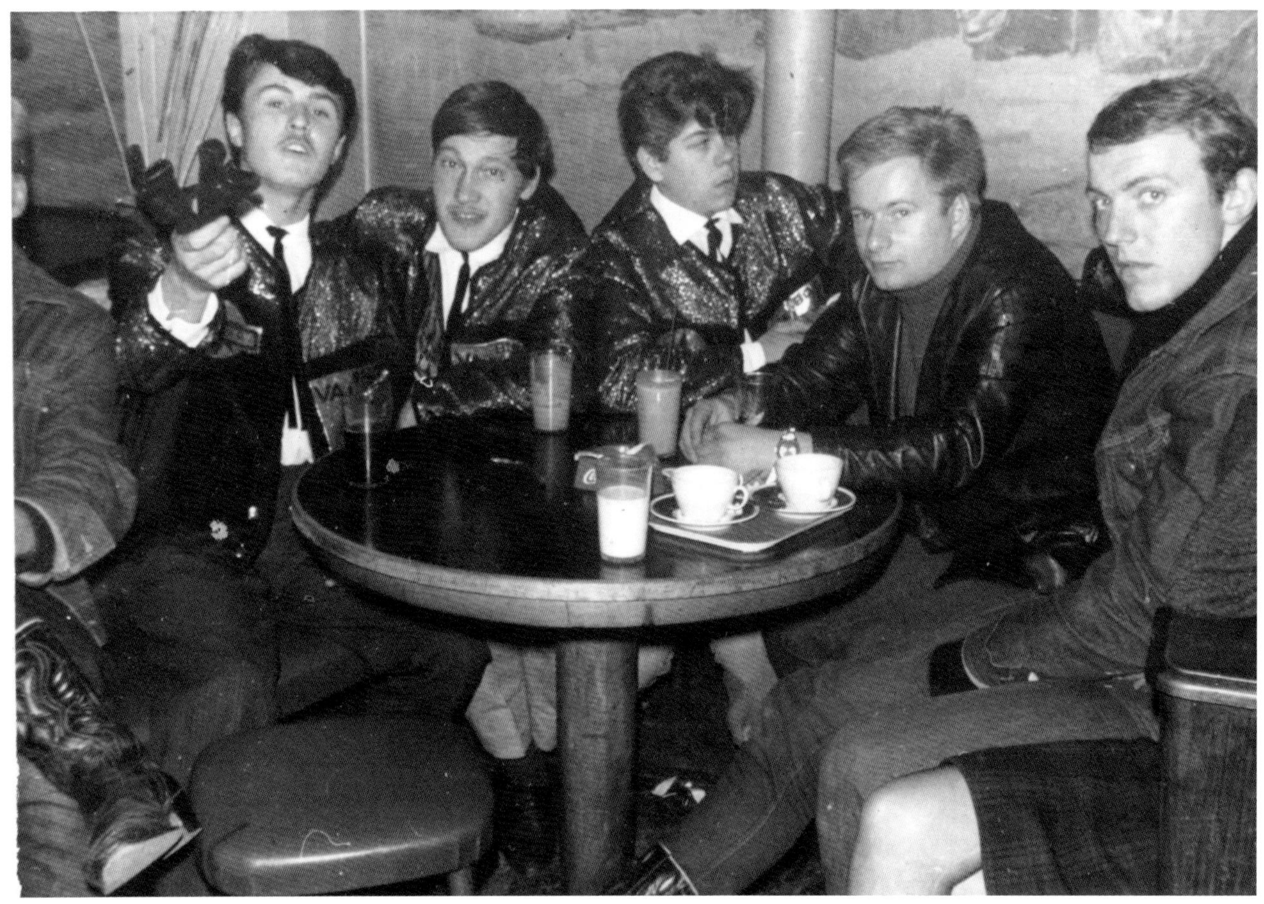

Cafe Oasis Basel (L-R) Dracula, Clochard, Muus (all three from Vampir Basel), Igel (no longer a gang member here) and Romeo (boss of the Revenger Gang Zurich).

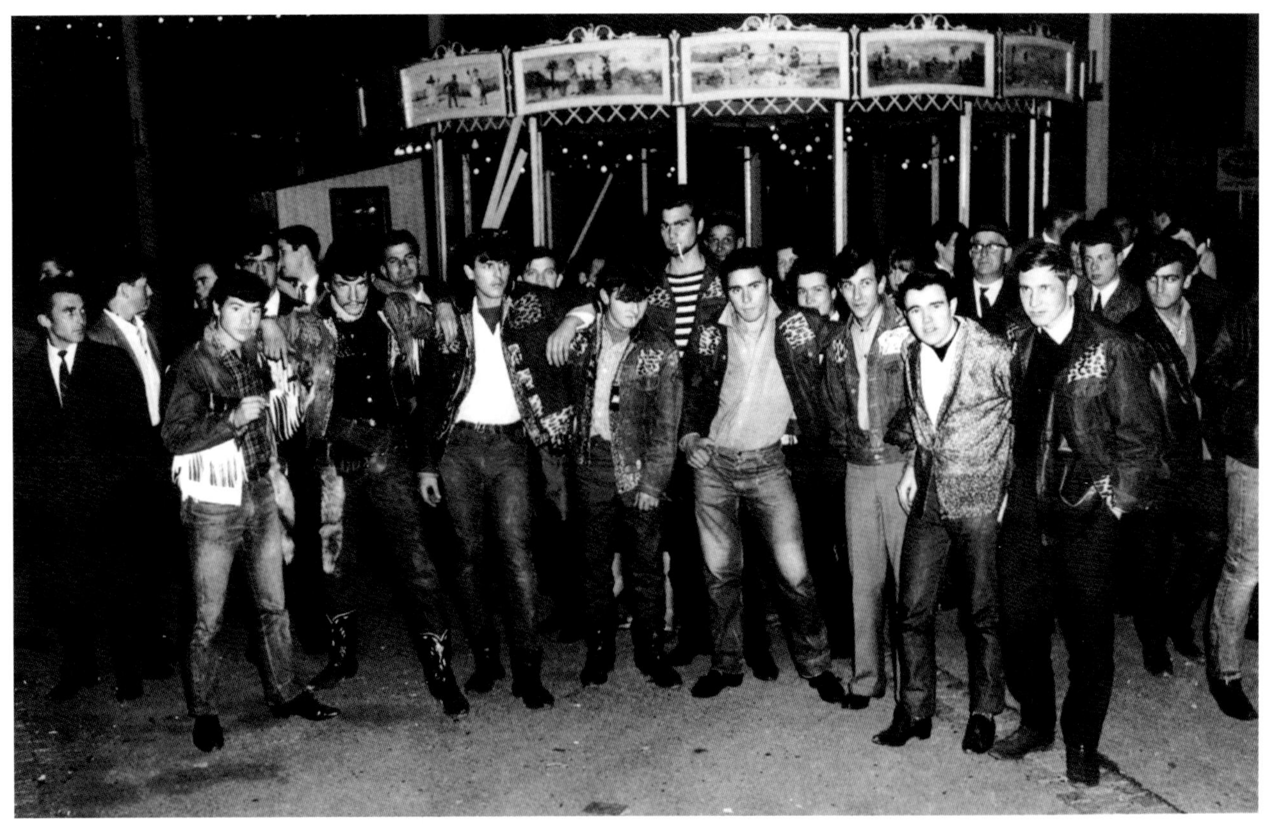

Six members of The Black Devil Gang Basel. Boss Mischuta is fourth from left. Photo from the collection of Peter “Rocky” Geissbuhler.

36/black devil gang, basel in aarau
around november 1964

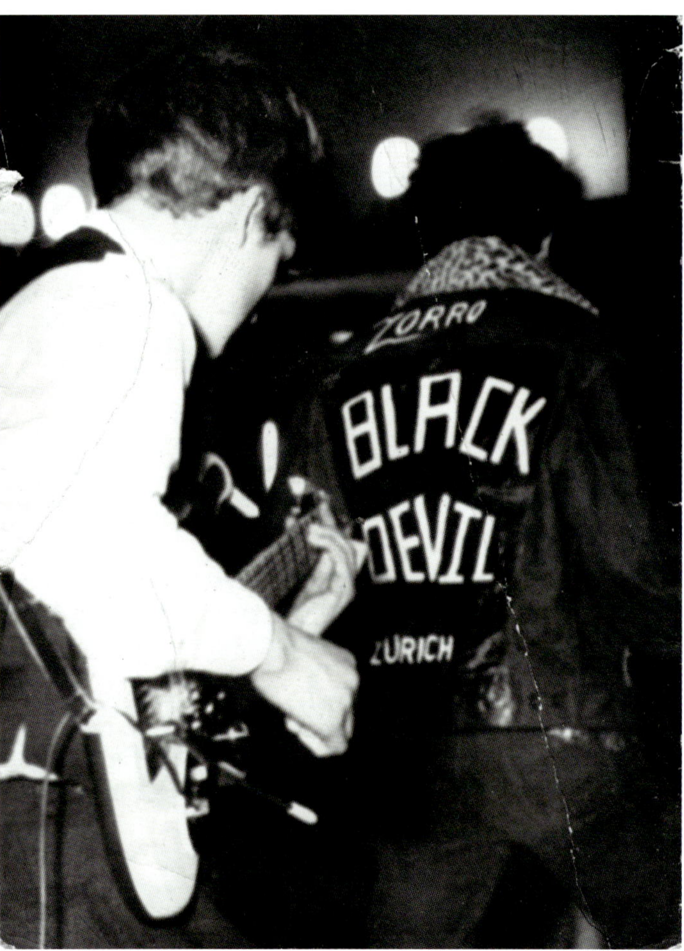

After Mischuta's move to Winterthur, he reformed his gang as the Black Devil, Zürich. Pictured is Zorro of The Black Devil, Zürich posing on stage at the Casino in Frauenfeld, while Roly (Roland) Schmid of The Mods delivers the goods.

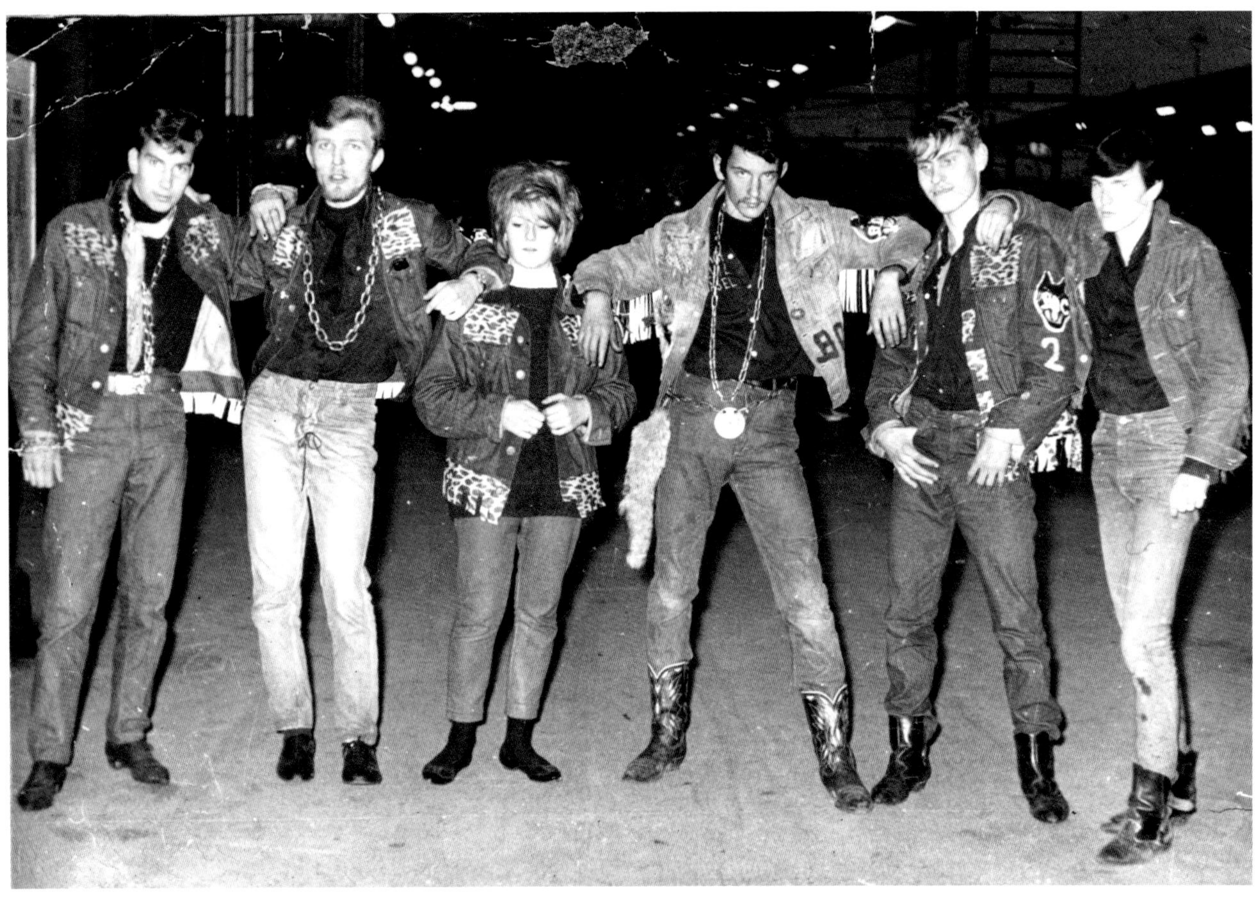

The Black Devil Gang Basel in Aarau, Oct/Nov 1964. Boss Mischuta Liechti is at the right of the young lady. Names of the other members remain uncertain. Photo by Peter “Rocky” Geissbühler.

1965

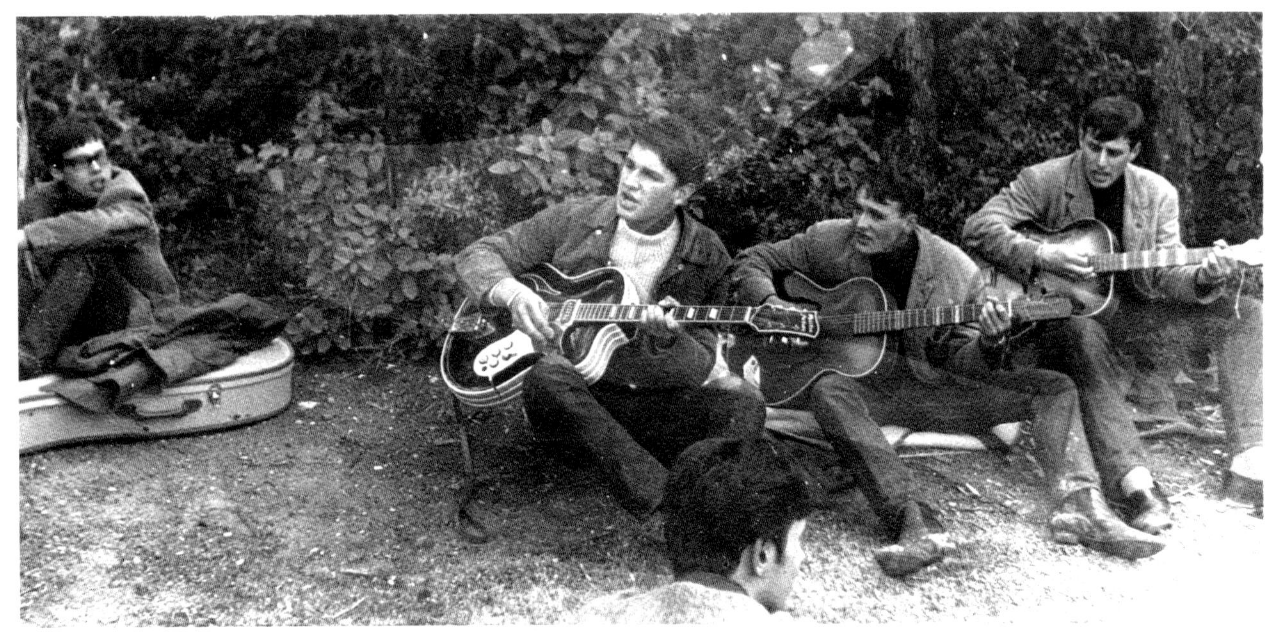

Members of the beat band The Red Devils from Basel entertain the Halbstarken gangs at St. Petersinsel.

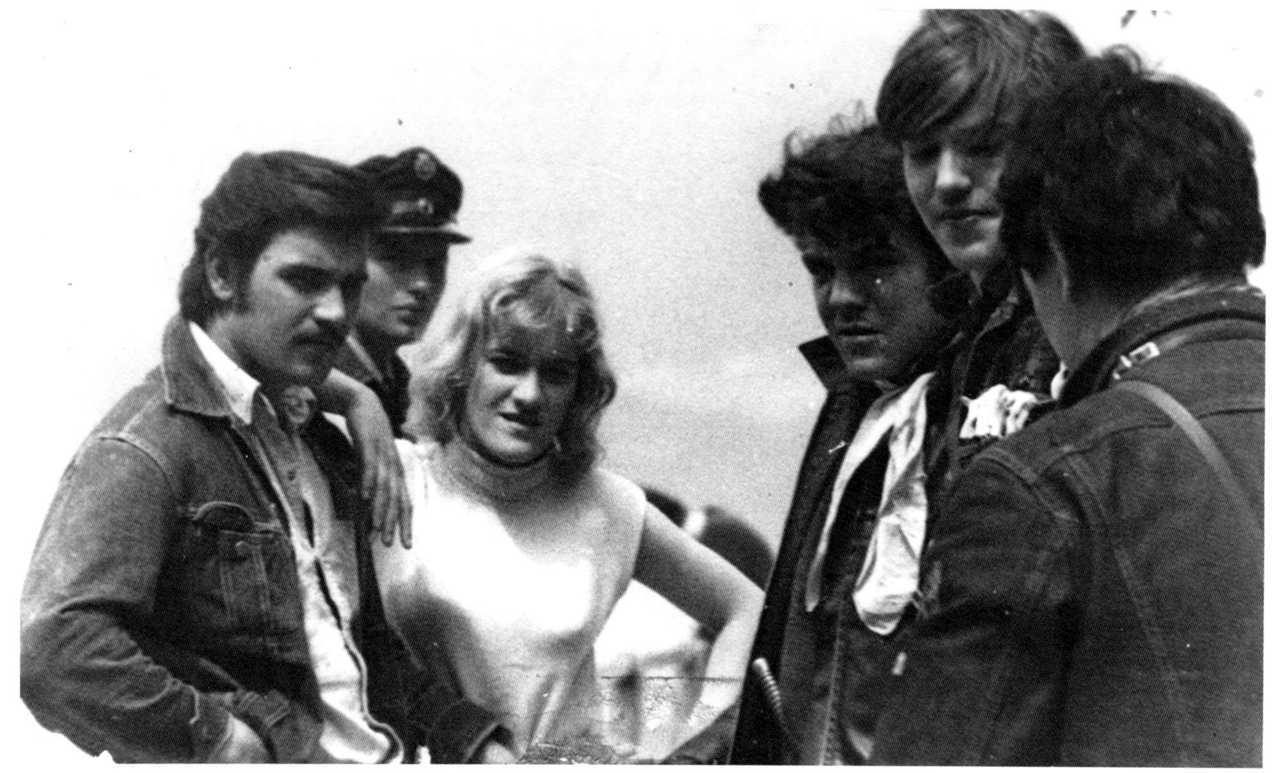

Various Halbstarken rebels from the third big yearly Swiss gang meeting at St. Petersinsel from June 6–7, 1965.

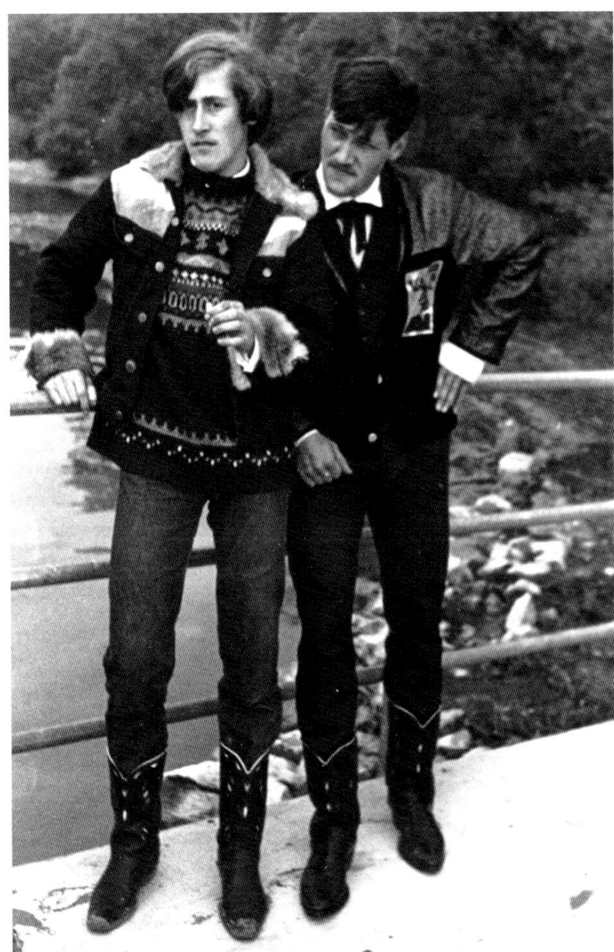

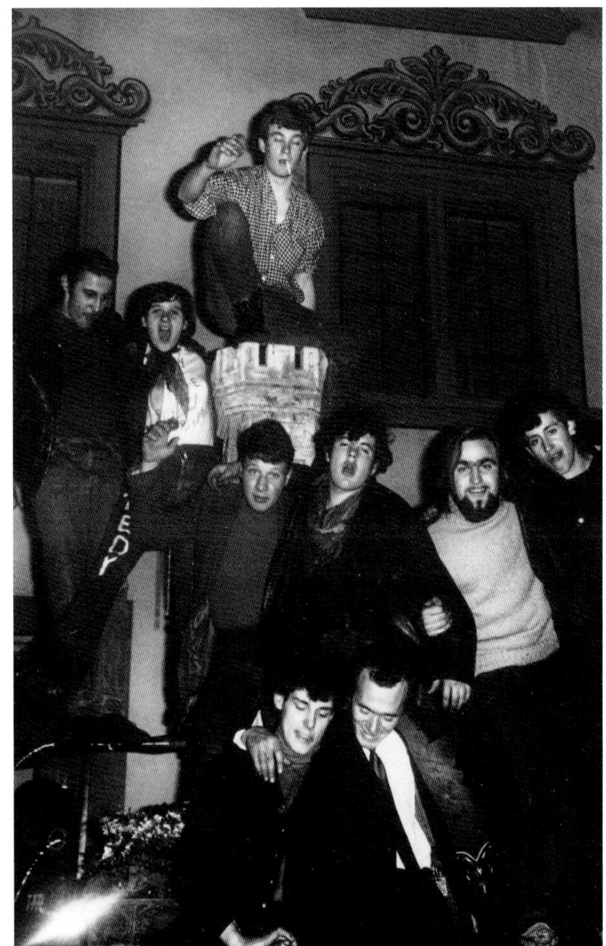

Left: 1965 photo of Hanspeter "Rio" Rütti (from the Black Star, Blizzard, and Vampir gangs), together with his brother René "Clochard" Rütti (from the Blizzard, and Vampir gangs). Right; The Black Star gang, Basel in around the mid 60s.

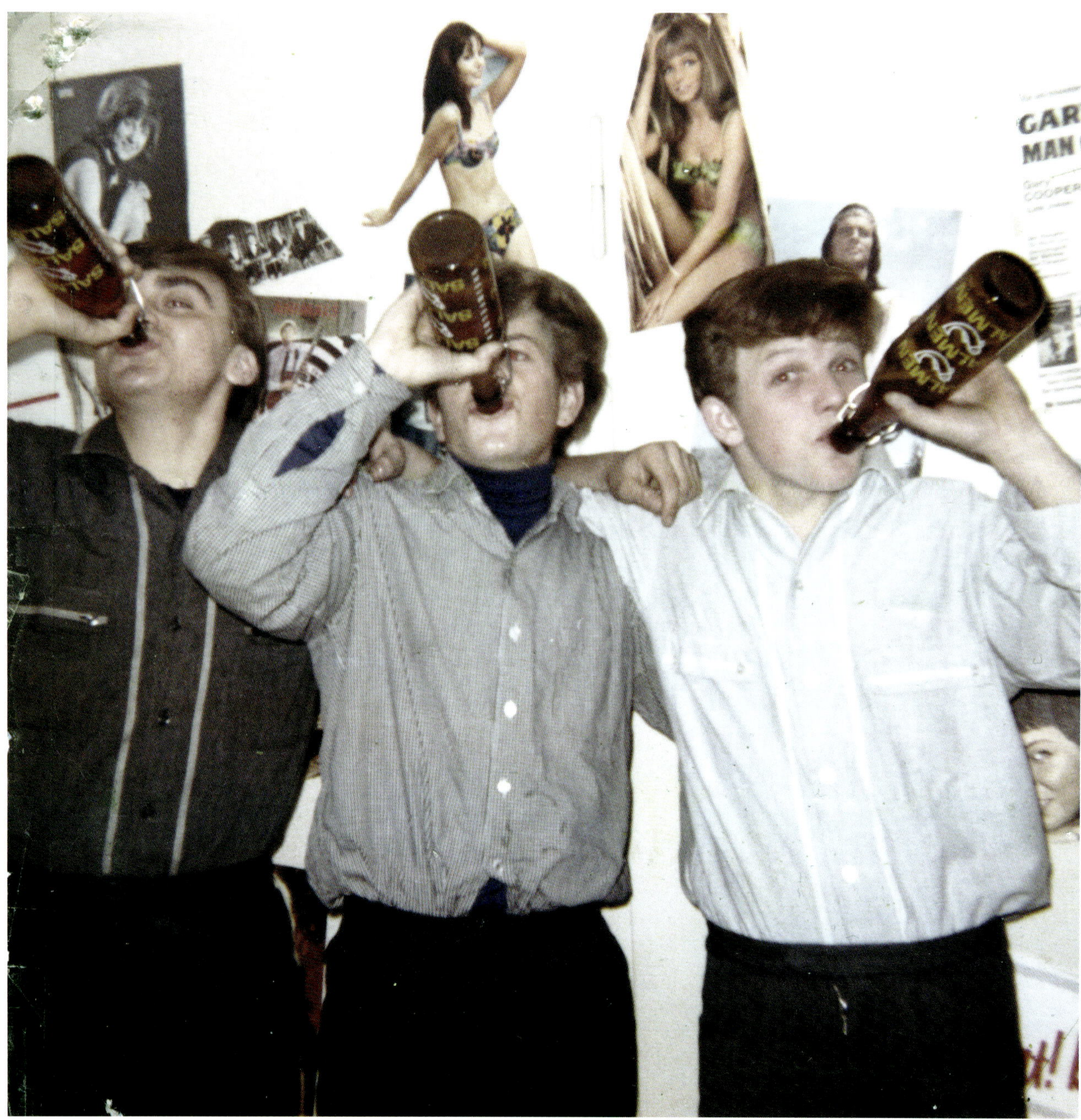

A button-down world in ’65 . . . but not for long.

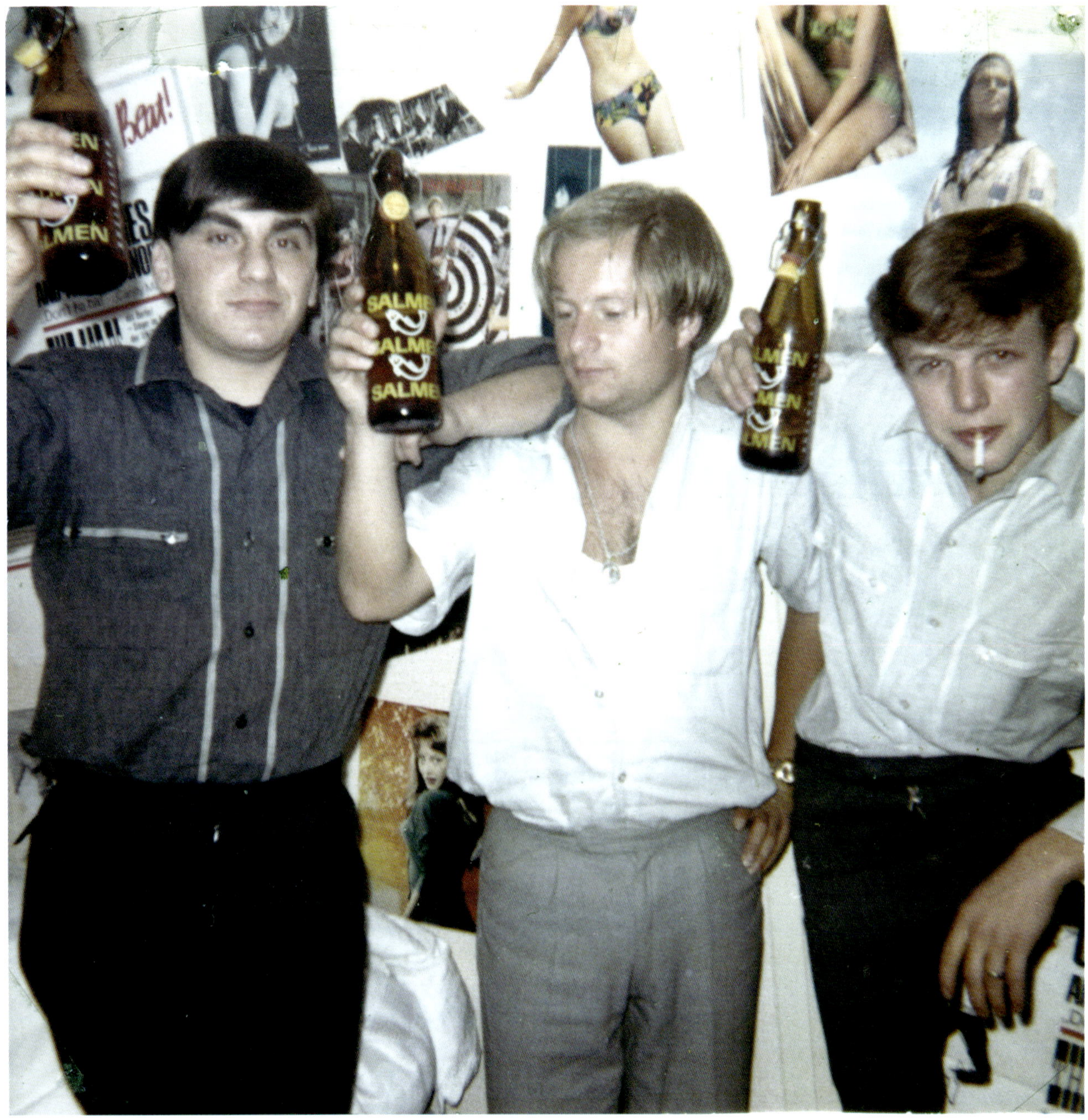

Pröschtli! Igel (center) and friends.

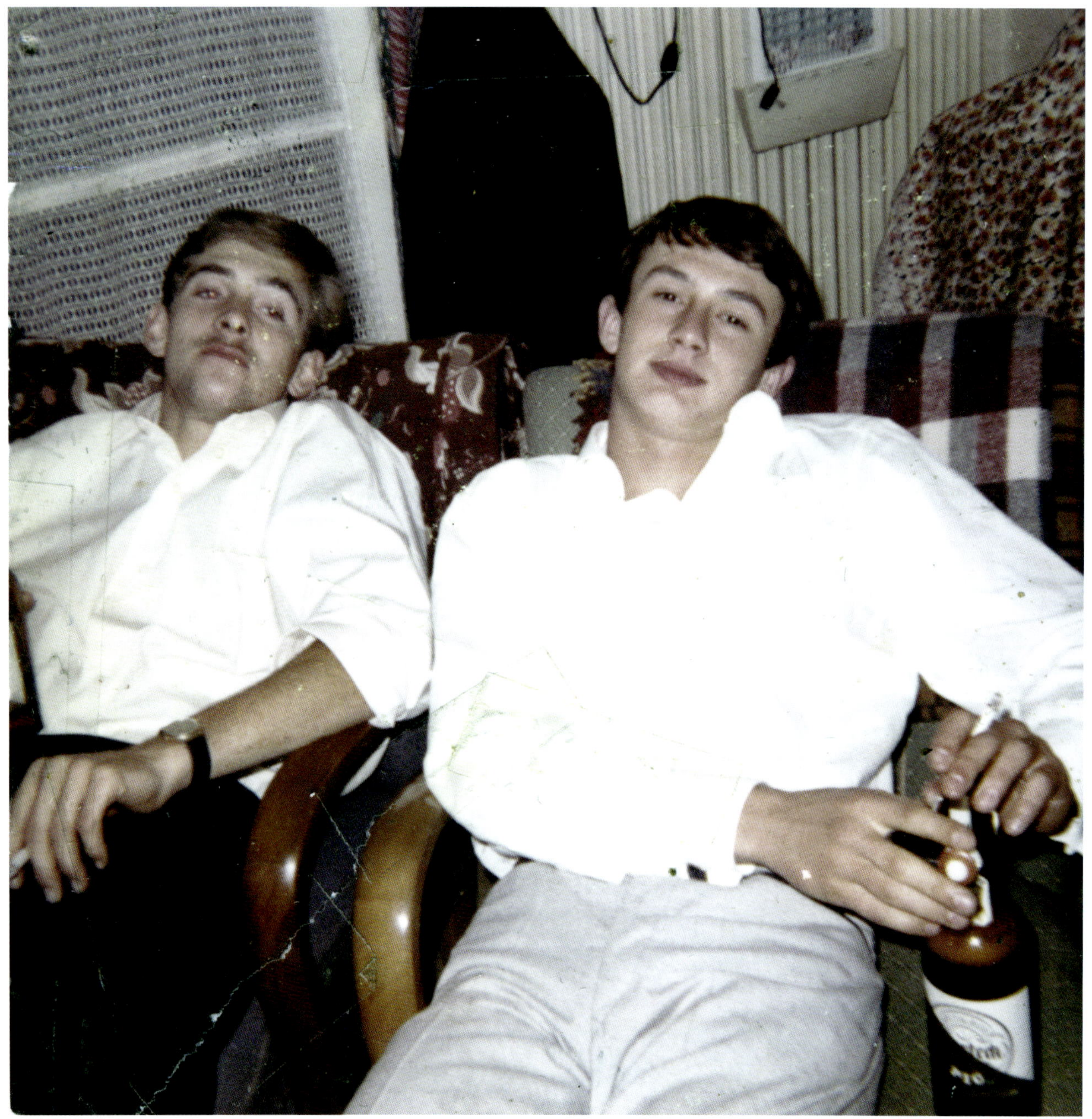

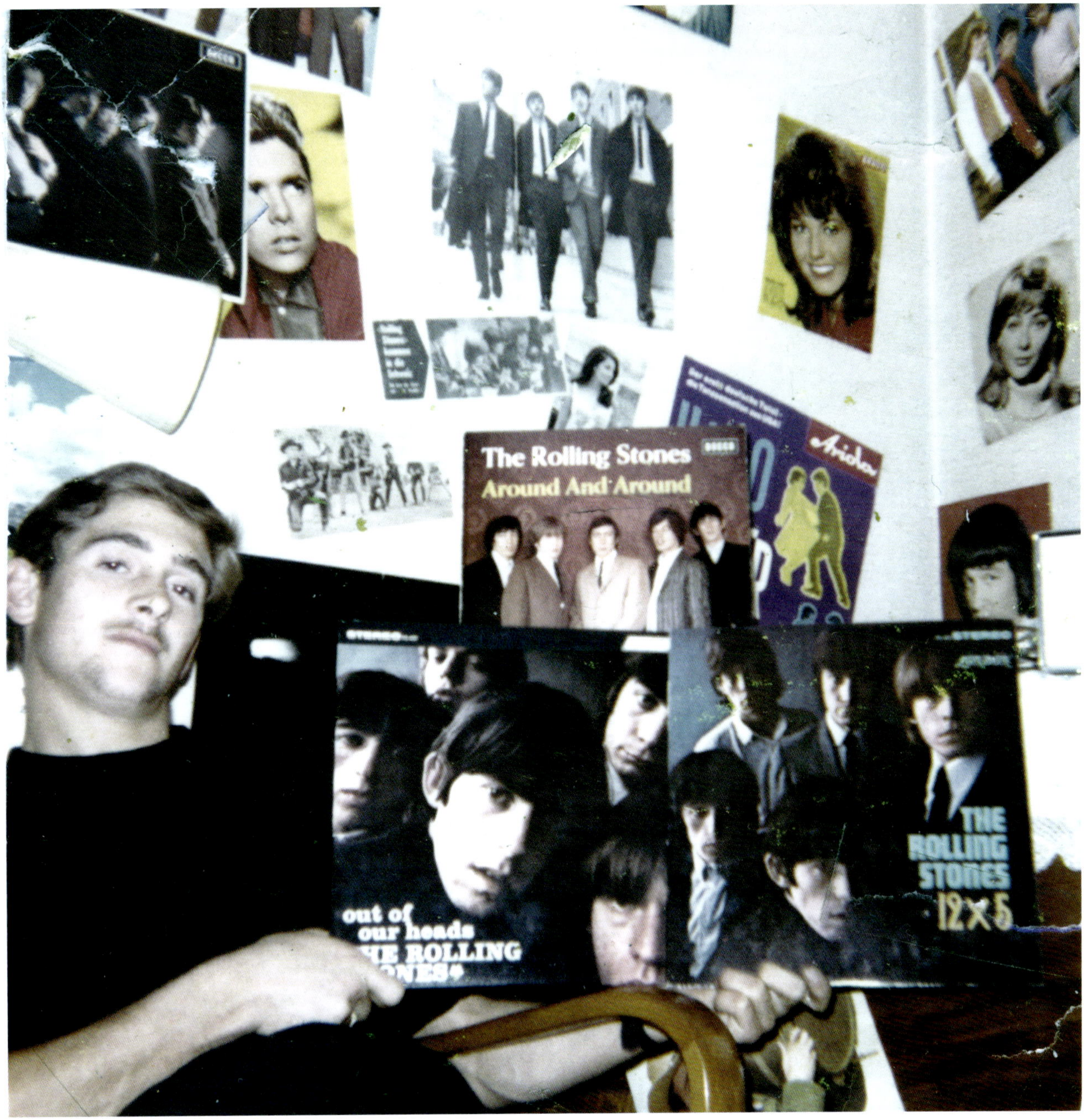

Get Off My Cloud.

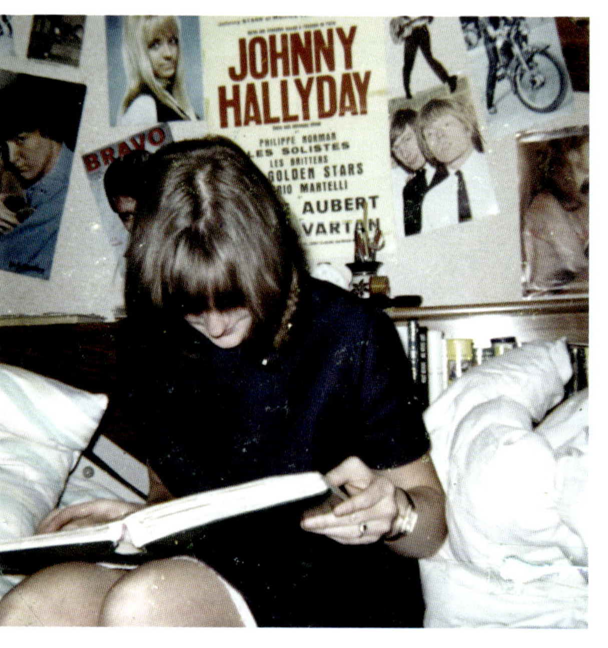
JOHNNY
HALLYDAY
PHILIPPE NORMAN
LES SOLISTES
LES BRITTENS
GOLDEN STARS
AUBERT
VARTAN
BRAVO

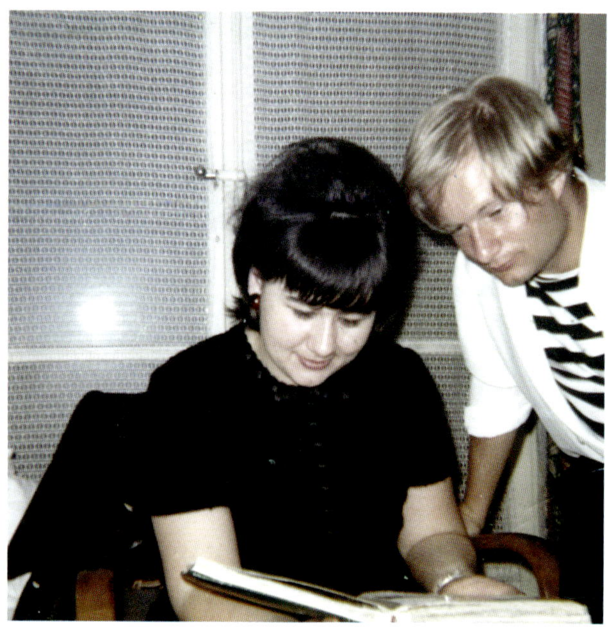

MUSTERMESSE BASEL
JOHNNY
HALLYDAY
PHILIPPE BORMAN
LES SOLISTES
CASEY JONES

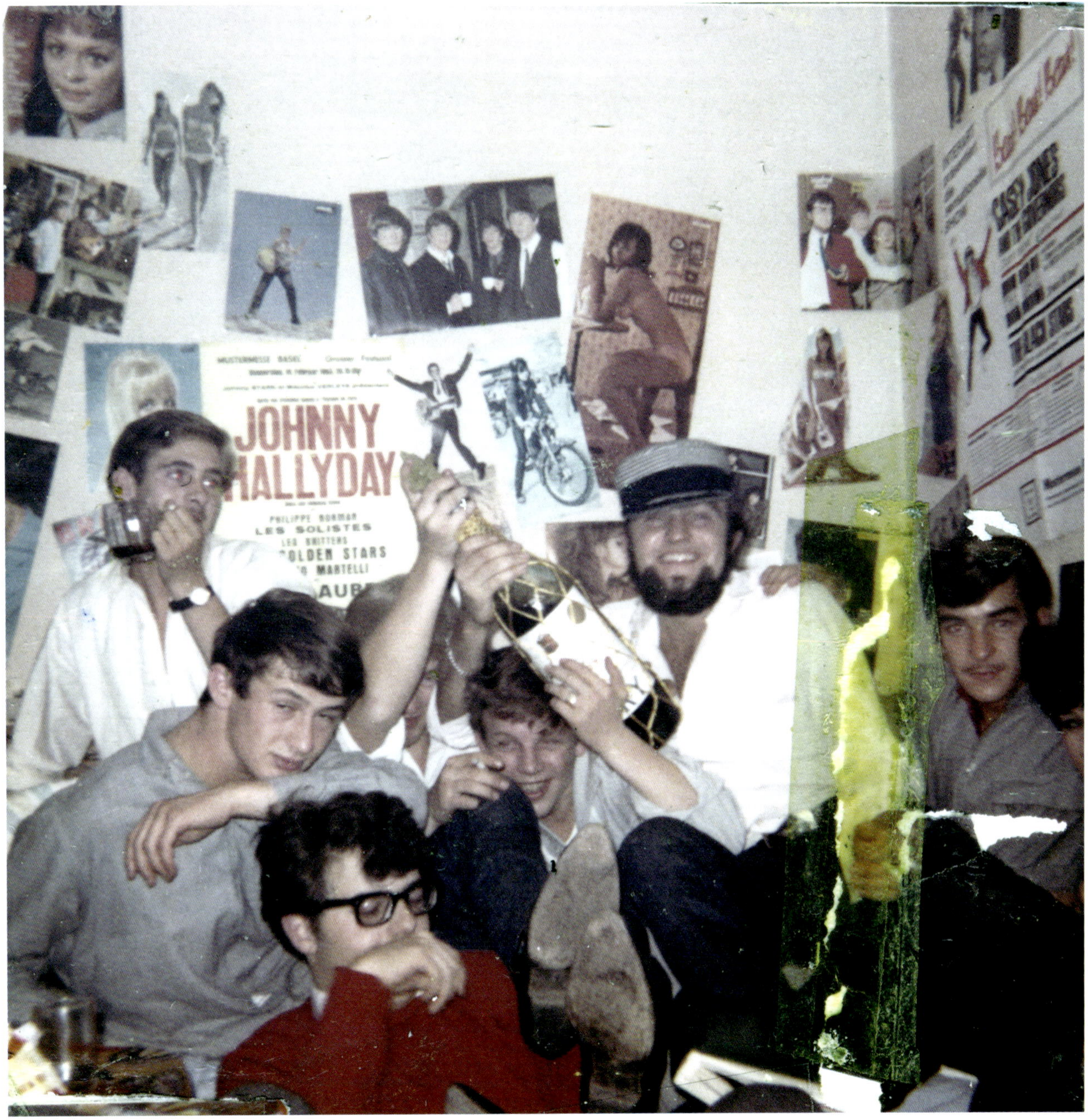

Booze party!

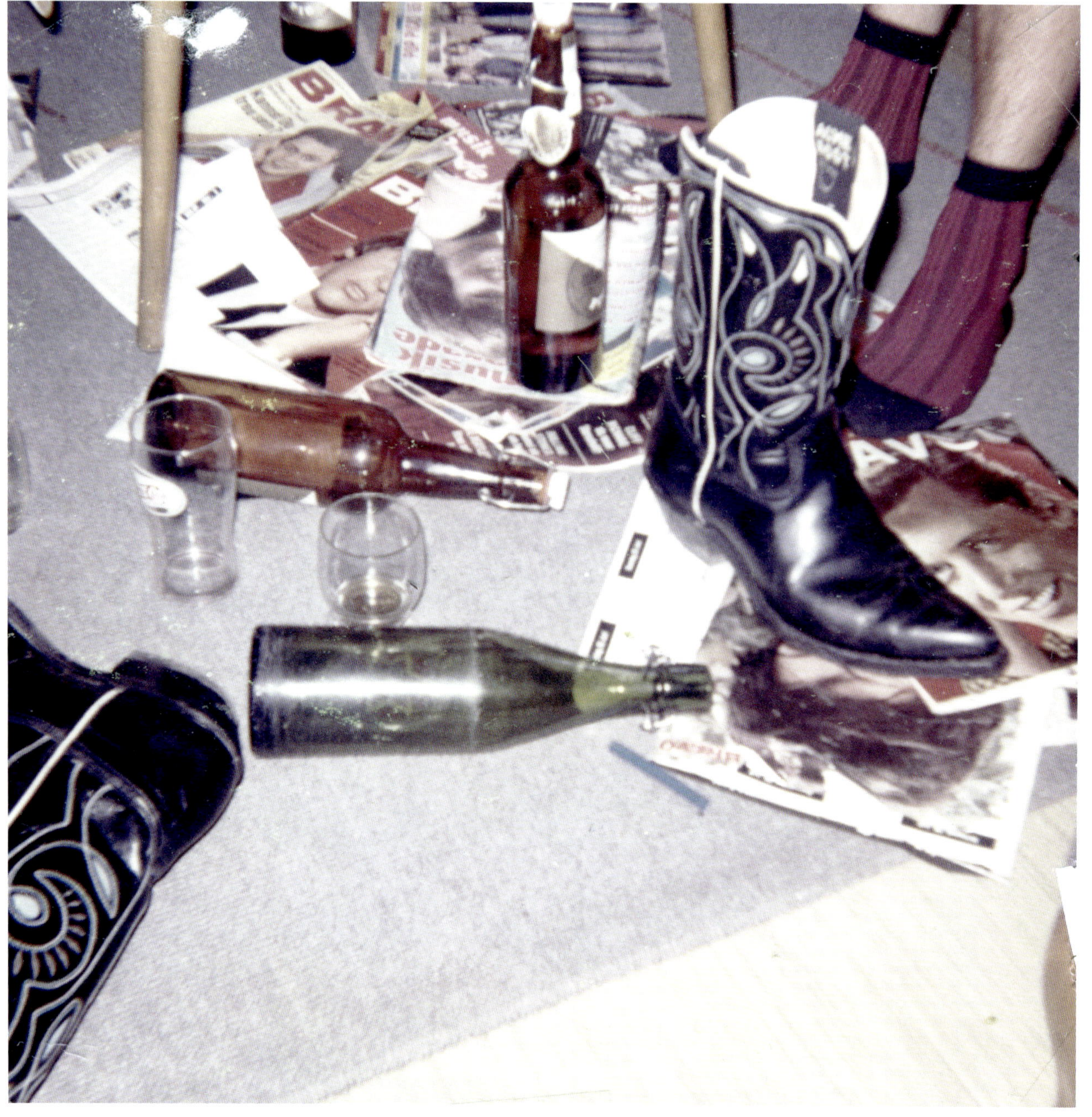

1966-67

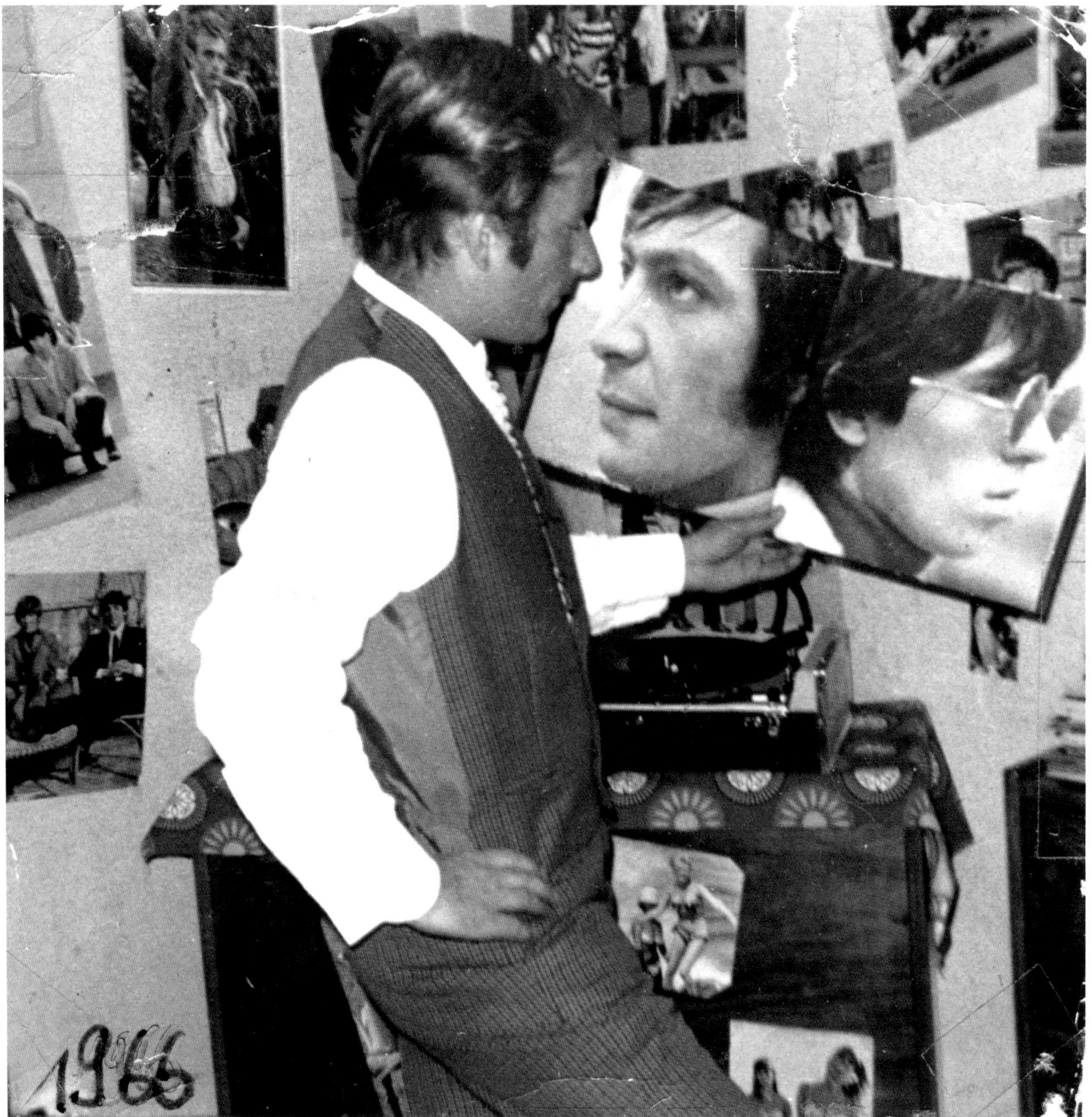

1966. Greaser Igel contemplates the future.

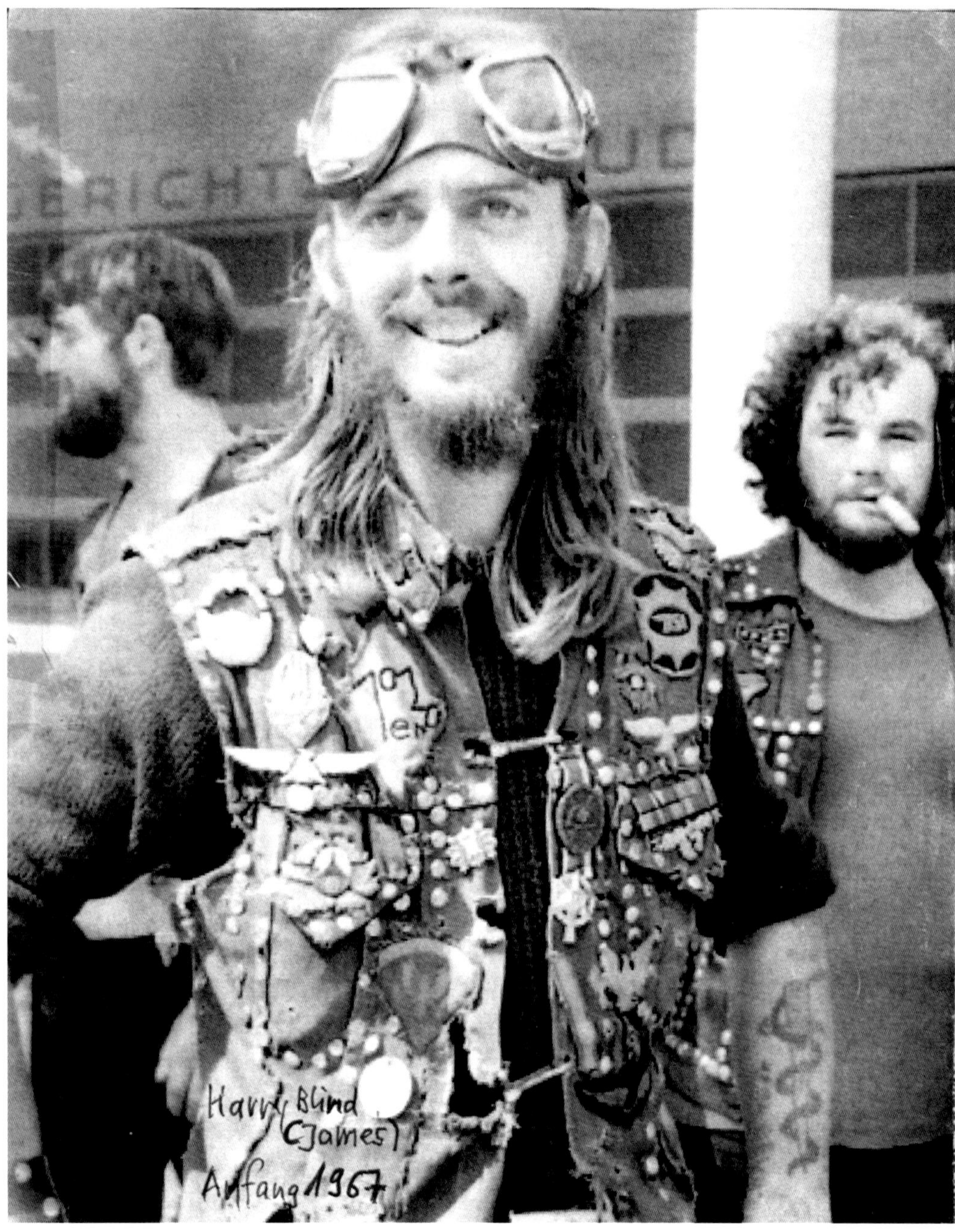

1967. Street gangs on wheels. Harry B in full regalia.

1972

38 / sky devils, basel
1972

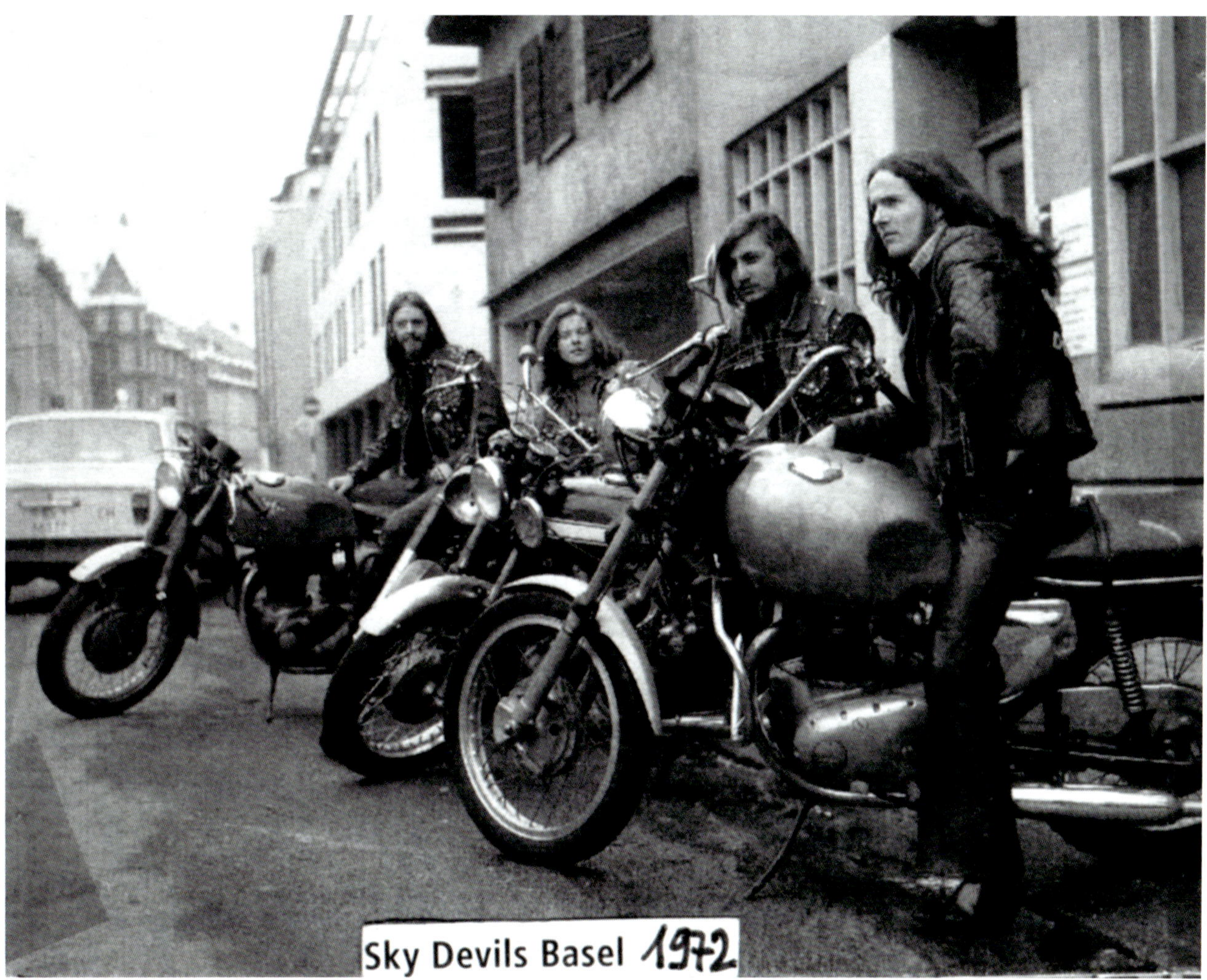

Aftermath. The gangs grow up—off the streets and onto the roads. Left to right: Four members of The Sky Devils Basel in 1972: James (real name Harry Blind), Bruno Meier, Zuggi, and Thomas Lindenmaier. Bruno came out of The Red Devil Gang Basel back in the late 1950s.

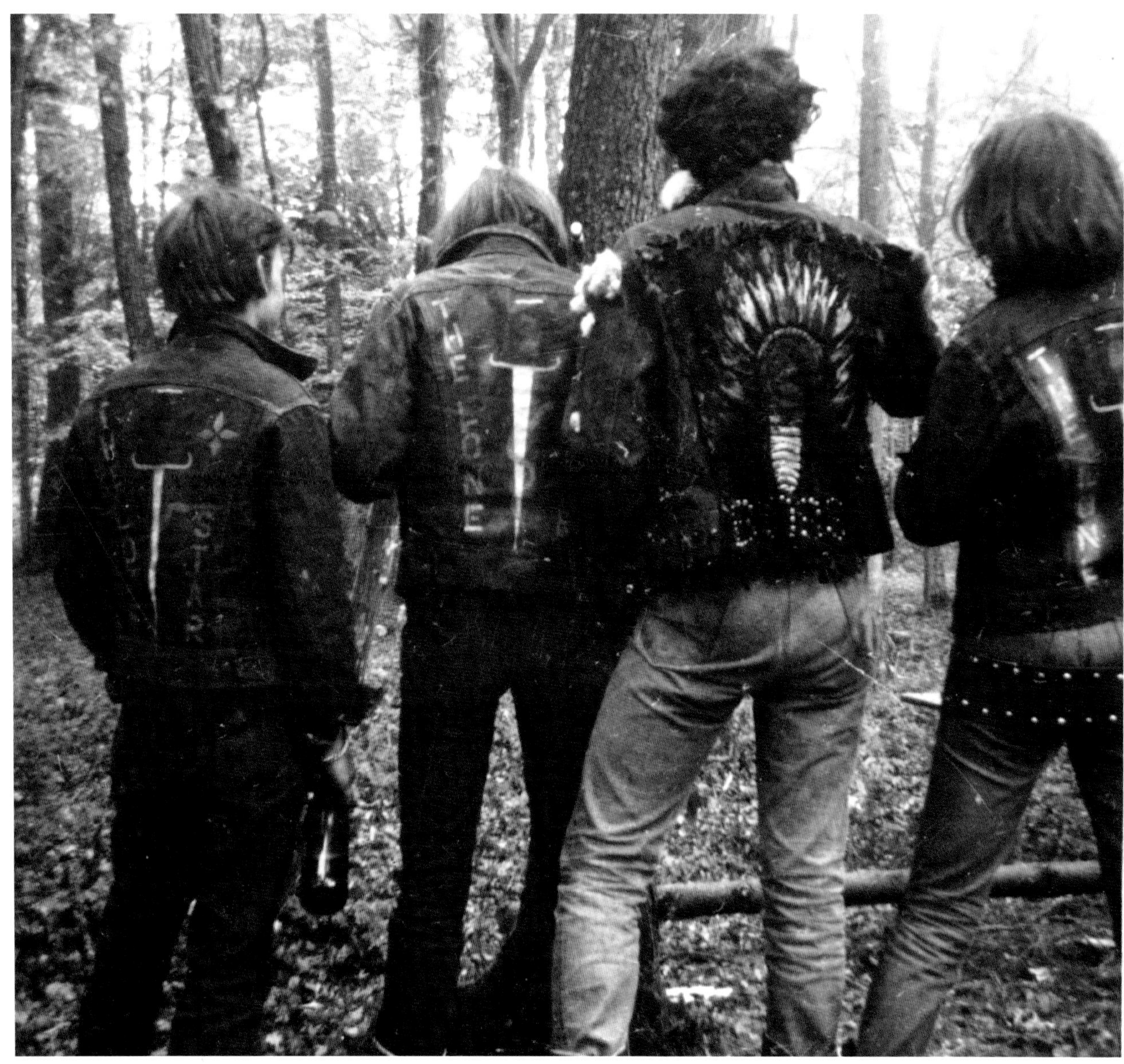

Tino wearing Romeo's Indian chief boss jacket, as the new boss of the Lone-Star Gang, Zurich back in around 1965/1966.

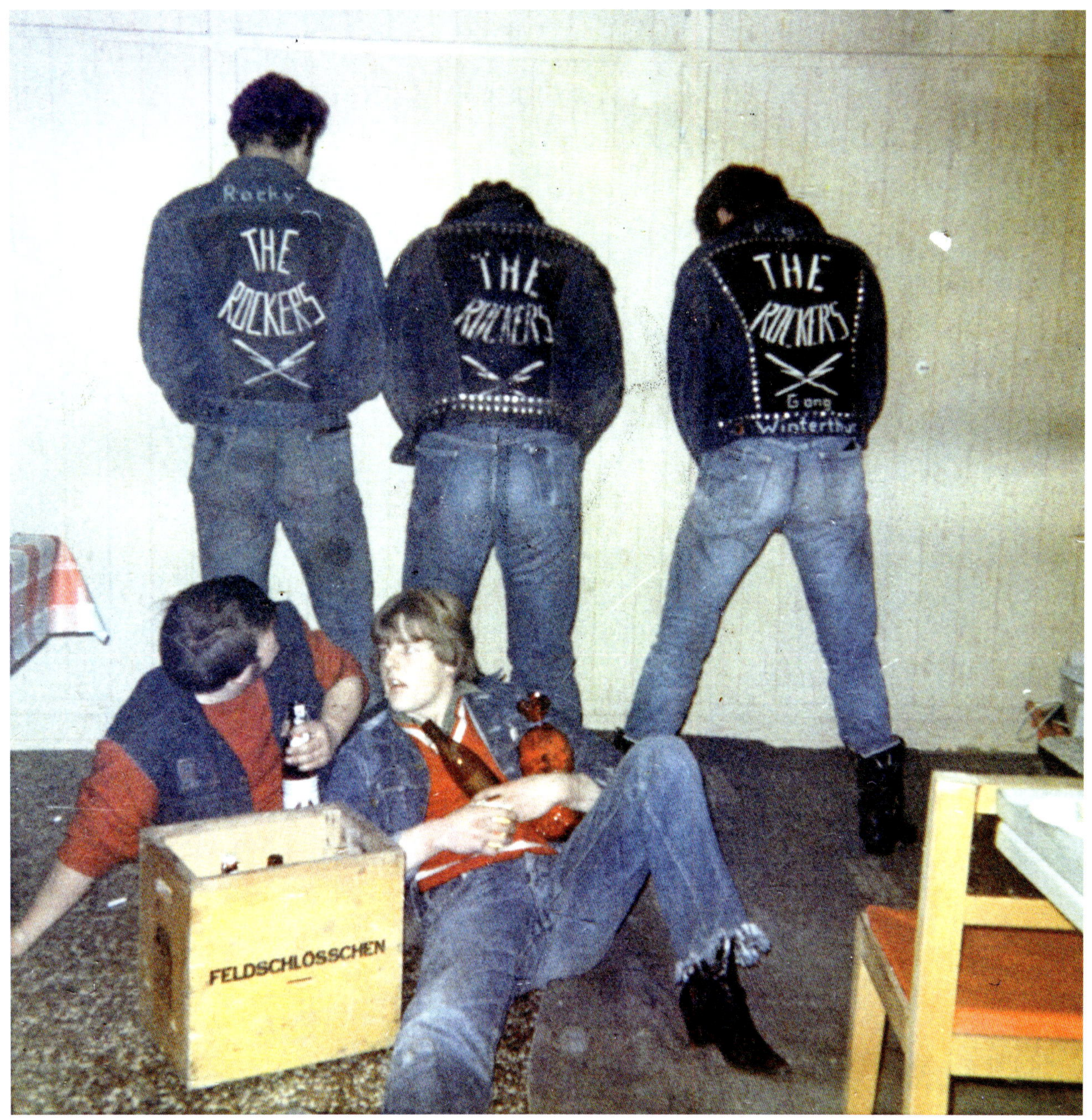

Rocky’s gang The Rockers (from Winterthur), Christmas Eve 1968.

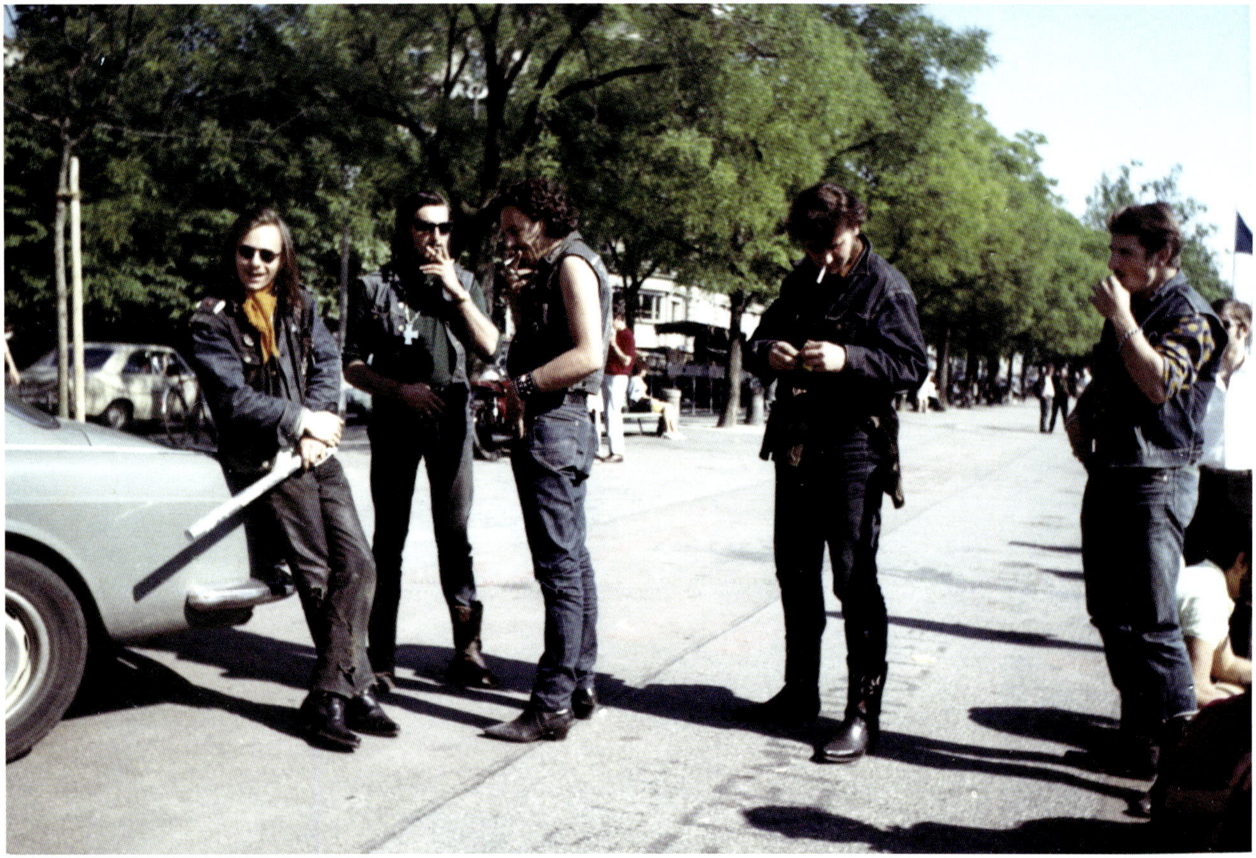

Above: Future Hells Angels the Lone-Star Gang, Zurich in summer of 1969. Left to right: Piol, Chris, Tino, Bulle, plus name unknown. Right: The emblem with the snake around the sword was first used by The Revenger Gang, Zurich, and then afterwards by the Lone-Star gang too. They've simply overpainted their new name over the old one on their jackets.

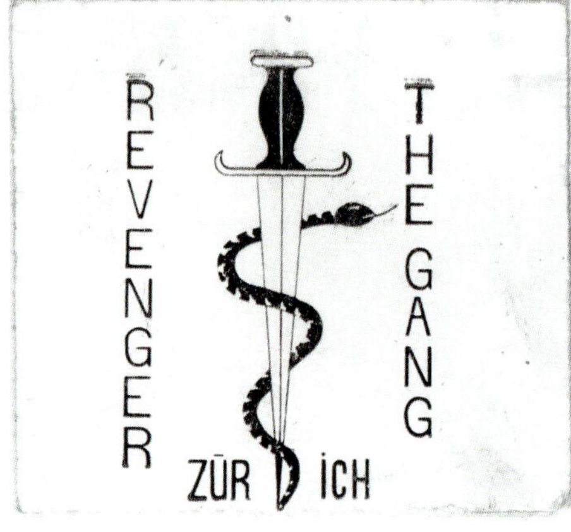

thanks

This book could not have been possible without Rolf Rieben, Lukas Mueller, Oliver Groth, Jeff Roth, Elizabeth Van Itallie, and Igel Erlich.

Thanks to Bruce Hackney, curator and U.S. Manager, Karlheinz Weinberger Stiftung, Zurich, whose expertise and support were invaluable.

Thanks also to Chiara "Kitt" Dona Dalle Rose, Matt Clarke, Johnny Aquino, Marc Miller, Howie "Pyro" Kusten, and Steve Rosen, for believing in this book, and to the players Gypsy, Hugo, Teelo, Rita, Mackey, Angel, Fritz, Rene, Raymond, Priska, Cliff from Lucerne and all of the Swiss rebels in these pages.

— Miriam Linna

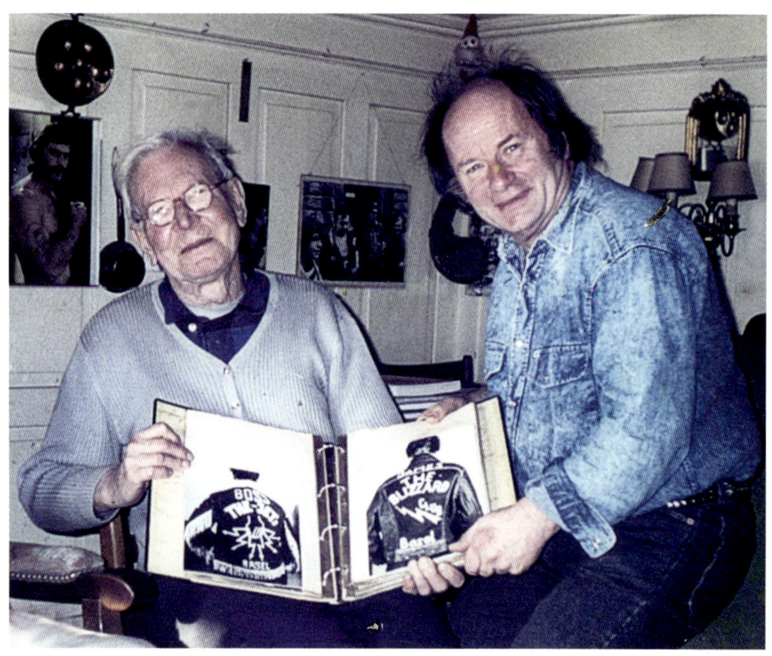

February 2000: Igel visiting Karlheinz Weinberger at home at Elisabethenstr. 26, in Zurich, Switzerland.